Written Out

# Written Out

## THE SILENCING OF REGINA GELANA TWALA

Joel Cabrita

Ohio University Press
Athens

Ohio University Press, Athens, Ohio 45701
ohioswallow.com


Printed in the United States of America
Ohio University Press books are printed on acid-free paper ∞ ™

31 30 29 28 27 26 25 24 23 5 4 3 2 1

*Library of Congress Cataloging-in-Publication Data*

Names: Cabrita, Joel, 1980– author.
Title: Written out : the silencing of Regina Gelana Twala / Joel Cabrita.
Description: Athens : Ohio University Press, [2023] | Includes bibliographical references and index.
Identifiers: LCCN 2022036096 (print) | LCCN 2022036097 (ebook) | ISBN 9780821425077 (paperback) | ISBN 9780821447895 (pdf)
Subjects: LCSH: Twala, Regina G., 1908–1968. | Anthropologists—Eswatini—Biography. | Social workers—South Africa—Biography. | Anti-apartheid activists—Eswatini—Biography. | Anti-apartheid activists—South Africa—Biography. | South Africa—Social conditions—20th century. | Eswatini—Social conditions—20th century. | Eswatini—Social life and customs—20th century.
Classification: LCC DT1949.T93 C33 2023 (print) | LCC DT1949.T93 (ebook) | DDC 323.168092 [B]—dc23/eng/20220816
LC record available at https://lccn.loc.gov/2022036096
LC ebook record available at https://lccn.loc.gov/2022036097

*To Thato Sukati,*

*with gratitude for friendship and*

*intellectual camaraderie*

# Contents

# Illustrations

## Figures

## Maps

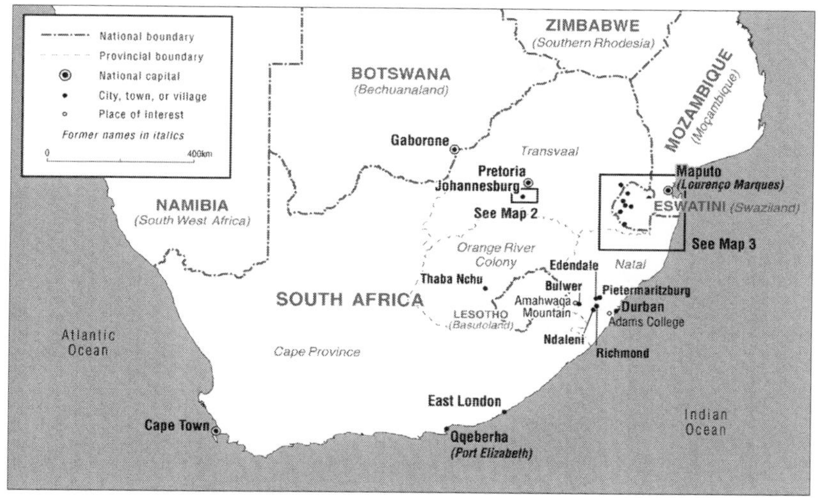


MAP 1. Southern Africa

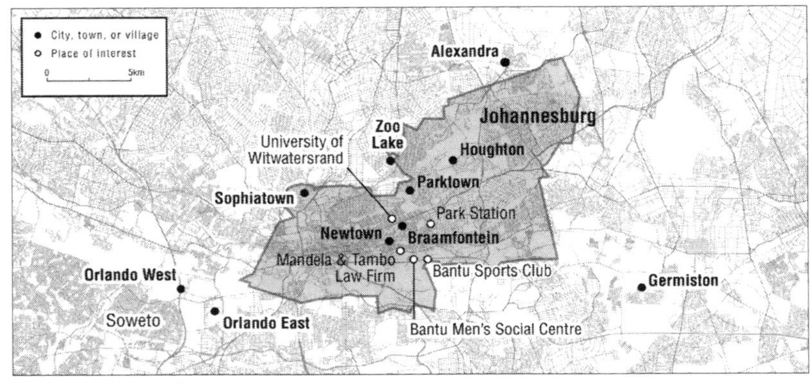


MAP 2. Johannesburg

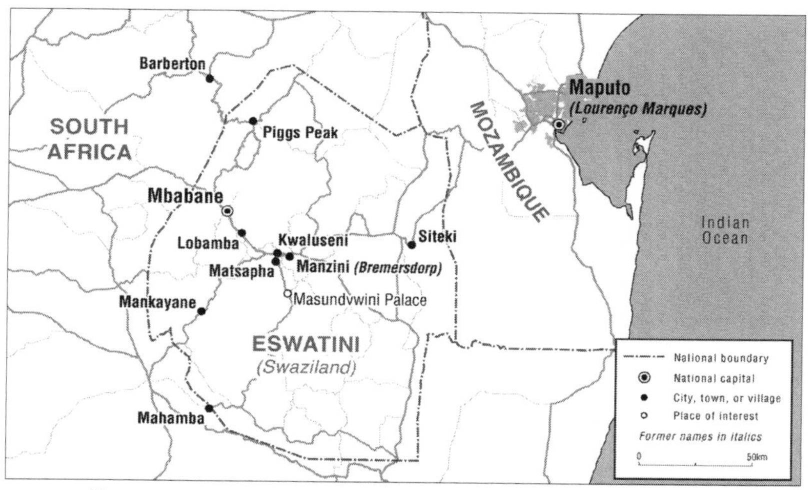


MAP 3. Eswatini

# Acknowledgments

There are very many people and institutions behind my writing of this book. First and foremost, my largest thanks are to the Twala family for their support and generosity. I am particularly grateful to Regina Gelana Twala's granddaughter and heir, Pinokie Gelane Twala, for her kind permission to cite from her grandmother's work. I am also indebted to Zanele Twala, Anne Twala, and Mary Twala for their generosity in sharing family documents and memories in the form of interviews. Sadly, both Anne and Mary died before this book went to press.

I am also grateful to other individuals and institutions for mediating my access to Twala's and other related writings and images. They include all the individuals in Eswatini and South Africa whom I interviewed, including many of Regina Twala's extended family members, neighbors, and friends. I am most grateful for their generosity in sharing their time and memories. I am also thankful to Diana Wall, Johannesburg, who kindly opened her home to me for preliminary viewing of Regina and Dan Twala's letters. My thanks are also due to Veit Erlmann, University of Texas; Brian Willan, Rhodes University; the Uppsala University Library Archives; the University of California, Los Angeles (UCLA) Archives (especially Molly Haight); the Historical Papers Research Archive, University of the Witwatersrand (especially Gabriele Mohale), where the Regina Twala Papers (RTP) are now kept; the University of Johannesburg Archives (I am grateful to Natasha Erlank for assistance in procuring issues of *Umteteli wa Bantu*); the National Archives of Eswatini at Lobamba; the National Library of South Africa, Pretoria; the Cory Library, Rhodes University, Grahamstown; Bob Forrester in Eswatini; Fiona Armitage and Peter Davis in the United Kingdom; Franek Rozwadowski in Washington, DC; the School of Oriental and African Studies (SOAS) Archives; the London School of Economics and Political Science (LSE) Archives; the Institute of Commonwealth Studies, London; Karen Fung, Stanford University; Ludo Kuipers in Australia; the Killie Campbell Library, Durban (especially Senzosenkosi Mkhize and Emily-Ann Krige); the University of KwaZulu-Natal Archives, Pietermaritzburg; and the National Archives of South Africa, Pretoria.

As with many works of scholarship, I am indebted to the individuals who provided paid labor in service of the research and writing of the book: Rozelle Bosch (transcription of interviews); Josie Brody (legal research on copyright law in Eswatini); Clinton Chiruta (research in the National Archives of Eswatini and the National Library of South Africa); Kyle Harmse (high-resolution scanning of images and research in the National Archives, Pretoria); Miles Irving (creation of maps); Talia Lieber (research in the UCLA archives); Sue Ogterop (research in the Methodist Archives, Cory Library, Grahamstown); Chandra Otto (also research in the Methodist Archives and in the Historical Papers Research Archive, University of the Witwatersrand); Thato Sukati (research in the National Library of South Africa and the National Archives of Eswatini); Glede Wang (website development); Carla Cabrita and Ibrahim Ameen Al-Hashimi (procuring photographs for me in Eswatini when I was unable to travel due to the pandemic), and Sibongile Zondi from S. C. Zondi Attorneys, Eswatini (offering legal opinion for copyright issues).

Finally, I am grateful for those colleagues who read portions and/or the entirety of this book and provided extraordinarily helpful feedback, both in the context of institutional seminars and individually. Thank you to the convenors of workshops and seminars who invited me to present my research while still in progress. These include Stanford's Historical Conversations Series, as well as its Junior Faculty Reading Group, Berkeley's Center for African Studies, the University of Copenhagen's Center of African Studies, the Radcliffe Institute, the Southern African Historical Society, the University of Johannesburg's Department of Historical Studies (which has also generously hosted me as a senior research associate), and the Yale Council on African Studies. I am also grateful to those individuals who provided research advice and leads. My largest debt, as ever, is to Tarik O'Regan, who remains my most inspiring interlocuter. My book has also greatly benefited from the input of Ed Porter, and from his expert reading of my manuscript and his instructive suggestions for its improvement. I'd also like to highlight the help of J. P. Daughton, who perceptively read the manuscript in its entirety, as well as to my colleagues who constructively engaged with the manuscript under the auspices of Stanford's Manuscript Review Workshop (Jim Campbell, Clifton Crais, Gabrielle Hecht, Isabel Hofmeyr, Ato Quayson, Richard Roberts, Pamela Scully). I list here all to whom I'm additionally grateful: Greg Ablavsky, Doo Aphane, Leo Arriola, Andrew Bank, Nora Barakat, Felicitas Becker, Ruby Bell-Gam, Catherine Burns, João Cabrita, Betty Sibongile Dlamini, Nhlanhla Dlamini, Rowan Dorin, Ainehi Edoro, Natasha Erlank, Harvey Feinberg, Bob Forrester, Jonathan Gienapp, Abby Gondek, Liz Gunner, Bruce Hall, Sondra Hale, Shireen Hassim, Meghan Healy-Clancy, Elizabeth Jacob, Destin Jenkins, Cherif Keita, Jill Kelly, Jenny Kuper, Peter Limb, Hugh Macmillan, Dan Magaziner, Ayanda Mahlaba, Athambile Masola, Sisonke Msimang, Maxwell Mthembu, Sinenhlanhla Ncube, Siphiwokuhle Nzima, Sue Ogterop, Kathryn Olivarius, Jacob Olupona, Derek Peterson, Charles Prempeh, Steven Press, Bongile Putsoa, Maria Saldana, Martha Saavedra, Nafisa Sheik, Stephen Sparks, Thato Sukati (to whom this book is gratefully dedicated), Ann Swidler, Julie Taylor (thank you for opening your home in Johannesburg to me so frequently), Lynn Thomas, Liz Thornberry, Chepchirchir Tirop, Charles van Onselen, and Mikael Wolfe.

Stanford University's History Department provided a welcoming and collegial home for the research and writing of this book. I am grateful for the support of my colleagues and especially for the assistance I received from the History Department staff, including Burcak Kozat, Brenda Finkel, and most especially Maria van Buiten in processing invoices.

At Ohio University Press, I am thankful to its former director and editor in chief, Gill Berchowitz, for her enthusiastic support of the project in its early stages. Rick Huard, Beth Pratt, and Sally Welch have carried it to completion, and I am most grateful for their supportive work. Thank you also to Laura André and Jeff Kallet for publicizing the manuscript, Anna Garnai for her assistance with copyright and permissions questions, Tyler Balli for his efficient management of the production process, and Don McKeon for his expert copyediting. Of course, any remaining errors are entirely my own responsibility.

# Biographical Notes

Aphane, Janet—Regina's Kwaluseni neighbor (1928–2020)

Bhengu, Nicholas—South African church leader (1909–85)

Campbell, Killie—South African collector of "Africana" (1881–1965)

Couzens, Tim—South African historian who stored the Twalas' letters in his home for many years (1944–2016)

Dhlomo, Herbert—South African writer (1903–56)

Dhlomo, Rolfes (R. R. R.)—South African writer (1901–71)

Junod, Violaine—South African sociologist (dates unknown)

Kumalo, Percy—Regina's first husband (dates unknown)

Kuper, Hilda—Anthropologist of Eswatini, based at UCLA for many years (1911–92)

Majozi, Muriel—Regina's mother (dates unknown)

Malcolm, Daniel—Chief inspector of Bantu Education (b.?–1962)

Matsebula, J. S. M.—Historian and scholar of Eswatini (1918–93)

Mazibuko, Joseph—Regina's father (dates unknown)

Mpanza, James—Orlando community leader (1889–1970)

Ngcobo, Selby—South African economist (1909–d.?)

Nquku, John—Founder of the Swaziland Progressive Party (1899–d.?)

Phillips, Ray—American missionary and social worker in Johannesburg (1889–1967)

Sobhuza II—Hereditary monarch of Eswatini (1899–1982)

Sundkler, Bengt—Swedish church historian and missionary of the Church of Sweden (1908–95)

Tyrrell, Barbara—South African artist (1912–2015)

Twala, Anne—Regina's daughter-in-law, married Vusi Twala (1944–2021)

Twala, Dan—Regina's second husband, manager of the Bantu Sports Club (1906–86)

Twala, Elizabeth and Shadrack—Dan Twala's brother (Shadrack) married to Elizabeth; parents of Mary and Zanele Twala, although Zanele's father was Dan, not Shadrack (dates unknown)

Twala, Margaret (née Mmope)—Dan Twala's second wife (dates unknown)

Twala, Mary—Regina's niece, adopted by Regina and Dan (1940–2020)

Twala, Pinokie Gelane—Vusi and Anne Twala's daughter; Regina's granddaughter (1970–)

Twala, Regina Gelana—South African/liSwati author, social worker, and politician (1908–68)

Twala, Vusi—Regina's only biological child (1946–77)

Twala, Zanele—Dan Twala's biological daughter and Regina's stepdaughter, raised as her daughter (1958–)

Zwane, Ambrose Phesheya—Founder of the Ngwane National Liberatory Congress (1922–98)

# Introduction

> No one is ever entirely the author of her life.
>
> —Talal Asad, *Genealogies of Religion*

This was the sixth phone call I'd made. My question was always the same. Have you heard of someone called R. D. Twala, who ran as a candidate in the 1963 legislative elections in Eswatini, a country in Southern Africa?[1] Twala had lived in the small town of Kwaluseni, on the outskirts of Eswatini's second-largest city, Manzini. Whoever this person was, Twala was also an accomplished anthropologist whose work was published in the prestigious journal *African Studies* (in which no biographical detail accompanied its articles). I had also come across R. D. Twala in the Uppsala University archives of the Swedish historian Bengt Sundkler. Twala had worked as a researcher for Sundkler in the late 1950s, sending the Swedish scholar meticulously crafted reports on religion in Eswatini. Whoever they were, woman or man, R. D. Twala was intelligent, erudite, politically active, and highly opinionated. My curiosity was piqued. I wanted to learn more about them.

But the answer to my question was also always the same. The historians whom I asked (both professional and lay), the journalists, the political activists, and the Kwaluseni residents all hesitated, thought for a few seconds, and then—I could sense it on phone calls—shook their heads and gave me a no. R. D. Twala was someone about whom they knew nothing at all. The name didn't even elicit a stirring of vague recognition. A complete blank. I was surprised. I had expected that a candidate in Eswatini's first semi-democratic elections—a momentous occasion for the country, just five years before it gained independence from Britain in 1968—and an individual who was a rare published Black African anthropologist of the 1950s would have left some imprint in public memory. Eswatini, moreover, was not a large country—only seven thousand square miles, slightly smaller than the state of New Jersey. My experience of growing up in Eswatini in the 1980s and 1990s was that this was a country where it was hard to remain anonymous.

My sixth phone call broke my streak of bad luck. I was contacting Professor Bongile Putsoa, an academic in her eighties who had taught at the country's university for many years (the university was in the small town of Kwaluseni, adjacent to busy Manzini). I had been directed toward Putsoa by an old school friend of mine, Thato Sukati, who had been married to Bongile's son for some years. As Thato listened to me bemoaning my difficulties in finding more about R. D. Twala, she suddenly thought of her former mother-in-law. Putsoa had not only had grown up in Kwaluseni (Twala's hometown; I at least knew this small fragment from the election bid) but was also deeply knowledgeable about local history. If anyone knew about R. D. Twala, Thato assured me, it would be Bongile Putsoa.

I rang Putsoa and gave my usual explanation. But before I had finished, Putsoa laughed and cut me off: "Oh, you must mean Regina!" For the next fifteen minutes, Putsoa spoke about a woman called Regina Twala who had lived in Kwaluseni in the 1950s and 1960s and who had died in 1968. (I later found out that Regina was born in 1908, placing her at an early sixty when she died.)[2] Putsoa had been a young woman in the 1960s, and her memories of Regina energetically striding around Kwaluseni were still vivid. In Putsoa's recollection, Regina was a social worker engaged in uplift of the community, although she did also hazily recall that Regina was active in politics. One thing in particular stood out in Putsoa's memory. Regina had founded a small library, certainly the only one in Kwaluseni and one of only a very few in the entire country in the 1960s. The tiny building still stood today, Putsoa told me, although now a broken shell with a tree fallen through its roof. She would take me to see it.

I met with Putsoa a few days later, and she did indeed take me to see the old library founded by Regina Twala. It was now a sad ruin under the Kwaluseni sun. A fading name in peeling paint read "Prince Mfanyana Memorial Library." Regina had named the library after Abner Mfanyana Dlamini, the first liSwati man to gain a university degree. Inside I could still see ancient, overturned bookshelves. I would later learn that Regina's founding of this library spoke to her lifelong dedication to the emancipation of the emaSwati people from British colonial rule and to her conviction that education was integral to this goal.[3]

Of even greater value were the introductions Putsoa made for me to Regina's family. There was Anne Twala, Regina's daughter-in-law, who around 1966 had married Regina's only child, her son Vusumuzi (known by family as Vusi). It turned out that Putsoa and Anne Twala were members of the same Methodist church. Anne still lived in the Kwaluseni house Regina had built when she moved to Eswatini in the 1950s. I then met Anne and Vusi's daughter, Gelane Pinokie Twala, who was named after her grandmother. (In later life, Regina used the name Gelana.) Regina never met Pinokie (as she prefers to be called), who was born about a decade after her death. Yet Pinokie was nonetheless Regina's heir. Vusi—Regina's only child—had died in a car crash several years after Regina's death, and Pinokie was his only offspring. Later on, it would become intensely important for my research that in name, as well as in the eyes of the law, Pinokie was Regina's sole heir and her grandmother's legal, intellectual, and spiritual representative.

Meeting her family helped me further unlock the mystery of R. D. Twala. I was subsequently able to also track down the existence of very many letters exchanged between Regina Twala and her second husband, Dan Twala. It is hard to overstate the significance of this collection. It is a unique epistolary archive unmatched in African history for its volume (there are nearly one thousand letters), its chronological longevity (the letters were written throughout a thirty-year period from 1938 to 1968), and for the distinctive voices of its interlocuters. Regina and Dan were both leading figures of twentieth-century Southern Africa, connected to key social and political transformations and figures of their tumultuous era. Regina, for example, was a friend of both Nelson Mandela and his wife, Winnie. It is a collection of letters entirely without peer; I know of no similar correspondence between two figures of twentieth-century Africa. Yet echoing the theme that I was fast coming to see defined Regina's existence—both during her life and posthumously—the letters are completely neglected. Nearly every historian of Southern Africa whom I spoke to about these letters simply had no idea of their existence.

What explains historians and the public's wholesale ignorance of this remarkable collection? For more than fifty years, the letters have been kept in the Johannesburg home of the South African historian Tim Couzens. Couzens had twice interviewed Dan Twala in the late 1970s (about ten years after Regina's death) and had planned—with Dan's blessing—to publish his and Regina's correspondence. Couzens was at the time doing research on Black male playwrights, and Dan was a leading figure in Johannesburg's theater scene, being a founder member of the city's Bantu Dramatic Society in the 1930s. But for some reason, after his interviews of the 1970s, Couzens never returned to the topic of Regina Twala.[4] Instead, Couzens spent much of the 1980s researching his biography of Trader Horn, an early twentieth-century European ivory trader based in Central Africa. Regina and Dan's letters languished in Couzens's study for many decades, and Dan would die in a car crash in Eswatini in the mid-1980s, seemingly putting the final nail in the project's coffin. Couzens himself died in 2016, and ever since, Diana Wall, Couzens's widow, kept the letters in large cardboard boxes in her husband's study. The storage of these letters for fifty years or so in a private Johannesburg home was a double-edged sword. It undoubtedly preserved an important historical collection for posterity. But with the letters locked away and inaccessible, it also contributed to the ongoing public amnesia about Regina Twala. In time, as work on my book progressed, I would also come to appreciate the painful resonance of Regina's legacy—that of a Black female intellectual—being in the ambiguous safekeeping of a white South African academic.

Obscurity and marginalization (frequently at the hands of white scholars) are themes that shape Regina Twala's life and legacy. While a prominent historian like Couzens had at least deemed Regina worthy of passing interest, this was not a widespread sentiment. My initial experience of realizing few people had ever heard of Regina Twala would be repeated very many times as I worked on this book. I became used to politely blank faces as I described the woman I was writing about. I was a biographer whose subject was invisible (or, more accurately, had been made invisible, a process that this book will document). Outside of a minuscule circle of family members, no one in either Eswatini or South Africa (where Regina was born and spent the first forty years of her life) had ever heard of her. Bongile Putsoa would remain a rare exception as someone who had either known her personally or who still remembered her work and her legacy. Kwaluseni's residents knew about the ruined one-room library built by Regina, standing off their main thoroughfare, but all daily passed it by, uncurious and unknowing.

Bringing marginalized people into focus is not a unique predicament for a biographer. There is an entire genre of biography that tells the little-known stories of ordinary women and men, deliberately eschewing attention to the elite, the famed, and the celebrated. Many of these biographies focus on quotidian figures as a way of illuminating a particular period or region. Biographers select "ordinary" people not for their extraordinary features but rather for their everyman qualities.[5] But Regina Twala does not fit this pattern of an obscure woman being clawed from the blank forgetfulness of the past by a dedicated historian. As I was fast finding out, she was far from an ordinary woman. Regina was part of a tiny group of middle-class professional Black women of twentieth-century Southern Africa. In her company were the first female nurses, doctors, teachers, politicians, and social workers, pioneering figures who pushed the boundaries of what was considered acceptable feminine behavior. Yet even among this illustrious company, Regina stands out as exceptional. A cursory examination of her life shows a truly unique figure in the history of twentieth-century Africa.

Born and raised in a Zulu family in the small village of eNdaleni in the Midlands of South Africa, Regina Twala would be only the second Black woman to graduate from the prestigious University of the Witwatersrand in Johannesburg, emerging with a degree in social studies (a mixture of sociology and anthropology). Throughout Regina's life, she wrote prolifically, producing perhaps as many as six book manuscripts (only two survived, one only partially) and over one hundred journalistic and academic articles. Alongside her academic interests, Regina was also an active political figure, protesting for many decades against the racism of the South African apartheid state and against the British colonial state in neighboring Eswatini. Regina also emerged as an outspoken critic of the traditional Swati monarch, Sobhuza II, who seized absolute power after the departure of the British. Regina's personal life was just as extraordinary. Those who knew Regina remember her as stubborn, opinionated, passionate, determined, and difficult. She could be kind to those in need and bitingly dismissive of those in power. Briefly married and subsequently divorced in the mid-1930s, Regina braved societal censure against women who left their husbands. She chose the prospect of a better life against the known reliability of an unhappy marriage. Regina's second marriage to the prominent Dan Twala—a thirty-year-long relationship—was a rich and multilayered intellectual, emotional, and physical union, marking the pair out as one of the power couples of midcentury Southern Africa.

Yet *this* was the woman whom history seemed to have forgotten. What was I to make of this puzzle? How was it that a woman as talented, unusual, memorable, and prolific as Regina Twala had been so thoroughly erased? She was a political leader in an era where few women occupied leadership roles, an intellectual luminary, an author of multiple works, an outspoken journalist, a university-trained anthropologist, and an unconventional defier of norms for women. Regina was certainly not an "ordinary" woman, not by the standards of the 1950s and not even by criteria of the 2020s. Regina, rather, was a blazing star, someone who pioneered numerous firsts for Black women in two different countries in Southern Africa. That a woman did nothing "exceptional" of course does not make her life any less worthy of remembering. But taking into account Regina's many accomplishments does make her invisibility to contemporary audiences all the more puzzling.

Yet the erasure of Regina Twala is a predicament shared by very many African women of the twentieth century. Generations of accomplished female professionals—writers, artists, doctors, and politicians—are virtually unknown outside of their immediate families. One way to measure what writer Zukiswa Wanner calls Black women's "constant flirtation with erasure" is these women's difficulty in gaining the attention of biographers.[6] While biographical coverage of African men is regionally uneven (South Africa predominates, while other parts of the continent are relatively unrepresented; the last biography of a liSwati individual was published in 1981), biographies of African women from anywhere in the continent are still a vanishingly rare species.[7] Of the 225 biographies published of South African figures since 1990, I count only ten that have focused on women.[8] Prominent women like Charlotte Maxeke—a US-educated teacher, social worker, and activist and probably the most famous Black woman in early twentieth-century South Africa—only received a full-length biographical treatment in 2016. Currently, it is not even distributed outside of South Africa.[9] In the rare cases where women are biographers' focus, these are largely women linked to prominent political men—what one historian dubbed the "lives and wives" approach.[10] There are more biographies of Winnie Madikizela-Mandela, for example, than of any other South African woman.[11]

One might argue that African women's biographies remain unwritten because there is simply not enough material with which to construct their lives; sexist societies have undoubtedly marginalized women from written official records. But the biographers of a nineteenth-century South African Khoikhoi woman, Sara Baartman, still managed to write her story despite a nearly complete lack of written documents for a biographical subject who had died two hundred years ago.[12] And historian Athambile Masola reminds us that the chroniclers of African women should search for their stories in locations that are far from obvious. Often women's lives appear in the footnotes of written records more concerned with documenting the deeds of men.[13] Scarcity of materials, moreover, was clearly not an issue for Regina Twala. I have already mentioned her hundreds of letters, her unpublished manuscripts, and her published journalism. This is not a woman whose written output has disappeared or that did not exist in the first place. Moreover, Regina's prominence in social and political life—her university education, her high-profile political activity, her social work—all meant that her activities were frequently covered in newspapers in both South Africa and Eswatini. Indeed, it is rare to write about a Black South African woman who has left behind quite so much trace of her life, both archival and published. How, then, are we to explain the silence about her, given there is simply so much material for a curious biographer to get on with?

Making the fact of Regina Twala's obscurity my focus rather than merely an odd sidenote (and recognizing this is a predicament shared by many other Black women of the twentieth century), this biography answers the questions of *why, how, when,* and *by whom* she has been so thoroughly forgotten, both within her own lifetime and after her death. Far from being a puzzling oddity, Regina's erasure came to me to signal the primary dynamic of her entire life. What follows is both a standard biography that relates the life of its subject, situating her in her context and time period. But it is also a broader meditation on remembrance and forgetting and on the gatekeeping mechanisms that ensure some individuals are celebrated long after their death and others are entirely erased. The anthropologist Michel-Rolph Trouillot memorably writes that "presences and absences . . . are neither neutral or natural. They are created. . . . One 'silences' a fact or an individual as a silencer silences a gun."[14] Telling Regina's story also means telling the story of how she has actively been written out of history, including identifying those responsible for this.

By adopting an agnotological approach (one that foregrounds inquiry into the production of ignorance), I will show how Regina's posthumous obscurity has neither been the product of chance nor the supposedly natural outcome of a little-known figure. Regina was the opposite of little-known: she was a prominent woman. But she was also one who has been deliberately written out of history, of memory, and of public consciousness, a process that began even while she was still alive. Ignorance of Regina Twala has been purposefully constructed. The public, scholars, and political powerbrokers have all engaged in a "sanctioned forgetting" of her legacy, both during her lifetime and afterward.[15]

Yet we usually think of caliber as more important in determining whose legacy endures and whose fades. One of the regular questions I was asked when writing this book and when I mentioned Regina Twala's difficulty in finding publishers, was the variation of "but was her writing any good?" The politics of merit are particularly fraught in a racist and sexist society like twentieth-century Southern Africa. Far more important in determining the success or failure of an individual's legacy than their merit were the facts of white rule over a Black majority population. Since the seventeenth century, Black South Africans had been subject to the imperialistic designs of both Afrikaners—the white settlers that had populated Southern Africa for several centuries—and Britons. In South Africa, this culminated in the election of the Afrikaner National Party on its platform of apartheid, or separate "development" of the races, in 1948, which brought into being one of the most viciously systematic systems of racist segregation the world has ever seen.

In neighboring Eswatini, the Swati monarch Sobhuza II always held nominal powers, meaning—on paper at least—that Black oppression in Eswatini was not on the same scale as in neighboring South Africa. Moreover, under the dubious patronage of the United Kingdom (Eswatini was one of Britain's colonial protectorates until 1968), the country managed to retain some measure of autonomy from South Africa, which had long desired to absorb its tiny neighbor into its own borders. Yet despite the much-vaunted progressiveness of Eswatini on matters of race (an attitude that still persists today), ordinary life in twentieth-century Eswatini was—for a Black person—little different from what lay across the border. Racist segregation laws existed in the country until 1963. EmaSwati had no voting rights until that same year. Violent killings of Blacks by whites—usually punished, if at all, by a minimal sentence or fine—were widespread until independence in 1968. Black women, in particular, were bereft of legal protection and at the whims of their male guardians and traditional chiefs.

Regina Twala's life thus underscores that Black women experienced the horrors of apartheid and colonial rule very differently from Black men. Racism was not gender blind. Being a Black woman under white rule in Southern Africa of the twentieth century meant having even fewer legal rights than a Black man, possessing the legal status of a child, and being unable to inherit or own property in her own right. Regina, however, was part of a tiny minority of women who were granted the status of "exempted" individuals by the British colonial state—a distinction reserved for Western-educated women—and thus she could enjoy the right to own property. But legal status gave Regina scant protection throughout her lifetime. Black women of Southern Africa still had to contend with the misogynoir of the white colonial and apartheid regimes and their anxiety over Black female sexuality and the independent activities of autonomous women.[16] Women like Regina also had to contend with a lack of solidarity from Black men, who were often intent upon compartmentalizing Black women into confining boxes of housekeeper, mother, and sexual object.

In short, a joint whammy of racism and sexism—what feminist scholar Frances M. Beal referred to as "double jeopardy"—made it punishingly difficult for Black women like Regina Twala to establish themselves in all kinds of professional spheres until well into the last decades of the twentieth century.[17] This was certainly true of authorship and academia, two of Regina's chosen spheres. Literary scholar Barbara Boswell documents the astonishing fact that by the 1980s only six books had ever been published by Black women writers in South Africa.[18] Writers like Regina and a handful of others had to contend with sexual harassment, patronizing attitudes, censorious moralizing, and jealous territorialism on the part of male publishing gatekeepers, both white and Black.

The literary gatekeepers of the racist and sexist society of twentieth-century Southern Africa clamped down by quite literally writing her out of the region's record. Regina is not unique among Southern African women writers in never finding a book publisher and being one whose work was consequently buried and near lost. (Even the rare writer who was published—the first English-language book by a Black woman appeared only in 1975—soon found herself out of print.)[19] The literary activist Goretti Kyomuhendo, who worked with women writers in Uganda in the 1980s and 1990s, told me of countless unpublished manuscripts of women writers that had simply never seen the light of day.[20]

Politically as well as intellectually, Regina's career was marked by many defeats. Her experience echoes that of the very many women throughout the continent who found themselves excluded by men from their own national liberation movements in the twentieth century.[21] Regina eventually withdrew from politics in Eswatini, defeated and bruised by the relentless hostility of the men she worked with. Regina's failed efforts at reputation creation during her own lifetime—her doomed work at cementing herself as a Black intellectual and political activist—would be echoed after her death. Regina's last breaths were quite literally taken up with her efforts to ensure her last book manuscript would be published. This work—an important ethnographic opus that would surely have established Regina's reputation as a foremost scholar of Eswatini—was posthumously forwarded to a white anthropologist of Eswatini, the eminent Hilda Kuper at the University of California, Los Angeles (UCLA), for publication. But instead of publishing Regina's work, Kuper buried the manuscript in her UCLA study for many decades. Regina had comparable experiences with other white academics, gatekeeping individuals unwilling to cede ground to Regina as an intellectual and researcher in her own right. Many of Regina's so-called allies—"progressive" white academics who repudiated apartheid and colonial rule—could in fact be her worst enemies, motivated by jealousy and intellectual territorialism.

Given Regina Twala's bitter experience with white scholars, my own role as biographer is an uncomfortable one to occupy. If Regina is a woman written out of history—both in her own lifetime and afterward—what does it mean that her reintroduction to history is being mediated through myself, a white academic? I am a professional historian residing in North America and employed by a prestigious university. I am, moreover, of white Southern African ancestry: my parents—one an Afrikaner, the other a joint national of Portugal and Mozambique—moved to Eswatini in 1982 when I was two. I lived there until 1998 and on and off since then. My bringing Regina's work to light is thus shot through with inherited issues of race and privilege. My family's and my story are part of the history of white supremacy in Southern Africa.

So, however important it is that Regina's story is finally coming to light, that it takes the mediation of a white academic from the Northern Hemisphere to do its telling would surely have rankled Regina. For all her desires to publish her corpus, manage the narrative of her life, and consolidate her legacy, the task of telling her story and of bringing her work to public attention has been taken up by another—and, what's more, by an academic employed by the kind of well-funded institution at which Regina was never able to find work. These are dynamics intensely familiar to African studies as a whole, a field of study historically dominated by white scholars (many in the northern hemisphere) telling the stories of Black African individual and communities. When viewed in this light, it is hard to view my biography of Regina in a straightforwardly rehabilitative sense, to laud it as a worthwhile restoration to memory of an important lost figure. Instead, my biography begs difficult questions about continued white privilege in telling the stories of Black historical subjects and of the entrenched institutional power of the universities and presses that have supported my career while spurning individuals like Regina Twala.

Even while I have wrestled with the implications of my telling Regina's story to the world, it has been clear to me that there is also one other party intensely interested in her public reputation. This is, of course, Regina's family—most of all her granddaughter, Pinokie Gelane Twala, and her two stepchildren (Dan Twala's biological daughter and niece, respectively), Zanele and Mary Twala. (Mary died during the writing of the book.)[22] Living in both Eswatini and South Africa, Regina's family are intensely proud of their mother and grandmother, recognizing her extraordinary talents and eager for the world to know more about her. The family has granted me access to family papers and interviews, in large part because they view the book as a means to bring Regina Twala to a wider audience. Pinokie Twala is a trained *sangoma*—a diviner and healer—whose guiding spirit is her deceased grandmother. Pinokie tells me that Regina in fact has selected me as her biographer. In the family's eyes, I am Regina's chosen instrument for at last ensuring her work is known to the world.

At the same time, Regina Twala's family also recognize the ways in which they run the risk of disempowerment in the managing of her posthumous reputation. Undoubtedly, they are cognizant of Regina's own maltreatment at the hands of the literary-academic establishment, an experience shared by very many Black women of the twentieth century, in South Africa and elsewhere.[23] The fact that the family has long been unaware of the letters kept in Tim Couzens's study is a sore point for them. And for my part, I am both a platform for Regina's legacy as well as a potential exploiter of their beloved relative's story.

Echoing these tensions, the pages that follow do not provide readers with a celebratory narrative of an indomitable woman who triumphed against the odds. Regina Twala was a powerful woman who was silenced by even more powerful forces. She was a prominent woman whose legacy has been obscured by those who sought—and still seek—to promote other agendas. The traces of her that survive are so hard to find, so locked away from the world that she is all but lost, save to those like myself equipped with privileged networks that gain them access to deceased white historians' studies and the ability to travel to international archives.

Some might find controversial my choice to frame both Regina's life, as well as my telling of it, as a tragedy. Critics might feel my approach places too much emphasis on the victimhood of Black women rather than their strength. Even the title of my book, *Written Out,* in the passive voice, suggests defeat rather than agency. The small number of biographies of Black African women—and more broadly scholarship of African women—prefer to tell far more celebratory narratives. Scholars offer stories of resilience, perseverance, and triumph against the odds, success despite challenges, rising up despite defeat.

As valuable as these stories are, it is important not to immediately fold vulnerability into triumph. The stories of silenced women deserve to be told without too quickly burnishing them into stories of resistance. In large part this is a question of ethical accountability. The forces that silenced Regina in her lifetime are still active today. Eswatini is today as much in the grip of the traditionalist monarchy as it ever was. As I write this introduction in mid-2021, the kingdom is undergoing a turbulent uprising as emaSwati citizens protest the absolute monarch, Mswati III, son of Sobhuza II. More than sixty emaSwati are reported to have been murdered by the country's army. The country is seeking proponents for democratic reform—such as Regina would surely be—but still grappling with the repressive silence the state imposes upon any discussion of these figures. Few in official circles in Eswatini today would be comfortable with celebrating a dissenting figure like Regina Twala. Regina was out of step with the politics of the 1960s; tragically, she is still out of time in contemporary Eswatini. Across the border, postapartheid South Africa has never gone through a true accountability process. The question of reparations has never been seriously discussed, and many of the economic and social inequalities of the twentieth century persist today. African studies—in the United States, at least—is still dominated by white academics. To simply celebrate Regina's triumphs draws our gaze away from those culpable for her silencing.

Telling the story of a written-out woman thus leads us straight to the crucial question of agency. Since the 1980s, as part of the broader shift toward "history from below," scholars have celebrated historical actors' possession of agency and the fact that even the most oppressed individuals are able to assert autonomy and self-determination.[24] Yet, as the literary scholar Naminate Diabate powerfully claims, "There is no agency outside of restrictions."[25] We might also think of the words of anthropologist Talal Asad cited at this introduction's outset: "No one is ever entirely the author of her life." I do not intend the title of this book to suggest a passive lack of agency. But I do mean it to convey that however creative and resourceful Regina Twala was, it was nonetheless impossible for a single Black woman to transcend the racist and sexist constraints of her time—and, indeed, of our time too. And even posthumously, the fact of Regina's mediation through me, a white academic, suggests the continued persistence of those structures of power. Following Diabate's construction, agency and restriction always unhappily coexist. This, then, is the story of an invisible woman, an erased woman, a silenced woman, a woman whose fate was for the telling of her story to be always in the hands of others. This is the story of a woman written out of history, and this is the story of how she was written out. This is Regina Gelana Twala's story.

# 1

## eNdaleni

> [They said,] Gelana you should learn to sit like a mature woman, one leg on top of the other, or else pull down your dress or sit with your legs stretched, a woman's underwear should not be visible when she is sitting down, those are habits of promiscuous women who just sit without care.
>
> —Regina to Dan, July 2, 1939 (RTP)

From an early age Regina learned what Southern African society expected of Black women. Her lessons on femininity came from two quite different, yet strangely compatible, sources. The first was the conservative Christian teachings of the rural Methodist mission where she was raised. Black Christian women were taught by white missionaries that their spiritual virtue mapped onto feminine domesticity. Then there was the fact that Regina came of age in the middle of a neotraditionalist cultural revival, one that harked back to the lost glories of the Zulu monarchy now extinguished by British guns. Both Christian missionaries and Zulu traditionalists invoked women as the backbone of the home, the latter claiming the Zulu nation would only be rebuilt if its womenfolk dedicated themselves to marriage and motherhood.

However far Regina would travel from this ideology, we cannot appreciate the forces that shaped her unless we understand this: hers was a society that believed women belonged in the home.

This is what we know of the first years of her life. Regina Doris Mazibuko was born in 1908 at Indaleni Mission Station, South Africa.[1] The mission was situated in a remote spot of the Natal Midlands, a swath of fertile hills extending upward into the country's interior from the coastal city of Durban. The British Methodist missionary James Allison had originally situated his mission in Mahamba, in nearby Eswatini, a future British protectorate. But Allison and his small band of converts faced growing hostility from the then Swati monarch, who, like many other African hereditary rulers of the nineteenth century, was decidedly unsure about Christian proselytizers. Allison gathered a small group of converts—mostly emaSwati but also a band of Hlubi refugees from Natal, members of a lineage displaced by warfare between their king, Langalibalele, and the then mighty Zulu nation under King Mpande.

Allison fled with the band into the hills of neighboring Natal, already under British rule.[2] Regina's own grandfather was one of this group, having been a Hlubi "warrior of King Langalibalele," as she remarked in later life. Given Regina's later reinvention as a patriotic liSwati, it is fitting that her distant forebearers had in fact arrived at eNdaleni in South Africa via Eswatini. While many politicians in her lifetime, both Black and white, would argue that ethnicity was an immovable entity, Regina's own biography illuminates just how fluid the labels of "Zulu," "Swati," and "Hlubi" were for those who inhabited them.

Once the refugees arrived in Natal, in 1847, the British colonial state awarded Allison six thousand acres of land. Allison promptly named this Indaleni, possibly after the thick mist forests that still grew in the area.[3] Within a year or so, a neatly laid out village emerged atop eNdaleni Hill. There were sixty whitewashed cottages, a chapel, and a school nestled in the green foothills of the massive Drakensberg Mountains with views of the valley below.

A community of prosperous isiZulu-speaking farmers, teachers, and craftsmen emerged. Like many other settlements across Southern Africa, the mission's goal was to create a new community of Christian Africans. Detached from old allegiances to tribe and chief, loyal to the new Christian God, these individuals became known as *amakholwa*—"the people who believe." Indaleni's residents—including its first Christian chief, Majozi—purchased small plots to farm. Individual possession of property, contrasted with the Zulu system of communal land ownership, was a defining feature of the mission.[4] Amakholwa also hoped for equality with whites. In amakholwa's opinion, their Christianity—and the associated skill of literacy—marked them out as equals of any people in the world. These Christians distanced themselves from their compatriots, denounced old traditions, and celebrated their status as civilized moderns. The small community flourished remarkably. Allison approvingly observed "the native Christians have been most industrious . . . cultivating their own gardens and building their own homes, now properly clothed in articles of British manufacture."[5]

Black women experienced Christian conversion in particularly acute ways. Missionaries found it was women who flocked most readily to their missions, many fleeing unwanted marriages or the stigma of widowhood.[6] Upon arriving at the mission, women were taught reliance upon Christ. But they were also taught to write and read, most of all the Bible. Conversion thus introduced gendered and generational tensions, upsetting the balance of power in Zulu society between elders and youths, men and women. The young Regina would not have been unusual in performing the powerful task of reading and writing for her unschooled elders (in her case, the grandfather to whom she daily read the newspaper). Yet countering this whisper of independence, missionaries also pounded into Zulu women's minds the importance of domestic virtue. In common with nineteenth-century Christian women worldwide, Indaleni's females were taught that piety was as much domestic as spiritual. Reading the Bible was no good if one could not sew or bake. The Allisons established a Manual Labour School, training girls as dressmakers and cooks. The result of all this was the formation of new Africans. Regina's ancestors were Christian women and men adapted to Western ways, who aspired to a universalist belief in the equality of the races, who absorbed the Victorian ideology that a woman's place was in the home, and who embraced private entrepreneurship.

But danger loomed. By the time Regina's mother, Muriel Majozi, was born in the 1880s, the mission had undergone a reversal of fortune. A European farming settlement named Richmond sprung up across the valley, barely two miles from eNdaleni. Richmond's whites looked jealously at the success of their African neighbors. They complained that the prosperity of Indaleni's Black farmers made them reluctant to work on European farms, leaving them short of labor. The dream of equality of the races was fast fading. Colonial policy soon targeted eNdaleni and other communities of successful Christian farmers.[7] Authorities passed laws reducing Africans' access to land and undercut their economic independence, forcing them into European employment on farms and in the nearby towns of Pietermaritzburg and Durban.[8]

The century into which Regina was born saw colonial repression of its African subjects reach new lows of brutality. Regina's birth year, 1908, marked the end of the Zulu Rebellion, an African uprising against British rule in Natal. The rebellion had started at Richmond when local men—likely linked to eNdaleni—killed two colonial tax collectors. Similar acts of defiance erupted throughout Natal.[9] After the British brutally put down the rebellion by killing four thousand Zulu men, they were even more determined to limit Black economic success. Amid worsening land shortages for Africans, patriarchs like Majozi lamented the unraveling of rural society and their diminishing control over their subjects.

The draconian 1913 South African Natives Land Act was a further blow to Natal's Black residents. The act divided South Africa's land between Blacks and whites in a dramatically unequal fashion: 7 percent for Blacks, the majority of the population, and over 90 percent for whites, who made up less than 20 percent of South Africans. As formerly prosperous settlements like eNdaleni declined, these inexorable forces propelled Africans into towns and cities for employment.[10] The pieces of a grim puzzle were moving into place: land shortage and rural poverty, the hollowing-out of rural families as men moved to cities for work, the diminishment of traditional authorities, and the resurgence of the politics of traditionalism with its attendant gender conservatism. All of these were the forces shaping Regina's early years.

Regina seems to have been Muriel Majozi and Joseph Mazibuko's only child, and Joseph either died or disappeared shortly after her birth. The disappearance of male family members was not uncommon in these years of chronic labor migration to industrial centers. In later life, Regina never once mentioned her father, though she would often affectionately call her second husband, Dan Twala, "Daddy." At times Dan occupied a distinctly paternalistic role in relation to his wife. But being the sole child of a single mother was not an insuperable handicap because, as a member of the prominent Majozi family, Regina's mother was well connected to the mission's elite.

Like for many eNdaleni women, economic duress obliged Regina's mother to work as a domestic servant in a white household in Durban.[11] Rural poverty meant it was not just men who left home for employment. The prevalence of African women who left families to work alone in towns, housed in the mean back rooms of white employers or in "girls' hostels," triggered debates about Zulu society's breakdown. Men lamented the autonomous women who repudiated their duties to pursue independent incomes in the city. Once these women were in town, free of husbands and fathers, many men feared for their virtue and for Black society's stability. One newspaper commented, "We have been recently impressed by the rapid decline in the morality of Native girls who live in the towns. . . . Under native custom, a woman's place is in the home, where they attended to their husbands or parents and brought up children."[12]

While we do not know what Regina made of her mother's absences in Durban, it meant she was raised by her maternal grandparents in eNdaleni, a common intergenerational arrangement in rural South Africa. Despite long periods apart, Regina was close throughout her life to her mother, as she was to her grandparents. Regina grew up in her family's cottage, one of a cluster of houses where the oldest residents of the mission lived. Situated in a "secluded corner of the Mission," the Mazibuko home was named "Cool Hill Cottage," suggesting its situation atop the hill and its enjoyment of welcome breezes. (eNdaleni was punishingly hot in the summer months of December to February.)[13] Regina's adult memories of eNdaleni were glowingly positive, almost rose-tinted, casting it as idyllic. She would remember the "simplicity of country life" at eNdaleni, eulogizing her luck in "breathing the fresh air and inhaling the mist drops that veil the vales and dales."[14] Throughout Regina's decades in Johannesburg, eNdaleni remained a powerful countertype to the city, a symbol of a slower and more gentle life. Perhaps it was her early eNdaleni attachment that so disposed Regina toward the quiet rural life of Eswatini in the 1950s and 1960s.

But Regina was not merely going around "inhaling mist drops." School kept her very busy. The mission's primary and secondary schools were located up the hill from the Mazibukos' cottage. There was a collection of white buildings with a large, two-story edifice in the center; this served as the main dining hall and central classroom. In 1914 Regina enrolled in the primary school around the age of six and remained there for ten years. She left the high school at the age of sixteen, in 1924. Regina's decade at Indaleni School exposed her to the missionary truism that education for girls should be "industrial," not "academic." Such views reflected the Christian consensus that women were innately disposed toward domesticity, suited for housework rather than books. The preference for industrial education also spoke to missionaries' affinity with white settlers' economic ideology: Blacks should be trained for lives of servitude. If a girl did attend school, she should be prepared for domestic service—to a white employer before marriage and for a husband after marriage. One European educationalist summarized Indaleni's goals thus: "[Education] will make the native girl more valuable to her community. . . . [She] will be able to keep her house better and be of service to white people."[15]

In this sense, one way to understand Regina's decade-long education at Indaleni is as training in a conservative vision of African Christian womanhood—exactly what she would rebel against in later years. Preparation for future domesticity—and most probably, service in a white household—was paramount. At both primary and high schools, Regina learned cooking, knitting, dressmaking, and basket making, as well as Indaleni's speciality—spinning with wool from local sheep. She probably boarded in one of three large, airy dormitories edged by verandas. Days began at a bleary-eyed 5:30 a.m. Thereupon followed a short prayer service, scripture class, and from 7:30 a day of classes, sports, music lessons (Regina learned how to play the organ here), cleaning, strenuous clothes washing in iron buckets around the outdoor water pump, and ironing. Nighttime devotions divided the days.[16] The British principal, Rev. Arthur Cragg, and his wife oversaw the students. Cragg was given to bouts of melancholy triggered by the challenges of a dipsomaniac deputy headmistress and an endless rotation of staff who left, deterred by low wages and the mission's remote location.[17]

Cragg's relationship with Regina and the other girls was both affectionate and paternalistic. Hugs and cards greeted Cragg's homecomings to the school after absences. When students struck in protest of the poor food, they subsequently sent a repentant note to the Craggs, "our dear parents," asking them to "take us as your dear children, we promise to try be good."[18] Above all, Cragg and his teachers kept an eagle eye on the girls' sexuality. Edwardian Christianity mandated a girl preserve her virtue for marriage; girls were taught to fiercely guard their purity. Regina and her classmates dressed severely: calf-length black skirts and starched white blouses buttoned up the neck.[19] In later life she remembered being scolded by teachers to "sit like a mature woman" so her underwear did not show. Otherwise, she would be marked out as a "promiscuous woman."[20] Cragg expelled girls for meeting with boys from eNdaleni village at night, one of his recurring problems. ("It seems hopeless to expect decent behavior from these girls," Cragg gloomily mused.[21]) Regina, however, passed through her years at Indaleni without any disciplinary missteps of this nature.

While she excelled at spinning and dressmaking, the teenage Regina stood out from her peers as both academically talented and intent upon further education. A photograph of Regina in her teens—the earliest I have found of her—shows her wide-set eyes calmly surveying the photographer. She has a small nose and a determined chin and mouth. She would not be deterred from pursuing her interests. Even an industrial school like Indaleni included options for "advanced academic subjects," offering a select group arithmetic, literature, geography, and history alongside domestic science and homecrafts.[22] Yet the bulk of Regina's education, as for intelligent girls throughout the world, was carried out through books devoured in her free time, late at night in her dormitory bed with a flickering candle for company. While a prominent colonial official claimed, "Zulu people are not readers to any great extent, they prefer to sing or dance or talk,"[23] the truth was that from a young age Regina read voraciously.[24] In the words of Dan Twala, "that girl was a reader."[25]

The teenage Regina belonged to a minuscule group of literate women. By 1931 only 12 percent of South Africa's adult African population could read, most of whom were men.[26] The very few female readers of the early twentieth century almost exclusively belonged to Regina's Christian mission–educated younger generation. Growing numbers of children were attending elementary schools, but far fewer—especially girls—went on to secondary schools like Indaleni. This was largely due to their cost (in 1907, Indaleni's fees were £8 per year, about one-third of an annual Black salary)[27] and prejudices against female education. From 1901

FIGURE 1.1. Regina Mazibuko, ca. 1920 (RTP)

to 1934 only 253 Africans in the entire country passed the highest graduation exam. While we don't have a gendered breakdown of these numbers, we can safely assume the vast majority were male.[28]

Newspapers, novels, and the Bible made up the bulk of the young Regina's reading matter. Scripture, as we know, was drilled daily into Indaleni girls, largely through recitation exercises in the spacious central classroom. Cragg referred to the "hours spent studying the grand old stories of the Old and New Testament" and his habit of "dropping on an inattentive child for an unexpected answer."[29] Regina read aloud the Zulu weekly, *Ilanga lase Natal,* for her unschooled grandparents, humorously "disgusted" that her grandfather made her read every inch, even the advertisements. We get a sense of the wider horizons beyond eNdaleni this opened for Regina: reading for her grandfather meant absorbing "news from our country" as well as from "overseas."[30] In addition to the expansive effects of reading, readers like Regina and her peers stressed books' companionate and self-improving effects. As one contemporary newspaper column on this advised, "A live book is more to a man than his best friend. . . . It comforts, cheers, inspires cautions and advises, it imparts light and understanding."[31] The author of this piece was Rolfes Dhlomo, a leading literary figure in the early twentieth-century Zulu Christian elite—and a future intellectual nemesis of Regina's. Dhlomo, moreover, placidly assumed it would be a man who benefited from a good book.

In fact, evidence from Regina's habits suggests literate Black women were also picking up mysteries, romances, poems, and plays. Like many others, Regina loved Georgette Heyer, a pioneer of the historical romance genre and a popular author of this period.[32] But men worried what would result from women reading too much, especially "unedifying" novels. Moralizing voices warned women against the "mischiefs of bad reading," no doubt indicating the popularity of low-brow fiction.[33] And while Regina could easily quote Romantic poets such as James Henry Leigh Hunt, her favorite books in her teenage years were Christian pulp fiction novels.[34] She adored the Cornish Christian novelist

Joseph Hocking who, almost unknown today, was one of the most popular authors of the interwar period. Hocking's books blended syrupy Methodist piety and historical romance.[35] Perhaps tellingly, Regina's favorite of Hocking's many books was his 1922 *The Girl Who Defied the World*—a stirring tale of female autonomy inspired by Christian ideals.[36]

In 1925 Regina did what many of the tiny number of academically inclined girls produced by mission schools across South Africa did. She decided to embark upon a career as a schoolteacher. Most Christian girls of this time were similarly plumping for a career in either teaching or nursing—although both were undertaken with the tacit understand that careers ceased after marriage. Tapping into stereotypes of women as nurturing caregivers, teaching and nursing were careers that still affirmed women's supposed affinity for homemaking. Black teachers and nurses were also paid far less than their white counterparts.[37] For a white state unwilling to invest money in Black social services, it was cynically convenient that teaching and nursing were so enthusiastically embraced by Black women. It was just as convenient they were paid a fraction of what white women earned.[38]

Regina enrolled at elite Adams College, an American missionary school on the Indian Ocean coast, sixty miles east of eNdaleni. Regina must have been tremendously excited to arrive at Adams in January 1925. Housed in an imposing building with gabled rooves, it was Natal's premier and oldest college for Africans, already famous in the 1920s for educating Black society's future leaders. Thirty years later, in 1956, the school would be closed by the apartheid government for its crime of daring to give Africans a decent education. But this was far in the future. Right now, in the 1920s, the college's prestige was impressed upon new students like Regina in annual events like the "Centenary of Pioneers," in which staff and dignitaries eulogized founding members with great gravitas. Regina and her friends irrepressibly giggled through the ceremony, tickled by the occasion's pomposity—"of course we were punished accordingly."[39]

Like other South African institutions run by white liberals, Adams was a paradoxical place. It was neither wholly emancipatory nor entirely repressive for its Black students. Under the direction of white American missionaries, Adams stressed a vocational education that trained Africans for their "station in life." In this respect, Adams subscribed to the racist ideology that taught Africans were mostly destined for manual labor. But there were also more hopeful opportunities for Black students. From the mid-1920s—when Regina entered the school—the well-known Black educator Z. K. Matthews was controversially reorientating the school in a more academic direction. As headmaster, Mathews emphasized literature, history, and geography, insisting Black students be taught to value the life of the mind as well as practical skills.[40] Alongside woodwork and dressmaking, teachers fed students Romantic poets: Wordsworth, Shelley, Keats, and Longfellow.[41] Perhaps significant for Regina's embryonic authorial ambitions, the school under Matthews's directorship stressed creativity, encouraging students to write poems, short stories, and plays.[42]

Adams, moreover, was a particularly mixed bag for its female students. Its records disappeared in a fire in the 1970s, making it impossible to reconstruct a female student's life during the 1920s. But we can glean something of what Regina's days would have been like from the account of a near contemporary. Ellen Kuzwayo was a political activist who attended Adams in the early 1930s. Her memoirs, written at the height of her fame in the 1980s, describe a utopian progressive environment where staff and students celebrated Africans' equality with Europeans. But even Kuzwayo's glowing account admits contradictions. While staff emphasized racial equity, female students were considered by many as men's intellectual inferiors. Teachers encouraged girls to substitute domestic science subjects for scientific ones and to embark upon industrial courses rather than enroll in the academic high school.[43] Disturbingly, girls at Adams didn't feel physically safe. Sexual harassment from male students and teachers was common. Kuzwayo remembers more than one occasion when school leadership dismissed male teachers for this.[44]

Yet for all this, Adams was an environment that stressed female intellectual accomplishment far more than Indaleni—with its spinning and dressmaking—had ever done. By the early 1930s, a few years after Regina left, the school got its first female teacher with a BA degree, the remarkable Ellen Ngozwana, a graduate of Fort Hare Native College and a future Ugandan politician by virtue of her marriage to a Ugandan national. Ngozwana provided an inspiring example for Adams's female students; Regina, surely, took note at what a Black woman could achieve.[45] By 1934 the college was lauding its female graduates in a range of professional spheres, while also regretting there were—other than teaching and nursing—still "few occupations open to Native girls as yet."[46] And Regina's time at Adams was not all work. She experienced her first romantic relationship there, with a young Zulu man called Selby Ngcobo, from Pietermaritzburg. The romance was short lived, but Regina would feel its legacy for many years. By the 1930s Ngcobo would be a thorn in Regina's side, a prominent member of the Zulu intelligentsia who could not—would not—take female intellectuals like Regina seriously (perhaps speaking to Ngcobo's early formation in Adams's misogynistic environment).

Regina completed her teachers' training course in 1926, after two years at Adams. By 1930 there is a definite record of her being employed as an isiZulu teacher at her alma mater, Indaleni High School. Regina gracefully accomplished the transition from former student to successful teacher, popular both with the two-hundred-odd students and her colleagues.[47] Dan Twala remembered that "Rev Cragg and his family used to respect Gelana very much; she was a hard-worker, a decided character, very practical, in the church."[48] Regina's lifelong qualities of resourcefulness and practicality were already evident. Her faith was also important to her; Regina frequently volunteered to lead prayers in the school chapel and played the organ for services. At this stage in Regina's life, all evidence suggests she wholeheartedly subscribed to the tenets of early twentieth-century South African Methodism: belief in a God who saved her from her sins, who demanded high standards of personal piety from his followers, and whose will could be divined via regular solitary Bible reading and prayer.[49]

Alongside spiritual formation, tennis was also a major part of Regina's time while teaching at Indaleni. While we don't know for sure when she learned the sport, by the early 1930s Regina was an accomplished player and a member of Indaleni women's Sunbeams Lawn Tennis Club.[50] Dan Twala called his wife's tennis prowess "wonderful."[51] A photograph from this time shows Regina with her club-mates. She is dressed in a knee-length white dress wearing a jaunty hat that shades her eyes from the sun; her right hand grips her racket, suggesting she finds being photographed tiresome and would much rather be on the court. For a small group of Black middle-class women, tennis became a marker of femininity (it was one of the only competitive sports considered "womanly") and of class (tennis-playing signaled leisure and sophistication).[52] The chief of eNdaleni, and Regina's kinsman, Gilbert Majozi, was also committed to the sport; his

FIGURE 1.2. Regina Mazibuko playing tennis (*far left*), ca. 1925–30 (RTP)

influence meant the mission had excellent tennis courts.[53] Regina enjoyed the competitive Black tennis scene of the 1930s, regularly traveling with her fellow Sunbeams to play other clubs around Natal and in cities like Pietermaritzburg and Durban.[54]

During her time as a teacher at Indaleni, Regina gained first-hand experience of what happened to African girls who bucked the day's sexual codes. Shortly after her arrival at the school, Reverend Cragg charged Regina with the sensitive task of escorting home a young student expelled for being pregnant (surely a sign of Cragg's regard for his new teacher). Regina took the train with the dejected girl from eNdaleni to the port city of Durban. There she waited with the girl for her boat back to the Eastern Cape, where her family lived.[55] Falling pregnant before marriage was the worst fate for a girl of the 1930s, a blow to her reputation and with dire consequences for future marital prospects.[56] The experience made a strong impression upon Regina; the girl's humiliating ostracism powerfully embedded in her memory. This, however, is not to say that Regina—a pious young Methodist woman—disagreed with the girl's fate. At this point, Regina was also a branch leader for the Wayfarers, a racially segregated South African version of the international Girl Guides movement. The Wayfarers aimed to neuter youthful female sexuality, preaching the domestic gospel to thousands of African girls across Natal: devote yourself to home-crafts, and zealously guard your chastity.[57]

While immersing her in the conversative Christianity of British Methodism, teaching at Indaleni School also exposed Regina to new currents in South African politics. By the 1930s the region was experiencing a Zulu cultural renaissance, exemplified by a political organization called Inkatha ye Zulu. Inkatha sought to combat Black social disintegration precipitated by racist legislation, rural poverty, and urban migration by reviving Zulu culture. This also meant enforcing "traditional" (read "domestic") roles for women. These Zulu patriots considered the fate of the Zulu nation and the discipline of its womenfolk to be tightly intertwined. In this respect, Inkatha was not a lone phenomenon. There were

FIGURE 1.3. Regina Mazibuko with fellow Wayfarers (*back row, far right*), ca. 1920 (RTP)

many other Zulu cultural movements of the 1930s that similarly stressed "traditional" gender values as a way of ameliorating social erosion. The Zulu Cultural Society, founded in 1936, lamented that "home life is losing its time-honored grip. . . . Who will mother the Zulu Nation?"[58] There was also the Bantu Youth League, formed by the Zulu social worker Sibusiswe Makanya (who had trained at Columbia University), which tackled female "immorality" in towns and "aimed to keep the girls pure in the right way."[59]

eNdaleni played a key role. Reflecting the period's unlikely alliance between Zulu Christians and traditionalists, eNdaleni's Christian chief, Gilbert Majozi, occupied the prominent role of chairman of Inkatha. The white state's hardening segregation, combined with worsening rural poverty, distanced Christian elites from their former confidence in their identity as civilized new moderns. In an era of urgent need, alliances with rural traditionalists seemed an appealing idea for Christians like Majozi.[60] At the very least, Christians and traditionalists shared similar ideas on women, the family, and female chastity. It was thus that Majozi directed Inkatha's major fundraising initiative of this decade, erection of a commemorative statue of the nineteenth-century Zulu king Shaka kaZulu.[61] Majozi hosted the paramount chief, Solomon kaDinuzulu, at eNdaleni, an occasion upon which kaDinuzulu addressed the whole school and at which Regina would certainly have been present.[62]

Regina was profoundly shaped by this convergence of conservative Christianity and Zulu nationalism. In many ways, her Indaleni career gives the impression of a conventional Zulu Christian woman of the 1930s. This was a woman who was a respectable schoolteacher, who guarded her virginity for marriage in keeping both with the teachings of her church and the dictates of Zulu society, and who expected to give up work after marriage. Regina was genuinely enthusiastic about homecrafts, something that would persist for her whole life. Even at the height of her political career in Eswatini in the 1960s, she hoed, planted, weeded, and cooked and made beadwork on a nearly daily basis.[63] Regina particularly excelled at dressmaking, sewing Indaleni children's costumes for plays and fancy-dress days, as well as organizing handmade prizes for sports day.[64] Regina was also a great admirer of Zulu culture, reflecting the neotraditionalist mood of the day. She singlehandedly organized a fundraising concert of traditional Zulu songs by Indaleni girls in Durban (whose success led Cragg to enthusiastically pronounce, "Miss Mazibuko is just 'it'"[65]). Regina also immersed herself in local history and folklore, on her own initiative interviewing eNdaleni elders to record the history of the Hlubi people in Eswatini.

But Regina's destiny would not be defined by these notions of womanhood. She would neither fit into the mold of compliant Christian homemaker nor docile Zulu daughter of her elders. Not least, this was because in just a few years—as a divorced woman—Regina would feel profoundly betrayed by the Zulu Christian elite's complacent consensus on female virtue. But this was in the future. Right now, Regina was fast absorbing a different stream of ideas about modern African womanhood, ideas emerging amid the migration of women to cities like Johannesburg. Regina's world was much wider than both her quiet mission station and the politics of Zulu cultural nationalism. In addition to traveling to tennis tournaments across Natal and Zululand, on several occasions she visited the gold-mining metropolis of Johannesburg.[66]

Most of all, it was Regina's life as a reader that introduced her to new and exciting notions of female independence. Regina's grandfather had jokingly warned her, as a child, against bad behavior on the grounds that "the newspaperman will write about [your] behavior in the paper for the whole world to read."[67] While this suggests a young girl who was lively and mischievous, it also hints at how the Johannesburg newspapers would become Regina's entry point into "the whole world," a far wider stage than her quiet eNdaleni life. By day, Regina taught, sewed, led prayers, played tennis, and organized "traditional" Zulu dances and craft activities. By night, reading alone in her quiet schoolteacher's room, Regina pored over debates about modern Black women in Johannesburg newspapers like *Bantu World* and *Umteteli wa Bantu*. And Regina would soon enter the fray, penning her own contributions to these same newspapers.

# 2

# Mademoiselle

> "I am planning to get married but I can't find a suitable girl. I want a girl of good character and so far I haven't succeeded in getting one." The above words were uttered by one of the many young men we meet daily, who are in search of a rose without a thorn. The question is: Will they recognize her when they happen to meet her on the way? I always wonder whether these men really know what a good character is.
>
> —"Young Men Look for a Rose without a Thorn: But Look in Vain," by "Mademoiselle," *Bantu World,* April 14, 1934

In the early months of 1934, a compelling new column appeared in the pages of the popular newspaper *Bantu World.* Its pseudonymous author, "Mademoiselle," sketched out a new African female who took the lead in matters of the heart. This was not a "simpering silent woman" but rather someone who held firm opinions and expressed them to her man. Mademoiselle wrote about love. But not old-style courtship between Zulu women and men, decorously supervised by vigilant elders. No, Mademoiselle's topic was modern African love, carried out between women and men as equals and played out in the big city of Johannesburg, far from the watchful eyes of parents. The column offered advice to modern women about how to steer romantic relationships in the new environment of the city—how, for example, to gracefully handle the advances of unknown men while riding on a tram. The column also prescribed new norms for modern domesticity. Mademoiselle suggested African men pitch in with housework and dandle the baby to give their wives—who might, after all, have work commitments of their own—a break. Mademoiselle's readers, largely women, loved the column. One letter to the editor enthused that Mademoiselle's "advice was beyond description."[1]

Mademoiselle was none other than Regina Mazibuko, devoted follower of *Bantu World* from the remote mission station of eNdaleni. And from 1934 Mademoiselle was also one of the newspaper's best-known female writers. Regina's early adulthood years had coincided with a great blossoming of African newspapers. While very few independent African periodicals had survived the Great Depression, the early 1930s saw several new ones emerge, most based in Johannesburg. These newspapers addressed their readers as urban moderns, living in worlds far removed from the repressive rural tribalism of the colonial imagination. The earliest of these newspapers was *Umteteli wa Bantu,* founded in 1920. But the most popular was *Bantu World,* founded in 1932, whose main readership was in Johannesburg and surrounding gold-mining conurbations as well as in the neighboring territories that supplied labor to the city. In contrast to regional newspapers like the Zulu weekly *Ilanga lase Natal,* whose content was largely in isiZulu (with a few English pages scattered throughout), both *Bantu World* and *Umteteli* were distinguished by their use not only of English but also of no fewer than six other African vernaculars.[2] Newspapers such as these were transcending older notions of insular ethnic identity, styling themselves and their readers as transnational and multilingual. Their readers were the new urban Black middle classes that had emerged in Johannesburg during the interwar years, individuals pushed to the city by the failing rural economy and pulled by the allure of better wages and independence from male elders.

Regina joined many women of the 1930s in devouring these publications, especially *Bantu World,* which was the first of the city's newspapers to appreciate its female readers, both in the city and farther afield. Women, of course, had lived in Johannesburg since its founding in the 1880s. But it was only in the 1920s and 1930s, accelerated by the Depression, that increasing rural poverty drove tens of thousands of women to Johannesburg. They came from rural provinces like Regina's own Natal as well as from the neighboring countries of Lesotho (then Basutoland), Eswatini (then Swaziland), and Botswana (then Bechuanaland). For the first time, the city had a significant Black female population. Women took up jobs in domestic service, teaching, and nursing. Yet the astronomical expenses of city living meant these poorly paid professions were simply not sustainable for many women (and in any case, teaching and nursing were only open to the educated elite). Large numbers of women turned instead to the illicit and more lucrative realms of beer brewing and the keeping of shebeens (informal drinking establishments run in Southern Africa out of a woman's home). White municipal administrators in vain tried to thwart beer brewing, seeing this a way to stem the tide of rural women flowing into the city. Their disapproving view, shared with Black men in the countryside, was that single women in the cities undermined societal cohesion and patriarchal power.[3]

For women like Regina, newspapers powerfully reflected this massive demographic and cultural shift. In 1932 *Bantu World* introduced its first Women's Pages (*Umteteli* followed in 1933), featuring advertisements for cosmetics and kitchen appliances.[4] An enthusiastic response meant the number of pages devoted to female issues rose steadily. A popular women's beauty contest invited women across the country to send in enticing photographs of themselves for the readers to judge. Riding this buzz, *Bantu World* launched a dedicated women's supplement called *Marching Forward,* its name exemplifying the sense of self-improving modernity that urban African women of this period espoused. Reflecting its more conservative views and rural readership, the isiZulu weekly *Ilanga lase Natal* did not introduce a dedicated women's page until 1937.[5]

Regina was an ardent reader of these newspapers and especially of their Women's Pages, viewing them as contact with an urban world far removed from the mission's parochialism. Newspapers were her link to "town people." eNdaleni, by contrast, was an uncivilized "forest." But it was not always easy to buy newspapers in rural eNdaleni, and so she relied upon friends in the city to send them. This way of procuring newspapers could be frustrating when contacts neglected to keep up a steady supply. Regina reproached one friend, "You are very funny though, because you won't even send me papers, Umteteli and Bantu World, where do you expect me to get information that would interest town people in the forest? Please dear, do make it a point to send me some copies of the papers."[6] Elsewhere she wrote of feeling sadly estranged from "civilization," unable to access Johannesburg newspapers: "Send the Bantu papers, I feel so lost and away from civilization like Tarzan of the Apes."[7] Regina's reference to the 1912 novel by Edgar Rice Burroughs highlights the aspirational status of Johannesburg for Black mission-educated middle classes of the day. Stranded in eNdaleni, Regina was desperate to access the cosmopolitan delights of Johannesburg, mediated through newspapers' pages.

The pages of these periodicals were also Regina's conduit to heated debate about educated women whose horizons were greater than child care and cooking. There were, it is true, the two professions considered sufficiently feminine to be allowable by the day's standards: teaching and nursing (beer brewing, needless to say, being wholeheartedly condemned by the middle classes).[8] But public opinion was far more divided over whether these women should work after marriage. Almost all who read newspapers like *Bantu World* and *Umteteli* were united in their opinion that education for women was a desirable thing in order to avoid an outcome whereby—as was pithily phrased by one journalist—"only one half of the race would be clever and well educated and the other half will know very little."[9]

But should an educated nurse or teacher continue in her vocation after marriage? Many in Johannesburg (both men and women) were not so sure. They bemoaned "modern girls" who contributed to the demise of the family by not "[going] domestic after marriage. . . . They yearn to work outside the home instead of inside it. . . . We are confronted with the spectacle of hundreds of women who leave children and houses while they run tea places, beer places, setting up furniture shops and what not. This is a great disappointment to husbands."[10] Elsewhere, "bluestockings"—Regina would surely have recognized herself in this scathing label—were attacked in the newspaper for "nursing disdain and contempt" for the institution of marriage, "not prepared to adapt themselves to the bread and cheese marriage."[11]

Others argued there was value in married women who worked. Many parsed this in terms of the utility of a working wife to her husband. One Mrs. Maria Piliso commented, "My husband must support me while continuing in my career, for how else will I understand his own crises in his career and professional life?"[12] Other contributors surmised a wife "who has a profession at her fingertips . . . will probably help [a man] emerge from [his] professional difficulties."[13] Above all, the career success of women—both married and not—was linked to the progress of the Black people of South Africa. Educated Black working women would lead Africans in the correct direction. While supposedly most ladies only cared about "fine dressing and love affairs," many affirmed the need for "more married women like Mrs. Maxeke and Mrs. Tshabalala [leading social workers] to make contributions to our progress as a race."[14] A much-repeated idiom was that "no race will rise above its women."[15]

From far-off eNdaleni, Regina intently followed these debates. Her own view was that a woman could both be married *and* work. Certainly, this was not an opinion Regina would have learned in the conservative milieu of the mission or perhaps even from studying at Adams. Regina may have been inspired by the example of her mother, Muriel Majozi, an independent woman who raised Regina without a husband. Perhaps Regina rebelliously thought of the strictures girls faced at Adams, talented young women harassed for daring to imagine themselves the equals of male students. Anne Twala, Regina's future daughter-in-law from Eswatini, told me she was convinced that her mother-in-law was born with something stubborn and defiant engrained in her personality, nothing to do with nurture or environment: "She was just a very strong and clever somebody."[16] Dan Twala held a similar view, maintaining his wife "was independent from her early days. . . . She had to struggle for her education, she was outstanding person with her own will."[17] And there was the fact that of all the women likely to defy social conventions, it was someone from Regina's class and background who had the confidence and emotional resources to do so.

Regina thus bemoaned women who stopped working after having children. This was something she regularly observed among her colleagues at Indaleni School. As she wrote in a confiding letter to a friend, there was "one girl [who had] the highest school marks in Natal. . . . She got the baby on her first year out teaching and she had to be married, and that was the end of those brains. Shame."[18] While these radical views would have found a chilly reception in eNdaleni, Regina used the platform of a Johannesburg newspaper to air her opinions to a more sympathetic audience. In 1935 Regina wrote to *Umteteli* to defend professional women against the charge they neglected home duties, pointing out teachers' training courses (such as she had completed at Adams) still required women to learn "domestic science." "Women teachers," she argued, could also be "efficient housewives."[19] In the same year, she wrote to *Umteteli* advocating for "educated women of the Race," arguing against the view of a male correspondent that "they are empty-headed and shallow-minded, as thinkers they are nowhere—when they attempt to write they usually commit plagiarism—they show little capacity for reading and serious study." Regina angrily retorted, "I dare say that many a good reasoning woman will side with me in saying they would rather read constructive criticism than destructive, unfounded, bombastic, good-for-nothing sweeping statements like those."[20]

Regina would even copy out by hand those newspaper articles that particularly impressed her. Examining these careful transcriptions gives insight into what mattered to Regina and the affirming pleasure she felt in having her views on modern women echoed in print. This hand-copied fragment of Regina's, culled from the Women's Pages of *Bantu World,* celebrated women with strong tastes. This was a paean to women who opted for the spicy rather than the bland: "I like the modern girl because she is a sport. . . . She can talk of interesting things as well as any man alive. She knows her own mind and doesn't simper and look vacant when you ask her what chocolate she wants. She smiles brightly and says, 'Chocolate Gingers please.'"[21]

By early 1934 Regina had decided to take things further. Rather than just reading the papers and occasionally writing to the editors, Regina took the bold step of becoming a regular contributor. Underlying Regina's careful tracking of debates around professional women was her own fierce ambition to be a writer—as Dan Twala would proudly dub her, a "Bantu Woman Journalist."[22] In aspiring for this, Regina was fighting perceptions that rural Zulu women were less progressive than their Johannesburg sisters and less likely to distinguish themselves professionally. The editor of *Ilanga lase Natal* bemoaned that while "our sisters in the North have taken the lead in wielding pens to spread knowledge," by contrast "nowhere in South Africa, are women as backwards as they are in Natal and Zululand."[23]

Regina, nonetheless, was determined. She would have taken great encouragement from the other women who had recently begun writing for newspapers. More than merely providing the platform to debate independent professional women, *Bantu World* and *Umteteli wa Bantu* were crucial for their very manifestation. They provided an entry point for women writers in an extremely difficult publishing market. The few presses publishing African authors were run by European missionaries who censored manuscripts for inflammatory political content or antimissionary sentiment. This led to many fallings-out between European missionaries and aspirant Black writers. A few authors self-published, but for most this was prohibitively expensive.[24] Faced with a bleak publishing landscape, newspapers were the lifeblood of African literary experiments. Only two books were published in his lifetime by Herbert Dhlomo, probably the period's most famous Zulu writer. Yet Dhlomo had a prolific output of short stories, essays, and serialized novels published in *Bantu World* and *Ilanga lase Natal*.[25]

For all this, contemporary newspapers were still dominated by male contributors. Many "female" contributors were men clothed in feminine pseudonyms. Male editors defended this practice by arguing there were not enough women writers to populate its pages.[26] One example of this was the "Editress" of *Bantu World*'s Women's Pages, where Mademoiselle's columns appeared. It was an open secret that this person was the well-known journalist and writer Rolfes Dhlomo (brother of Herbert). Such pseudonyms allowed men to attack educated career women for "immoral" behavior—as the decidedly misogynistic Editress did—while taking refuge under the pretense of offering friendly woman-to-woman advice. One Jane Coka was known for "her" scathing attacks on modern women. Women readers smelled this out. Many—including Regina—wrote in, denouncing "Jane" as a man, confessing that their "blood boils at his statements."[27]

But there was a small number of women who had long written for newspapers. The first poem by a woman was published in *Ilanga lase Natal* in 1913; throughout the 1920s *Umteteli waBantu* published the poetry of a Johannesburg-based Xhosa woman, Nontsizi Mgqwetho.[28] Alongside these cheering examples of women authors, Regina would have been helped by the fact that women readers across the country were pleading for more female-authored content. Reader Henrietta Molapene's feeling was "some of our women are, I am positive, better writers than our men writers, and their contributions to the Native Press would enhance Native literary standards."[29] Even the conservative *Ilanga* published a letter from a woman reader expressing "regret womenfolk haven't yet joined men in writing for the columns of our newspapers."[30] Regina herself wrote to *Umteteli* expressing her view that "we must fight for the women's pages and only women's views should be expressed therein."[31]

Sensitive to these criticisms, *Bantu World*'s editors called for "women readers to send notes on their activities."[32] The Women's Pages also ran a series on "hints for the journalist"—for example, reminding "lady journalists that in their haste to fill pages, they forget what an important part punctuation plays."[33] *Bantu World*, in particular, began to feature actual women writers, not just men disguised as women. There was "Miss Gloria Molefe," an enthusiastic reader of *Bantu World*, who "just loved writing articles."[34] The talented Johanna Phahlane, founder and manager of all-female singing troupe the Merry Maker Girls,[35] was another prominent contributor, penning articles on topics "social, literary and educational." Like Regina, Phahlane wrote under a pseudonym, calling herself "Lady Porcupine."[36] Another writer was Ellen Ngozwana, Regina's old teacher from Adams. Ngozwana's pen name was "Pat," and she wrote rousing statements on the "emancipation of women."[37]

Taking her cue from Lady Porcupine and Pat, Regina began to write her own column, somehow finding time amid her teaching schedule, chapel, sewing, and tennis and her commitments to Wayfarers. Perhaps she snatched time between lessons or after the school day, or possibly she woke before the 5:30 morning bell to write for an hour or so. Regina may have received a small fee for her columns, helpfully augmenting her modest teacher's salary.[38] Via the small network of mission-educated elites, Regina had links to prominent journalists in Johannesburg. These contacts included both Rolfes Dhlomo and his brother, Herbert, also on the staff of *Bantu World* and her contemporary from Adams. It is quite possible the Dhlomo brothers provided a point of contact for her first publishing efforts.

What lay behind Regina's choice to write as "Mademoiselle" rather than as Regina Mazibuko? Mademoiselle was not a ruse. *Bantu World*'s readers knew Mademoiselle was Regina Doris Mazibuko, a schoolteacher in her twenties from Indaleni Girls'

High School in Natal. In covering Regina's writing successes, *Bantu World* nonchalantly mentioned "Miss Mazibuko is known to readers of these pages as Mademoiselle."[39] It is true some women writers—like men—used pseudonyms as protective devices, a way to maintain anonymity when publishing controversial views.[40] Certainly, women writers who aired critical views of men found pseudonyms useful. One "Maritzburg Woman" directed reproachful criticism "against young men who neglect their womenfolk." In doing so, she greatly angered *Bantu World*'s male readers. So, she reasoned, "Why should I reveal my name when my words are clear. . . . The newspapers are the mouthpiece of our people, if we do not say our say through them, where else can we say them?"[41]

For Regina, though, a pseudonym was not meant to obscure her identity. Rather, it expanded her sense of self. For 1930s readers, "mademoiselle"—French for an unmarried woman—implied glamorous sophistication, a knowing wink at a cosmopolitan world beyond racist South Africa. Regina's pseudonym also bore a faint echo of her family nickname. Regina's family called her "Gelana," or "Little Girl" ("ana" is isiZulu's diminutive form, showing endearment). In later life Dan Twala claimed that the nickname stemmed from Regina's small face and the girlish appearance she carried with her into adulthood. These, then, were Regina's two names that—although proximate—suggested two different interpretations of young womanhood. Mademoiselle, a sophisticated unmarried woman, at ease in Johannesburg as well as Paris. And Gelana, a vulnerable girl from the South African countryside. Regina could both be the schoolteacher Miss Mazibuko of rural Natal and the glamorous Mademoiselle of Johannesburg.

Mademoiselle's columns—twenty-three in total, appearing from 1934 to 1936 in *Bantu World*'s Women's Pages—were pioneering in their forthright celebration of female independence. In humorously sarcastic tones, Mademoiselle advised her women readers that correct behavior for the modern girl was premised upon professional autonomy and financial self-reliance: "Ladies, pay for your own fare in buses, tram cars, taxis and at functions."[42] But it was not all hard work. New ways of organizing leisure time were also important for the modern woman. Numerous Mademoiselle columns recounted "thrilling" matches of women's tennis followed by long parties of women chatting and listening to music all night. "What Fun!" exclaimed Mademoiselle. Fun—alongside financial independence—was emerging as part of the lexicon of the modern African woman.[43]

Mademoiselle also extensively discussed women's clothing, a topic she frequently and lovingly dwelled upon in her writings throughout her whole life. African women were restyling themselves as emancipated beings of the city, frock by frock. Mademoiselle devoted many lines to the dresses of modern African women, celebrating new European-derived styles and the pleasures of dressing beautifully. Mademoiselle dubbed these "a picturesque of all the latest shades in the fashion world," both "a magic carpet" and a "fairy land." A new grammar of femininity was crafted, peppered with an enticing vocabulary of georgettes, necklets, coatees, and crepe de chine. Mademoiselle's account of an eNdaleni birthday party is worth quoting (not least for her knowing reference to the dress of one "Miss R. D. Mazibuko"):

> Miss Manquele wore a green tight-fitting frock, ankle-length which gave her a carriage of distinction. Miss Mayeza appeared in pink georgette, with a white rose for her necklet. Miss Dhlamini wore yellow, an ankle-length frock with a frill curving from the waistline and finished with a heavy-laced bottom. Miss Ngubane appeared in a blue tight-fitting frock with a black velvet coattee with white fur whilst Miss Mabandla chose a blue crepe de chine with white spots and Miss R. D. Mazibuko preferred light pink with lace and a star necklet to tone.[44]

Most of all, Mademoiselle wrote of modern love. Her columns criticized African men's notions of marriage, suggesting what they really wanted was a glorified domestic servant. In searching for a life mate, they betrayed their true values—namely, their desire for a submissive homebound mouse. This was Mademoiselle's satirical account of the "ideal" woman:

> She must be good natured and timid, she must always listen to what I tell her to do and never, never contradict me. She should not travel too much about the country but stick to her home. She should take no interest in sport, e.g. tennis, and she should have only female friends. She should not be jealous even if I am in love with half a dozen girls and she is the seventh. She must wait for my decision to marry her when I feel like it. It may take me approximately two to six years.[45]

The ideal women the column conjured was basically everything Regina was not. Mademoiselle, on the other hand, offered women an alternative manual for love, one premised on a strong and outspoken woman who was financially independent. Her columns supplied advice for how women and men should meet and court in the city, an interaction that assumed the autonomy of the woman and stressed the necessity of men's respectful behavior. Mademoiselle's column of December 1, 1934, instructed men how to behave around women they met on the city's thoroughfares: "Young men should never take advantage when a lady is traveling and has to be helped. . . . It must be understood such an acquaintance ends at the platform of the terminus and needn't be a recurring decimal."[46] The column explained at what point a man's pursuit of a potential love interest turned unwelcome, asserting the necessity of men respecting feminine boundaries: "A person who regards you with as much interest as a piece of furniture is quite peaceful without your kindness."[47] Once introductions and courtship were negotiated, Mademoiselle was arbiter of the modern marriage. Her columns advocated egalitarian relationships in which both worked and both contributed to housework. She advised husbands to "sometimes feel young and naughty, give your wife a surprise by laying the table and telling her a fairy did it."[48] In words that would have been heard as revolutionary by both African mothers and fathers, husbands were urged to "have a share in the bringing up of the baby, don't stand stiff, arms akimbo and look at your own baby as if it would defile you to touch it."[49]

Women adored Mademoiselle's subversive column. *Bantu World* counted Mademoiselle one of most "our popular contributors."[50] This was an era in which African city women were regularly attacked by Black critics and white municipal authorities for "loose morals." Grateful letters thanked Mademoiselle's outspoken advocacy for the modern girl and her efforts to rehabilitate retrograde men. One reader wrote to "thank Mademoiselle for sound advice for husbands."[51] So popular was Regina as a writer that she made *Bantu World*'s "Who's Who in the Women's World," listed alongside Johanna Phahlane and Ellen Ngozwane as "a prominent rising woman journalist and essayist."[52] By the end of 1935 Regina's reputation had grown such that *Bantu World* devoted an article to an account of her writing career, accompanied with a jaunty photograph of Regina with her parasol. "Miss Mazibuko . . . has achieved for herself wide recognition. . . . Her articles . . . created great interest among our readers," the newspaper declared. Mademoiselle was evidence of the heights attained by African womanhood, proving "that Bantu women, given opportunities and encouragement, are capable of great things."[53]

Mademoiselle was not Regina's only pen name. From early 1935, still writing from quiet Indaleni Mission, she started writing a women's advice column for Johannesburg's second popular weekly, *Umteteli wa Bantu*. Throughout 1935 twenty-five columns appeared by the pseudonymous "Sister Kollie." (Once again, it was common knowledge that this was Regina Mazibuko.)[54] These pieces shared much with those Regina wrote as Mademoiselle. Both explicitly addressed women readers, and both aimed to equip women to negotiate modern love in the city. But Sister Kollie differed from Mademoiselle in several important ways.

For one, Sister Kollie's focus was sexual temptation—how girls were to navigate courtship while maintaining "purity." As she put it in her first column, "The writer wishes to publish a series of talks which may be of help to young girls that are growing in

THE BANTU WORLD JOHANNESBURG, SATURDAY, DECEMBER 21, 1935 PAGE 11

# Satin Dress Brings Emily Love

## Our Christmas Short Story

A Wedding And A Shop Window.

(By PANSY.)

Emily Maplank pressed her nose against the shop window and gazed with longing eyes at her dress—she felt it was hers the moment she set eyes on it. It seemed that for years she had been longing for a pale pink satin evening dress trimmed with twig rosebuds and chiffon flares; and now, here it was, before her very eyes; waiting for her to walk in and claim it as her own! She pictured herself at the forthcoming Christmas Party—dressed in the pink satin, she would surely attract all eyes! She imagined herself floating round the room in the arms of her partner, with the lovely chiffon flares swishing round her ankles.

Emily made a note of the name of the shop; gave a last look at the Dream of Pink, and hurried off down the street with tightly compressed lips—that dress had to be hers—the skies might fall, or a world war might break out—but that dress had to be hers!

For the rest of the day Emily was dreamy and absent-minded. Her mother noticed the change. "Really, Emily my child, you are behaving like a half-wit to-day! What ails you? Are you in love?" Emily gave a short laugh. "Yes! I'm in love all right—desperately in love—and before Christmas Eve the object of my affections is going to be mine!"

"Oh and is he a handsome man?" "It's not a he—it's an it."

"Emily! What are you talking about?"

The daughter laughed softly and put a coaxing arm round her mother.

"Oh mother, it is a dress I am in love with—a beautiful pink satin evening dress. It was made for me, I am sure! And I want it so badly for the Christmas Party."

Mrs. Maplank looked thoughtful. "I know your green dress is very old and shabby... but a new one will cost a lot of money, Emily. I am afraid to ask your father."

"Oh mother! Just come with me tomorrow and look at it! It is marked at twenty-five shillings but I am sure it is worth four pounds. Wouldn't you like your daughter to look really beautiful at the party?"

Her mother smiled. "Emily, you vain child! who said you could look beautiful?"

"I would, in the pink dress," replied Emily, with confidence.

And so the next day, the mother and daughter paid a visit to a certain shop window. Emily was fearful lest some lucky girl had already bought it, and she heaved a sigh of relief when she caught sight of the familiar pink satin in the window.

Her mother had been a great beauty in her day, and she still loved pretty clothes.

"Why, Emily! What a beautiful dress! It's cheap at twenty-five shillings. Isn't the rosebud trimming sweet? And look at the chiffon flares! It is too

flares floated out as she whirled excitedly in front of the long mirror.

At the Party, all her friends gazed at her in amazement.

"Why! I didn't know that Emily Maplank could look so beautiful! I wonder where she got that lovely dress."

And there was a certain young man who thought Emily the prettiest in the room...no, she was the prettiest girl he had ever seen...as a matter of fact, she was so enchanting that he was determined to play the charming gentleman to Emily!

He played it so well that our Emily of the pink dress thought him quite the nicest man she had ever met...and so handsome!

By the end of the evening they were the closest of friends and David Moteane (for that was his name) made a vow to himself that before the New Year Emily would be his promised bride.

On a certain Saturday afternoon, six months later, wedding bells were pealing out their silvery chimes as Mr. and Mrs. David Moteane stepped from the church porch out into the brilliant sunshine. Every one wanted to kiss the radiant bride, and a friend of Emily's whispered in her ear, "How did you get such a handsome husband?" Emily laughed proudly and whispered back, "Pink Satin!"

## Just a Smile, Please

The story is told that when a bishop was riding on a train out west a big strapping rough fellow came in and sat down beside him. Then he said to the bishop, "Where in hell have I seen you before?"

The bishop replied, "I don't know; what part of hell are you from?"

"Why do you refuse to have any business relations with that man Riggles?"

"I always avoid a man cleverer than myself."

"In what way is he cleverer?"

"Why, he once had the chance to marry my wife, and didn't."

Teacher: Now, Tommy, if I lent your father ten shillings, and he promised to pay it back at two shillings a month, how much would he owe me in three months?

Tommy: Ten shillings.

Teacher: You don't understand arithmetic, Tommy.

Tommy: You dont understand my father.

## Miss R.D. Mazibuko

(By THE EDITRESS)

Although this brief sketch of the activities of Miss Mazibuko, of Indaleni Mission Station, Natal, does not fall under our feature series, I take this opportunity to introduce you to her. Miss Mazibuko is one of our most versatile young women.

At present she is teaching at Indaleni High School where, in fact, she has been teaching successfully for many years. Inspite of her teaching duties Miss Mazibuko still finds time to enjoy her greatest hobby-Journalism. She is a very successful young writer and has achieved for herself wide recognition in the literary field by winning almost all literary competitions she has joined.

Miss R. D. Mazibuko—a photograph taken some time ago.

To crown her success this year, she has been awarded 2nd Prize in the 1935 May Esther Bedford Fund Literary competitions for the best original unpublished work in prose in Bantu language, with English translation, held at Fort Hare this year.

The title of her work is "Tales of Swazi and Hlubi-Land."

This is a great honour for a young woman of her age. In fact, it serves to prove what I have consistently tried to prove on these Pages that Bantu women, given opportunities and encouragement, are capable of great things.

Miss Mazibuko is known to readers of these Pages as "Mademoiselle." Her articles under this pen-name created great interest among our readers.

Apart from these activities she still finds time to take piano-forte studies with success. Her outdoor hobbies are tennis and Wayfaring.

"The Bantu World" congratulates Miss R. D. Mazibuko and wishes her all success in the future.

## Secrets Of Good Cake-Making

If you would delight your guests with dainty little cakes of your own making you must remember that cake-making is an art; it is useless to expect a cake to be a success if the ingredients are just mixed together anyhow.

Let us take for instance the simple but popular sandwich cake. The ingredients usually are flour, sugar, butter, eggs, baking powder, milk and flavouirng.

First measure out the flour into a bowl and add a pinch of salt; then cream the butter and sugar; this word 'cream' means melt the butter very slightly and mix it with the sugar by pressing it about in a bowl with a knife; this should be done properly as it improves the texture of the cake.

Then take eggs and beat them very well with a fork or an egg whisk and add to sugar and beat for about five minutes—this is important to make the cake soft and light. Then add the flour, a little at a time while you are beating, then the baking powder and the flouring and go on beating for a couple of minutes. Very often cakes are spoilt by sticking to the pan so to avoid this it is best to line the baking dish with a piece of greased paper—just ordinary white paper rubbed over with a little butter or fat will serve the purpose.

The layers of a sandwich cake are thin so they should not bake longer than a quarter of an hour or twenty minutes. A good way to test if a cake is baked enough is to take a thin straw of grass and insert it into the centre of the cake—if the straw comes out quite clean you can be sure that your cake is sufficiently baked. Never put the filling or icing on until the cake is quite cool, otherwise it becomes heavy and 'soggy'

Before you commence to make your cake make quite sure that you have all the utensils and ingredients on the table, otherwise half beaten eggs will go flat in the dish while you search wildly for baking powder or flavouring!



FIGURE 2.1. Miss R. D. Mazibuko, *Bantu World*, December 21, 1935 (Historical Papers Research Archive, University of the Witwatersrand)

ignorance and have no idea of what people mean when they talk 'of the world and its temptations.'"[55] Her tone and content leave us in no doubt that Regina repressively disapproved of women having sex outside marriage. However progressive her views were, Regina still espoused classic 1930s Christian-infused sexual morality. It would have been nearly unthinkable for her to do otherwise. We might think here of her continued involvement in the conservative Wayfarers organization throughout these years.

But Sister Kollie's tone *was* radical in one important way. Most commentators—both male and female—laid the blame for sexual misdemeanors on women themselves, pointing fingers at their moral weakness and lustful appetites. Sister Kollie entirely disagreed with this. She took it as her starting point that the guilty party was almost always the man. Her default position was sympathy for women, for whom she counseled a state of wary vigilance. As she reminded her readers in one column on this, "let us always be on the alert, because we might find in one whom we once thought to be a friend a fiend. There is but little difference in the spelling of these two words; it is even so in reality."[56] And bucking the day's prudishness, Sister Kollie insisted women should receive frank, intelligible education on sexual matters: "It is of vital importance that girls should have a thorough knowledge of those facts that affect their own lives."[57] Female empowerment was still a key theme.

Sister Kollie's second innovation was to experiment with how newspapers united women into new feminine solidarities. She invited women to write with their problems—although cautioning them "not to use their real names. . . . No one will ever know who the real writers are. . . . I therefore offer my time to be a pen friend to all lonely women who wish to ask for advice or sympathy in whatever sphere of life they may be." Disarmingly, Regina confessed, "I do not profess to be a very good person myself nor do I deceive myself that I shall be able to answer complicated questions because I am but a human being. Still, I promise to extend my love to all women of the Race without prejudice."[58] These "Pen Friends" wrote to Sister Kollie with questions ranging from whether to start a relationship with a man with a child to whether to breast-feed or bottle-feed their babies.[59] Through the warmly supportive space of her weekly column, Regina was drawing together an imagined community of new "sisters," all cloaked in pen names (self-protection here being a real concern given the intimate nature of their questions) and who could offer each other support. While critics accused modern women of estrangement from older traditions, writers like Sister Kollie used words to create new circles of womanly sociability. Freed from old names and casting off old identities, these anonymous women of the newspaper joined together as modern beings, sisters of the city.

While Mademoiselle and Sister Kollie pioneered new definitions of womanhood, it would be inaccurate to pigeonhole Regina as allied with all that was progressive and modern by our contemporary standards. Regina dwelled at length upon the continued saliency of the Zulu past and of African tradition and custom for modern city dwellers. We see this in Regina's efforts for the new institution of the "essay competition," a device pioneered by *Umteteli* and *Bantu World* as a way to increase readership. Regular competitions offered readers small cash prizes for the best essays on topics like "harmony between the races" and "the past, present and future of African art." Regina began to enter these, succeeding in winning a clutch and even beating university-educated men. (She was hugely proud of this aspect of her triumphs, even more so than the cash prizes.)[60] Some competitions, it was true, were solely aimed at women, inviting submissions on whether higher education should be accessible to them (for which Regina won fourth prize) and thoughts on the care and feeding of infants (which Regina pointedly did not enter).[61]

Regina's greatest triumph was her success in the London-based May Esther Bedford Prize contest. This was a prestigious essay competition run out of the University of London, which offered a staggering prize of £25—a year's salary for a man in Southern Africa—for the best submission in literature, art, or music from either a woman or a man. Reflecting the interests of London's anthropological set of the 1930s, the competition aimed to stimulate Africans to rehabilitate cultural traditions thought to be dying out. Literary submissions had to be in an African language, for the goal was "to encourage original works of a distinctly African culture."[62]

While the first prize went to the renowned male poet S. E. K. Mqhayi, the committee was so impressed with Regina's submission that it took the unprecedented step of awarding her a second prize. Titled "Tales of Swazi and Hlubiland," Regina's essay was based on her interviews with elderly family members at eNdaleni whose ancestors hailed from Eswatini and the kingdom of the Hlubi. Only a fragment of Regina's essay has survived, buried in the letters between her and Dan stored in Tim Couzens's office for many decades. Helpfully, the existing pages are the essay's introduction, and they list Regina's aims in writing the piece: "To reveal stories that may be forgotten in the future, and for them to be told from our perspective as black people. To show our ancient practices. . . . To discover and spread the language of our forefathers, because our language is being forgotten due to contact with other languages from other nations and those of the West." We can assume that Regina's essay, located between ethnography, oral history, and folklore, powerfully tapped into the contemporary fashion for reviving African tradition and custom, for countering "detribalized" urban Africans who had "forgotten" their stories and language due to contact with the West.[63] The forward-looking and subversive columnists Mademoiselle and Sister Kollie were very different literary personae from the prize-winning "Miss R. D. Mazibuko," dutiful scribe of her village elders and of African oral history.

Around this time, perhaps emboldened by her professional successes, Regina applied to be emancipated.[64] Natal's 1891 Code of Native Law had enshrined African fathers' and husbands' control over women by stipulating that a "native woman was a perpetual minor by law . . . with no independent powers save as to her own person." However, the government permitted women who could demonstrate "good character, education and thrifty habits" to apply for exemption for this kind of control. The number of African women who succeeded in doing so each year has never been counted, but it must have been minuscule—probably never exceeding double digits.[65] In 1935 Regina joined their elite ranks, emerging as a woman who could own property in her own right as well as undertake independent legal action. As we shall soon see, this would have fateful consequences for her.

# 3

# Johannesburg

I am a black woman, the curse of South Africa.

—Regina to Dan Twala, 1938 (RTP)

In June 1936 Regina arrived at Johannesburg's Park Station, the terminus for Southern Africa's railway traffic and freshly overhauled by architect Gordon Leith for its sixteen million annual passengers.[1] The station's sunken concourse was already famous, a majestic structure that an architectural historian of the city likened to "vast Roman thermae."[2] Now Regina was one of these millions of transiters passing through Park Station en route to her new life in the city—although, like all Black passengers, she was banned from the concourse as well as the swanky new dining area, the Blue Room, named for the blue-painted tiles lining its walls. Regina, moreover, exited the great station using different doors than those allocated for white travelers.

Regina dressed with characteristic care for her arrival in the city: a calf-length green woolen dress, this being winter (Johannesburg's June early morning and evening temperatures can be freezing), tightly gathered at the waist and ruched at the sleeves. Three embroidered flowers studded her scooped neckline. On her head, Regina wore a closely fitting white turban, held in place with a heavy brass pin. Her legs were covered by silken stockings, and she clutched a rectangular snake-skin purse. Regina was no stranger to Johannesburg. But now she was here to live. She was newly married to Percy Kumalo—a man she "idolized"—and had a new position at an American missionary school.

First things first: Regina needed to make her way to her new home with Percy, who—as a clerk on a gold mine—lived in a small house in Robinson Deep Mine south of the city.[3] Perhaps Percy came to meet her at Park Station, or perhaps Regina undertook the fifteen-minute walk solo, climbing up the station's marble steps to the shopping hub of Eloff Street, briskly striding to Diagonal Street in Newtown to catch a tram to Robinson Deep, "the place where hundreds meet and part for Sophiatown, Martindale, Newclare, Western Native Township . . . seething with people, screeching voices, incessant rush."[4] Perhaps she caught a glimpse of skyscrapers, the soaring ziggurats of Escom House, Anstey's, Lewis & Marks, and Chrysler House, built in invocation of Manhattan, affirming Johannesburg as Africa's preeminent city.[5]

In 1936 Regina's published musings on love had taken on a new dimension: she fell in love and married. Percy, her beau, was a member of Natal's mission-educated elite. Like many young men, he had moved to Johannesburg and taken up work in a gold mine, in his case as a clerk, an occupation marking him a member of the city's small middle classes—although scarcely better paid than an underground miner.[6] Percy was a handsome, snappy dresser. Pictured in figure 3.1 with Regina, he wears a stiffly collared white shirt with a dark blazer. *Bantu World* frequently chronicled Percy's activities, noting "this young man looks well and has as promising future. . . . [He is] well known in local sporting and social circles."[7] An office worker by day, Percy was a popular vaudeville stage dancer by night, performing with Griffiths Motsieloa's jazz band, De Pitch Black Follies. His vaudeville career frequently took him to the cities of Bloemfontein and even Cape Town.[8]

In early 1936 Percy left Johannesburg to visit his Natal family. While there, he visited his Indaleni cousin, Dora Kumalo, who taught at the high school with Regina. (Additionally, Percy's uncle was one Reverend Xaba, the mission's African minister.[9]) While Regina must have been struck by the dashing dancer, Percy was equally compelled by the talented writer, fresh from winning her Esther Bedford Prize and the subject of a recent *Bantu World* spread. As Dan Twala mused, Percy was irresistibly drawn by "Miss Mazibuko of Natal fame—her beauty and her social status."[10]

FIGURE 3.1. Percy and Regina Kumalo, 1936 (RTP)

While there is little record of their courtship, by June *Bantu World* announced the marriage of two stars of the Black elite: "Mr. Percy Cameron Kumalo leaves this weekend for Natal to make preparations for his wedding to Miss Regina D. Mazibuko of Indaleni . . . a gifted writer whose pen has won her prizes in literary competitions."[11] On July 1, 1936, the pair married in Indaleni Mission Station's stone chapel. No records of the ceremony survive. But contemporary accounts of Black society weddings suggest Regina's nuptials would have featured the trappings of popular "white weddings," including an ornate dress with a multitiered cake.[12]

Regina then moved to Johannesburg to live with her new husband. In typical fashion she defied the orthodoxy that married women cease working outside the home and started in a position at an American Board mission school.[13] (The couple would have struggled to survive on Percy's meager earnings.) While *Bantu World* presented Johannesburg as an enticing city for Black women, Regina found a different reality. The year 1936 was a bleak one for Johannesburg's Black residents. The Black middle classes' hopes for equality with Europeans were fading. Whites united to further disenfranchise Africans, ensuring they and their labor would be offered to industry and agriculture like lambs to the slaughter. The government passed two of the infamous Hertzog Native Bills, formulated in response to South Africa's economic downturn during the Depression, in 1936; the third would be passed the next year. The bills removed voting rights from Africans, prohibited Black purchase of land outside "native Reserves," and largely stopped Blacks from buying land in urban areas. This last fact reflected deep official unease about urbanized Africans, despite the mining industry's need for proximate labor.[14] While Europeans belonged in towns, Blacks' supposed natural home was rural "tribal" areas. For Regina's class, a demographic that had long prided itself on its affinity with "civilized" peoples, meticulously marking its distance from "heathen" tradition, this was a blow. *Bantu World* editor R. V. Selope Thema expressed widespread outrage: "Many worked to break down tribalism, yet the Bill worked in flat contradiction by orientating progressive peoples back to the tribal environment."[15]

And while women like Regina hoped to find autonomy in Johannesburg, the reality was that life in the city had never been harder for its Black female residents. As the last chapter outlined, recent years saw a tremendous surge of women moving to Johannesburg for employment. Both white officials and Black middle-class society viewed this as a serious problem. The European-led municipality worried about consequences for the disappearing "traditional" social order, playing up the specter of the independent urban woman unchecked by father or husband. Many within the Black establishment shared these fears. Editorials and opinion pieces in newspapers like *Bantu World* and *Umteteli wa Bantu* blasted city women who "lost responsibility and decency . . . who let strange men talk to them on the streets, going about with a cigarette and having their face painted."[16]

Multiple laws conspired to make Johannesburg's Black population—especially Black women—feel uneasily out of place. The 1923 Urban Areas Act restricted where Africans could work and live. Black residents had to perpetually carry identification documents, certifying their usefulness as workers. Without these, or if found out of order, imprisonment and expulsion from the city was a certainty.[17] Given the hostile mood to urban women, Black females were particularly vulnerable. By the 1930s Johannesburg women had to always carry a "certificate of approval," stating that a father or husband was employed in the city.[18] One of the hated "pickup vans" could arrest any African without their documents on a whim. In 1934 the persecution of a nurse, Sister Mbatha, outraged the city's middle classes. Mbatha was returning from an evening concert with a taxi-load of other professionals. A pickup van stopped and detained her; her crime was not having a "special pass" for an evening excursion.[19] Regina herself had many frightening experiences of dodging pickup vans—"running for her life," as she put it in one letter to Dan Twala.[20]

Regina found professional opportunities for Black women seriously limited. The municipality tolerated small numbers of Black women to meet white domestic labor needs. Most women went into this profession; in 1936 around twenty-two thousand—90 percent of Johannesburg's Black women—were employed in a white household as cook, cleaner, or nanny. (Until the 1930s the majority of domestic servants were male.)[21] Wages were pitifully low, and conditions were punishing. Yet even the lucky few who belonged to the educated elite—teachers and nurses—and who were married with a husband to guarantee their right to live in the city struggled. As a teacher, Regina received dramatically lower wages than her white counterparts, part of a strategy of "keeping the African in their place." Regina and Percy, along with many friends in the city, were perpetually cash-strapped. Johannesburg's astronomical cost of living—it was one of the most expensive cities in the world at the time—meant they struggled to afford necessities and attain the lifestyle they believed their education and "civilized" status required.[22] Despite yearning for middle-class respectability, poorly paid clerks, interpreters, teachers, craftsmen, shopkeepers, and ministers lived in the city's worst parts alongside the unemployed and destitute.[23]

All this reminded Regina and thousands of educated Blacks—especially women—that they did not belong in the city. In the end, all their progressiveness meant little to the authorities. Later that year, Dan Twala wrote to Regina of their mutual friend Mark Rathebe, the new secretary of the hub of Black middle-class conviviality, the Bantu Men's Social Centre. Rathebe had recently returned to South Africa after studying in the United States. Dan's bleak view was this: "I'm very sorry for [Rathebe], he has to now live the life of a K****r and forget that he is a Negro. South Africa will not care for all his degrees."[24] Regina's aspiring class was thus an insecure one, blending imperceptibly into the humble working classes.[25] One "respectable" Johannesburg woman lamented that despite her ambitions for a better life, she had to still take in laundry, "[standing] here day after day and kill[ing] myself washing."[26] Many women turned to illicit yet profitable beer brewing. This only added to the demonization of urban Black women as a social menace.[27] An American missionary in Johannesburg noted the wife of "one of the best educated and cultured native men" was "a liquor seller. . . . Their home is now a regular den."[28]

Amid these challenges, Regina found the city's Black middle classes obsessively preoccupied with respectability. "Spare" time was an opportunity to differentiate oneself from working-class brethren. Middle-class Johannesburgers frequented a circuit of worthy activities like lectures, debates, discussion, and reading groups. Church lay at the heart of such self-improvement activities, linked to Christian notions of progress and uplift, and structuring social activities like baptisms, marriages, and funerals. As we know, Regina was a devout Methodist, attending services where she heard an intertwined gospel of salvation and middle-class respectability. Christianity was also important to the city's working classes, but this was a different faith from hers. Via American missionaries, the 1930s brought Pentecostal Christianity, preaching the miraculous intervention of the Holy Spirit. Hundreds of churches sprouted up, most under prophets who shouted healing benedictions on devotees in cramped houses and on open hillsides. Working-class adherents eager for miracles gathered at Wemmer Pan, a lake south of the city in an area of grassland. Here outdoor baptisms in the freezing waters occurred, as did screeched exorcisms of evil spirits. Regina and most middle classes steered clear. In later decades, however, Pentecostalism would become an important force in her life.

Many self-improvement events were funded and organized by Johannesburg's white liberal set, a group who shared a close and frequently uneasy relationship with Black middle classes. These were philanthropic do-gooders—mostly linked to churches, like the American missionary couple Frederick and Clara Bridgman—who positioned themselves as allies of Johannesburg's Black population. They spoke against the Hertzog Bills, they lamented attacks on African life in the city, and they provided facilities to mitigate bleak circumstances. Collaboration between liberals and Black middle classes was exemplified in the "joint councils," organizations bringing together the races in regular discussion to "remove causes of irritation and improve racial relations."[29]

Yet for all of this group's liberal credentials, there was a profoundly conservative vision at their core. They were responding to the political and labor militancy that characterized South African cities during World War I. Reacting to dire poverty, a massive African mine workers strike occurred in 1920, involving seventy thousand miners. The following year a radical millenarian Christian movement called the Israelites emerged in the Eastern Cape near Queenstown. It soon clashed with the government, leading to white police murdering 171 of the Israelites in the Bulhoek Valley. Liberals saw softening the difficulties of Black life a way to forestall unrest. The joint councils put it thus: "Our greatest need is for an increase in the number of Europeans and Natives who have confidence in each other, and who can co-operate to avoid conflict."[30] There were also social welfare and educational institutions—maternity hospitals, women's hostels, social clubs, libraries, sports facilities—targeting the supposedly moderate middle classes, trying to convince them that white rule was—against all appearances—in their favor.

At the forefront of this was the missionary Ray Phillips, a man described by a colleague in 1930 as "young, virile, athletic, of magnetic personality and tireless energy."[31] In coming years, Phillips would be patron to both Regina and her future husband, Dan Twala. Employees of the American Board of Missions, Phillips and his wife, Dora, arrived in Johannesburg in 1918, fresh-faced Christian workers from Minnesota. Inspired by their American Board mentors, the Bridgmans, the Phillips sought to devise a "social gospel" to solve "the whole great problem of moralizing the leisure time of natives in the city."[32] The Phillips were unstinting in their condemnation of "Moscow emissaries" who might radicalize the middle classes. Their focus was on ameliorating Black living conditions and providing uplifting activities in the hopes this would ward off political "agitators."

Phillips's views on women were particularly pernicious. He portrayed Johannesburg's women as "hopelessly driven by an unquenchable attraction to lust, luxury, and criminal pursuits." He argued that Black women fled the countryside not because of rural poverty or to avoid arranged marriages but because towns were filled with "activity and excitement, fine clothes, and love making."[33] Once in town, unattached women became a "perplexing problem" for the Christian missionary, finding beer brewing and prostitution more profitable than wholesome employment. Short of barring female migration to the city, Phillips's solution was to provide uplifting activities and moralizing lectures on chastity, which he hoped would direct women's proclivities in more fitting directions.[34]

By 1924 Phillips had founded—with the help of Johannesburg's authorities, alert to the political advantages of the social gospel[35]—the Bantu Men's Social Centre. This was a modest two-story brick building in the southernmost part of Eloff Street, strategically adjacent to Johannesburg's mines. The center's goal was to uplift Black life in Johannesburg, providing films, concerts, lectures, and debates for the middle classes. Regina probably used its well-known lending library—the only such institution in the city for Blacks—and attended its concerts. Perhaps she also attended Dr. A. B. Xuma's lecture on the Native Bills held that year, or she and Percy may have been in the audience for the Bantu Dramatic Society's performance of *Lady Windemere's Fan*, not realizing that among the actors she gazed at on the floorboards was her own future husband, Dan Twala.[36] An institution like the social center exemplified the contradictions of white liberalism. Addressing the uplift of the city's Black population, the center also sought to redirect Blacks from politics. In racist terms, Phillips boasted his screenings of Charlie Chaplin films during a 1922 strike calmed the "animal energies" of Black mine workers.[37]

Regina also partook of Johannesburg's dances, films, dances, walks in the park, tennis matches, tea parties, and soccer games. Sunday—a "gala day for the Bantu"—was when many of these activities took place. The Johannesburg Zoo and the inviting slopes of nearby Zoo Lake—never segregated—were popular destinations for many. From the 1930s a tram ran to the zoo's red stone entrance, disgorging well-dressed men and women who picnicked on Sunday afternoons, strolled on the flower-hemmed lawns, and napped, lazily "continuing until late making whoopee."[38] (We can assume Regina and Percy, with their middle-class hang-ups, would not have been among the numbers enjoying the latter.) One of Regina's favorite pastimes was watching movies. Like novels, films offered a glimpse into a world of alternative lives, of imagining yourself someone else. If lectures and debates promised to elevate Africans via the intellect, movies and novels offered imaginative escape. In addition to the films shown at the social center, cinemas open to Africans were scattered throughout Johannesburg, screening Hollywood Westerns, romances, and Charlie Chaplin (colloquially known in isiZulu as "isiDakwa"—the little drunk man[39]). Friendships—both imagined and real—between Black South Africans and Black Americans were strong in these bleak years of increasing segregation, and many looked to Americans as role models for Black achievement. The films of American actor Paul Robeson were especially popular in 1930s Johannesburg. Regina was surely not alone in having a treasured "snap" of Robeson, which she would passionately kiss—perhaps while Percy's back was turned.[40]

The line between uplifting versus salacious activities was a fine one for these status-insecure classes. The middle classes thought a select few activities—educational, artistic, and religious ones especially—would uplift them to new heights. Other activities were disapprovingly labeled unbecoming of a people under pressure to certify their progressive credentials. A new variety of the blues known as "marabi" was the focus of intense debate. Linked to nighttime revelry and sensuous dissipation and thought to provoke immorality especially in female listeners, the music was disapproved of by many of the Black elite. Middle classes were scarcely more comfortable with marabi's slightly more respectable cousin, American-style jazz. *Bantu World* writer Rolfes Dhlomo expressed a typical view when he lamented, "This jazzing madness has its victims in its octopus-like grasp."[41] Yet even critics could not deny marabi and jazz were wildly popular, especially among Johannesburg's youth. And despite their solid middle-class status, Regina and Percy were fans. The couple attended jazz parties at the Inchcape Palais de Dance—also known as the "Ritz," "the mecca of pleasure-seeking Bantu"[42]—located on Polly Street in Johannesburg's oldest part. The Ritz hosted weekend concerts and dancing. Groups like the Rhythm Kings, the Jazz Maniacs, and De Pitch Black Follies looked to the big-band ensembles of Harlem for inspiration and played to packed houses.[43] Regina was married to a semiprofessional dancer, and perhaps she and Percy clung to each other in the Ritz or another dimly lit venue, swaying at the ubiquitous "concert and dance" that wrapped up at four in the morning.[44] These occasions cut across the city's class stratifications. While teachers and clerks frequented the Ritz, so did the city's working classes, with *Umteteli* commenting that dance parties allowed those on society's margins magical opportunities for reinvention via fine dress: "Dora the housemaid in Parktown dressed in all the finery beloved of her sex, in ankle-length evening dress and silver or gold brocade shoes, Jim the waiter and garden boy, complete in tails and boiled shirt, strutting the floor."[45]

If life in Johannesburg wasn't hard enough for Regina as a Black woman of the 1930s, she soon had new problems. Regina was devasted to learn that shortly after her arrival in Johannesburg, Percy had resumed a relationship with an old girlfriend. As she later reflected, "My fiancée [*sic*] wasn't brave enough to tell the other girl he was through, he just let things hang on indefinitely. . . . Then he came down to Natal to go over the marriage vows with me and on returning he met the same girl."[46] Percy quickly moved on from this initial relationship, starting affairs with other women. His work as a vaudeville dancer took him away from home on weekends and during holidays, including to faraway Cape Town. The problem, according to Regina's cousin (whom historian Tim Couzens interviewed), was that Percy could not resist temptation when away from home.[47] Sensitive Regina was devastated, lamenting, "Here is a man I idolized. I made him my hero, I gave him my soul. What has he done[?]"[48] Regina bitterly summarized her ill fortune in unwittingly marrying a serial adulterer: "When I met Percy [he was with another woman], as soon as he saw another feminine gender, he let drop, so he married me, and as habit will allow, he met another feminine gender, so he forgot me. Still another feminine gender appeared in the form of the present one and as natural as breathing he forgot my rival gender and he is going to stick faithfully to this one until another pattern is found. That's my man."[49]

Regina's options were limited. Johannesburg society of the 1930s had little to offer women whose husbands were unfaithful. One of the hottest debates centered around divorced women. Black commentators—largely male—noted the "appalling" rise in divorce in Johannesburg, arguing "in this place of ever-increasing pleasure, it is difficult for people to behave like married people, here they begin flirting."[50] Most blamed women, with their supposedly innate lasciviousness. Several commentators pointed fingers at educated women, casting them as entitled beings who wanted more than their proper due from husbands.[51] While unstinting in their condemnation of women, these same critics presented male infidelity as an inevitability of modern marriage. The problem (according to Rolfes Dhlomo) lay not with unfaithful men but with "women who needlessly break up the homes when their husbands do a little philandering."[52] With breathtaking double standards—female infidelity was "amoral," male infidelity normal—*Umteteli* bemoaned "divorce notices crowding the newspaper," offering a patronizing "exhortation to our womenfolk ignorant of proper duty and behavior after marriage. A good wife must make her home the seat of happiness."[53]

Regina was having none of this. She rejected Johannesburg society's prescription of a docile wife remaining silent about a "little philandering." In furious retribution to Percy, now absent from their home, she even started her own love affair. This was a startling move for a woman who until now fulfilled contemporary expectations of virtuous Christian femininity, which gives some sense of the emotional pressures Regina was enduring. As she wrote to Dan Twala the following year, women were both vulnerable to predatory men and were shamed when they trusted those men: "I wish for Christ's sake I would turn you miraculously into a woman and a pretty one too and let you off in the world so that you can meet men and be our example of goodness."[54]

Regina had no shortage of admirers.[55] Their attentions were a balm to the sting of rejection from Percy. Fittingly, given her love of pretty clothes, her new lover was a local dressmaker, a Mr. Makutso, who had been besotted with Regina for years but was himself married. Makutso was a well-off Johannesburg businessman and had two shining cars he used for orders to his dressmaking shops. It was one of Makutso's cars that Regina used to cart off her belongings when she finally stormed out of her and Percy's house in 1937. This was Regina's spirited justification (made in an early letter to Dan) for matching Percy's infidelity with her own. Her betrayal, hurt, and anger at Percy—the man "to whom [she] gave [her] soul"—are painfully evident: "Why should I save my womanhood for a swine? Why shouldn't I give this man [Makutso] a reward, when I had given my best to a man, married him, and he didn't appreciate it? My lawful husband didn't want my womanhood."[56]

In June 1937 Regina began the process of suing Percy for divorce, something she could do in the Supreme Court as an emancipated woman. Her grounds were desertion, a common complaint of Black women. (Percy had left their home to live with his new girlfriend.) Regina engaged the services of Hymie Basner, a well-known liberal European lawyer who had a reputation as a defender of Africans and was an active member of the South African Communist Party. (In 1952 the newly qualified Nelson Mandela briefly worked in Basner's law firm.)[57] The process, however, was far from straightforward, with Regina—along with many other women—complaining of its labyrinthine complexities.[58] The state was opposed to granting African women divorces, fearing this would lead to a tide of emancipated urban females independent from male guardians. The state made its resistance known in the snail-like pace of proceedings and by chronic underfunding of the African divorce courts.[59]

Divorce was also unaffordable for most women. A divorce in the Supreme Court cost nearly £20, with court fees and trips to

Pretoria (around forty miles from Johannesburg) included.[60] As a point of comparison, the best-paid African in Johannesburg was the writer Herbert Dhlomo, a librarian at the Bantu Men's Social Centre. Yet even Dhlomo was only earning £15 per month. An average worker was subsisting on £5, so we can assume Regina earned somewhere in between.[61] Regina explained her predicament in an early letter to Dan. We can hear her desperation and a new tone of disillusionment with the middle-class Christian consensus that stigmatized deserted women: "How can a native woman deserted by her husband pay a sum of £17 12d . . . that is to come from a deserted woman who is claiming for freedom because of failure of maintenance! And having been unsupported for eighteen months or so. Where is justice? Where does Christianity come in?"[62]

No longer supported by Percy and now paying lawyer's fees to Basner, Regina found it impossible to afford rent on her meager salary. She turned to the Black community leader James "Sofasonke" Mpanza,[63] who helped her petition the courts for support from Percy.[64] Mpanza, well known for riding his horse through the new African township of Orlando (ten miles southwest of Johannesburg), had been a legal clerk, racehorse trainer, interpreter, convict, photographer, evangelist, and teacher—a career path that nicely illustrates the checkered fortunes of the besieged middle classes. Mpanza was originally from Natal and had studied at Indaleni School; perhaps this is where Regina met him.[65] But Mpanza's efforts were unsuccessful, despite him being, in Regina's estimation, "a very clever man at law."

Regina now left her job at the American school. Her puritanical employer may have been displeased at having on its payroll a deserted woman seeking divorce.[66] And in unsuccessfully applying for future jobs, Regina made the unpleasant discovery she had to present her marriage certificate to potential employers, suggesting their preference for respectably coupled teachers. In any case, Regina was unable to do this as her certificate was far away, filed by Basner in Pretoria for the court proceedings.[67] The law also stipulated Percy had eighteen months' grace before the divorce went through. In the meantime—although Regina's mind was set—Percy oscillated between wanting to return to his wife and staying with his new girlfriend.[68]

Regina was bitterly disappointed in her lawyer. Regina felt that Basner, ostensibly a "friend of the African" (as the public dubbed liberal whites—or they dubbed themselves), wasn't taking her case seriously or pushing for its speedy resolution. Her caustic take was this: "I am a black woman, the curse of South Africa, and he is a white man, and of course a N****r has no feeling."[69] Regina's disillusionment with Basner was a foreshadowing of her future tensions with Southern Africa's white liberal set, a pattern that would become more pronounced in coming years as segregation tightened its grip upon Black lives.

In desperation, Regina started a position as a domestic servant for a white family in Johannesburg's leafy northern suburbs. This was the only way she could stay in the city. The thought of returning to eNdaleni—a year after her nuptials, in shameful humiliation—was too dreadful to contemplate. Domestic service would waive the requirement for a "certificate of approval" from her spouse and would offer Regina accommodation in the form of a mean backroom behind the main house. Her new employer lived in the posh suburb of Houghton, newly built on a tree-dense ridge above the city and dotted with art deco villas, many featuring swimming pools, tennis courts, "circular driveways and double garages for Dodges, Plymouths, Buicks, and Cadillacs."[70]

For Johannesburg's status-conscious world, this was a great fall from grace, illustrating the treacherous ease with which downward social mobility occurred. Regina went from being a teacher at a respected mission school, a journalist, and a literary competition prize-winner to a humble "kitchen girl" whose "legs were all swollen up" from kneeling scrubbing a "cement floor."[71] She loathed her "haughty European mistress," who worked her past nine in the evening without overtime.[72] From the perspective of an elite woman relatively protected from the harshest realities of Black life, this was a terrible shock. Some sense of Regina's reduced circumstances can be gleaned from contemporary newspaper accounts snobbishly praising teachers and denigrating domestic workers. Statements like this must have been painful for Regina, reading the newspapers in her small servant's room in the dim light of dawn: "We Bantu haven't a higher class of women than our teachers and nurses. They are intellectually and socially better than our domestic servants, nurse girls and kitchen girls [who are only] servants and work for the good of their European mistress."[73]

In becoming a domestic worker, Regina joined a generation of Black women—including her own mother—traumatized by the profession's loneliness, physical hardship, and stigma. When American political scientist Ralph Bunche visited South Africa in 1937, he was taken by a local psychiatrist, Wulf Sachs, to tour the women's ward at the "Mental Hospital for Natives in Pretoria." Bunche found many women were former domestic servants, now "spend[ing] their entire days on their knees with pails of water, scrubbing the floors. . . . One has been doing it for seven years. Dr Sachs likens this to Lady Macbeth's washing her hands all the time."[74] Regina was one of the lucky few. She would only be a domestic worker for a few torturous months. Yet brutalized working women's plight was something that would galvanize her later social and political work in South Africa and later Eswatini.

Given all this, it was no wonder that when Regina met Dan the following year, she made him swear to secrecy her "shame" of being a servant.[75] Her authorial dreams had come to nothing; she considered burning the book manuscript she had worked on for the past year, writing, "Never again in creation will I be afforded the opportunity of finishing my ambitions."[76] Perhaps Regina was deep in clinical depression, so extreme was her despair. This may have been her own brush with the epidemic of mental illness that Bunche had astutely linked to being a Black woman of the 1930s. At Regina's lowest point, she bought a "revolver, a heavy one . . . a loud thug" and contemplated shooting Percy and herself.[77]

# 4

# Dan

I had gone so far Dan, when you came to be my redeemer.

—Regina to Dan, August 28, 1938 (RTP)

Regina was miserable and friendless; she called herself "a pathetic figure in a melancholy mood." In an effort to lift her spirits, in early 1938 Regina began playing tennis at the Bantu Sports Club. The club was in downtown Johannesburg, on Van Weilligh Street near a mining abutment and five minutes' walk from the Bantu Men's Social Centre. (Regina would have taken a bus to the club from Houghton.) The club had soccer fields, space for five thousand spectators in its stands, and the sole tennis facility for African women in the city. *Bantu World* noted, "No three tennis courts [are] so extensively used throughout the whole of the Union of South Africa by Bantu womenfolk."[1] There was also a "sociable" clubhouse, which *Bantu World* lauded: "Newspapers and scribbling papers [are] neatly arranged on tables, on the walls hang beautiful pictures that lend charm and dignity."[2] The gardens were extensive and welcoming; "a variety of differently shaped lawns bordered with large stones and planted with flowers and soft grass . . . altogether a delightful scene."[3]

Part of the same white liberal push toward "edifying" the leisure of Johannesburg's African population that had resulted in the Bantu Men's Social Centre, the Bantu Sports Club opened in 1931. It received funds from Johannesburg municipality, but its grounds were donated by Howard Pim and J. L. Hardy, two wealthy Johannesburg philanthropists. The powerful Christian social worker Ray Phillips was key to the club, which was, in its early days at least, linked to the social center. While the social center offered intellectual entertainments, the sports club sought to edify the body. Johannesburg's welfarists were convinced urban ills—"loose" women, family breakdown, political unrest, crime—could be ameliorated via leisure. It was a conservative vision, steering clear of criticizing policies degrading African life and focused on placebos like sports facilities for bored and lonely women and men living in grim one-room accommodations in their white employers' yards or in the prison-like dormitories of mining compounds.[4] Municipal officials approvingly noted "the moral effect of sport has been very marked. Instead of the weekends developing into beer parties . . . the youth are now sober sportsmen."[5]

The club especially focused on the city's domestic servants, both male and female (existing in equal numbers by the mid-1930s).[6] Both white liberals and municipal officials viewed the club as vital to neutralizing the threat of unattached urban women. Providing women with wholesome occupation for their Sundays would, it was thought, prevent them from engaging in beer brewing or parties. Welfarists ultimately envisioned a string of tennis courts and soccer grounds reaching deep into the white suburbs—areas like Saxonwold and Orange Grove—to entertain and uplift Johannesburg's servants.[7] Dan Twala, manager of the club, recalled how he and his colleagues would boost membership by riding on motorbikes to the "kitchens"—white suburbs north of the city where Black domestics worked—and spread word of the new club.[8]

Despite protests from white residents who alleged that crowds spilling into Van Weilligh Street threatened their children's welfare,[9] the club flourished. This was due to the backing of the municipality and the powerful Chamber of Mines; both recognized the club's political value.[10] But the club also thrived because its patrons loved its offerings. On weekends and holidays, thousands poured to the club from white suburbs, doling out 4d for bus fare and a further 6d for the popular soccer matches (a tenth of a monthly wage).[11] Soccer matches were more akin to festivals than sporting events. To the cheering of thousands, teams were escorted onto the pitch by mascots and bands of miners bearing lanterns, and evenings saw grand "concert-and-dances" in the social center, "a fine show with beautiful lighting and decorations . . . fine speeches interspersed melodious musical items and delicious refreshments." The most popular of the Black jazz bands, the Merry Blackbirds Dance Orchestra, would play into the early hours, strains of piano and trombone floating out the windows.[12] For the many women who annually passed through its gates, the club was a respite from domestic service and the racism of the outside world.

Regina was one of these women. More important than its tennis courts, the club also allowed Regina to meet the good-looking Dan Twala.[13] Born in 1906 (two years before Regina), Dan was one of the city's most beloved personalities, frequently featured in the who's who pages of *Bantu World* and *Umteteli*.[14] Like Regina, Dan's family were from Eswatini, part of the same African Christian aristocracy. Tragically, both Dan's parents died within days of each other during the 1918 influenza pandemic. This was a loss not only for Dan and his four brothers but also for society. His father, Reuben Twala, was one of the first Black Methodist ministers in Eswatini—later transferred to South Africa—and had been the religious adviser to the Zulu king, Dinuzulu kaCetshwayo.[15] His mother, Julia Msimang, belonged to a prominent South African Methodist family. Her brother—Dan's "Uncle Richard" Msimang—was a founding member of the country's first Black political organization, the African National Congress (ANC).[16]

A bursary allowed Dan a place at leading African mission school, Lovedale, in the Eastern Cape. A further scholarship took him to do his matriculation exam at the University of Fort Hare, formerly the South African Native College. Like Regina, Dan belonged to the narrow slice of educated Black South Africans, an elite by birth and education. After graduation, Dan began a brief career as a Johannesburg soccer player. (Athletic talent ran in the family. Dan's brother Shadrack "Up and Down" Twala was a well-known footballer.)[17] In 1936, at the age of thirty, Dan ascended to the prestigious role of manager of the sports club, the first Black individual to hold the post. Through networks linking Black elites and white liberals, Dan had been introduced to Ray Phillips, who took a shine to Dan, becoming "particularly fond of Dan and [having] high aims" for the young man.[18] Recognizing that Dan was both talented and hardworking, and had a natural sports aptitude, Phillips handpicked him for the role. Dan was now responsible for organizing sports for the club's thousand-strong membership.[19]

Phillips also saw a political ally in the young man. Dan exemplified the moderate ethos of many Black elites. Organizations like the ANC were largely quiescent in the 1930s. The short-lived All-Africa Convention was founded in 1935 in response to the Hertzog Native Bills (Dan attended some meetings), but its middle-class character meant it never gained popular urban or rural support.[20] Intensely affected by segregation—how could he not be?—Dan saw uplift for Black South Africans in a different direction than the political. Dan viewed neither political agitation nor economic change as solutions to urban problems. In common with many, he identified the city as the cause of Black social ills. The town was cast as an alien environment for those whose "natural" home was the countryside. And sports facilities would ease this jarring adjustment from rural life to city. Rather than higher wages, what was needed was an ineffable change of "morals," something the playing field supplied. Dan proclaimed, "We have to do everything to reinstate the morals of our people. Town life has demoralized them and the only hope of uplifting them is not to imprison them, add more police, or pay them more wages, but to awaken their morals, bring about personal pride in their being."[21]

FIGURE 4.1. Dan Twala at the Bantu Sports Club Johannesburg, late 1930s (RTP)

In his quest to "awaken morals," providing what Phillips called "clean, wholesome, and character-building activities,"[22] Dan focused his efforts on female domestic servants. He chaired a new African Domestic Servants League, the first effort to organize the large group of workers. This was an organization aimed at—as Dan put it—"protecting the interests of women labourers who live under unfortunate conditions in the back yards" and providing training through cooking classes.[23] Yet it was not clear whose interests the league served—the white employer or the Black woman servant. One goal was to "address the friction that arises whenever houseladies have to deal with impertinent and cheeky servants."[24] An advertisement for a cookery demonstration, circulated by Dan, urged employers to "send your servants to come and learn to be of greater service. . . . Cheeky servants must go!"[25]

Dan's interest in urban women—expunging their "cheekiness" and cultivating Christian character—went beyond the professional. When he met Regina, he was romantically linked with Bella, a "stout, robust, dark-haired lady," a domestic servant whom he met through the club.[26] Dan dubbed Bella a "fallen woman," and in the moralizing eyes of middle-class Johannesburg she was just that, being an unmarried mother of one. Over time, Dan housed and provided for Bella and her child, and in return she did his cooking and cleaning, also becoming sexually involved with him. Dan conceived of the relationship as a magnanimous gesture on his part, an act of "social welfare." Complacent in his Christian virtue, Dan defended his involvement with Bella in a letter to Regina, casting his affair with an unmarried woman as "an invaluable service to Christianity": "When I meet a woman like Bella who has had moral weakness to fall in her maiden days and try to raise her up to respectability and restore her self-pride, providing a home for her and her young one, I think I have rendered an invaluable service to Christianity and social service."[27]

Despite his involvement with Bella, Dan took immediate interest in the beautiful Regina, whom he already knew—as he did Percy—via the small world of elite Johannesburg. Perhaps he caught sight of Regina's strong serve while sitting at his desk overlooking the tennis courts. Or perhaps he glimpsed her at a weekend dance, swaying with one of the men who queued up to partner her. He was intrigued. Yet in Dan's clear-cut moral universe, he knew Regina was a "fallen woman." All Black Johannesburg knew Regina was suing Percy for divorce. Dan was certain of his moral high ground. Thus, Dan proclaimed to Regina, after meeting her, that "as a man, I can safely say that our girls are a real disappointment to our civilization and to our race." Furthermore, "our girls" were bucking their time-honored role of conjugal deference: "You find them all trying to entice the man to love them and after that they want to rule, govern, control, and domineer the very man they say they love! There is nothing I hate more than a woman who tries to play the BULL for her lover."[28] Dan placed on Regina full blame for her marriage's breakdown, despite recognizing Percy's infidelity. He sternly lectured: "I am sorry you have not had the courage the stand the test of enduring marriage. . . . You have failed dismally to be loyal to the man you chose. We are not interested whether he was a bad choice. Since you had made it, it was your duty to stick to it."[29]

Even worse, Dan saw Regina continuing this downward trend—as he harshly put it, "disgracing yourself as a loose man-hunting prostitute."[30] Perhaps Dan heard rumors of Regina's relationship with Makutso. Dan's pronouncement was this: "I am afraid your name is already in the gutter. . . . You have been discussed as a great disappointment to Society and to African civilization."[31] There was a humiliating episode at the club when a man called Conference (probably Conference Setlagelo of Thaba Nchu, a small town four hundred miles southwest of Johannesburg)[32] made a disparaging comment to Regina about Makutso. To her horror, Dan joined the mocking, suggesting she stay behind with Conference as "all men are the same to you." Outraged and hurt, Regina wrote a blistering letter to Dan, accusing him of portraying her a "real backyard prostitute—a man hunter—a wash out of a woman that has no feeling."[33]

Yet Dan was no paragon of sexual monogamy. His relationship with Bella was one of several. As he lamented to Regina, "I have at least four women—all ready to pounce on me for marriage." There was Sannie Tayise, a domestic servant who frequented the club. Dan thought highly of Sannie—"She is a masterpiece of womanhood so far as character goes"—but found "somehow I cannot appreciate her sufficiently to sacrifice my choice upon." Clearly Dan was sensible to his high value as an eligible bachelor, determined to linger in deciding who the lucky recipient of his "choice" would be. Another interest was Nettie Nkosi, whom Dan, however, dismissed as "an old spinster mistress . . . on the oldish side."[34] Dan, moreover, was already a father, having a daughter with Chloe, an old flame.[35] Dan later reflected on his bachelor days, remembering, "I was an expert at the woman-game, having studied and passed all examinations in flirting, philandering, spooning, fornication, promiscuous sexual intercourse, and raping."[36] What to make of Dan's flippant reference to "raping"? Rape was as much a crime in 1938 as today in South Africa. Yet sexual violence was part of daily life for Black women. Courts seldom stepped in to defend them, perhaps especially if the perpetrator was a renowned personality like Dan Twala.

Dan's sexual interests were not limited to women. While historians know laborers in Johannesburg's mines had same-sex relations, they usually cast this as "situational homosexuality" (men having sex with other men because they had no other options).[37] While this analysis ignores that men may have preferred sex with men, it also leaves us in the dark about same-sex relations in Johannesburg in residential parts of the city among middle-class men and women. Yet this is the world Dan was part of. He was close to R. G. Carroll, a European mining geologist and club donor. Dan commented, "Carroll thinks I am a remarkable fellow . . . the first black man he has seen with so wide a vision."[38] Carroll became a mentor, advising the young manager to procure grounds outside the city (reiterating stereotypes about the city corrupting Blacks): "The Sports Ground is too centrally situated, you collect all the town stiffs who contaminate the law abiding ones. . . . Keep the people's minds clean."[39] Dan regularly socialized with Carroll—calling him "my dear friend"[40]—together attending concerts at the club and visiting Carroll's farm at Lyndhurst, north of Johannesburg, for overnight stays.[41]

Carroll and Dan's friendship not only crossed racial lines—itself startling—but also sexual ones. Carroll's farm was their base for assignations, with Carroll urging him to visit regularly: "I long to see you."[42] Regina was cognizant of all this, referring to Carroll in letters to Dan as "your sweetheart."[43] She confessed she had spied a moment of passion between the two at Johannesburg's train station, seeing your "mlungu [European] friend kissing you at Park Station."[44] Dan, meanwhile, admitted Carroll "loves me very jealously." He was "praying [Carroll] should not be disappointed in my falling for a woman."[45] The geologist was indeed displeased to hear of his protégé's love affair—he "thinks [by falling in love with you] I'm doing a great mistake"—and warned Dan their intimacy would be constrained. Dan told

Regina, "As soon as I am married [to you] I will have to cut myself away from him, as he cannot then harbor the same freedom with me."[46] Surprisingly (for it contrasted with Regina's attitude to Dan's affairs with women), Regina treated all this with humorous equanimity. She advised Dan to "tell Carroll he shouldn't be jealous. . . . We can share you comfortably."[47] Perhaps Regina's relaxed attitude reflected the period's homophobic sense that male love affairs were not the "real thing." So far outside the boundaries of acceptable relationships, Dan's affair with Carroll was merely fun, not threatening in the same way Dan's affairs with women were. Carroll being white surely only heightened Regina and Dan's sense this was a nonviable relationship.

So, Dan was a hypocrite when it came to sexual morality. But he also realized Regina was an exceptional woman, shining among her peers. With many of his circle, Dan noted the absence of "African talented women," lamenting the lack of a "Bantu Woman to make a stand for her people."[48] Despite disapproving of married women who worked, many Black intellectuals nonetheless felt that the progress of their race would be mirrored in the achievements of their womenfolk. In the talented Regina, Dan thought he had found that exceptional woman. Dan knew Regina's reputation as a writer; her success in the Esther Bedford Prize competition ensured that. He applauded her talents: "I admire your intellect, your literary capabilities and your fine personality. These good qualities in you I believe can still be saved for humanity."[49] Linking himself with a woman like Regina appealed to Dan's pride. Theirs was a relentlessly aspirational class, and marriage was a vehicle for professional and social success. Suitably redeemed, Regina would be a fitting partner. As Dan told Regina, "I need a real, sincere friend—one I can share my views of progress with—and I think I have found that friend in you."[50] As fond as he was of Bella, that "she is illiterate and unskilled" meant Dan viewed her as unsuitable; otherwise, he said, "I would have banked all my future on her."[51]

Dan adopted Regina as his new "social welfare" project. He felt being a domestic worker was intolerable for such a talented woman (a snobbish view reflecting their class's prejudices), writing to Regina, "I loathe the idea of you classed as an ordinary backyard woman when I am convinced of your wonderful capabilities."[52] He thought Regina should resume her writing career, which had ceased since her arrival in Johannesburg. Her final Mademoiselle column was published before marriage to Percy; nothing appeared after 1936. But Regina had not abandoned her dream of authorship. The last year's despair had blocked her writing, but she was slowly coming back to creative life. Regina shyly told Dan about her ambitions in one of their first letters. She hoped Lovedale Press—the preeminent missionary publishing house for Black writers—might want her manuscript, an expansion of her Esther Bedford Prize submission: "Confidence No. 1. I have a book written half-way. You know the Topic with which I won the Esther Bedford Prize. Lovedale [Press] is waiting."[53] Dan warmed to the idea, insisting Regina come to his club office on Sundays to work on his typewriter and adamant that Regina "reach for [her] literary glory once more."[54] He warned Regina that his office was noisy because sound from festivities from the gardens would drift in. Regina replied undaunted, "Don't tell me it's noisy because concentration is in my capillaries."[55] A pattern ensued whereby Regina visited the club every weekend to play tennis and write.[56] As dismissive as Dan could be of her as a "fallen woman," Regina of 1938 was a traumatized creature who responded eagerly to his support.

Dan also connected Regina to his own powerful patron, Ray Phillips, inaugurating a relationship that would shape Regina's life for many years. After a nighttime event at the club, Phillips drove her home to Houghton; it was late, and the dangers of the pickup van loomed. But instead of quickly jumping out, Regina sat discussing her predicament with Phillips in hushed serious tones. When Regina at last emerged from the dark car, she felt dazed—not only by the electric lights streaming from her employer's house but also by the kindness she had experienced. She had expected Phillips to denounce her as "the most wicked woman in the world, I deserve no sympathy, and I should go to the devil." Instead, he listened sympathetically, suggesting Regina go to Johannesburg's native commissioner for her divorce rather than wasting money on lawyers. (This came to nothing.) Phillips even promised to speak to Percy, whom he knew, "so that he should not stand in my way at all," and to help Regina find employment outside domestic service.

Phillips offered Regina a rare show of Christian mercy. Despite his harsh views on single women, his tolerant stance toward Regina fitted his Christian belief in "repentance, redemption, and beginning again with a new life." Yet the events of the last year had nearly driven Regina from her faith. She was embittered by the Black elite's moralizing, caustically remarking to Dan "some of the Holy Saints of this world will not come to the house of a wicked woman like myself."[57] She had not renounced the faith of her girlhood entirely. She still thought "religion is very important and necessary"—but "not as it is carried out today." In her opinion, churches were too preoccupied with legalism and harsh judgment.[58] Regina's curbside encounter with Phillips reminded her that her faith was not lost. Several months later, while visiting eNdaleni, Regina heard a moving sermon about the Prodigal Son. The preacher described how "we were created in the image of God and as we lose ourselves the Godliness in us fades. . . . Then comes that one time when we must retrace our steps to the Grace of God and make our lives afresh."[59] Phillips's kindness reminded Regina she could indeed make her life "afresh." But I also detect the strategic interest of a proselytizer in a high-profile convert. Phillips discerned Regina's value as an inspiring example for other similarly "degraded" women. As Regina confided to Dan, "[Phillips] says I could be a living example of a life preserved to pull through even after so great a disappointment."[60] Yet there was surely a sting in being cast as a fallen woman, albeit one redeemed.

Despite Regina's protestation that friendship was "far better" than "sex love," she and Dan quickly became involved. Regina initially resisted this, with Dan reproaching her "if there is to be real friendship between me and you, it was must genuine, true and natural sexually."[61] But Regina's resistance did not last. Within a month, they were lovers, meeting in Regina's cramped backroom rather than Dan's shared house in the African suburb of Sophiatown. (He lodged with a family, and privacy was unavailable.) Regina rationalized her new intimacy with Dan, "What is there to prevent us from such a joy as well? We cannot run away from it or despise it for it is human nature."[62] Their physical relationship gave them both great pleasure. As Dan put it, "I have never tasted anything like the joy—the sensation—the passion—the madness of Gelana."[63] In another letter: "The mating we have together is the best any couple can desire and I feel I cannot have enough of my Gelana. . . . You make me intoxicated with your kisses, your touch makes me see heaven."[64] This was a sexual relationship that Regina enjoyed every bit as much as Dan. Her letters reference her "spasms of desire," confiding "your touch, your kisses, are enough to finish Gelana."[65]

Alongside this physical pull, Regina and Dan's relationship was deeply companionate. This reflected the mood of Johannesburg's Black elite that "progressive" marriage should encompass friendship as much as reproduction. *Bantu World* tabulated "rules for married couples," including the admonition to "be perfect friends with each other . . . be a helper and proud of one another."[66] Regina felt this was why her marriage to Percy had failed. She reflected to Dan, "Do you know why marriage seems to prove a failure nowadays? It's because there is but love and no friendship or companionship, just like eating a piece of cake and no tea to swallow it down." Her time with Dan was both cake and tea. This was a couple who discussed books, who clipped out newspaper articles for the other, and who swapped opinions on politics in South Africa and internationally (the buildup to World War II being much remarked on in local newspapers).

Quite simply, thirty two-year-old Dan had never met a woman as talented, educated, and unusual as Regina: "I desire uplifting companionship, none of these [other] women give this to me. . . . Your letters are always thought-provoking, they make me proud to be connected with so erudite a woman as you."[67] While Regina was far from conventional, for all of Dan's prejudices about divorced women, he was as willing as Regina to contemplate a relationship escaping gendered norms. Dan's opinions defy straightforward categorization. He both hated a woman who played "bull" as well as loved a woman's "fighting pride." A letter to Regina encapsulates Dan's paradoxes: "You are a very difficult woman to please and once you are bent on having your satisfaction, it will take a man's whole day labor to keep you from your want." So far, so normal. But then: "Although I would love you less if you had to be all willing all yes yes yes and all humble to whatever I arrange for you. I like your fighting spirit, your pride and your independence."[68]

Both saw their relationship as more than merely a love affair. A sense of social duty for the "welfare of the race" preoccupied them both. Snobbishly confident of their superiority with regard to their compatriots, Black middle classes saw as their vocation uplifting their people. In T. W. Skota's who's who of 1930—a compendium of the Black elite—a common phrase used to describe the elites peopling its pages was their "keen interest in welfare."[69] Being elite meant great responsibility to uplift others less fortunate, through teaching and medical, religious, and social work. Regina and Dan were aware they were talented and educated and that their union would create an exceptionally accomplished family. Perhaps they had in mind other African power couples—Barney and Mabel Ngakane, for example—both social workers who were part of the city's Black elite (and later active in the ANC).[70] This is how Dan put it: "Let us combine to do something definite and do it for the common good of our advancement and social betterment."[71] Their romance should be a vehicle for their people's uplift: "Let us help solve our social problems by serving the community through our companionship."[72]

It is hard to find Regina's voice at this stage, so dominant was Dan then. A compliant Regina was swept along in these grand plans, writing to Dan that her only desire was "to be your helper in every sphere of life more so as you are so ambitious and determined about your future, then I shall have something definite to live for."[73] This was a relationship in which power was decidedly skewed in one direction. Regina looked to Dan as her savior and her educator, referring to him as "her hero."[74] Regina was grateful for Dan's kindnesses, however patronizing: the use of his typewriter, his encouragement of her writing, his advice about her divorce, his introduction to Phillips, and his interest in her, a "wicked woman." She had been at her lowest when she met Dan, and then—"a hand came to pull me out of the deep—that was [Dan's] hand."[75] As another letter put it, "I had gone so far Dan, when you came to be my redeemer."[76] Regina gratefully accepted his advice on "every topic of importance affecting me, dress, habits, thrift, home life, and my ambitions as a whole. . . . Where can I get a friend so sincere as my darling Dan?"[77]

With ambitions as grand as these, the dependency as acute, and the sex so good, the relationship was destined to become serious. The two decided to marry once Regina was free of Percy. But frustrations thwarted them. The lovers were unable to spend much time together. Regina worked throughout the week and could only come to the club on Sundays. White employers didn't allow female domestic workers male visitors to their backrooms, a major contention between women and their employers. African critics exhorted European employers to show "friendliness and love . . . not threaten these poor girls with immediate dismissal or the prosecution of their boyfriends when found in the premises."[78] Dan's surreptitious visits to Regina in Houghton were thus infrequent. As Dan put it, "Here I am ready to take care of you, but because your mistress will not let you have men visitors I cannot be with you. . . . What hypocrisy!"[79]

Within several months, Regina and Dan decided she should leave Johannesburg until her divorce went through. From rural eNdaleni, the city had seemed an alluring citadel of opportunity. But two years later, the city had become a prison. There was no prospect of immediate release from Percy or marriage to Dan. They both hated the humiliations she suffered as a domestic worker. Regina was overwrought with emotional stress, writing to Dan of the "terrible scoldings" she received from her mistress, how she was "worked like a horse. . . . Isn't she terrible. Oh Dan, I can't stick it."[80] For his part, Dan wrote of his distress in spying her take out the garbage: "I nearly cried when I saw you [outside your employer's house]. . . . It seemed very cruel to see you draw that heavy load of rubbish out in the open air."[81]

Dan and Regina settled on her going to eNdaleni for a holiday while they decided her next steps. Rural eNdaleni would be an antidote to her demoralizing city life. "A rest at home where you have no anxiety about your livelihood may help you to overhaul your principles and give you moral strength," Dan wrote here.[82] Both moralizingly pitted the city against the countryside. The former represented degenerate wickedness for single women, the latter a restorative sanctuary (despite while actually living in eNdaleni, Regina had disparaged the rural mission as uncivilized). This glowingly romantic view also papered over the impoverishment of South Africa's rural areas, hollowed out by migration. Nonetheless, Regina's Johannesburg trauma and the moralizing consensus about cities combined to persuade her she would be better off at home. Dan advised, "You are degenerating whilst in this town. . . . Breathe much more fresh air, get out into the open and commune with the sages, the saints, the beauties of mother nature."[83] The change of scene seems to have had the desired effect. At home after quitting her soul-crushing job, Regina was filled with renewed optimism: "My mind is perfectly clear now, Dan Dear, I have forgotten my affliction."[84]

Regina only stayed a few months at eNdaleni. By August 1938 she was recruited by the Polela Institute, a Presbyterian school in the mountain hamlet of Bulwer, Natal, near the border with Lesotho. Regina would teach isiZulu to secondary school students. Bulwer was near eNdaleni, and perhaps Regina's excellent reputation carried her over any doubts regarding her personal circumstances. Or perhaps Johannesburg news hadn't seeped into rural Natal, given Regina pretended the nearly daily letters she received from Dan were missives from her husband. The school was also desperate. The Zulu teacher—a young woman named Dora Msomi—had fallen pregnant and gotten married. (That she might continue to work while married seems to have been unthinkable.) The school "begged" Regina, and she accepted, telling Dan, "I would be the salvation of those poor children left in a hole by their teacher who thought it best to become pregnant and marry in haste."[85] Just as important, the job came with accommodations.

Despite its proximity to eNdaleni (about forty-four miles west and deep into the massive Drakensberg escarpment bordering South Africa and Lesotho), Regina had not visited Bulwer before. She took the train from Pietermaritzburg, trying to avoid conversation with her compartment mate—"an insignificant gentleman who wore spectacles"—reread letters from Dan, and "dozed like a tired child." Occasionally she opened her eyes and watched the Natal countryside—"glimpses of nature"—flash by the window: "meanderings of rivers—African boulders—cattle ranches. . . . It seems very clear I am going further away from civilization."[86] While she hoped the countryside would restore her, we can still hear a poignant note of loss for what Johannesburg offered her, an educated woman. It was, after all, "civilization."

The Bulwer train station was fifteen miles from the school, so the final leg of Regina's journey was undertaken in the back of an open truck, into which teachers and students were piled like cargo. Regina's sense of exile was further confirmed upon arrival at the school. To her horror, she found Bulwer's lone shop sold neither writing paper, envelopes, nor hot-water bottles (the last the most urgent, given the freezing temperatures). The remote settlement was overshadowed by Amahwaqa Mountain, a massive, rock-capped twin edifice regularly covered with winter snow. In time, Regina would find her solitary walks up the mountain the most comforting moments of her time at Polela. But when she was newly arrived in the cold August weather, the hulk of rock added to her foreboding. At least she had her own secluded room within the gabled building, partly making up for the terrible food, weather, and equally chilly welcome from her new colleagues (not "even a bite" before bedtime, not "even a cup of tea on a beastly cold wet day as this").[87]

Regina was also woefully outnumbered by male teachers and students. The only other woman on staff was the nurse, who hadn't yet arrived. Regina felt deeply uncomfortable. Taking a walk when the weather warmed to explore the thick forests surrounding the school, she took off her stockings to wear "short tennis socks." On her way back, "one of the boys saw I had bare legs and he ran to tell the others to come and see Mrs Kumalo without stockings. Think of a group of boys all rushing towards me to come and admire my legs—I felt so small. They were all talking with each other—I will never do it again."[88] A woman fearfully outnumbered by men, heartsick at her separation from Dan, despairing at her divorce's slow pace; it was her letters with Dan that became Regina's lifeline.

# 5

## Letters

> Thanks for your snap. . . . I am still going to kiss it often, Dan, I looked at this body and found such beauty was wasted on a man, such round smooth shoulder, such shapely legs, would pass for a belle of a maiden.
>
> —Regina to Dan, April 26, 1938 (RTP)

Physically distant, the lovers now depended upon letters for contact. Regina and Dan were in good company. South Africa was a country marked by labor migration and hence also by letters. Throughout the twentieth century, written missives were the lifeline connecting displaced wives and husbands, children and parents, across the entire country and especially between industrial hubs like Johannesburg and the countryside.[1] Recognizing the significance of letter writing for their rural workforce, some recruiting companies for Johannesburg's gold mines even provided free writing paper, envelopes, and postage.[2] And the early twentieth-century South African postal service was far superior to what it is today. Postal workers collected and delivered the mail several times a day. This meant nearly daily letters—sometimes more than one a day—flew back and forth between Regina in remote Bulwer and Dan in Johannesburg. In August 1938, six months after meeting and just after her arrival at the Polela Institute, Regina joked to Dan that he must have "letter indigestion. . . . You get letters every day from me."[3]

Such frequency meant that Regina and Dan felt occasional delays in the postal service as excruciating lapses in their intimacy. After a seven-day silence from Dan, Regina took to her bed "for two hours to drown my disappointments" and obsessively fingered a ring Dan had given her. ("The only token I have as comfort is the ring which I keep on turning round and round in my fingers.")[4] When it was his turn to suffer a lapse in communication, Dan wrote reproachfully to Regina how "very discouraging [it was] not to get a letter from you."[5] But a delay in mail meant several letters might arrive all at once, and a bumper crop of letters was cause for rejoicing. Regina would "jump with joy to see [she] had such a fat mail."[6] Sometimes she couldn't find the self-discipline to wait to read them in her room alone at night and instead greedily pored over them in study hours with the students, stifling laughs "in case I spoil the discipline of these children."[7]

Regina and Dan's letters, especially this early in their relationship—their correspondence would thin out after the initial heady years—were long, often running to five or even more pages and written in both English and isiZulu, as well as a mixture of the two. Often when Regina was writing something particularly sensitive, she wrote in isiZulu and then returned to English once she had closed the topic. Their letters were both typed and handwritten; Dan had his office typewriter, while he lent Regina his personal machine to use during her absence from the city. She would tap away at night, when everything was silent, and the school tucked into bed. Both wrote by hand as well, using conventional writing paper as well as whatever stationery Regina could find. Regina was without much of a shop at Bulwer, and so she relied upon Dan to keep her supplied with a steady stream of stationery including pens, notepaper, and school exercise books. Parsimonious with her writing materials, Regina tended to recycle paper, sometimes writing on the back of letters received already from Dan on Bantu Sports Club letterhead. They usually wrote their letters late at night when the day's work was ended, although it was a mark of their passion that they snatched moments to scribble a letter to each other while at work. (This was Regina: "Dan you ask for a letter when I am at work, ngiyibhale nini? [when am I to write to you?] The whole day I have been mad over thoughts for you.")[8]

A further favored venue for letter writing—for Regina, at least—was the Amahwaqa Mountain. Soon after her arrival at the school, Regina began taking regular bracing walks right up the peak—about five thousand feet above sea level—to be "all by myself with Mother Nature." Some patches were so steep that she had to scrabble on her hands and feet lest she lose her balance and fall: "Feeling giddy . . . I dared not look back."[9] Listening to "calls and songs of birds in all keys," Regina would settle down for a bout of letter writing to Dan. At times like these, Regina would communicate through pictures as well as words; several of her letters to Dan from atop the mountain include her Biro pen sketches of the twin peaks of Amahwaqa. The quiet of the summit seemed to her the perfect place to reflect to Dan on their joint life thus far: the ardors of the climb recalled both their personal difficulties and their hopes for eventual triumph. ("The climb has given me a hope that I shall reach the summit of my desires.")[10]

The mountaintop was also a place that stirred Regina's deep-rooted spiritual sensibilities, with the views inspiring her to "quote the Psalmist, 'I will lift my eyes unto the hills from whence cometh my help.'"[11] In general, Regina's time at Polela—a Presbyterian school—was one of renewed commitment to her faith and an urgent sense that her deliverance from her marriage to Percy would only come about through the power of prayer. She regularly attended church services in the school's chapel, enjoying the "good sermons" she heard there. Regina seems to have now fully embraced the evangelical Christian teaching that she had committed a sin in leaving her husband. ("I must retrace my steps to the Grace of God and confess, 'I have sinned Father, make me

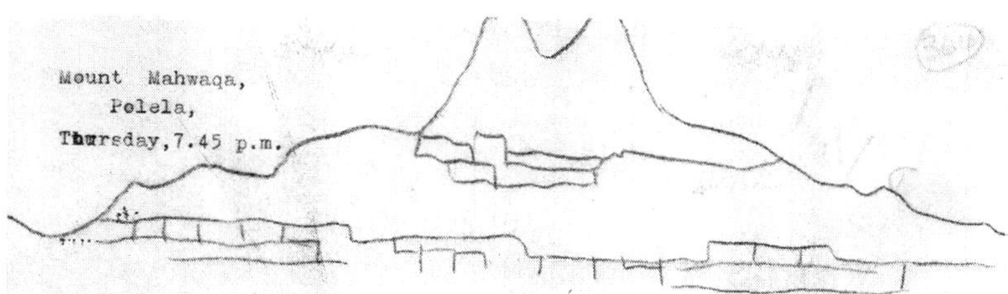

Mount Mahwaqa,
Polela,
Thursday,7.45 p.m.

Beloved Daly.,

Ihave just finished a very long letter to Mother , after along silence on my part , it had to do with some home matters mostly, and about her Cousin and son-in-law. She wrote to tell me that they have to meet Marjories executor, this week , and that an announcement for the Reserve yearly rent £1 has been made.

In answer to her I got an opportunity of saying all what I have been wanting to say about my Dan. I told her of her sonn's ability , as a dramatist , of my book that Iam sending to the printers soon , of our mad love with Dan ,that he has placed his cards on the table to his relations and is stubbornly going to have no one else but Gelana . That her daughter has definitely made up her mind to go up to her Dan this December come what may , divorced or not divorced , sin or no sin. God will just have to to make up his mind whether to curse or to bless . Also that I am loosing my right of getting my restoration of funds because of this infernal case. I have been telling her all that.

I went as far as describing to her how happy this boy was when he spent his holidays with Gogo , that every single day we slept with laughter in our hearts , because of Dan's silly ,boyish jokes. How Gogo fell desparately in love with you in so much that when I left she charged me that should I find discomfort where I am II must go to you for help and protection. Mother knows all that now.

Igot a letter from Lizzie telling me that she has sent your jersey and she had no money she had to borrow from someone , and that she has eaten all that money she has hardly a stamp now , so please refund her the money for postage she must have been afraid to direct that to you , all she could ask for was stamps. I hope that thing will fit you now.

Look at the crooked lines its the ribbon getting finished ,the new one mind you I have been tyiping like the duce I tell you and By next week Ishall have finished my Zulu Book .To-day I met Mr. Malcolm and we discussed the book he tells me it must go through thehands of the Department and the Zulu Society to ensure a sale.I pointed out that t he Language used

FIGURE 5.1. Letter from Regina Kumalo to Dan Twala, 1938 (RTP)

afresh, and give me another chance.'") At the same time, she felt peace, certain that she had found forgiveness: "The answer to such a contrite heart is always give him the best robe, a ring, new shoes, let us kill a fatted calf and rejoice."[12] Resting in her new spiritual calm, Regina urged Dan to join her nightly—from Johannesburg, whether in his office at the Bantu Sports Club or in his lodgings in Sophiatown—in a few minutes of joint prayer, separated by hundreds of miles but together in spirit. Not only letters but also shared supplication to God united the couple: "Oh Dan, pray with me as I asked you to join me everyday at 9pm. I have never failed a day to observe that hour. Dan I believe we haven't as yet prayed enough or else we would have been rewarded."[13]

Not all their letters possessed such an elevated otherworldly tone. In common with the long history of love-letter writers everywhere, Regina and Dan discovered that these letters—eagerly anticipated and greedily devoured—could feel remarkably like the body of the sender.[14] In showing physical affection to the letter, one was in effect caressing the loved one. Upon finding inky thumbprints on a letter from Dan to her, Regina showered kisses on them, realizing "maybe your thumb had the ink."[15] She commanded Dan to "kiss your signature in my letter" before sending it off to the post office, and the mere sight of Dan's handwriting "makes my heart miss a beat." "Sleeping with [your letters] under my pillow" was a way of imagining herself lying in bed with Dan.[16] Photographs tucked into letters also conveyed the physical presence of the longed-for lover in a particularly intense way. Opening a letter and finding an unexpected "snap" of Dan inside made Regina "scream with joy."[17] Regina also sent photographs of her own to Dan, including nude photographs, suggesting perhaps the existence of studios in early twentieth-century Johannesburg or Pietermaritzburg where such portraits could be taken.[18] He found he "could not stop kissing that image. . . . You made me feel very naughty."[19]

Letters could hold emotional significance as well as functional utility. Complicating the notion that letters were a means to bridge physical distance, some of Regina and Dan's most heartfelt correspondence was in fact written during an intense vacation spent together in Natal rather than during the long months she was at Polela. Dan used his precious two-week winter vacation to visit Regina in eNdaleni just before she started her post at the Polela Institute. This was their first time reunited since she had fled the city a few months earlier and Dan's first opportunity to meet her family and see her parental home. They reunited in Durban and together undertook the train journey to eNdaleni. Their time spent at Cool Hill Cottage entered their personal couples' mythology as one of the most prized moments of their relationship. Regina called it the visit that "changed us completely."[20] Part of the significance of the visit lay in the couple's relief at escaping Johannesburg, echoing stereotypes of the uplifting effects of country life. As Regina put it, "I have been able to know you [Dan] in a new light, the simplicity of country life minus all the artificiality of town sophistication has revealed to me the real man in you."[21] They walked in the wintery Midlands hills and climbed the peaks around eNdaleni. Dan spent hours chatting with her by then elderly grandmother (whom he "fell in love with"), he chopped wood to keep the small cottage stove burning, and although they had sworn off sex until Regina's divorce came through, they found themselves unable to remain apart during the cold nights. For Dan: "I'm like a fly in the milk, I'm caught in the act—I can't resist you."[22]

FIGURE 5.2. Dan Twala and Regina Kumalo, probably 1938 (RTP)

That Cool Hill Cottage holiday was also one of their most intense periods of letter writing—this despite the fact that these conversations could much more easily have been had in person. Yet there was something about letter writing, and the possibilities it offered, that was hard to pass over. Writing to each other, even while together, was a treasured route into expressing their growing love. These letters were ruminative meditations on their feelings for each other, their despair that Regina was not free from Percy, their anger at the injustices she faced in trying to end her marriage, and their hopes for a joint life. In later years, Regina would refer to the Cool Hill Cottage letters as the "best in the whole history of our love," and she would often return to them in times of sadness, feeling that "reading them is like being in a sanctuary."[23] This is one example, taken from a letter Dan composed to Regina at Cool Hill Cottage, secure in the knowledge that the beloved recipient of his letter was in the next room—he wrote at the table in the living room while she prepared food in the kitchen—and that the missive would be safely delivered by him into her own hand: "Use me, Gelana, yes, use me as much as you can. For your carnal and your beastly desires. I am here. For your spiritual and cultural yearnings, I am here. For your motherly embraces, your material inclinations, your anything, I am here."[24] A letter such as this shows Dan's tender appreciation of Regina's complexity (whom he called by her isiZulu family nickname of Gelana, the name that Regina would in later years permanently adopt). Dan was aware Regina could simultaneously be many things at once: carnal, beastly, spiritual, cultural, motherly, material, both Regina and Gelana—anything at all.

The theme of multiple identities is not limited to this letter. Indeed, reading their letters, it is hard to believe this was the correspondence of only two people. The letters seemed to contain a multitude. Regina signed her letters off not only as "Regina" but also as "Reggie," "R. D.," her middle name "Doris," and her isiZulu nickname of "Gelana." There was also "R. D. Twala" and "Mrs. Twala"—both before her marriage, in joyful anticipation of her union to Dan, as well as after, in confirmation of her marital status. And then there was "Wife," "Mummy," and "Sisi [Sister] Gelana." For his part, Dan was variously "Daly," "Daly Mail," "Daddy," "D. R.," "Buti" (Brother), "Hubby," and "Beloved." In a letter of June 1939, imagining the happily-ever-after of their marriage, Dan "much amused" Regina by playfully listing no fewer than thirteen names by which she would be called after their nuptials: "Mrs Regina Doris Twala, Mrs RD Twala, Mrs Dan Reuben Twala, Mrs DR Twala, Mrs Regina Doris DR Twala, Mrs RDDD Twala, Mrs Gelana R. Twala, Mrs RD Gelana Twala, Mrs DR Gelana Twala, Mrs DR Regina Twala, Mrs Regina Doris Mazibuko, Madam Gelana, Mdme Gelana." Dan finally settled on a francophone name that invoked her Mademoiselle identity of old: "I have at last decided to address you officially as Mdme Gelana."[25] Both made much of the interchangeable nature of their initials—Regina's were "RD" (Regina Doris) and Dan's were "DR" (Daniel Reuben)—and they punned repeatedly on this happy coincidence. Regina "delighted in signing myself RD RD Twala, that is RD reduplicated of course."[26] And piling yet a further name on, Regina often signed herself off as "Reggie," one of Dan's favorite pet names for her, along with Gelana. While games with names were a source of amusement, they also played with nomenclature in other ways. Dan frequently addressed her as his "Mother" in letters, while Regina could sign herself off as "your daughter, mother, sister, wife."[27] A letter by Dan of 1940 (after their marriage) addressed Regina as "an ass, a fool, a conceited thing . . . to think I am going to be your husband, your slave, your playboy, your Dry Cleaner."[28]

Photographs could also transform letter writing into role-playing. Dan often sent Regina a range of photographs of himself in different costumes and moods—"my snap where I have a hat on . . . makes me look a real naughty scoundrel . . . then a snap of mine in a rather serious mood—a change from my usual cheery attitude."[29] Regina loved receiving these and—demonstrating her subversive sense of gender play—joked that Dan was so beautiful he should have been a girl; indeed, he *was* a girl: "Thanks for your snap. . . . I am still going to kiss it often, Dan, I looked at this body and found such beauty was wasted on a man, such round smooth shoulder, such shapely legs, would pass for a belle of a maiden."[30] Regina could also play this game, sending Dan photographs of herself dressed up in traditional Zulu garb and even—startlingly—as a mermaid with bare breasts and a long glittering skirt, an image that "filled [Dan] with praise and pride that I own that Mermaid all toes and legs, breast and head."[31] While their letters and photographs experimented with the boundaries of male and female identity, photographs such as these also pushed the limits of what was considered "human," playing with Regina as a hybrid creature, half fish, half woman.

Many scholars seeking to understand the rise of letter writing have linked the genre to the emergence of private individualism. In their view, writing a letter was a way to initiate a one-on-one conversation, far away from the prying eyes of family and household members. In the process, one's own sense of interiority was solidified; one became a concrete "self" through the exchange of private letters.[32] But Regina's dispatches to Dan Twala tell a very different story. Far from evoking a stable and self-possessed self, Regina used the genre of the letter to imagine being an entire cast of characters, both human and nonhuman, as well as muddling femininity and masculinity. Letter writing seemed to be Regina's way to free up—rather than delineate—new horizons of selfhood, seemingly boundless and frequently transgressive. After all, everything is up for grabs in a love letter: who you address as your love, how you address the beloved, who you are when you sign off, the entire range of fantastical scenarios you create in your letter.[33]

Yet as freewheeling as Regina's letters to Dan Twala were, they were also undeniably the product of a certain time and place. As we have already begun to see, 1930s South Africa was the era during which a highly repressive white government was narrowing the parameters for Black self-expression, a process that would culminate in the election to power of the National Party in 1948.

African women such as Regina would increasingly struggle to articulate any kind of aspirational identity: the range of names available to Black women was ever shrinking. Racism was allied to patriarchy: the segregationist vision of the apartheid state would imprison Black women into straitjacket identities of docile wife or mother, safely exiled to the rural "tribal" reserves away from the temptations of the city.

In the context of such serious challenges, a pseudonym appears as deadly serious rather than merely playful. As Regina dreamed of herself in her letters to Dan as a new being—a man, a woman, a wife, a writer, a maid, a poet, a celebrated seventeenth-century playwright, an American millionaire divorcée—white authorities in twentieth-century South Africa were trying to compartmentalize Africans—and especially African women—into dehumanizing boxes. In this sense, Black reinvention through letters was a political statement as much as it was a private undertaking or an exploration of interiority. In 1930s South Africa, the personal *was* political. Epistolary self-invention became Regina's way to escape and to challenge the identities thrusted upon Black people—especially Black women—by a racist white regime as well as patriarchal men of her own racial group. Her letters reveal her as the woman of letters, twisting and turning through her dance of epistolary noms de plume, intent on thwarting the snares of race and sex.

Just like Regina (and perhaps this is what made them so well suited), Dan was also deeply interested in what it meant to try on new identities, both gendered and otherwise. In addition to his role at the Bantu Sports Club, Dan was also a keen actor. In fact, he had been one of the founding members of Johannesburg's new Bantu Dramatic Society, an organization that had staged plays with all-African casts since 1932. (The playwright Herbert Dhlomo was also a member of the society, and many of its first productions were Dhlomo's plays.) Throughout the 1930s, Dan played numerous characters: an eighteenth-century playboy (Tony Lumpkin in Oliver Goldsmith's play *She Stoops to Conquer*), an

FIGURE 5.3. Dan Twala in *Lady Windermere's Fan* (*second from left, holding hat in hand*), Bantu Men's Social Centre, late 1930s (RTP)

English aristocrat (Lord "Tuppy" Lawton in Oscar Wilde's *Lady Windermere's Fan*), and an adviser to the king of the Southern African kingdom of Basutoland (the part of Mofokeng in Herbert Dhlomo's play *Moshoeshoe*).[34] Further expanding his theatrical sensibilities, moreover, Dan also had a burgeoning career in film. He had both played a Zulu warrior in a 1930s Afrikaner film and later on in the decade, in a government health-education film, a naive country man who comes to the city and is corrupted by a degenerate "modern girl."[35]

Their back-and-forth letters became a playground for both Regina and Dan to imagine radically different selves. This could be profoundly gender-bending. Regina invited Dan to consider himself a woman, and she called herself his husband. Dan addressed Regina as a man and labeled himself her wife. Regina wrote letters for Dan's former male lover, pretending in them to be a man, Dan. Regina called herself Rudyard Kipling and William Shakespeare. In one of the earliest correspondences of their relationship, Regina wrote a wild letter—desperate at Percy's infidelity, desperate at her job as household servant, and desperate at the failure of her divorce to come through—accusing Dan of having no idea of the difficulties a Black woman of the 1930s faced from predatory men. Her letter passionately urged Dan to imagine himself a woman; we might think of the extract I already cited in a previous chapter: "I wish for Christ's sake I would turn you miraculously into a woman and a pretty one that, I'd then let you off in the world so you can meet men."[36]

Dan, likewise, used letters to invite Regina to imagine herself as something other than the docile woman lauded in both Black and white public opinion of the day: "Please know that you are capable of doing anything a man is capable of. . . . Just because you have different garb to him, it should not be his reason to assume superiority."[37] As we have already seen in chapter 4, Dan's stance on emancipated women was paradoxical: he was both misogynistically opposed to "women who played bull" while at the same time he warmly encouraged Regina to pursue her professional ambitions. While Regina was away from Johannesburg at the Polela Institute, Dan was researching employment possibilities for her. He found a potential job at a new, privately funded social welfare society for Africans. He wrote to Regina immediately, full of excitement at the prospect of her new identity as a "modern woman" (and one that would exclude the usual occupations of cooking and childrearing): "How do you like the idea? No cooking, no children, no romancing for you. Can you sacrifice all of these for service? You shall have a car and be able to move about freely. This will make you a liberal-minded, modern useful woman. Are these all dreams? Tell me, am I crazy?"[38]

Yet other letters from Dan cemented traditional gender roles, even while superficially subversive. These missives can be taken as premonitions of the couple's future clashes over Regina's career in the outside world. A year later, when they were at last married, one of Dan's first letters to his new wife continued the theme of reinvention that had characterized their correspondence of their courtship. Written from the kitchen of their new shared home in Orlando, a suburb of Johannesburg, Dan wrote in anticipation of his new spouse about to walk into the house after a day away at work. Yet it was not Regina whom he called his wife but rather himself, and it was Regina whom he labeled as his new "husband." For all this, though, Dan's letter still reveals his ultimately conservative vision of womanhood. He celebrated the domesticated "proper wife," one who ultimately "think[s] only of [her] Husband":

> Here I am, acting the proper wife to you, Gelana. I cleaned up the home, I swept, cleaned the pots, washed the dishes, swept under beds, removed shoes, made up some potatoes, put them in the meat pot. . . . I am now longing for you, waiting just to hear your voice and then go to sleep. I am trying to be a Good Wife to you—looking after the pots, cleaning the house and just thinking only of my Husband. With loving kisses, your wife, DRT.[39]

These fictive selves could be drawn from many sources. Both Dan's and Regina's letters allowed them both to inhabit characters from books and novels and even mimic real-life celebrities and famous personalities. Drawing on her long history of religious education at Methodist schools, Regina admiringly wrote to Dan that he reminded her of the biblical Daniel: "Your name, Daniel, your nature and character, typical of the Daniel of old who was very brave, stood alone, protected principles." And in the same letter, Regina likened her anxiety about her impending divorce to a character in a fairy tale: "I feel as foolish as the lady in the fairytale, worried that the mallet will come down and kill my lover."[40] Dan was especially fond of imagining himself and Regina to be perhaps the most famous lovers of the 1930s: the former British king Edward VIII and his American divorcée wife, Wallis Simpson. In typically grandiose style, Dan impressed upon Regina the social risk he was taking in associating himself—the great Dan Twala of the Bantu Sports Club—with a divorced woman. Dan phrased it thus: "Like the Prince of Wales, I am faced with a real critical decision and the question is whether my Mrs Simpson will stand by me faithfully and stubbornly when I abdicate my Throne and become a commoner for *her* sake?"[41]

Most of all, Regina and Dan wrote most of their letters throughout 1938 and 1939 against the backdrop of characters in Dorothy and DuBose Heyward's famous American play about Black American life, *Porgy* (by then recently adapted by George Gershwin as an opera, *Porgy and Bess*). Written by two white American southerners, the play tells the tragic love story of Bess, a prostitute and cocaine addict, and Porgy, a disabled beggar who makes his living on the streets of Charleston, South Carolina. The opera was immediately criticized by leading Black composers, including Duke Ellington, who famously declared that "the times are here to debunk Gershwin's lamp black Negroisms." In an age of caricatured representations of Black American life, the play and later opera—both created by an entirely white team of writers, composers, and librettists—reiterated racist tropes of Black criminality.[42]

Black readers, playwrights, and audiences in South Africa took careful note of this, as they did of many cultural innovations coming from across the Atlantic. Yet interestingly, Black South African responses to *Porgy and Bess* seem to have been warm, with none of the critique offered by Black American intellectuals. While in Johannesburg, Regina had practiced her new typing skills by typing out sections of the play for Dan; eventually, Dan's Bantu Dramatic Society adopted the play for its own production. Directed by Dan, Johannesburg rehearsals were ongoing throughout their courtship. The play was an opportunity for the Bantu Dramatic Society's actors to comment upon themes of segregation and racism, strikingly parallel in the United States and South Africa. Yet this exploration was nonetheless couched in the safe distance of material that dealt with the United States rather than South Africa. And there is no hint of criticism of its stereotypical portrayal of Black southern life. Indeed, many of its tropes of Black vice were near identical to the discourse of South African intellectuals like Regina and Dan with respect to the breakdown of morality in the city. In fact, the play became a route for the South African couple to measure their distance from the impoverished world of the American South, reflecting upon what seemed to them their relatively better state: "Now we are not as badly off as those two, and we have the good fortune of coming from good homes and civilized surroundings."[43] Regina and Dan thus upset the usual hierarchies of 1930s Black South Africa, which more often than not assumed the superiority of Black Americans to Africans. In Regina and Dan's reading, it is they who are civilized, not the Americans. And alongside sparking this complex transnational conversation on race and progress, the play also became a way for Regina and Dan to probe the depths of their own love affair, imagining themselves as a latter-day Bess and Porgy, mired in intense love and immense challenges. Dan compared Regina to the much put-upon Bess, confessing, "I could not help but admire Bess for her simple and sincere affection for Porgy, the cripple and how she tried hard to be a real partner to him."[44]

As well as comparing themselves to literary characters—indeed, they used letters to imagine themselves to *be* those other characters—both Regina and Dan referred to their letters in ways that attributed "literary" qualities to them. They viewed their letters as a complete coherent corpus—a book, in other words—rather than an aggregate of individual missives. Challenging usual designations of women's love letters as an ephemeral "nonliterary" genre, we see that both Regina and Dan treated their letters to each other very much as literature.[45] They variously referred to their collection of letters as "volumes and volumes" and as a "memoir."[46] For Dan, their value was greater than a "real" book, even the greatest book of all for a mission-educated Methodist boy. As he wrote to Regina, "Somebody reading your letters may feel a bit disappointed because there is so much real mischievousness about them, but to me I would not exchange the Bible for them, so valuable they are."[47] Both Regina and Dan, moreover, thought carefully about the aesthetic qualities of their letters, paying careful attention to questions of craft rather than solely content.

Regina, for example, could reproach Dan for a letter that was "dry, no details, and yet I want to create an imaginative picture of your environment."[48] We might also think here of Dan's father, the Methodist minister Reuben Twala, who had commented, decades earlier, on the importance of well-crafted letters: "The important thing is to look for good or beautiful words."[49]

Good and beautiful words deserved to be kept for posterity. Both diligently archived their correspondence. Dan, in particular, seems to have played the role of secretary in later years, collecting his letters to Regina from her and filing them away with her own to him. (Indeed, it is thanks to Dan's careful preservation that the letters have survived intact via Tim Couzens after so many years.)[50] In this way, the couple created an epistolary archive to which they returned in times of sadness, loneliness, or simply to remind each other of the fundamentals of their relationship.[51] Their letters from the other were a precious book that required reading in consecrated spots. Once at the top of Amahwaqa Mountain, Regina would not only write letters to Dan; she would also reread older ones from him she had already received, absorbing them afresh amid the peacefulness of the summit: "I have some of your letters, [Dan], to read and be able to live in your spirit once more."[52]

Letters like these surpassed the boundaries of the strictly private. From time to time, Regina and Dan dared imagine a wider readership. Books, after all, were meant to be published and read by others. It was their common practice to also enclose letters from others—friends and family members—into the envelopes carrying their own love letters to one another; letters were items to be circulated around and widely commented on by a broader circle of readers than just the sender and recipient. Awareness that their letters would be read by more than just them led to deliberate acts of self-censorship and autoediting. When writing angry words to Dan or dealing with a sensitive subject (such as a young woman at the Polela Institute who fell pregnant and was immediately expelled), Regina's habit was to separate out this portion of text and write it out on a separate page, in order that Dan might destroy it after he read it without doing harm to the larger letter. (Evidently, in many cases he did not.) Regina's rationale was that someday others might read their letters—she showed remarkable prescience in imagining myself as her future biographer rifling through these one day—and so she treated their correspondence simultaneously as intimate private letters and as a more public text aimed at wider readership: "Dan when you write on a wayward subject please write on a separate page will you? One day our letters may be collected as a memoir and some such rubbish is not becoming."[53] Dan, likewise, when reminiscing about wild nights spent with Regina and extolling her "sexually sensitive nature," would then rebuke himself and remind them both, "Let us forget this side of our nature, it is too bad to be chronicled in ink."[54]

Regina's determination to create a permanent record of her writing—"to be chronicled in ink"—only strengthened during her time at Polela. More than merely writing and archiving their letters, her goal was to write a *real* book. Her dream was to be published, for her words to live between two covers, to send her writing out into the world, and to fearlessly meet the critical gaze of real-life readers. Regina was about to write her first book.

# 6

## Kufa

Authorship is my dominating aim and desire.

—Regina to Dan, May 26, 1938 (RTP)

Letters weren't Regina's only literary output of these difficult months. Remote Polela Institute was ideal for other writing too. She had aspired to write a novel since at least her Johannesburg days. Amid her austere existence, she made quick progress with this new project, called "Kufa" (titled after the male protagonist). Regina had correctly foreseen this happy state of affairs, predicting that away from Johannesburg's cinemas, jazz concerts, and lectures—not to say her grindingly tiring days as a domestic worker—she would progress with her work: "When I am at Polela I shall get a good environment for writing with no distraction, that is what I really like about College life."[1] Her exile from the city was an opportunity for writing: "I knew that if I waited, I would lose the swing of the thing. . . . I was only on Chapter One and there were Sixteen Chapters waiting for me."[2] In less than four months—August to early December 1938—Regina produced nearly twenty-thousand words, holding to a strict schedule detailed in a letter to Dan: "A glimpse into my personal timetable. 5 am alarm, 5:15 am devotion, Daly, 5:30 am bath, 6:30 am supervision, 4:30 pm typing exercises, 5:30 pm supper, 6 pm clean teeth, 7:15–9 pm Kufa, 9 pm Daly, 9:30 pm Devotion and Repose."[3] While dawn and bedtime meant Regina's letter to "Daly" (her pet name for Dan), she allocated nearly two hours for writing. She worked in her small cell. ("The only good thing about the school . . . [the room] is secluded, away from the noise, and the bedding is blue, my favorite color.")[4] Not having a desk, Regina sat on her iron-framed bed with the rough blue blanket, fingers clicking the typewriter Dan had lent her (but only after she promised to use it for her novella and not solely for lovelorn letters). He also supplied her with typewriter ribbons and folio paper—purchasing either in Bulwer was impossible. Regina had learned to type during the afternoons at Dan's office and continued to schedule a daily hour for "typing exercises." But she still struggled with the machine, discovering "the shift for capital would not work unless I held it with my hand. . . . Look at the irregularity of the margin line." But, as she philosophically concluded to Dan, "Rome was not built in a day. . . . That little machine is so handy, it sits so comfortably on my bed as I type."[5]

Regina peppered her letters to Dan with references to "beastly cold" and "freezing fingers . . . barely able to hold a pen." She must have written in woolen socks and dressing gown for insulation from Natal's winter, perhaps huddling the hot-water bottle she requested Dan urgently send within hours of arriving at the school. These silent nights yielded an exceptionally productive period: cold, isolation, and yearning for her lover did her writing good. Sometimes Regina was too exhausted after a day's teaching to muster the energy: "I didn't feel in the mood at all tonight. . . . I was made cross by the kiddies, they were so insolent."[6] At times like these, "Kufa" was "simply draining" to her.[7] But mostly, as Regina proudly confided to Dan, "Thoughts just flow out of me." Dan was delighted at her progress: "I am pleased you are finding time for your [novella]. . . . Keep it up, let me see your name in gold and your deeds in reality very soon, I am dying for that."[8] Ideas were so copious that Regina simultaneously worked on several books, although with varying intensity. ("Kufa" is the only book manuscript of this period that she completed.) As she told Dan, "I have so many ideas for books that Mammy gave me a thorough scolding for having too many irons in the fire. . . . She says I should do one thing at a time, and do it well."[9] Nonetheless, "Kufa" was her main project, and she found inspiration flowed as freely as water:

> These lines came to me anytime, even when bathing before bed. I would manage 7 lines, then sponge myself. Then when I was having a wash, [the rest] came flowing. I put down my face towel and sat down naked to scribble. I continued with my ablutions. Before I finished, something else came while I was drying myself. I rushed for the pen and I wrote. Such things come as a dream that can never be repeated. . . . If you lose time about them, they go.[10]

Regina's authorial ambitions crystallized during these Bulwer months. She was already, thirty years old, an experienced newspaper columnist. Now she aspired to write actual published *books*. While I hesitate to reiterate stereotypical hierarchies elevating books over newspapers (Regina's columns were as important as her book writing), she herself viewed book authorship as the pinnacle of literary accomplishment. Just two months earlier, she had avowed to Dan that book "authorship is my dominating aim and desire."[11] Now she was passionately pursuing this. We should not forget how unusual this ambition was for a 1930s South African woman. A handful did publish books, but they were almost exclusively white women like Olive Schreiner and Sarah Gertrude Millin.[12] While there were increasing Black female journalists, by the 1930s the number of Black women who published actual books—sheets bound between front and back covers—was only three in the whole country (all of these books are either out of print or lost).[13]

For Black men, on the other hand, the 1930s saw a relative flowering of book production. S. E. K. Mqhayi, A. C. Jordan, Thomas Mofolo, Sol Plaatje, and John Dube were all publishing books in isiXhosa, isiZulu, and, increasingly, English.[14] This small renaissance of Black (male) writing was partly because mission presses—especially Lovedale Press under R. H. W. Shepherd—now viewed promoting indigenous "good literature" as key to Black progress.[15] Shepherd was "broadly sympathetic to the needs of literature rather than to narrow concerns of the missionary."[16] There was also the determination of Black writers themselves. Figures like Herbert Dhlomo and R. V. Selope Thema, editor of *Bantu World*, called upon aspiring Black writers to produce indigenous literature. Rebuking the racism of figures like Shepherd, these Black intellectuals rejected the notion that African culture had no intrinsic value. Instead, they sought a new synthesis of the best of indigenous and African values. Their goal was to create a distinctively Black African literary idiom that reflected African tradition—all that was valuable about it—and the modernizing changes of the last century. Black literature would thus be a microcosm of Black South Africa's progress. As Dhlomo reminded *Bantu World*'s readers in 1933, "The future history of the African depends upon his achievements in art, literature, music, and invention."[17]

Regina took careful note of these debates. Many conversations occurred in the pages of periodicals like *Bantu World* and the more highbrow *South African Outlook*, both of which she regularly read.[18] Judging from the familiarity with which she wrote about Sol Plaatje and Rolfes Dhlomo (brother of Herbert) in letters to Dan, I am guessing she also read English-language novels like Rolfes Dhlomo's *An African Tragedy* (1928) and Plaatje's *Mhudi* (published in 1930, although written ten years earlier). Both novels celebrated African history, culture, and traditional rural life, casting European influence in largely negative terms. These same preoccupations also threaded through Regina's early literary efforts. Yet for Regina, born and bred in isiZulu-speaking Natal, the theme of reconciling tradition and modernity was inflected with her homeland's regional politics. Regina didn't think in general terms of "African" literature but specifically puzzled over what it meant to be a Zulu writer.

Polela was fertile ground for these reflections. Located in isiZulu-speaking Natal, its staff and students were nonetheless a diverse crew, recruited from far and wide.[19] Yet Polela's diversity paradoxically cemented ethnic differences. Both staff and students strictly self-segregated. As Regina explained to Dan, the common room had two fireplaces: "one occupied by Zulus, the other by Basuto." The unfortunate Xhosa students were left to be "eaten by the cold."[20] A student's birthday was celebrated by her own ethnic group but not students more broadly.[21] As Polela's isiZulu teacher—and a Zulu herself—Regina became mentor for Polela's Zulu students (many affectionately called her "Mother"). She reminded students who misbehaved in an unnamed "dreadful affair": "The Zulu race has always carried itself with pride, and where many tribes mix there is no excuse to forget one's custom and be wayward."[22] Back in Natal for the first time in two years, Regina confessed to Dan, "Since I came here I have discovered myself afresh that I am a Zulu and no other thing."[23] Zulu nationalism could have an ugly face. Regina's letters chronicled violent "faction fights" where Zulu students "gathered sticks" and Basutu students "stones"—"We shall have to pass a Disarmament Act," she joked. Anti-Indian sentiment, however, united all groups, with students debating topics like "Are Indians of any benefit to this country?" Responses ranged from "Indians have a smell that perfumes all Africa" to "They refuse utterly to use toilet paper." (Regina dismissed these offensive sentiments as "childish arguments.")[24]

Several projects reflected Regina's interest in what Zulu identity meant in modern South Africa. One was a Zulu school reader; Regina knew publishers were more likely to accept manuscripts that could be prescribed for students.[25] The reader was an extension of her Esther Bedford essay, an isiZulu collection of folklore and regional history. Her second was a nonfiction book called "eNgilandi" (England). This related the life of one of Regina's students at Polela, a Zulu boy born a twin, something traditionally despised by Zulu culture. Abandoned by his parents, he was adopted by a European missionary. At the age of eight, the boy moved to England with his adoptive parents for several years—meaning "he can hardly speak Zulu correctly"—and then returned to South Africa. Regina was fascinated by this tale of loss and adaptation, busily "collecting from this boy all I can. . . . I hope to make a book about his experiences."[26]

These ideas—cultural transformation amid colonization, the impact of Christianity, and an ever-shifting landscape of Zulu tradition—were not just abstract concepts. Regina's experiences at Polela immersed her in debates about Zulu identity. Moreover, since the beginning of the century, eNdaleni had been gutted by migration to Johannesburg. As she lamented to Dan, "all the men are away from home and their women and children suffer in their education, their home discipline and their upkeep."[27] Regina parsed her own marital woes through the prism of cultural erosion. Traditional Zulu marriage had protected women from male infidelity. As she wrote to Dan, "during the days of our grandparents, there was mutual understanding and love. . . . The husband could make sweetheartings [*sic*] and the wife would take it as a joke. The heathen marriage has the best principles for avoiding friction that we educated people overlook." Regina thought of her own marriage to Percy when she instructed Dan to compare the regulated sanction of a Zulu polygamous marriage with the chaos bred by "modern" Christian unions. Here her tone is far from Mademoiselle's joyous celebration of the modern. Bitter from two disastrous years with Percy, Regina was disillusioned with European-style marriage, arguing it damagingly elevated the "sweetheart": "You marry a woman, you call her your wife, then you get a sweetheart and she calls you a husband, she competes with your wife, she boasts about it so your wife is despised and becomes a public laughing stock trying to compete with this young girl. . . . Your husband remarks his wife is jealous. These sweethearts are a curse."[28]

More positively, Regina also addressed how Black people could productively live amid the demise of traditional norms. Another book manuscript was an isiZulu math guide titled "Isihluthulelo

Sezibalo" (The key to elementary arithmetic). An experienced teacher, Regina had long noted "the difficulties our children get in making sums." She now wrote an isiZulu teaching text "so our African children will not be fools when it comes to percentages, formula and fractions." Regina proudly reported to Dan, "I have invented real appropriate words for numbers, factors, composite numbers, denominator, numerator, approximation, reduction. . . . I guarantee the book will sell like hot buns and will lift the standard of mathematics among Africans." Regina was thinking big: her plan was to translate the text into seSotho—one of South Africa's other widely spoken African languages—and "it would be a key book for all South African Native Schools on the Mastery of the Principles of Arithmetic."[29]

With her "eNgilandi" and the Zulu reader, Regina focused on safeguarding a fast-disappearing culture, exploring how Africans were alienated from their heritage. In her math textbook, Regina explored the flipside. Devising isiZulu vocabulary to express mathematical concepts was part of a broader project—undertaken by many African intellectuals—of updating "tradition" to align with "modernity." Regina may have read the debates on this topic between writers B. W. Vilakazi and Herbert Dhlomo in *The South African Outlook* in 1938 and 1939. These two leading literary figures respectively argued for modernizing African "tradition" (Vilakazi) versus imprinting African idioms upon European modernity (Dhlomo). In reality, these two positions were closer than they appeared. Both Vilakazi and Dhlomo agreed African language and culture should be adaptive rather than ossified.[30] For all her eulogizing the lost beauty of traditional Zulu custom, Regina's stance was similarly more complex than nostalgic neotraditionalism. Interest in *both* the conservative and the modernizing exemplify Regina's approach during these years and, indeed, for many decades to come, including while in Eswatini.

Regina's novella, "Kufa," wove together these interconnected ideas. Here she focused on how Zulu identity—encompassing marriage, women's welfare, family life, bodily health, and personal and societal morality—was under threat in the big city of Johannesburg. In Regina's view, rural Africans moved to the city and were beaten down by doing so. This, moreover, was a novella born directly from her own experience of heartbreak and humiliation. Her Mademoiselle columns had been glowingly romantic portrayals of Johannesburg, painting the City of Gold as a place of opportunity for young women seeking love, adventure, and careers. In "Kufa," by contrast, the very idea of the city had turned sour in her mouth. Evoking the idyllic rural life so beloved by intellectuals of the day, Kufa lived a simple existence in Zululand—"spending his days hoeing, grinding, chopping." Yet like many men of the era, Kufa soon went to Johannesburg to work on the mines to support his young family at home. After that, everything went wrong for him. Upon arrival, Kufa encountered city "hooligans," who took advantage of his rural naïveté and robbed him. On Kufa's first payday, walking outside the mining compound with wealth heavy in his pockets, he was robbed again, losing all his precious pay (and also depriving his hungry family in the countryside). Kufa was then injured in the hazardous underground world of the mines and forced to return home in defeat, a maimed shadow.

The themes Regina touched on—tradition's breakdown, the city, mineral capitalism—were explored by nearly all contemporary South African writers. One such effort was Guybon Sinxo's 1933 isiXhosa novel *Umzali Wolahleko* (The misguided parents); another was Peter Abrahams's 1946 *Mine Boy*. Both described the innocent abroad and the tragedies that befell them. South Africa's Black writers were using the novel to reflect on the link between tradition and modernity, between rural life and the city. What did it mean to be an African in an era of intense economic exploitation by Europeans? Writers created characters who were consumed by the city and whose sole hope lay in returning to country life. Ironically, this was also a classic government trope, feeding the segregationist discourse that Africans belonged in rural areas.

The closest parallel to Regina's manuscript was Rolfes Dhlomo's 1928 novel *An African Tragedy*, the first English-language book published by a Black author and a book Regina had read. We already know Rolfes Dhlomo as the pseudonymous "Editress" of *Bantu World*'s Women's Pages and are acquainted with his moralizing disapproval of Black urban women. Dhlomo's neotraditionalist concerns were evident in other writings. By the late 1930s, Dhlomo branched beyond journalism to publish books on past Zulu kings, eulogizing a pristine African culture uncorrupted by Europeans.[31] *African Tragedy*, an earlier effort, reflected Dhlomo's unease over the corrupting effect of the city. It also echoed the views of his European missionary–printer patrons at Lovedale. The publisher's note at the book's start—probably written by Shepherd—praised Dhlomo's book "as a contribution towards staying the decline of Native life in cities and towns." Dhlomo calls Johannesburg "that most unreliable city"—in a chapter titled "The Evils of Town Life"—and his protagonist, Robert Zulu, newly arrived from rural Zululand, is "plunged deeper into its vice and evil."[32] Dhlomo's cautionary tale concludes with Robert infecting his rural bride with syphilis and himself dying in agony.

But Regina's "Kufa" did more than parrot literary conventions. Her novella was also inspired by her growing politicization. Doubtless the result of her time in Johannesburg, Regina recognized how South African cities—and those who ran them—mercilessly oppressed society's vulnerable, especially Black women. During her Polela months, Dan supplied her with newspapers such as *Bantu World, Umteteli wa Bantu, Sjambok, The Forum*, and *South African Outlook*. Regina read these intensively (afterward sharing them with students and other staff; "as soon as I finish with my papers, I distribute them. . . . Dan sends his rays like the sun, and the far-off parts are illuminated").[33] She absorbed reports of the new All-Africa Convention and the joint council meetings, the multiracial committees set up to debate social, economic, and political issues of Black life. She registered the chronic underfunding of Black health care in Johannesburg, finding herself "very touched by articles on slum conditions and poverty. . . . Economic conditions really are very bad."[34] She also attended meetings of the Polela teachers' association (these groups acted as hubs for politicization throughout South Africa), having explained to her the Natives Land Act of 1913 that dispossessed Black South Africans of their territorial inheritance, making rural prosperity so impossible.[35] Regina lamented the segregated educational system that employed her—"the Education system of the Bantu is rotten"—and confided in her lover, "You know, Dan, I don't feel educated because the [Teaching] Certificate I have has an Adjective 'Native.'"[36] Rather than dismissing contemporary critiques of cities as "tribalizing" tropes, we should note Regina's words: she shows what good reason Black intellectuals of the 1930s had to condemn urban life.

Yet for all this, the tone of "Kufa" was humorous rather than tragic. While it is hard to be certain (given the lack of a manuscript), a surviving fragment suggests her treatment of these dark themes was lighter than Dhlomo's *African Tragedy*. This portion of the novella (preserved in a letter Regina sent to Dan) is a comedic account of Kufa trying on a pair of trousers for the first time. This is Kufa's first morning waking up in the mining barracks, far from Zululand's green hills:

> Kufa pushed his legs into one [trouser] leg and that sent him flat on his face. Then he got up again and was puzzled, so he stood for a while and watched what others were doing. . . . He saw a Shangaan trying his on so this time he tried again, but with caution and he succeeded in pushing one leg with no accident this time, then he tried another with good results.
>
> Experience is the best teacher, so he must be careful with the shoes, and if they don't seem comfortable take them off and try again. . . . With a smile he jumped up and started walking towards the door. He couldn't walk fast, his trousers were cutting him and hurting. He examined his own pants.
>
> Yes, there was a difference between his and those of other people which had charms in a row in the front and these made them walk fast. He looked once more at himself and the

> charms buttons were at the back. So he sat down again and pulled them off to face the front and then he wore them.[37]

The extract suggests Regina's eye for farce. Despite her plot's pathos, Kufa is no tragic hero. Regina portrays Kufa as a naïf, having her hero play out the bodily comedy of pushing two legs into a single trouser leg and buttoning his pants the wrong way. He falls to the ground heavily. The reader laughs uproariously as they realize he has no idea the "charms" are buttons. While Dhlomo saw urban Africans as tragedy, Regina was using different weapons—buffoonery and clowning—to offer equally scathing commentary on Africans' experience in Johannesburg.

As Regina progressed with "Kufa," Dan was a constant supporter. He cheered her on when she was despairing, reminded her she would "have some money and some independence" from it, and told her "my ambition is to see you an independent woman, not relying on men who would only use you as their tool." Dan's exhortations were tinged with nationalistic fervor. Echoing Dhlomo's equation of literature with national progress, Dan believed Regina's writing career would contribute not only to her own advancement but also "to the advancement of Africans in this land of our fathers."[38] Dan's help was also practical. With no carbon paper, Regina was unable to make duplicates of the novella, so she asked Dan to type each chapter afresh using carbon paper—"what a dear." (The manuscript's disappearance suggests he didn't do this.) Dan also sent Regina's manuscript to sympathetic white liberals. Given white monopoly over publishing, it was unlikely Regina would succeed without these contacts. As Dan put it, "I have started to get you introduced to the authors and publishers in town, getting them ready to publish your work and place your writings in their lists."[39] Dan sent the manuscript to one "Miss Goetz, my German friend," to "criticize [its] techniques of story writing."[40] Dan identified another patron, one who would play a major—ultimately poisonous—role in Regina's future career. This was Hilda Kuper, a young South African social anthropologist at Johannesburg's University of the Witwatersrand doing ethnographic research in Eswatini. Kuper belonged to the liberal network of white philanthropists, missionaries, and academics working to "uplift" Black South Africans. Kuper would become one of Regina's most important academic mentors, both at the university and afterward.[41]

Dan also provided extensive editorial assistance. Regina sent him draft chapters, nervously requesting he "tell me exactly what you think, don't be afraid to speak your mind if it be utter nonsense." She pleaded for assistance with her woeful spelling, wryly proclaiming it sick beyond cure, "kepa ispelling [but the spelling], it is a disease."[42] Dan offered Regina advice on words, diction, and plot: "Concentrate more on your ideal and moral in the story and see that words and diction do not carry you away from your Main Plot." Echoing contemporary debates within Black literary circles, Dan encouraged Regina to imbue her writing with a distinctively "African" idiom, reflecting the concerns of the Dhlomos and Vilakazis with a vernacular tradition: "Develop the African Tradition to a great length, to give your story a natural African surrounding with a purely African air and taste."[43]

But Dan's role went beyond encouragement. He became intensely involved in the novella's conceptualization and production. Dan perceived the value of Regina's work as fodder for his own Bantu Dramatic Society, desperate for material produced by African playwrights. This realization had taken place early on. Soon after they'd met, Regina shyly shared her writing with Dan. Lacking in confidence, she asked whether he thought her drafts had any future. Dan had "looked over my papers and we reasoned together as to what use they may be." After "sometime puzzling over it," Dan "brightened up," saying, "I think we have a play here!"[44] In crafting Regina's work as a play for his dramatic society (the slippage between "Kufa" as novella and as play offers an interesting parallel to *Porgy and Bess*'s own dual life as both opera and play), Dan hoped "Kufa" would be as much his triumph as Regina's. It would mean he had pipped the more famous Herbert

Dhlomo to the goal of producing an African-authored play. As Dan explained to Regina, "I want to picture myself reading your play to the group [Bantu Dramatic Society] one day, explaining to them just the parts and scenes connected with the staging of the production. Get busy."[45] In fact, their joint effort would even better Dhlomo's. Dhlomo controversially insisted on writing solely in English, arguing only English allowed an African author to find large readerships and develop a "modern" literary idiom. By contrast, Regina and Dan's play would be a truly African production as it would use isiZulu, a vernacular language. Dan hoped that although "today one man rules [Dhlomo] and the other perishes [Dan]," Regina's book would change all that: "Please get busy with your Kufa and help us follow in the steps of Dhlomo with something real and light and symbolic of the people your character represents. . . . It will have to be done in Zulu."[46]

Regina agreed, committing to the use of isiZulu. She avowed herself "against taking a native story and putting it in English," as the famous Dhlomo did. Grandly, she gave Dhlomo points for effort: "At any rate, Bravo Dhlomo. You have tried something better than any of us. It may be a poor attempt, but it is some effort."[47] But by the time Regina moved to Polela, she abandoned "Kufa" as a play in favor of a novella. Possibly Regina's distance from Johannesburg and the Bantu Dramatic Society were the reason. More probably, Dan was himself growing disillusioned with the society. It was riven with rivalries, and Dan resented that he did the bulk of its administration, especially given his arduous job at the Bantu Sports Club.[48] And while Dan did not cease acting, he was gravitating toward film rather than theater.

But Dan still viewed "Kufa" as in some sense "his," interchangeably referring to the novella both as Regina's and "ours." Dan exhorted Regina to drop her other commitments and focus only on "your novel, I mean our novel, KUFA."[49] In December 1938, as Regina neared completing the novella, she wrote that all she needed was a final addition from Dan: "I am waiting for you to expand just on this chapter and then OUR Kufa is finished."[50] Dan tied their literary endeavors to their social consciences, an African couple working for the race via "our" literary work: "Let us be among the few trying to raise the nation, let us make the [Zulu] Reader our beginning, from there Kufa, from there Journalistic Qualifications in collaborating in 'Social Research Work.'"[51] While a published novel would benefit the "nation," it would also be a personal boon. Regina confessed she "dreamt of seeing revenue from publication of our books . . . the joy of finding my bank account swell up all of a sudden, not feeling the anxiety of an insecure life."[52] Dan hoped "Kufa will bring in money and there will be a clamor for more novels of this type. . . . There is no telling what treasures we can reap."[53]

There was some justification in Dan's claim this was a joint production (again, another point of comparison with *Porgy* the play, which was written by a husband-wife team, the Heywards). Regina recognized herself unable to write sections dealing with male migrant life in the city. ("I have a very shallow idea about life in a compound," she confessed.) She asked Dan, with his knowledge of mining compounds gleaned through his work with the sports club's clientele, to supply her this material: "Dan, beloved, I want you to write the part on Kufa coming into town as a recruit and put in a detailed account of all that takes place in a compound."[54] Although Dan was "frightfully busy" in Johannesburg, "he drafted something that gave me some idea of life in a compound." Then Regina did—as she put it—"the digesting of the whole business and interpreted it within her story." The addition worked well: "That chapter of Kufa on the mines became the longest one of my whole novel."[55]

In addition to writing prose, Dan supplied Regina with other materials to weave into the novella. For her account of Kufa's education at a Natal mission school, Dan sent her a small pamphlet he had picked up when attending the Annual Missionary Conference of 1937 (invited by the white Christian liberals who organized it, as a leading Black social worker): "What I want you to do is read it, then to take extracts for your book Kufa, where it explains the influence of the Church on the life of the Heathen people. . . . You will find very useful material here, don't you think I'm a godsend to you?"[56] Other advice streamed forth. For Regina's Zulu reader, Dan instructed her to conduct further interviews with elders from eNdaleni to deepen her accounts of local history: "Collect material from the Old Ladies at Richmond. . . . We could compile a book of folklore, legends and other historical narratives. We could even make them into plays."[57] Dan urged Regina to take "trips for research work," probably for the reader. She should use holidays from teaching "to do as much informative discovery as she could." And if she needed cash: "Please just say how much and do not be shy to ask for my aid in any respect."[58]

Dan positioned himself not just as Regina's critic but also her teacher and mentor. An uncomfortably patronizing tone emerges, a persistent dynamic in their relationship. As we have already seen, Dan rebuked Regina for her failed marriage and her affair with Makutso. Playing on stereotypes of fashion-mad women, Dan now criticized her for spending too much on stockings and a "frivolous hat."[59] As much as he admired Regina's "brains," he was comfortable in his knowledge that he was her intellectual superior, a "Fort Harean" and, of course, a man. Dan could also seamlessly appropriate Regina's words, passing them off as his own. Despite being a Fort Harean, he implicitly recognized Regina as the more skilled writer. Her talents could thus be used to advance Dan's own career. To this end, he repeatedly asked Regina to write material that he needed for his duties at the Bantu Sports Club, especially comedic dialogues for his new club bulletin.[60] More illicitly, when Dan was asked by the Transvaal Exam Board to "draw up 7 or 8 questions for the Std VI final exam in Zulu," he wrote Regina, asking for her help but warning her "not to discuss with anybody." He cheerfully signed off his request, oblivious to the implications of asking her to do work he passed off as his own, for which he was perhaps even paid: "Do your best now, Gelana dear, and let us have good questions—you know the kind of stuff to set for school children. Cheerio!"[61]

Regina's writerly voice could thus be hard to pin down, as in one poem she wrote for Dan. He wanted to give "an ode of praise" to his sometime lover and friend R. G. Carroll, in thanks for a trophy Carroll had donated to the club. Dan asked Regina to write the poem. Seemingly feeling no jealousy about her lover's attachment to Carroll, Regina obliged. But she did jokingly ask Dan whether, in making such a request of her, he thought she was "Shakespeare or Rudyard Kipling." Continuing the play on names, Regina called her final draft "Carala"—an amalgam of "Carroll" and "Twala"—and she composed it as a paean to the redemptive qualities of the playing fields at the club ("which will make sport a recreation / that knits man to man as a nation"). The poem left the mystery of her authorial identity unresolved. As she told Dan, "at the top, I wrote 'by' and I left that blank because you might have your own ideas."[62]

Regina oscillated between love-struck deference and hurt resentment at Dan's appropriation of her work. Regina genuinely felt Dan's influence as instructive, reflecting, "I shall never forget the kind of education I got from your letters during the past few years, these letters have changed me a great deal."[63] One letter of April 1938 exclaimed, "Good God, Dan, you are changing my writing completely!"[64] In another letter, Regina pleaded with Dan to "not let me float without your guiding hand. To you, I am but as a little child. I have my own opinions . . . but you are the father of my thoughts."[65] This sense of respectful obeisance is also felt in Regina's nickname for Dan: he is frequently her "Daddy," her all-knowing mentor. Other letters betray her resentment. Regina found Dan's criticism of her work abrasive, reproaching him for being "being extremely rude. . . . You did not try to help me, but told me the whole thing was rubbish." She declared, "I am telling you straight, I don't care for destructive criticism. . . . If you have the same spirit, please don't do a thing to my papers."[66] In another letter she accused Dan of "developing a habit of taking things for granted," citing his failure to thank or acknowledge an article she sent for his sports club's bulletin, "as though these things do not take my time and thought."[67]

Writing "Kufa" encapsulated Regina's tentative claims upon authorship and her difficulties in disentangling her own authorial voice from her male lover. She was hungry for literary success yet hesitant to inhabit this role. She could proudly affirm, "The fire kindled in Reggie is fast growing and it is going to consume all before it. You will have to be very firm to stop it."[68] At the same time, Regina's self-abnegation meant she ceded important ground to Dan as "co-author." Pseudonyms—both in Regina's letters and earlier newspaper columns—could be a liberating experience. The pen name expanded the possibilities of who Regina could be, at a time of diminishing opportunities for African women. But the dynamics at play in writing "Kufa" suggest the opposite was also true. An evasive literary voice signaled a lack of confidence and failure to claim autonomy as a writer. And Regina's anxieties around authorship as a Black woman were far from ungrounded, as we shall now see as she set about trying to publish her book.

# 7

# Failed

> Dan I seem to fail in everything, you wanted me to write books, to do some social work, but in all these things I am nothing by a disappointment.
>
> —Regina to Dan, March 11, 1940 (RTP)

By the end of 1938, Regina's self-imposed mountain exile had paid off. In December she finally completed "Kufa." She sent this exultant letter to Dan:

> It is approximately 17,500 words, I think a little more. It has seventeen chapters. All the rich words have been explained in the glossary at the end, their origin mentioned, their meaning too. All are arranged Chapter by Chapter. Ain't I clever? No, I am not—self-praise has no recommendation. But Paul did say, "I have fought the good fight, I have kept the faith and now there waits for me the crown." He wasn't boasting, he was in exuberance because of his achievements.[1]

This semihumorous letter speaks to Regina's fragile sense of pride in her literary achievements: "Ain't I clever? No, I am not." It also suggests the bolstering confidence she found in likening herself to more illustrious counterparts—in this case, a figure no less than the apostle Paul. While it was bad form to indulge in "self-praise," it was acceptable—was it not? Paul did it—to be "exuberant" over "fighting the good fight." One was female vanity, the other a commendably Christian celebration of perseverance and hard work.

In any case, Regina and Dan immediately set about trying to find a publisher for the manuscript, which was ultimately completed in isiZulu. Their hope that was that the Natal Department of Native Education—the primary publisher of educational books—would be interested in Regina's book as a school reader for teaching purposes. Despite the new interest of a few missionary presses, in general the publishing landscape for Black writers in South Africa was bleak. Around this time, the journalist and aspiring book author Walter Nhlapo lamented, "Bantu people have the material but no outlet, Bantu books are in demand but the publishers do not want the books. . . . The writer has no status, he is forced to hawk his wares from house to house, a greengrocer has more respect."[2] In the absence of an established literary industry for Black writers, it was instead schoolbooks that constituted the main opportunity for African authors of this period.[3] Leaning on her contacts with missionary educators at both the Indaleni and Polela schools, Regina managed to set up a meeting with Daniel Malcolm, Natal's chief inspector of Native Education before the end of the year.

While he was tentatively interested in the project, Malcolm's advice to Regina was that she should seek the sanction of the Zulu Cultural Society for her book.[4] Founded by the future Nobel Peace Prize winner Albert Luthuli as well as by other notables among Natal's Zulu elite, the society reflected the widespread concern for the preservation of African tradition amid cultural change. It had strong links to Natal's European administration—especially the division for African education—and it exemplified the aspirations of both Black elites and white liberals to forge a modern African identity that at the same time harked back to the glories of the Zulu past.[5] The society thus became a kind of gatekeeping organization for any effort to codify Zulu culture and history. As such, its approval was central to the willingness of education officials to publish Regina's book. It was not an impossible notion that the society might have been willing to sanction "Kufa," written in isiZulu and with its nostalgically romantic portrayal of rural Zululand and its corresponding polemic against the corrupting vices of the city. Accordingly, Regina wrote to Selby Ngcobo—one of the Zulu Cultural Society's leading members and a future university professor and illustrious MP in the KwaZulu homeland government—"to ask him if he [would be] willing to correct the manuscript and attach a Foreword and approval of the Zulu Society."[6]

In fact, Regina and Selby Ngcobo had a lengthy shared history. Born in 1909, Ngcobo was one year younger than Regina, and they had studied together at Adams College in the late 1920s. Ngcobo had also been Regina's first serious boyfriend and, while both were students at Adams, had proposed marriage to Regina. But Ngcobo's parents had scotched their romance. Selby was from a traditionalist Zulu family historically linked to the Zulu king, and they viewed Regina's Christian background as of inferior pedigree: "indoctrinated by the whites . . . not fully Zulu."[7] Regina, too, was ultimately unsure about the relationship. While she admired Ngcobo's talents and probably his prestigious family too, she found him overly "intellectual": "I could never get on with Selby in spite of his education—a fellow with such remote narrow-grooved ideas. So that was that."[8]

Regina's request that Ngcobo write a foreword for her book and offer the Zulu Cultural Society's sanction—thereby "giving it more dignity" in the eyes of the chief inspector for Native Education—disastrously came to nothing. Perhaps there was lingering tension between the pair or perhaps resentment on Ngcobo's part at Regina's rejection of his proposal. Regina was "disgusted" when Ngcobo—now married—responded to her request with a shocking sexual proposition. He said he would write the foreword—but only if she consented to "having an affair with him on the quiet."[9] This was an example of male arrogance at its worst. Regina fumed at Ngcobo's sense of both professional and personal entitlement: "that rubbish of a letter from Selby Ngcobo

BA and B Eco, a man under the impression he will be a great boon, a leader of Africa." As she protested angrily to Dan, "I wasn't appealing to his private person, but the whole thing was purely a business concern in that he is a member of the Zulu Council and well versed with the new orthography and has an ideal of the right standard of Literature."[10] Regina told Dan that Ngcobo was in urgent need of "a lecture on Husbandry in Marriage. . . . He must have a hide-and-seek-life with his wife. That is exactly the sort of partnership I do not care for in my own Married Life."[11]

Dismayed, Regina found that other members of the Zulu literary elite—all men—also closed rank against her. In fact, ongoing tensions between Regina and the day's male literary luminaries had marked her writing career from the start. Regina had frequently made scathing comments—at least to Dan in private—about the pretentions of what she called "the supposedly educated gang" who dominated Johannesburg's literary scene. She dismissed the output of the city's leading poet, the famed B. W. Vilakazi, as "just a lot of works arranged in English rhyme with no taste at all. . . . He may write a lot but he cannot be our Shakespeare in a true sense."[12] In fact, Regina had had—as she put it to Dan—"a great deal of difficulty from these male writers." From an early date, she had found the more established authors reacted jealously to her successes. Regina was acutely aware that she was stepping into an already overcrowded sphere, one characterized by intense rivalry: "It is true that the Zulu market is becoming full. . . . Everybody who can hold a pen is writing a book out here in Natal. . . . Every Tom Dick and Harry considers themselves a writer of literature nowadays."[13]

Nearly all these figures were male. According to Regina's tally, there was "R. R. R. [Rolfes Dhlomo], who has written more than a half dozen books" and the venerable John Dube in Durban, and "of course, the poems by Vilakazi." But there was "still only one lady writer, Miss V. Dube."[14] While we know nothing of Miss V. Dube's experience, we do know that for Regina, a rare woman in a practically exclusively male literary world, predatory sexual behavior threaded through all her interactions with male writers. Due to Regina's literary success, I can imagine the titans of this literary clique would have been reluctantly impressed by her well-publicized talents. At the same time, they could not see beyond her status as an attractive young woman and deployed a punitively aggressive sexuality to shame Regina and keep her in her place. These literary elites used "romance" to dismiss Regina as a sexual object and to negate her as a serious writer. One male writer—whom she "would not name"—"ran after me . . . like a sly fox . . . wanting to play love with me, so I could trust him, give him all my secrets. He knew that romance turned the hearts of the soldiers of Rome into water. Instead of fighting, the soldiers went fishing with Cleopatra on the Nile. He is afraid of competition."[15]

These jealous competitors also included the literary siblings Herbert and Rolfes Dhlomo. According to Regina, Rolfes Dhlomo was "flabbergasted" to learn she was writing and was greedy for more information. Regina worried that "those 'D' brothers may go to the extent of stealing my papers because I am the competition. [Rolfes] is so curious and upset about it."[16] As with Ngcobo, she also had a romantic past with Rolfes, although less enthusiastically entered into on her part. She had initially been "pen friends" with Rolfes and was "getting on very fine" with him. (It was probably during this period that Regina had sent him—as "Editress"—her Mademoiselle columns for *Bantu World*.) Trouble started when Rolfes made unwanted sexual advances upon her, shortly after her arrival in Johannesburg in 1936: "The whole matter got spoiled the day we met. . . . He thought friends of the pen can go beyond the pen. We had met on paper and should have stayed on paper."[17]

Disillusioned with the lascivious luminaries of the Zulu Cultural Society, Regina decided to send her manuscript to Daniel Malcolm, the chief inspector for Native Education. This, in fact, was Dan's advice to her: "To hell with your soft-soap graduates at the Zulu Society."[18] Concurring that Ngcobo and the others could "jolly well stay away from my book," she handed her manuscript over to Malcolm, who "promised to look at it." But Malcolm gave Regina scarcely more help. Government officials were increasingly scrutinizing the content of African educational books for anything subversive of white rule. Now a special board approved all new educational publications—a board of which Malcolm was a prominent member. In the same month that Regina submitted her manuscript to Malcolm—October 1938—the board refused Herbert Dhlomo's new play *Mfolozi* (part of his quartet of plays on great Zulu chiefs and which was subsequently lost).[19] This was on the grounds that it strayed too far into the unacceptable realm of "politics," perhaps being a little too effusive in its praise of past Zulu kings for white taste.[20] Political views loudly asserted could indeed block publication by an African author. One H. D. Tyamzashe, cowinner with Regina of the Esther Bedford Prize in 1935, recounted how, despite his early successful writing career, "I was suddenly dropped when I espoused the Native cause."[21]

Black public opinion exploded at the decision to block publication of Dhlomo's work, with the well-known journalist Walter Nhlapo writing in the *Bantu World* that "men with wrong psychology and perspective as to the type of literature fit to be read by Zulus are not to be entrusted to guide the destiny of Zulu literature. . . . Censorship will cripple Zulu literature and writers will have as many restrictions and shackles as the Germans under Nazi rule."[22] Regina also raged at the news, accusing "these Balungus [whites] of trying to suppress patriotism."[23] She angrily contrasted Dhlomo's rejected work with the poor quality of books much more easily accepted by education officials: "If they could hear what I could say about a Std VII Literature book [that they published], a rotten book—poor English—hopeless morals—no wonder the children today cannot express themselves."[24]

While Dan said, "Your book will have a better fate" than Dhlomo's work had, Regina correctly foresaw trouble ahead, worrying "my book has gone to the same society [as rejected Dhlomo's], perhaps they might pass it over."[25] As she bitterly reflected, "Ngiyabona ukuthi [I see that it is] the spirit of 'Keep the Native in his place.'"[26] And indeed, a long and ominous silence followed, with "the confounded Mr. Malcolm not answering me. . . . I wanted to know the position of my Manuscript, but he did not reply to my letters."[27]

While Regina underwent the agonizing wait for feedback on her novella from Malcolm, her divorce case was still churning through the South African courts. At the end of the year, she decided to resign from the Polela Institute and move back to Johannesburg. Now that she had completed "Kufa," she found the freezing isolation of the school unendurable. She also wanted to be closer to the court and her lawyer, as she hoped the culmination of her lawsuit against Percy was nearing. Dan set about finding her accommodations in the city. Regina, however, worried that a rented room in a cramped, shared house would not suit her intense writing schedule: "I would rather stay alone. . . . People I stay with would be fed up with my writings, typing and studies. . . . I have no time for gossiping, I am rather serious about life."[28] Eventually they decided that while Regina waited for her divorce's culmination, she should stay with Dan's brother and his sister-in-law.

Regina moved in with her future in-laws, Theo and Miriam Twala. The family lived in the nearby mining town of Nigel, part of the urban conglomerations making up the east–west mining seam of the gold-rich Witwatersrand. Theo was a prominent educator in Nigel, whom the government had recently appointed a supervisor of Native Education in the Transvaal.[29] This arrangement, however, was not a success, with Regina clashing with Miriam, complaining of their freezing house, and writing to Dan of the days she spent "crying in bed . . . [drinking] a drug to quiet my nerves and sleep."[30] (This is the only mention in their correspondence of Regina's reliance upon a chemical substance for her "nerves"; I have little other information as to whether this was a common contemporary practice.) Dan oscillated between worried tenderness and unkind impatience, curtly writing to her that "you are really depressed in spirits and in physique. That should not be so. I do not want to feel I am taking a very 'fussy, irritable and displeased' wife. For my sake try to make things bright and cheer up. . . . I hate to hear of your petty pains troubles and illnesses."[31]

Desperate for income to support her case against Percy, Regina began to look for a teaching or clerical job in the city (and of course, this would also enable her to afford rent there). She turned to her and Dan's contacts among the network of white philanthropists who oversaw African education in Johannesburg. But she woefully reported to Dan how white liberals drove her from pillar to post. It was painfully humiliating to be thrust into the world of white philanthropy, ostensibly surrounded by "friends of the native." In reality, as a Black woman, Regina was entirely at their patronizing mercies, enmeshed in a lopsided power dynamic masquerading as egalitarianism:

> I saw Ray Phillips and he pretended to have something for me, but it ended in smoke, he sent me to your Trustees [at the sports club] and even there they have no use for me. We saw Mrs Hellmann [Ellen Hellmann, a social anthropologist and prominent social welfarist] and she had no use for me, then Miss Jenish [Miriam Janisch, head of the "native welfare section" of the city's Non-European Affairs Department] who pushed me forward to Mrs Eddy and that lady too had no use for me—Carter too had nothing for me.[32]

Unsuccessful in looking for a job in Johannesburg, still waiting to hear from Malcolm about her novella, Regina turned to freelance journalism as an opportunity to get her work published and earn some money. Dan had long advised her to focus on the European papers in South Africa, as these "would certainly give you much more for your articles than any of the Bantu papers."[33] They both focused on *The Forum*, a highbrow current affairs and arts weekly review that they regularly read and enjoyed. Just launched in 1938, the magazine was a voice for white liberals in South Africa, exemplifying their aspirations for eventual equality between the races while still maintaining the basic edifice of white racial superiority (a publication that Ray Phillips, for example, would have read).[34] In writing for *The Forum*'s largely European readership, both Regina and Dan cannily recognized the contemporary appetite for exotifying tales of "native" life. As Dan put it, "It must be something 'original' and 'native' as these people are all crazy about 'Bantu Life and its Mannerisms.' I'm sure you can give us something very humorous and informative about the life of the jungle."[35]

Once again underscoring the dependency of Black intellectuals of the 1930s upon well-connected white liberals, Dan sent Regina's unpublished articles to the anthropologist Hilda Kuper at Wits University. Dan knew Kuper through their joint Eswatini connection: he was, of course, from Eswatini and, centrally located at the Bantu Sports Club, he had become something of a contact point for emaSwati in Johannesburg. For her part, Kuper had recently undertaken a major bout of ethnographic research for her PhD dissertation in Eswatini—she was a student of Bronisław Malinowski's at the University of London—and was now working on her thesis, which she would publish in 1947 as the universally acclaimed *An African Aristocracy*, a book that sealed her lifelong reputation as the foremost anthropologist of Eswatini.[36]

Dan and Kuper were on cordial terms—sufficiently so for him to think nothing of a three-hour visit chatting to her in her home. Dan first broached the topic of Regina's writing ambitions with Kuper during one such visit to her house in the white suburb of Westcliffe, a densely forested ridge, not far from Houghton where Regina had previously worked as a domestic servant and just north of the city. Dan's letter to Regina describing this visit is worth quoting in full, for it evocatively conveys the complex and uncomfortable ties of patronage, dependency, admiration, and resentment that characterized Dan and Regina's relationship with a white academic like Kuper:

> Today I went to see Mrs Cooper [*sic*] at Westcliffe. I found her busy on her book on the Swazis in the room upstairs. She was dressed in shorts and sitting on her desk with papers all around her. I could not help thinking of you in your shorts and also of the many papers we have had round us in writing KUFA. She had just returned from Swaziland and she has had no time to read your book again and make corrections . . . but she thinks she can help you in converting it to two or three short stories and getting them suitable for publication.

> She has also asked me to request you to write an article for The Forum on the "Future of African Women." It must be brimful of good and sound thinking. You will be paid for it. Mrs Cooper [*sic*] is dying to see what you have written in Zulu and just what you are capable of writing in English. She really wishes to make good friends with you and is trying to get you to trust her and confide in her all your journalistic and authorship difficulties. Please write her a sweet letter.
>
> She has a wonderful store of knowledge in Swazi culture, customs and mannerisms. She makes me shy, for a white lady of her type to know so much about my people, when I am trying to be a better authority on native life.[37]

There are many threads worth pulling out in this letter. First is Dan's admiring recognition of Kuper as both a formidable intellectual with her "wonderful store of knowledge" and an appealing figure in shorts atop her desk. Second is Dan's wistful yearning that Regina become precisely this kind of personage. When he looks at Kuper in her shorts, he thinks longingly of Regina dressed just like this. Confronted with her messy piles of draft chapters, he thinks of his and Regina's own writing and of their own pleasingly authorial scatters of paper as they worked on her novella. Third, Kuper's suggestion about converting "Kufa" into two or three short stories perhaps points to the editorial challenge of turning a short novella into a full-length book (possibly this also underlay Malcolm's evident reluctance to publish Regina's work?).

Next is the sense of dependence. However casual the friendship was, the truth was that Kuper wielded clout that Dan could never aspire for as a Black man in 1930s South Africa. Seeing "just what you are capable of writing" was no low-stakes proposition: Regina's publishing future rose or fell with what Kuper thought of her writing. No wonder Dan urged her to send Kuper a "sweet letter." And, finally, there is the unmistakable tinge of envy and perhaps resentment too. Dan—seeking to become a "better authority on native life"—felt "shy" when confronted by a white scholar's supposedly superior knowledge of his own people, the emaSwati.

Anger at white scholars' self-proclaimed expertise on African life is a theme Regina would repeatedly return to over the years—and especially with regard to Hilda Kuper, as we shall later see.

In the meantime, though, Regina was not yet sufficiently angry to object to Kuper's patronage of her "journalistic and authorship difficulties." She obediently wrote an article on this topic for *The Forum* and sent it to Dan—who typed it out for her, in the process adding many of his own amendments and "corrections." Dan expressed disappointed in Regina's first draft, proclaiming it "her worst" piece to date. He objected to Regina's perspective on the "future of African woman," accusing her of being glowingly uncritical of the contribution of white female missionaries who set up charitable philanthropic enterprises to uplift African women: "Please think independently, do not allow other people's thoughts to sway you. Avoid Missionaries and their Talitha Homes [a well-known Johannesburg 'home' for unwed mothers and babies], for these are the deeds of Mrs Bridgman [a white American missionary in the city] and others, not our own women."[38] Dan urged Regina to focus on Black women, not on well-meaning white liberals. Ironically—given the drastic reversal of coming years—Dan was at this time the more politically radical of the pair.

Kuper responded critically to this revised version. Yet she targeted most of her opprobrium at precisely those passages that Dan had added. Regina's indignant response to Dan gives the sense of an old wound reopened—her angry sense that her lover did not take her intellectual talents seriously—and of her own vindicated self-justification in finally having an external reader judge her efforts better than Dan's: "In trying to cut out what you thought was rubbish from my article, you put in some nauseating phrases instead. . . . Dan you don't know art my dear, don't deceive yourself that you can outstrip Gelana."[39]

Ultimately, however, Regina's efforts for *The Forum* were not a success, with the periodical rejecting all her articles. Dan harshly criticized her for what he—and perhaps Kuper?—considered an overly stilted writing style. Given the disappearance of these draft articles, it is hard to judge what Dan meant by his accusation that she was "suffering too much from 'European Standards of Expression.'" It sounds uncomfortably like his half-joking earlier recommendation that Regina only attempt "native" stories about the "life of the jungle." Instead of trying to write like a "European," Dan advised Regina to stick to her "own simple narrative manner of writing. Your letters to me are so sweet and free in style, but when you start writing an article or book you assume a 'dignified pure' style."[40] Years later, in Eswatini, Regina would receive similar criticism that her writing made her sound too educated and hence too "Western." This was a common criticism aimed at Black writers of this period, echoing segregationist ideology that Africans should "develop along their own lines." White reviewers of Sol Plaatje's historical novel *Mhudi* (1930) disliked Plaatje's "inauthentic" style of writing and advised him to "stick to your people and give up apeing the white man."[41] And when, in Regina's case, this did not yield any acceptances from *The Forum*, Dan confessed himself deeply "disappointed at your failure to pick up your freelance journalism"[42]

At this point, Regina slumped into a low period, reminiscent of the dark months of the previous year before she had met Dan. She was beaten down by her inability to free herself from Percy, demoralized at her rejection from magazines like *The Forum*, and depressed by her failure to publish "Kufa." "Failure" is perhaps the wrong word for an outcome so linked to factors unrelated to Regina's own efforts and talent. It may be more apt to label the nonpublication of her book as the fact she was herself failed—failed by the Zulu literary establishment and failed by the educational division as one of the sole publishers for African authors. Despite Dan exhortations to Regina to "please pull yourself together and do something," she confessed "her spirits were very low and sensitive."[43]

Partly due to the stress of these months, Regina's health declined. In around April 1938, she was admitted to Johannesburg's Non-European Hospital for surgery and brief stay. (Her malady was gynecological, an ominous foretaste of her travails in the coming years.)[44] From her hospital bed and groggy from the anesthetic,

Regina weakly fretted she still owed Kuper a promised piece of writing and asked Dan to pass on the message that she was unwell and presently unable to work. But he did not do this: "I am sorry to say I have not told Mrs Kuper about your health." This was his bleak reason: "I feel she will not believe me. She will think it is one of those usual excuses one gets from Natives."[45] However generous Kuper was in helping Regina and her writing, at the end of the day Dan and Regina acutely felt themselves to be—in her final estimation—just "Natives." They feared usual white prejudices would taint Kuper's opinion of them. Dan felt keenly for Regina's emotional and physical pain, empathically lamenting, "I feel even more sorry that your book should not be out now, to help you in your hour of need. It would have been a real triumph for you morally to know at least you achieved something before your illness."[46]

Regina had had such high hopes for her book. But after Dan's comment in early 1939 about "Kufa" not yet being published, the book is rarely again mentioned between the two of them. The trail to Malcolm also goes cold after Regina submitted the manuscript to him. Nor is there a surviving copy of the manuscript, with the extract I quoted from in chapter 6 (the snippet describing Kufa putting trousers on) being the only surviving fragment I have managed to find.

But "Kufa" endured in unexpected ways. My suspicion is that this, Regina's first book manuscript, may have survived in two different formats: as a play and—more surprisingly—as a film. In neither did Regina find any attribution at all—a pattern of neglect and marginalization that would continue beyond her death.

In January 1941, as we shall shortly see, Regina started a two-year course at Johannesburg's newly opened Jan H. Hofmeyr School of Social Work, South Africa's first training institution for Black social workers. In October of the same year, students of the Hofmeyr School—including Regina—put on a play full of "pep and life" (although the actors were badly afflicted by "stage fright"). *Bantu World's* review of the play told its readers about an urban morality play with a plot virtually identical to that of "Kufa."

Journalist Walter Nhlapo described the production as a "sketch depicting a country youth with a tribal background hoeing, grinding and chopping . . . who comes to the mines to earn money, undergoes a catastrophic accident underground and 'returns home disabled.'"[47] Was this Regina's "Kufa," returning at last to her and Dan's original vision of the story as a theatrical production, now carried out in the context of an amateur theatrical production and with the parts acted by her fellow trainee social workers?

Fast-forward eight years. A new film called *African Jim*, known popularly as "Jim Comes to Joburg," is released in South Africa. It has its packed premiere at the Rio, a famous "non-European" cinema on Market Street in downtown Johannesburg.[48] The Rio breaks its own audience records, reporting "the entire non-European population of Johannesburg is queuing up to see the film. Natives, Coloreds and Indians line up eight deep in efforts to get in."[49] It is partly so popular because it is the first South Africa film to have an all-African cast, although two white Britons, Donald Swanson and Eric Rutherford, directed and produced it. One member of the cast was Dan Twala, playing the second male

FIGURE 7.1. African Jim's production team, 1949, including Dan Twala (*second from left*) (Peter Davis, *In Darkest Hollywood: Exploring the Jungles of Cinema's South Africa* [Athens: Ohio University Press, 1996])

lead. But Dan was also an important fixer for the film. He procured acting talent for Swanson and Rutherford (including the female lead, the then unknown singer Dolly Rathebe, who would become one of the country most famous female vocalists, "South Africa's Billie Holiday") as well as arranged for two famous jazz bands—the African Inkspots and the Jazz Maniacs—for the film's nightclub scenes.

Aspects of *African Jim* are reminiscent of "Kufa" (although we should also bear in mind that the plot of "Kufa" was a classic storyline of this period). The opening credits proclaim that it is a "simple film . . . a quaint tale of the native and the sophisticated, a true reflection of the African Native in a modern city." The film tells the story of an untouched country boy—"Jim Twala"—who leaves his rural life to come to Johannesburg. There urban thugs rob the gullible rural boy, who eventually comes under the care of a kindly yet streetwise night watchman. (This is Dan's character.) Here the film diverges from "Kufa." Jim (played by the Ghanaian actor Daniel Adnewmah) finds his way to a Johannesburg jazz club where he falls in love with the glamorous Dolly Rathebe, a singer there. And while sweeping floors in the club, Jim discovers his own calling as a talented jazz singer. Unlike "Kufa," the film is a rags-to-riches tale, a fantasy of Black achievement in the city against all the odds.

The film's credits do not list any screenwriter. But we know that Dan's role in the film exceeded merely acting; he intensively helped with its conceptualization and production, even giving the lead character his—and by this time, Regina's—last name of Twala. We also know that Dan frequently presented Regina's writing as his own to outside patrons in the hopes of furthering his career. And the final clue. Watching the film carefully, I was startled to find Regina herself about halfway through. I have many photographs of her. But to discover Regina in black-and-white "motion" felt like our first meeting. The setting is a musical interlude in the nightclub. Dolly Rathebe is singing, her face slightly lifted up and her eyes closed, seemingly unaware of the six people seated around her.

FIGURE 7.2. Regina Twala (*standing*) in *African Jim*, 1949 (Villon Films)

But Rathebe is not, in fact, the center of this scene. Our eye is immediately drawn to a tall woman enfolded in a stiffly tailored dress, flaring out in a draping cascade. She is the only person standing in this scene; the others seem to be crouched in the vicinity of her waist. Regina listens to the music with a smile and her hands folded behind her. Without uttering a word, she reigns over the scene. Her face looks down at Dan.

June 1939 finally brought better news for the beleaguered couple. Regina and Dan had decided to replace the unhelpful Hymie Basner with a new lawyer, Julius Baker of Baker & Hellman. Baker succeeded in getting Regina's case to court in March 1939, and a divorce was at last granted. But section 3 of Law No. 13 of 1883 of the Laws of Natal meant the judgment was provisional for three months. On the June 15, 1939, two years after Regina's proceedings against Percy had started, her divorce became final. Dan and Regina had waited for this moment for close on a year. They thus lost no further time and married within days, sealing their bond at a Johannesburg Magistrate Court on June 19, 1939.[50]

# 8

# Orlando

> I reach the supreme height of my unhappiness . . . punctuated by the strongest desire for motherhood and the fear of being a barren woman.
>
> —Regina to Dan, March 11, 1940 (RTP)

In June 1939 Regina and Dan moved to Orlando, a newly built African residential area ten miles west of Johannesburg. Here they would start their life as a married couple; its streets form the backdrop for their life in the 1940s. Dan and Regina's new home was 7303 Orlando West, near the train station that connected them with downtown Johannesburg. As the name suggests, their house was in the western part of Orlando, an area that had the reputation of being more "upper class" as it was where most of the three-room houses were to be found. Their new house looked exactly like every single building on their street and on every street beyond their street. Still standing today, Regina and Dan's first marital home consisted of a red-brick box with a corrugated iron roof, a short flight of steps up to a cement-floored porch and inside three rooms: a living room combined with a kitchen area and two bedrooms. When Regina and Dan's niece, Mary Twala,

FIGURE 8.1. Mary Twala at 7303 Orlando West, 2019 (Joel Cabrita)

showed me round the house in 2019, I saw that the pit latrine was still in the small back garden and that bathing took place in a metal bucket in the kitchen behind a curtain. Their house had open rafters; Regina and Dan would have looked straight up beyond smoke-stained wooden beams to a metal roof that roared when it rained during the wet summer months. This was how the African middle classes of Orlando lived in the 1940s. By residing in a three-room house, they were the very elite of the elite.

Orlando had one outdoor water tap for each eleven houses. On average, each house had ten people living within it. That meant 110 people had to share one tap located on the corner of a street. For Orlando's nearly forty thousand residents, this meant queuing in the street for anything from one to two hours very early in the morning—freezing in the winter months of June to August—for their daily water supply, which would then be hauled back to the house—along unpaved streets—in heavy metal pails.[1] Flushable toilets, it goes without saying, did not exist.

Water was not the only thing in short supply. Hospital beds and doctors were scarce too. Two doctors were responsible for the health of tens of thousands of people. One clinic with eight beds serviced the whole of Orlando. Any serious case had to be transferred to Johannesburg's Non-European Hospital, ten miles away and itself under huge pressure: by the 1940s, the hospital's patients were sleeping stacked in corridors and under metal beds on mattresses.[2] And Orlando was not a community in good health. One of the leading causes of death in the 1940s was tuberculosis, born out of poor sanitation and overcrowding.[3] A horrifying report in *Umteteli wa Bantu* estimated over half of the patients admitted to hospital for TB would die within six weeks.[4] And while adults died, children starved. A round of government inquiries revealed time and time again that Johannesburg's African parents simply did not earn enough to pay for the basic nutrition required by their growing children.[5]

Situated ten miles southwest of the city of Johannesburg, Orlando was a vast and unbroken stretch of nearly identical cuboid houses, what one historian of the city has called "an extensive mass of little detached houses of monotonously similar design."[6] By the 1960s Orlando and neighboring Black urban townships were formally named part of the massive "South Western Townships" (or Soweto) agglomeration. But in 1939 Soweto had yet to come into existence, and there was only Orlando and the nearby area of Klipspruit.[7] Over three thousand houses mapped out a grid shape that was still surrounded, in the 1940s at least, by stream-threaded, high-altitude grassland. Most of the tiny matchbox dwellings measured forty square meters—the size of an average living room in a white middle-class house of the time. About a third of the houses had three rooms; most were two-roomed structures. Many residents moved into their new houses with high hopes only to find rough unplastered walls and floors sprouting green with grass.[8]

Orlando had been established by Johannesburg's city council in 1932 as a township for middle-class Africans. It represented a

FIGURE 8.2. Orlando Township, 1937 (Ellen Hellmann Papers, Historical Papers Research Archive, University of the Witwatersrand)

broader push toward urban segregation on the part of government officials. This was their effort to purge the city center of mixed-race residential areas and to place Africans at arm's length from white suburbs—but not so far away that they couldn't still commute in daily to perform the many labors that white life in the city relied upon. Despite this, many—including middle-class African patrons of the scheme—hoped that Orlando would come to rival international hubs of Black cultural and intellectual life such as Harlem in New York City.[9] The long-term admiration that Black South Africans felt for Black America was now expressed in their aspiration that this new township be the "Harlem of Africa." Boosters of the township did not foresee that Orlando would soon descend into extreme urban poverty. The start of World War II in 1939 catapulted into being a huge boom in the city's manufacturing sector. Combined with the continued decline of rural economies across South Africa, an unprecedented number of African women and men would stream into the city during the war years. Orlando and other Black areas were the destination of the rural poor from places like eNdaleni, women and men trapped by the endless consequences of the 1913 Natives Land Act.

The urban population explosion of the 1940s placed acute demands on Orlando's already limited resources. Houses overflowed, roommates stepping over you as you slept at night.[10] Water, wages, and health care were woefully insufficient for these conditions. By 1945 sixteen thousand people were on the Johannesburg municipality's waiting list for houses in Orlando.[11] From being the hope of the new Black middle classes, Orlando had become bleakly overcrowded and underserviced. The writer Es'kia Mphahlele, who lived in Orlando in the late 1940s, recalled "the mass of red-roofed blocks with a population of 100,000"—this ten years after Regina and Dan moved there—and how Orlando spread and mutated like a living organism, eventually meeting up and merging with other townships of refugees from the rural areas of South Africa.[12]

Unsurprisingly, 1940s Orlando was where radical African politics were starting to brew. During the 1940s the African National Congress awoke from its many years of dormancy to find a new assertiveness under more radical leadership. ANC Youth League leaders based in the new township, figures like Nelson Mandela and Anton Lembede, rubbed shoulders with Communist Party member J. B. Marks as well as with labor organizers like James Majoro, all uniting to launch the numerous strikes, protests, and petitions that marked this decade.[13] Popular disillusionment grew with the Native Representative Council, criticized by this new generation of young radicals as little more than a "college debating society." The council had been established in 1936 (part of one of the infamous Hertzog Native Bills) to ostensibly "represent" Africans in legislation affecting their welfare. In reality, by the 1940s the council was totally ineffectual and out of step with Black South Africans' extreme unhappiness.[14] Orlando was also where, in 1944, the same James Mpanza who had advised Regina on her divorce from Percy nearly ten years ago now led a populist "squatters rebellion." Three thousand Orlando residents camped in burlap sacks in the open grassland for many months in protest against the insufficient housing provided by Johannesburg's municipality. Mpanza's movement became known as "Sofasonke":

isiZulu for "We shall all die together."[15] Es'kia Mphahlele remembered the "squalid little settlement," born as a "mighty exodus" from the terrible overcrowded houses of Orlando. Looking down from the relatively higher-up ground of Orlando, the settlement consisted of some 250 shelters constructed of burlap, maize stalks, flattened biscuit tins, and bits of corrugated iron. Within a month its population had grown to twenty thousand residents.[16]

Given the acute predicaments that its residents faced in navigating daily life, Orlando was also an important crucible for emerging ideas of social welfare among all races. A powerful consensus was growing among both the more moderate strand of Black urban leaders and white liberals and missionaries, academics, and urban administrators. This twinned the notion that the state should be held accountable for its failures to provide for its citizens of all races, on one hand, with the conviction that Africans should take matters into their own hands, on the other. The era saw both an increased top-down commitment from the state to shaping society for the better as well as a growth in grassroots associations, mutual aid societies, and populist movements among Black urbanites themselves. But the contradictions were glaring. In its focus on social and economic improvements, "welfarism"—whether touted by Blacks or whites—largely avoided the harsh political inequalities that undergirded material suffering. In the words of one historian, "the recommendations of the welfare lobby were entirely compatible with the maintenance of a system of white supremacy, albeit one with a more humane face."[17]

In time, Regina would come to hold a similarly scathing view of the social welfare industry in white-ruled South Africa. But for now, she was caught up in the challenges faced by all who lived in places like Orlando. Both she and Dan hated Orlando.[18] They thoroughly agreed with the welfare lobby that township life corroded Black dignity. They hated its overcrowding, and they loathed the poor conditions of the houses and their terrible facilities. They, along with all other Africans who lived there, complained of the long distances they had to travel into Johannesburg not only to buy basic food supplies but also for work and study—Dan every day to his work at the Bantu Sports Club (although he at times had access to a car; when he did not, he endured an overcrowded, uncomfortable, and expensive train ride) and Regina by train to the University of the Witwatersrand a few years later.

Regina and Dan also hated Orlando's crime. From the 1940s onward, gangs of smartly dressed young men called *tsotsis* terrorized Orlando's residents. Many of them wielded switchblades and looked for inspiration to the New York gangsters whom they'd seen in black-and-white films shown at the Ritz or other "Non-European" cinemas. Walking at night down unlit roads often meant being accosted, robbed, and left stripped naked and beaten up.[19] By the early 1940s, the situation had grown so bad that Orlando's residents banded together to form night-watch patrols to guard against nocturnal thieves.[20]

Highlighting the idolized relationship that Regina had with the countryside, both she and Dan found their yearning for green hills and rural air increased during their years in Orlando. The coal and paraffin that Orlando's residents burned for heat and light meant a dark cloud of stench always hung in the air. Throughout the decade that this chapter covers, both repeatedly spoke about buying a home outside of the city in order to access "fresher" air. Dan, with his roots in Eswatini, dreamed of buying land and building a house in the mountainous protectorate. And for Regina, her eNdaleni home continued to be a place where on her regular visits from Johannesburg she felt "healthy," "free," and "spiritually purified"—all words she used to describe her visits there during these years in letters to Dan. In Regina's account to Dan of a tranquil holiday she spent at eNdaleni in 1942, she describes the quiet reassurance of attending a service in the church where she was baptized and grew up taking weekly communion: "The country folks have a steady life. On Sundays everybody goes to church, as the bell rings, they sit in the same old firm seats, after service they shake hands with everyone, inquire into health and get the same answers all round. I am happy to be home."[21]

But despite Regina's negative feelings about city living (in her letters to Dan, she referred to the "dreaded Orlando"[22]), she loved the domesticity of finally being married to Dan and sharing a home with him. She and Dan named their little Orlando house "Ntokozo Home"—"Home of Happiness." They chose the name "so that we shall be happy no matter what may befall us."[23] Regina and Dan's choice of name for their new home surely speaks to the many trials they'd gone through to get to this point and their relief in finally being legally united. Trying to mitigate the bleakness of their new home (to make it what she called a "joy to the eye"), Regina took great pride in their little handkerchief of a garden, planting not only vegetables and fruit trees but also flowers and shrubs. She was in good company. Many other Orlando residents of this period were devoted gardeners, to the extent that the white-run municipality ran regular competitions for the prettiest garden. (One imagines this was part of a cynical official strategy for reconciling Orlando's residents to their underserviced living conditions.)[24] Busying themselves with domesticating their home, the newly married couple quickly settled into a companionable routine. Dan adjusted to the novelty of being married to as strong-willed and unusual a woman as Regina: "Your attention to me, though very cheeky at times, is on the whole very original and independent. I like you for that."[25] For her part, Regina found the intimacy totally blissful, writing in a haze of dreamy domesticity that

> it has been a joy to wait all evening for the screeching of the gate, and then the heavy footsteps and the well-known knock of a lover. We sometimes make big noise when we are told a woman's place is in the kitchen, but who can tell the joy one feels of arranging a meal for the dear one and then sit and wait, counting minutes and hours, til you meet again, anticipating a calm repose of two souls that have missed each other the whole day.[26]

But as happy as Regina was to be finally sharing a home with Dan, and as much as she embraced the novel "joy of arranging meals for the dear one" (suggesting that traditional "womanly" roles of the 1940s were not always distasteful to her), there was a stain on these early years of their marriage. Twinned desire and fear haunted her, both "the strongest desire for motherhood and the fear of being a barren woman."[27] The couple had started trying for a baby as soon as they'd married in June 1939. But six months later, by the end of 1939, Regina had still not fallen pregnant. Regina's self-professed "failure" to do so devastated her. She named it "my calamity at the end of every month."[28] For a woman to be perceived as barren was a huge stigma in twentieth-century South Africa. Regina's future academic mentor, Hilda Kuper, would even write an ethnographic play on this topic some twenty years later. Titled *A Witch in My Heart* and set in the British protectorate of Swaziland in the 1930s, Kuper's play explored male attitudes toward infertile wives and the traumatized state of women humiliated for their "failure" to bear children. Kuper's female protagonist, unable to have children, despairingly lamented, "There is a witch in my heart!"[29] Reflecting the intense pressure on women of the 1940s to start families, Regina was paralyzed by her sense of disappointing Dan, disappointing Dan's family (who made nasty comments to Dan about his new wife's infertility) and, finally, her own family in eNdaleni, who every time she visited "are disappointed by the one thing, I need not mention it."[30]

Throughout the first year of their marriage, Regina thought of little else herself. A photograph of them newly married in the early 1940s shows Dan wreathed in a smile while a moody-looking Regina has lowered eyes and a slightly knitted brow. It was hard for her to escape her continual feeling of failure. Dan, moreover, already had a child from a relationship that predated his acquaintance with Regina, so they surmised that their childlessness was not due to him. (One imagines that the existence of Dan's other children must have been extremely painful for Regina.) And, in fact, they did have a young child living with them in Orlando, although neither Dan nor Regina was the biological parent. During Regina's long years of trying to conceive, she and Dan had taken a young girl called Mary Twala—the daughter of Dan's brother,

FIGURE 8.3. Regina and Dan Twala, ca. 1940 (RTP)

Shadrack—to live with them at 7303 Orlando. This was in large part due to the fact that Shadrack and his wife, Elizabeth, had many children and almost no money, and Regina and Dan—as better-off relatives—took in one of their offspring as an act of kindness. Surely also the fact that they were longing for a child of their own played a role in the decision. Perhaps Mary played the role of a surrogate child for them both, as in later life Mary referred to Dan, at least, as a parent—"Papa."[31]

Dan also urged Regina to "get whatever medical advice and assistance you can get" and professed himself "also prepared to take any test that will assist you."[32] The round of doctors Regina and Dan consulted provide a window into the fertility options pursued by relatively monied African women and men of mid-twentieth-century Johannesburg. They saw the handful of European doctors in the city who took on African patients, and Regina also had several gynecologic X-rays taken at the Non-European Hospital in the city.[33] But Regina and Dan also turned to other sources of therapeutic wisdom. As well as Western biomedical treatments, they drew on a mix of "scientific," folk, and indigenous therapies. Regina, for example, carefully followed what she called "The Jewish Chart"—a month-by-month way of tracking her cycle—and commanded Dan to hold off from what they privately called "doodles" until that time of the month when "I am supposed to be very fertile and sex-minded and you have ready for me a matured stock for my consumption."[34] They both also had courses of injections from "a Chinaman, Dr Liang," who also prescribed an unexplained "red paint,"[35] and both Dan and Regina religiously took the internationally popular Dr. Williams' Pink Pills for Pale People, a patent medicine cure for "all forms of weakness in male or female."[36]

The couple diverged, however, on the question of seeking help from local African healing specialists. These were figures called *izinyanga,* ostensibly "traditional" Zulu healers who worked via the application of herbal remedies. By the 1940s—especially in a cosmopolitan place like Johannesburg—izinyanga were in fact highly eclectic figures who drew on a creative blend of the old and the new, the local and the foreign, incorporating indigenous, South Asian, European, and patent medicine therapies into their healing arsenals. Many among the Black middle classes regarded these figures with suspicion, feeling it wasn't quite the thing to solicit their help. Dan, for example, felt it unseemly that Regina should consult an *inyanga*, unbefitting of their status as the mission school–educated elite of Johannesburg's Black society. But Regina was adamant she wanted to try this route, although she "knew I shall be forcing you to do a thing you dislike . . . the humiliation of an inyanga." Regina admitted to Dan that she, too, had her doubts about izinyanga, and part of her wanted to dismiss them as the provenance of the uneducated and the superstitious: "It's not to say that I have any real faith in them." But Regina was desperate enough to try anything, willing even to sacrifice her precious identity as an educated, progressive African woman: "I believe that miracles do happen."[37]

But nothing—not the European doctors or the "Chinese" injections or the izinyanga or the pink pills—worked. Regina was devastated. And there were other disappointments too, this time in the realm of her career. Regina's disappointment with her book and her journalistic efforts meant that she was unenthusiastically contemplating going back to teaching at one or another missionary-run school in the city.[38] She didn't end up doing this, but in 1940 she did start a correspondence course in shorthand at the well-known Union College. But she soon gave this up because the couple found it too financially challenging to pay for her tuition. Dan tersely upbraided Regina for her lack of direction now that she had put her authorial ambitions aside: "Choose your career—perhaps teaching—perhaps Home-Craft at Miss Smith of the Joint Council does—perhaps Social Work with Mrs Kuper or Child Welfare Work with the Race Institute or Mrs Hoernle."[39]

Evidently, now that she would no longer be an author, Dan was keen for a wife with another prestigious professional tag attached to her name. "Social Work"—exemplified in the figure of the Wits anthropologist Hilda Kuper—or "Child Welfare Work"—embodied in the career of the anthropologist and liberal social welfare activist Winifred Hoernlé—ranked high in Dan's ambitions for Regina. So did the local joint council and the South African Institute of Race Relations, both liberal, white-run institutions that focused on issues affecting Black welfare. Dan now zeroed in on the possibility that Regina would become a social worker. A newly professionalized conception of social work as a career route for Black women emerged around this time, fueled by the explosive growth of areas like Orlando and the plethora of social problems they seemed to breed—up to this point, nursing and teaching being the two main career options for African women. As Dan put it to Regina in a letter written in 1940: "I would like you to take up some social upliftment work—something to help the kids, the poor people and the destitute."[40] Ever paternalistic, Dan had his eye on several potential opportunities for Regina. There was, for example, an upcoming job as probation officer for African women released from jail.[41]

Dan, however, was especially keen for Regina to work alongside him at the Bantu Sports Club. Given her own proficiency in tennis, he hoped she would take over the club's offerings in the sport (and hopefully in the process boost the club's membership numbers).[42] As we've already seen, Dan imagined his work at the club as a form of "social welfare." Christian philanthropists like Ray Phillips, the director of the club, were lynchpins of the lobby that saw improved leisure offerings as key to mitigating the social ills of urbanization and industrialization. Dan hoped he and Regina would become a joint social worker couple at the club, much along the lines of the well-known William and Mabel Ngakane of Orlando, who respectively ran a reformatory for young boys and a women's mutual aid society.[43] Dan hoped Regina joining him at the sports club would be financially more stable for them. It would also provide further leverage as he sought to persuade the club's white trustees that they should have a house built for them on-site.[44]

In 1940 Regina began her work at the Bantu Sports Club, taking charge of tennis as well as supervising the club's beautiful gardens. Enjoying her job for a time, one of her innovations was employing inmates from Johannesburg's Central Prison to work on the garden.[45] She seems to have been a success; the city's newspapers praised Regina's work at the club as "capable." She also wrote regular bulletins promoting the club's tennis news in a jaunty tone. Regina's first piece of writing published in *Bantu World* since her Mademoiselle days was pun filled and garnished with exclamation marks: "Good news!!! Tennis marriages are starting—mixed doubles. . . . We are pining to know the most successful exponents of true reliable Tennis matrimony."[46]

But Regina's interest in the club soon waned. Downcast by her continued inability to conceive, Regina also came into conflict with the other women on the staff—many of whom turned out to be ex-lovers of Dan. There was, for example, the glamorous Sannie Teyise, who had starred with Dan in Bantu Dramatic Society productions in the 1930s and now ran the club's restaurant, the Blue Lagoon.[47] Teyise had been devastated when Dan left her for Regina. Now Teyise and other former flames got their revenge by giving Regina unkind nicknames and talking about her behind her back. The name that hurt Regina the most was "Welana" (to rhyme with "Gelana"). This approximated the acronym for the much-hated Witwatersrand Native Labor Association, WNLA, pronounced "Wenela"—the organization that procured African men from around the subcontinent to work on Johannesburg's gold mines. Regina felt that her status as the wife of the club's manager meant she should be accorded extra respect. It also angered her that people around the club called her the informal and familiar "Sis Gelana" rather than "Mrs. Twala." Arguments erupted between her and Dan about the club, with him angrily proclaiming that she lacked a sense of responsibility and claiming to be hurt by her failure to show any interest in his own work there.[48]

But toward the end of 1940 an escape route presented itself. A new school for training African social workers would open at the start of 1941. Regina seized upon this opportunity with great relief. She could now both leave the sports club and qualify for her new career as a social worker.

# 9

# Jan Hofmeyr School

> My beloved Hubby, I have never had time to thank you for your sacrifice in making it possible for me to attend the School of Social Work. I know dear, you had to fight a quiet battle within yourself before you came to a decision. You had to think of money too. It will not be enough to thank you by word of mouth or script, but I shall endeavour to honour you by doing my very best. I am aiming to outclass our majority. Above all I am enjoying the classes immensely.
>
> —Regina to Dan, February 2, 1941 (RTP)

Regina sat in the very front row of the wood-paneled Great Hall of the University of the Witwatersrand. The back of her neck prickled as she felt the gaze of hundreds of curious eyes upon her and upon the other twenty-six other African students who sat in the front row with her. They were the pioneering cohort of the new Jan Hofmeyr H. School of Social Work, seated for the opening ceremony of the school in January 1941—what Dan excitedly called "a great affair." The school would be housed in the Bantu Men's Social Centre in downtown Johannesburg but, signaling the gravity of the occasion, the organizers deemed the university's impressive Great Hall a more fitting venue for the opening ceremony. The hall—the central meeting point of the university's campus, just recently built—was filled with a who's who of Johannesburg's white philanthropic set.[1]

The newspapers called the occasion an "inspiring scene." Wordy speeches praising the initiative were given by the minister of finance and education, the liberal Jan Hofmeyr (after whom the school was named), by the prominent liberal senator Rheinallt Jones, and by Ray Phillips, the American missionary who was the brains behind the project. They lauded the school as "the beginning of a great social experiment."[2] Dan was somewhere in the audience—crammed among municipality officials, academics like Hilda Kuper, and prominent "welfarists" like Ellen Hellmann, who headed the South African Institute of Race Relations—craning his neck to see the small figure of his wife way in the front and anxiously smoothing down his jacket. He had been fretting to Regina in the days leading up to the event that not holding a bachelor's degree he didn't have a graduation gown, all of his suits were dirty, and what on earth was he to wear?[3]

Dan's worries about his clothing hint at his anxiety about his own academic accomplishments. In starting on a two-year professional qualification at the age of thirty-three, Regina was poised to outstrip her husband in formal educational achievement. As much as Dan aspired for Regina's success, the prospect of a highly educated wife seems to have precipitated mixed feelings within him. As Regina put it to him in a letter, "You had to fight a quiet battle within yourself."[4] Perhaps Dan was expressing his own insecurity about the fact that *he* did not have a university degree. This was a topic the couple had discussed in the past, with Regina exhorting Dan to "pick up your threads in the Educational sphere, get it definitely impressed upon your mind that you will not die with that Matric of yours. . . . You have to qualify in Bachelor of Economics or Social Studies."[5]

Regina's ambitions for Dan were fueled—as were his for her—by a sense of competitive class consciousness, a determination

FIGURE 9.1. Dan and Regina Twala, 1940s (RTP)

that her husband "keep up" with the accomplishments of his peers. She cited men of Dan's age (thirty-five) and class who had gained university qualifications—for example, Mark Rathebe, manager of the Bantu Men's Social Centre, who had come back from the United States with a degree—and judged that "yet you have better brains than all of them put together."[6] But Dan was not interested. Unlike his bookish wife, Dan preferred a practical route to an academic one. He wrote to Regina that he had no desire "to be another Selby Ngcobo. . . . I want to be a leader in solving the social and economic life of the people. Who will employ your LLBs and your DPhs if the nation is starving, is weakened by social evils and degraded by [bad] environments[?]"[7]

Dan's ambition "to be a leader in solving the social and economic life of the people" was in keeping with the mood of the times. The opening of the Jan Hofmeyr School reflected a growing sense that the welfare of the city's African population should be in the hands of Africans themselves. Prior to this, no training facilities existed for Black social workers; welfare provision for the African community was almost entirely in the hands of Europeans.

There were, it is true, a few important Black figures who had done this work in the past years. Some were Black Americans who had spent time in South Africa: the YMCA organizer Max Yergan and the social worker Maddie Hall Xuma, who married the famous Edinburgh-trained physician Dr. A. B. Xuma (also president of the ANC) and who had started the Zenzele ("Help Yourself") organizations for women. And a few of the Black figures involved in social welfare work were local women, people like Sibusiswe Makanya and Charlotte Maxeke, both of whom had trained in the United States and subsequently returned to South Africa to work with rural women.[8]

But by and large, by the start of the 1940s, the welfare industry was a white one. The most prominent of these figures were sitting in Wits's Great Hall that hot summer's day in mid-January—missionaries who ran the Helping Hand Club for young women in the city like Clara Bridgman; wives of prominent liberal politicians like Edith Rheinallt Jones, who was involved in just about every welfare initiative for Africans in the city (including Wayfarers for girls); the English nurse Ruth Cowles, who had helped set up the new health clinic in Alexandra Township, just north of the city. With the exception of nurses like Cowles, many of them were not professionally trained—indeed, there *was* no professional training for social workers in South Africa until the 1930s—and they did their work on a voluntary basis, without payment—the quintessential hallmark of privilege meeting philanthropy.[9]

Also seated in the Great Hall that day was the preeminent queen of African welfare work. This was Ellen Hellmann, who had studied social anthropology at Wits University in the early 1930s (one of her classmates was a young Hilda Kuper) and who had subsequently researched Black women beer brewers in inner-city Johannesburg.[10] After the birth of her first child, Hellmann had "thrown herself into welfare activism," playing a prominent role in the South African Institute of Race Relations and becoming an outspoken liberal advocate for improving African living conditions in Johannesburg.[11] Indeed, Hellmann was a loyal champion of Regina's, being "very fond of her," and she was one of those who had encouraged her to enroll at the new Jan Hofmeyr School, "pray[ing] you qualify so that you may be an honor for African women."[12]

The fact that whites like Ellen Hellmann and Edith Rheinallt Jones had a near monopoly on questions surrounding African welfare had not gone without comment. Dan and Regina extensively discussed this between themselves, and they could not help but notice that the prevalence of European, largely female, volunteers effectively barred Africans—most of whom could not afford to undertake unpaid "work" as these white do-gooders could—from working within the social welfare industry. Dan was highly unusual in being in a relatively well-paid social welfare job at the Bantu Sports Club; there was simply very little funding available for salaried African social worker positions during this decade. The fact that there was an enthusiastic group of white women willing to work for no wages would have hardly helped solve this problem.[13]

Others shared Regina and Dan's observations. Resentment grew that Black welfare should be so exclusively in the hands of white philanthropists. Letters to editors in the Black press angrily debated whites' paternalistic attitudes and their self-proclaimed expertise on matters affecting Africans' day-to-day life. In 1940 James Korombi, a well-known community leader in Sophiatown, one of the oldest Black residential areas in Johannesburg, wrote to the editor of *Bantu World* denouncing "the many so-called experts on the Native Questions who sing to the top of their voices about African social welfare . . . [while] Africans are denied the right to work for social welfare on the grounds they are not qualified 'experts.'"[14] Readers like Korombi also fiercely criticized the fact that many white welfarists sought amelioration of poverty without attention to its underlying political causes: "The average social workers are under the impression they can succeed in their work even if they disregard the economic welfare of the race."[15]

When Africans did try to start welfare initiatives of their own, tensions often erupted between them and the gatekeepers of the white welfare establishment. One example was Mabel Ngakane's Orlando Mothers' Welfare Association, which the Johannesburg municipality tried—unsuccessfully, it must be said—to shut down on the grounds that it was overly critical of official policies. Officials accused Ngakane and the other women heading the organization of falling under "the subversive influence of certain African agitators whose policy is to oppose the Department whenever possible." Africans spearheading welfare work cast in safely apolitical terms was fine. Openly criticizing the policies of the white-led municipality was not acceptable.[16]

Black individuals had long tried to wrest control of social work from whites. The Hofmeyr School was not the first time a training institution for African social workers had been proposed by those who advocated for improved conditions for Black South Africans. About ten years earlier, the Black American YMCA secretary Max Yergan had tried to get a training scheme for African social workers off the ground in Johannesburg (at a time when white universities across the country were adding social work training and diplomas to their curricula). While Yergan's initiative had many supporters among the city's Black elite, white authorities in the city's Department of Education withheld funding and deemed the Black-led initiative, and Yergan himself, as simply too radical.[17]

The opening of the Hofmeyr School was the first sign that Africans would be trained and later paid to undertake social work in their own communities. The formation of the school reflected the widespread view that urbanized Africans contradicted the so-called natural order of things (Africans belonged in the rural countryside, not the city) and that specialized intervention was required to correct the social ills like crime, delinquency, and prostitution that arose from this. This view was shared by many Black intellectuals as well as white officials and social welfare; as *Bantu World* phrased it, "The impact of Western civilization upon us has uprooted us from the anchor of the ancient life of our race and thus has created social problems that can only be dealt with by trained men and women."[18] But to be clear, the "training of men and women" would still be conducted on terms entirely controlled by Europeans. Only three Africans sat on the twenty-six-member steering committee of the school. The government's Native Affairs Department supplied most of its funding (£2,000 per year from the NAD, £500 from the city municipality) on the grounds that unrest in Black urban areas posed a threat to white property and life.[19] The rationale for a school for Black social workers was ensuring "social stability"—code for good for white business interests—rather than any active interest in alleviating the suffering of the Black community.[20]

So, while white liberals hailed the opening of the Hofmeyr School, Black opinion was only tentatively optimistic. *Bantu World* professed itself "wholeheartedly glad" at the opening of this school but at the same time sounded a note of caution: "We hope these people [graduates of the school] will not be instruments of white social workers whose efforts . . . have served little purpose."[21] Regina's own experience of the school reflected these mixed feelings: glad to be receiving training for her new chosen career now that she had put writing aside but nonetheless increasingly skeptical of the principles underlying it. Her fellow Hofmeyr students—which included seven women in this first year—were drawn from a very similar social class as Regina herself.[22] Among the twenty-seven of this incoming year, for example, were a Mr. and Mrs. Poswayo from Johannesburg. Their backgrounds mirrored her own and Dan's: Mr. Poswayo was the head clerk at a mine, while Mrs. Poswayo was a schoolteacher; he was chairman of the local Gamma Sigma Club (a missionary-founded organization for debating and lecturing) and a leader in the Pathfinders movement (the boys' equivalent of Regina's Wayfarers). Both also "were talented musicians."[23]

Later the Hofmeyr School got its own dedicated building, but in these early years it was housed in the rooms of the Bantu Men's Social Centre, at 1 Eloff Street. The center was a large two-story brick building with a gabled roof with white trim. It

FIGURE 9.2 Regina Twala, 1940s (RTP)

was surrounded by a shaded garden and resembled nothing so much as a respectable mission boarding school. Today the street outside the center has hurtling minibus taxis, street vendors, and shops selling everything from tin kettles to tinsel decorations for Christmas. Eighty years ago, in 1941, the center would have been in a relatively quiet area, away from the main hustle of Johannesburg's downtown. Clutching her briefcase of papers and books, Regina would have traveled here daily from Orlando (taking the train from Phefeni Station near their house to nearby Park Station and either walking from there or taking a tram). Her school day would have begun with prayers at eight o'clock (meaning she would have had to leave Orlando around six or even earlier) and classes all morning.

Doing the two-year program in social welfare necessitated belt-tightening from the couple. The cost of self-improvement for the Black middle classes was significant. Regina spoke gratefully to Dan of his "sacrifice" that had made it possible for her to attend the school. Fees were high: £15 per year (equivalent to half a year's salary for most of the city's Black workers), one-half of which was to be paid on the first day of the school year in January and the rest before August.[24] This covered tuition, class materials, and provision of a midday meal. There were only a very limited number of bursary loans and "work scholarships" available for students in need (which we can assume were probably the vast majority of Regina's classmates).[25] Ray Phillips, the director of the school, supplicated potential donors by detailing heart-wrenching stories of students unable to continue with their studies due to the cost. One student wrote to Phillips that "I regret with tears and a broken heart that I'm being denied an excellent and invaluable training due to poverty." His brother had hitherto paid for his fees but now had to educate another member of the family in addition to supporting his mother, wife, and several children.[26]

In return for these fees, Jan Hofmeyr students received an intensive two years of classes provided by about twenty white academics, social workers, Christian missionaries, and government officials. There was only one African on the teaching roster, the prominent community worker Sibusiswe Makanya.[27] Ray Phillips led devotions—a requisite each morning—as well as taught courses in sociology, social pathology, group work, and modern penology.[28] Representing the contemporary confluence between social anthropology and social work, the anthropologists Ellen Hellmann and Hilda Kuper both taught classes.[29] Kuper's was the social survey requirement (two hours per week, plus fieldwork), instructing students in the basics of the "theory and planning of the social survey," including how to design a questionnaire and reminding students of the "difficulties of objective observation."[30]

A month into her course, Regina professed herself to be "enjoying the classes immensely." She didn't mention which were her favorites, but we can imagine that she would have been greatly excited by courses like Introductory Sociology and Law and Social Legislation, given her keen sense of social change and her appreciation of the complex dynamic between urban and rural areas. She must have also enjoyed the intermingled theoretical and practical aspects of Hilda Kuper's social survey class, given that she would choose to study with Kuper at Wits University when she embarked upon her BA degree there in several years' time. Initially, Regina flourished, thrilled with the rigors of academic study and all her competitive instincts aroused: "I am aiming to outclass our majority," she informed Dan a couple of weeks into the course.[31]

But Regina's feelings soon changed once she realized the nature of the training she was being given. Ray Phillips had declared from the outset that the school would offer "an extremely practical course with just enough theoretical teaching to enable the [social] worker."[32] And the school was indeed light on theory. The schedule—designed by Phillips—awarded classes on sociology and law a stingy one or two hours a week. The most class time was spent on the courses Arts and Crafts (ten hours per week) and Physical Education (six hours per week). Regina was finding that the school did not expect a properly trained social worker to be very knowledgeable of the legislation that made African life in cities such a challenge. But its leaders did think that skills like gymnastic tumbling, clay modeling, and working with papier-mâché were indispensable for their profession. This, of course, reflected the contemporary liberal consensus that social work was more about moralizing leisure time than affecting any political or economic change.[33]

Even the so-called theory classes steered clear of anything remotely political. Phillips was clear from the start that his conception of social work avoided politics—this was on the grounds that it would result in "misleading and mischievous" activism on the part of students.[34] The class Introduction to South Africa's Economic Problems began with "feudal and domestic economic relations in England" and drifted to the "laws of supply and demand in South Africa" and then on to "determining facts in low and high income." Lecturers made no mention of segregation, racial protectionism in the labor market, legal disenfranchisement of Africans, or systematic attacks on African landownership in rural areas. The economy existed in a vague moralizing bubble, and "social problems" could be ameliorated by better morals, Christian virtue, and wholesome leisure pursuits. In 1944, when the school had been three years in operation, a Wits-hosted conference on social welfare work in Johannesburg found Hofmeyr's two-year program "deficient" and out of step with the emerging social science discourse because analysis of the root causes of poverty was entirely absent.[35]

There was, however, one aspect of her training as a social worker at the Hofmeyr School that Regina found truly life-changing and whose effects stayed with her for a long time. In addition to the morning classes, afternoons and evenings were devoted to practical fieldwork in social welfare institutions around Johannesburg. (Presumably, this was the purpose of the social survey training students received from Hilda Kuper.)[36] Regina was assigned to Mtutuzele, a home for unmarried mothers in Orlando with beds for twenty-four women and run by a Mrs. Elliot.[37] As she told Dan, she immediately "fell in love with this kind of work. . . . It is definitely for the fallen, the unwanted and the despised." The experience brought to her mind the words of her "Master," Jesus Christ: "The stone the builders rejected has come a cornerstone. . . . [Among] those 'unwanteds' there may be gold hidden by mud." Perhaps Regina was thinking of her own recent experience of being a member of the "fallen, unwanted and despised." As she walked Mtutuzele's corridors, her early days in Johannesburg—an abandoned wife and humble domestic worker—surely must have been in her mind, the self that she had been before her ascent to the wife of the sports club manager. The women she worked with at the home must have aroused her own sense of the injustices contemporary women faced: predatory men, hypocritical attitudes from society regarding different sexual mores for men and women, and social ostracization if you bucked the rules.

Regina, moreover, also appreciated Mrs. Elliot's progressive views on African involvement in the enterprise. As she reported to Dan, Elliot told her that "we Africans must work amongst our people, she has made a start, now we must pick it up." The home, it must be said, also had "babies by the dozen," some of whom were without mothers: "They were picked up from the streets or have mothers who died." She could not help think sadly of her own childlessness. As desperate as she was for a baby, here were scores who were unwanted. There was always adoption as a "last resort." As she confided in Dan: "Yes dear, when I saw those innocent babies lying there unclaimed, I thought to myself that if it comes to the push, we may come with you to pick one or two to bring them home, that is the last resort."[38]

The enticements of Mtutuzele's "innocent babies" aside, after Regina's first excited response to starting the program, her tone cooled considerably. By August 1941, about eight months into the program, she was sarcastically referring to Phillips as Dan's "father"—an allusion to the patronage relationship between the two men—and expressing her disillusionment with Phillips's cozy stance with city officials, what she called his tendency to "praise the Municipality in flowing language."[39] The other clue we have to Regina's more cynical take on the school was her dismissal of the graduation certificate she received at the end of 1942 as "nothing so wonderful." And this is Regina's desolate account of her graduation day ceremony at the end of 1942, held in the Bantu Men's Social Centre: "I spoke to no one, just went out and left the crowds and rejoicings to find my way to the station."[40]

All the graduates were immediately placed in social welfare positions in Johannesburg and across South Africa. About half took up positions as "Directors of Native Recreation" in local town municipalities across the country.[41] But not Regina. Her academic performance at the school had been outstanding, yielding her a clutch of distinctions and placing her at the top of her class, outstripping all the men.[42] Clearly, while this had been a program that hadn't stressed theory, its academic rigor had nonetheless been where her true interests lay. Regina was still deeply interested in the idea of social work—her philanthropic impulse to work for the uplift of her people, most especially "despised" women, was still there—but she was craving a more theoretically critical version of this than the safely paternalistic version offered by Ray Phillips and the Jan Hofmeyr School.

Toward the end of 1942, Regina—with Dan's encouragement—applied to, and was accepted at, Johannesburg's University of the Witwatersrand to begin its new BA degree program in social studies. This was an applied sociology program taught by the leading minds of the day. She would be the first Black woman to ever take it and one of only a handful of Black students at the university. (Now known colloquially as "Wits," in the 1940s it was simply "the university.") But despite Wits's reputation as a liberal funk hole, a refuge for young men evading military service, and a "pro-black, pro-Jewish" school (in the words of right-wing Afrikaner critics), Regina would soon find that the so-called liberal university had distinct limits to its liberalism.[43]

# 10

# Wits

> I am beginning to adjust myself gradually, icuriosity kubelungu iningi kabi [the whites' curiosity about me is really terrible].
>
> —Regina to Dan, February 11, 1943 (RTP)

Lecturers asked Black medical students at the University of the Witwatersrand to leave the room when European cadavers were cut open and splayed out for observation. They were also asked not to wear their white medical coats as they entered and left Johannesburg Hospital. This was so European patients could remain unaware that African doctors-in-training were in the building. White lecturers and professors also commonly asked their Black students to sit at the very back of lecture theaters. And when Black students used the university's library, the authorities expected them to sit in a separate "Non-European Reading Room." Swimming pools, sports grounds, and university dances were all barred to Black students. Regina may well have continued playing tennis, but regulations would have forced her to walk to a single "non-European" court at the far end of the campus.[1] Such were the realities of being a Black student at Wits in the 1940s.[2]

South Africa's entry into World War II marked a watershed in the history of the university. This was the start of the so-called open years, a period during which the university admitted Africans into the medical school for the first time, and the number of African students in other schools also grew. This change was partly due to the fact that Black medical students had previously trained overseas—something that was now impossible due to wartime restrictions. And partly the newly permissive attitude toward admissions lay in the obviously desperate need for more doctors and social workers in Black urban communities as cities like Johannesburg grew exponentially during the war years.[3] By 1945 there were 156 "non-white" students (a designation that included African, "colored" [i.e., mixed-race], and Indian-descended students) out of a student body of three thousand.[4]

But while in theory admission may have been possible for Black students (although not equal treatment at the university once they arrived there), the prohibitive cost of a degree meant many could not dream of entering. For Regina's degree in social studies, tuition was probably about £50 a year, around three times the cost of her social welfare diploma from the Jan H. Hofmeyr School.[5] Her degree would take four years—years during which she would not be earning or contributing to the household's finances. And money was still very tight for them. Despite Dan's elevated status, he still struggled each month to reconcile his accounts—a common predicament for Black professionals in Johannesburg of the 1940s. Throughout the years that he supported Regina at both the Hofmeyr School and at Wits, Dan repeatedly asked the sports club's trustees for raises "in order to keep up the dignity of my position as Manager of the Club."[6] Their financial situation was further complicated by ongoing medical expenses for them both. Regina continued to see an army of doctors throughout for help with conception. And on Dan's part, a devastating (and highly common) diagnosis of TB in 1942 meant new costs in connection with that: "The question of my health at this time when there is no £-s-d is a big problem. . . . I only pray it may end quick, now that it has been discovered."[7]

Regina's prospects for further education were saved only by the announcement in October 1942 by the Johannesburg branch of the all-white South African Association of University Women that it would be offering a "bursary for a degree course at the University of the Witwatersrand for a non-European woman."[8] However, the association required a matriculation certificate on the part of the successful applicant, something Regina didn't have. Here, Dan and her connections to the white philanthropic world who financed these kinds of opportunities was crucial. An introduction to Wits's influential Professor R. F. Alfred Hoernle—a philosopher as well as the then president of the Institute of Race Relations—seems to have secured her the scholarship. Regina proudly wrote to Dan after a meeting with university officials, "They say I can't waste such brains, I must be helped to further my education. There is your wife, Twala."[9]

But despite the scholarship, financial worries never really receded for all Regina's years at the university. It was only partial: amounts awarded ranged from £20 to £50 per year, meaning she and Dan still had to supply a significant sum.[10] At least once, Regina was on the brink of being barred from attendance for late payment of fees.[11] Such pressures were the norm among African students. The most famous example was that of Nelson Mandela, then a law student and who overlapped with Regina for nearly all her years at the university. Mandela's studies nearly bankrupted him. He had to sell his house in Orlando—very near the Twalas' home—as well as take out large loans. All this left Mandela "destitute and stranded."[12] Similar problems weighed on the Twalas. After several years of scrambling for fees, Regina wrote to Dan, "I am almost mad in the head to think about the hardships my man faces in funding my studies."[13]

In addition to fees, accommodations were the Twalas' other practical worry about the degree course. Most Wits students were not residential, as the university had only limited accommodations on-site. The majority of (white) students lodged in boarding houses in the conveniently located surrounding white suburbs.

Wealthier students opted for the large family homes of treelined Parktown while poorer, largely Afrikaner students lodged in the working-class area of Braamfontein, in which the university was itself located.[14] But urban segregation laws meant neither of these options were open for Black students. They had to live much farther afield in areas like Sophiatown or even Orlando. Travel was expensive and lengthy, and various permits had to be obtained to legally move between downtown Johannesburg and Black residential suburbs at night. And even when they had the necessary documentation, conductors and drivers frequently treated Black students badly on public transport. Again, Mandela's autobiography is illuminating. He describes being thrown off a "white tram" by its driver and frequently spending the night in a jail cell while traveling back home from the university after late evening classes in the 1940s.[15]

Regina and Dan fretted over this problem at some length. Where was she to stay? They both worried that Orlando required too long a daily commute and would eat into Regina's precious studying time. White liberals rallied once more—although in a typically ambiguous way. Ernest Jokl was a German Jewish refugee to South Africa. Jokl—a pioneering scholar of sports science—was introducing physical education to South African school curricula, including to Black schools. In connection with this, he worked closely with Dan at the sports club. Jokl and his wife, Erica, suggested a plan whereby Regina would stay in their centrally located house near the university and in exchange do housework in the afternoons and evenings after her classes were over. (The municipality offered exemptions for Africans spending the night in white areas if they were living on the premises as domestic workers.) This is Regina's matter-of-fact account to Dan of what even Jokl recognized as a "humiliating" offer:

> Jokl suggested I should stay with them and help with the house, and he would bring me to school every morning. I don't know whether this scheme will work, but I will try. Jokl suggested I

> go this week [to their house] and weigh the situation to find out if it will suit me because he says that Mrs Jokl thinks I might find it humiliating to take the place of a servant. . . . The path to success is not an easy one.[16]

Regina would ultimately refuse this offer in favor of the exhausting daily commute to Orlando—she had come too far to return to being a domestic servant in a white household. And once the logistical issues of money and accommodations were solved, Regina could prepare herself for the excitement of at last being a university student. Wits had previously offered a two-year diploma course in social studies that many of the Black individuals spearheading the new push toward social work had taken. For example, William Ngakane, husband of Mabel who headed the controversial Orlando Mothers' Association, had completed this.[17] By the late 1930s the university had inaugurated a new Department of Social Studies, part of the broader contemporary sense that massive urbanization and industrialization required a professionalized set of "scientific" skills. The department was thus hybrid in nature, balancing academic sociology with practical training.

But unlike the Hofmeyr School, social studies at Wits stressed scientific methods—statistics was part of the course offerings—and religious teaching was entirely absent. It also lay at the heart of a powerful network of white liberals, leftists, and radicals at the university. It was staffed by figures like the sociologist Henry Sonnabend (whom Regina glowingly called "a lecturer and a half" on account of his powerful oratory),[18] an outspoken critic of the government's policies toward Black South Africans. Social studies students also had to take courses in social anthropology with Hilda Kuper. Many South African anthropologists of the 1940s—Kuper as well as Ellen Hellmann—saw their discipline as a profoundly applied one, a tool to further ameliorate Black living conditions as well as to critique the segregationist policies of the state. Kuper, for example, used her lectures to lambaste biological concepts of race as entirely lacking in scientific validity.[19]

Kuper also led groups of students to do research projects in Black townships, focusing on topics such as women liquor producers and formulating critical responses to government policy.[20] The atmosphere could not have been more different from the stuffy, conservative Christian flavor of the Hofmeyr School.

Who were Regina's classmates? In 1948, the year Regina graduated, there were sixty-four students in all the four years of the social studies BA program, meaning she would have been in a cohort of around sixteen students.[21] Most were women, part of the new influx of female students to the university during the war years. Presumably the female bias of the course also reflected the sense that welfare was a "woman's career."[22] Regina would also have encountered a peppering of white female welfarists attending her lectures, including a doyenne of welfare work in Johannesburg: Edith Rheinallt Jones, founder of the Wayfarers, came with great dedication to lectures. And then occasionally there was a wife of a male faculty member who attended classes for they "had heard they may be stimulated."[23] Regina, moreover, was the only Black woman in the entire social studies program and the first Black woman to ever achieve this particular degree.[24] Almost certainly, she found few soul mates among her fellow students, most of whom were much younger than she was and many of whom were there in the spirit of a finishing school or for mental "stimulation" rather than in preparation for future careers.[25] The anthropologist Audrey Richards, who taught at the university in the late 1930s, had this to say of her female students: "All are very self-possessed, posé, and charming, but minds as blank as boards. . . . The girls are beautifully dressed and I feel quite shabby, they look like a set of rose buds on a stalk."[26]

Rather than studying with the sweetly pink "rose buds," Regina had hoped to be placed with the African medical students for her science classes. (She was, for example, required to take botany in her first year.) There was even another woman in this group, Mary Malahlela, the first Black woman to train as a medical doctor in South Africa and who would graduate from Wits a year before Regina, in 1947.[27] But to Regina's dismay, a timetable clash made this impossible. So, Regina stayed with the white students for her botany classes, although with great reluctance. She told Dan a month after starting, "I am beginning to adjust myself gradually, icuriosity kubelungu iningi kabi [the whites' curiosity about me is really terrible]."[28]

Regina, however, did make at least one new friend at Wits. This was the soon-to-be-famous Ruth First, a fellow student in her social studies degree program, with whom she would overlap with by two years. (First would graduate in 1945.)[29] It tells us something about Regina's burgeoning political consciousness and her rejection of white liberalism that it was First with whom Regina formed her most serious Wits friendship. First represented an entirely different kind of politics from that represented by liberals like Ellen Hellmann and Hilda Kuper. She was an active member of the South African Communist Party (her Eastern European immigrant parents had been founder members of the party in Johannesburg in the 1920s), and she was also romantically involved with a Wits Law student of South Asian descent, Ismail Meer. Both First and Meer would become important figures in the ANC. Indeed, First's life would end violently in 1982 as she unwrapped a parcel bomb sent by South African apartheid operatives while she was in exile in neighboring Mozambique.

Both her Communist allegiance and her interracial relationship placed First in a different world from the "rosebuds" of the campus. First sat at the heart of a politically radical group at the university that included Meer, First's future husband the Communist Joe Slovo, as well as Nelson Mandela, a fellow law student with Meer. Student politicians at Wits were inspired by the rise of populist Black-led movements in the city: First was one of several Wits students who volunteered for the miners' strike of 1946, for example, which involved more than sixty thousand workers, and Wits students had also used their and their parents' cars to give rides to those who boycotted the buses in 1944 (a protest against the high fares that devastated those who had to travel long distances into the city to work).[30] In an interview with Tim Couzens in the late 1970s, Dan stated—not altogether approvingly—that it was during her Wits years that Regina "got mixed up with Ruth First and the Trade Unions."[31] This should not be exaggerated: we know from her letters to Dan that she was largely preoccupied with studies during her time at the university and that her political commitments would only come into fruition after her degree. But we can nonetheless see Wits as an important experience in exposing Regina to radical politics.

On the academic front, Regina struggled quite considerably. Statistics were her greatest woe, a course that she succinctly described to Dan as "trouble" and correctly predicted failing in her end-of-year examination.[32] Her university transcript shows a borderline performance in her first year, with lots of third-class passes (49 for English, 40 for Sociology, 47 for Social Economics, and 47 for Botany), one fail (18 for Statistics), and a first-class (77 for isiZulu).[33] Regina's marks—especially her 49 for English—do raise the issue of how a system of assessment could possibly consider a talented writer like her worth barely a pass. A similar pattern repeated over the next few years.[34] The white Association of University Women, who partially funded her studies, were distinctly unpleased with the situation, pronouncing Regina "a great disappointment."[35] However, this unimpressive academic performance was not unique to Regina. A glance at the exam results for her cohort of sixteen shows that other students were also largely getting second- and third-class passes.[36]

Where Regina was unique was in that she—as the sole Black student in her class—not only had to contend with a grueling commute to and from Orlando but was also squeezing in her hours of study either in the very early hours, before she had to leave, or late at night, once she finally made it home. Even the Association of University Women could not deny that her poor academic performance was on account of her "liv[ing] in a township and not hav[ing] the necessary facilities for study."[37] While Regina left no record of her experience of these many hours of commuting, we can imagine what it must have been like from the famous photographs of Santu Mofokeng, who documented passengers on the Orlando-to-Johannesburg train route some forty years later. Mofokeng's photographs show women and men in overcrowded train carriages, slumped exhaustedly in seats and barely awake on their feet.[38] We should also think here of Nelson Mandela's defense of his own poor academic performance as a law student in exactly the same years (perhaps even traveling between Orlando and Johannesburg on the same train): "I resided in Orlando Location in a noisy neighbourhood. In the absence of electric light, I was compelled to study in the evenings with a paraffin lamp and sometimes with a candle light. I wasted a lot of time travelling between Orlando and the city and returned home after 8pm feeling tired and hungry and unfit to concentrate on my studies."[39]

During the first two years of her Wits education, moreover, Regina was also putting many hours into running the Bantu Sports Club while Dan was unwell from TB and being treated. (Dan spent some time in Rietfontein Hospital outside of Johannesburg. One of Dan's fellow patients would have been none other than Desmond Tutu, who himself spent two years in Rietfontein recuperating from TB.)[40] Added to all this, Regina was still trying to become pregnant. Throughout her Wits years, she frequently dreamed of walking through fruit orchards at eNdaleni, passing beneath trees laden with ripe mulberries, picking them, and eating them. She hoped this was a premonition of pregnancy, that these "funny dreams mean good."[41] Seeking a child meant more expensive doctors, tests, and medical regimes and more time-consuming appointments. Yet Regina felt unable to stop, arguing to Dan that without addressing their childlessness she wouldn't be able to concentrate on her studies: "If I am to do university work, I must be free in my thoughts and anxieties. . . . Dan, I feel things cannot go on this way forever. I must know the truth about myself, if the doctors condemn me, let me know about it and forget about it in time. This uncertainty is tedious and it is going to be a stumbling block on my way."[42]

So, Regina continued with the doctors. This time her physician of choice was Dr. James Moroka—future president of the ANC—who had trained at Edinburgh in 1918 and now ran a practice out of the small mountain town of Thaba Nchu, a day or so journey from Johannesburg. Along with Dr. Xuma, Moroka was one of the few African doctors for Black patients of the 1940s with means. Now Moroka took both the Twalas under his care, who seem to have temporarily based themselves in the Orange Free State. Perhaps they believed the mountain air would do Dan's lungs good. Moroka successfully treated Dan for his TB and diagnosed Regina with a "swollen part" that required surgery (although Moroka humiliatingly had to ask a white colleague to perform the operation as the "law does not allow a native to give instructions to white nursing sister [*sic*].")[43] All of this was very distracting, leading Regina to take weeks off from the university, missing lectures and failing to keep up with her statistics homework.[44]

But the cares of these years still could not quite erase Regina's joy in embracing her new vocation as a social worker. She discovered—unsurprisingly, given what we already know of her interests—that she was especially drawn to initiatives for women. The university required a number of practical case hours from students. Her professors either assigned Regina, or she herself volunteered, to work for the Children's Benevolent Society, an organization that supported children as well as their mothers amid the difficulties of city living. Dan fortunately preserved one of Regina's case reports from this exercise, so we are able to piece together something of her experiences. For the report Dan filed away, Regina's client was one "Miriam Mbelle [*sic*]," a single mother of three young children who worked as a domestic worker in a white family's home.

Regina's interview notes with Miriam—preserved in their entirety—tell a litany of the suffering Black women endured in the city. Miriam had been arrested by a pickup van for illicitly living in the city center, been imprisoned by the authorities for the offense, had undergone assault and sickness, received woefully insufficient medical treatment at the Non-European Hospital, and experienced poverty to the point that she had received food rations from the government for her and her children for about six months. Regina's response to Miriam was empathetic and perceptive, immediately grasping both the dimensions of the problem and acknowledging Miriam's bravery in caring for her children: "At present I may say that Miriam is in a difficult position of being an unmarried mother with illegitimate children. She is trying to live a good life in order not to put a further stigma on her children."[45]

These years were also when Regina began to experiment with ways to alleviate women's predicaments, finding opportunities to practically implement the skills she was learning at the university. The huge inflation of food costs in the city was one of the most crippling problems of the war years. Regina began to organize women in Orlando into "food clubs," in which they would contribute the small sum of two shillings each week to the fund. At their height, the clubs had a membership of 150. Regina—who served as the capable "Organizer and Cashier"—would take the funds on Saturdays to the local fresh-produce market. There she would haggle wholesale prices down as she made bulk purchases of vegetables for club members. Decades later, when she wrote as "Intombazana" about this experience for the *Times of Swaziland,* she recalled how she and her associates would shame buyers who tried to outbid them, shouting, "Hawu, hawu, hawu!"—an iziZulu exclamation of shock or disgust.[46] The vegetables would then be divided among the club's members, with an estimated "double value for their money" compared to women who bought food for their households individually. In Intombazana's words, by "forming food clubs . . . [they had] saved train fare, cartage and being crushed by big purses."[47] *Bantu World* glowingly described Regina as "the energetic Mrs Twala who procured quantities of vegetables that attracted many families to the Club. . . . Numbers continue to grow."[48] The complete absence of white welfarists was a notable feature of the endeavor. This was African women organizing to help themselves.[49]

The last months of 1945 brought the best news possible. In September 1945 Regina and Dan finally managed to conceive a child. In the understatement of the interview, Dan told Tim Couzens that he and Regina "got a surprise" when the doctor finally informed her she was pregnant after seven years of trying.[50] Regina and Dan's son, Vusumuzi Ntozonke Carrolton Twala, was born on June 9, 1946. His carefully chosen name was rich with meaning: Vusumuzi means "building up a home," Ntozonke "you are everything," and Carrolton was in honor of Dan's long-term friend and sometime lover, the geologist Gerald Carroll. The inclusion of Carroll in their son's name once again suggests Regina's acceptance of Dan's relationship; a jealous wife surely would have objected to her much-anticipated son being named after her husband's ex-lover. On September 22, 1946, Vusi was christened in the Methodist church in Pimville (formerly known as Klipspruit, adjacent to Orlando). Along with five other babies, he was baptized with water from the River Jordan—brought back from the Holy Land by a South African soldier stationed there during World War II. Vusi was wrapped in a lacy white cloth and held tightly by Regina. Afterward, Regina and Dan held a grand christening party at their house in Orlando, attended by the cream of Black Johannesburg society.[51]

Vusi's arrival meant Regina took five years to complete her degree, rather than four. But by early 1948, she had graduated in triumph, one of only four Black students to graduate that year from Wits and the only Black woman of the year, second only to the physician Mary Malahlela in the history of Wits (Malahela graduated in 1947). We know from contemporary accounts of other graduations that these occasions took place in Johannesburg's impressive City Hall.[52] Both *Bantu World* and *Umteteli wa Bantu* reported on Regina's graduation, a mark of the rarity of her achievement.[53] And the Bantu Sports Club held a grand ball in Regina's honor, in recognition of the talented

FIGURE 10.1. Regina Twala upon graduation from the University of the Witwatersrand, 1948 (Pinokie Twala)

wife of its manager, Dan Twala. A "Mrs Malie"—probably the wife of Julius Malie, the then manager of the Bantu Men's Social Center—who was herself a BA holder from Fort Hare University, made a speech in celebration of Regina, noting "that such occasions as these when honor fell upon an African woman were very rare."[54]

But a bitter note sounded amid all the celebrations. In advertising the "graduation ball," *Umteteli wa Bantu* noted that "Mrs. Twala is not only a scholar, but a competent housewife and mother."[55] Regina had just achieved what no Black woman in South Africa had ever achieved before. But the gatekeepers of Black society were still insistent that scholarship had its limits. What finally mattered more than anything else, in the end, was the home and the children.

U Nkosk. R. D. Twala, B.A., ekuzakuba umqolo wenamba egameni lakhe ngokuhlwa nje, ukuvuyisana naye ngokuphumelela uviwo. U Nkosk. Twala asisiso sityudaka kupela-nje, ikoko yinkosikazi yendlu yayo ekwa ngu nozala. Ubonwa apha ekunye nonyana wake.

U Nkosk. R. D. Twala B.A., ekuyakuba ne dance ayenzelwayo ukujabulisana naye ngokuphumelela ezinfundweni eziphakeme kusihlwa nje. U Nkosk. Twala akakhuthalele zimfundo kuphela nekhaya ulikhuthalele kanjalo. Ubonwa laph[illegible]endodana yakhe.

Mrs. R. D. Twala, B.A., whose graduation is to be celebrated by a ball in Johannesburg this evening. Mrs. Twala is not only a scholar, but a competent housewife and mother. She is seen here with her little son.

Mof. R. D. Twala B.A. ea etsetsoang mokete oa ho thabisana le eena ka ho tsoella lithutong tse phahameng mantsiboeng ana. Mof Twala ha a khohalla lithuto feela le lehaeng o joalo. O bonoa mona a ena le mora.

FIGURE 10.2. Regina Twala and son, *Umteteli wa Bantu,* January 1948 (Zanele Twala)

# 11

# Regina to Gelana

> Unless these obnoxious laws are exposed and their injustice opposed, there can be no hope for future of our South African nation.
>
> —Gelana Twala, *Advance,* December 11, 1952 (RTP)

In 1952 Regina changed her name. No longer using the English "Regina," she would now publicly embrace her isiZulu name of "Gelana." This would be much more than a mere change of name. Regina's preference for an isiZulu name symbolized her political and personal transformations of the 1950s. These were years during which she lost faith in South Africa's powerful white liberal elite. She would now view their well-meaning efforts at Black uplift as thinly veiled racism. Amid the early years of apartheid, these were also years when Regina would embrace the newly radicalized ANC, seeing direct political opposition as the only viable course of action when confronted by a racist state. Finally, this was when Regina's marriage to Dan Twala would fall apart, crushed by Dan's infidelity and his resentment at his newly politicized wife's ambitions outside the home. Regina, the pliant protégée of Dan Twala and white philanthropists and missionaries, died. Gelana—politically radical, outspoken, independent—would be born.

All this lay ahead. First, Regina had to secure work after she got her BA degree. After her graduation from Wits in 1948, the same network of white female liberals who had supported her over the past decade—however ambiguously—once again rallied. This time it was to help Regina find her first salaried position as a social worker. Violaine Junod—daughter of Henri Junod, an esteemed Swiss-born missionary, linguist, and ethnographer—had briefly overlapped with Regina in Wits's social science program.[1] After Junod graduated in 1946, she ascended to position of director of the new Family Welfare Centre in Alexandra Township, a private endeavor supported by Wits students' fundraising efforts.

"Alex," as the township is called, is ten miles north of Johannesburg.[2] It was at the time one of the most densely packed African residential areas in Johannesburg, a conglomeration of tin and burlap shacks crisscrossed with unpaved roads, lived in by eighty thousand people.[3] Alex was desperately poor. In 1952 the Family Welfare Centre commissioned a study of four families. This showed residents were not making enough money to supply basic food needs. Malnutrition was widespread among both children and adults.[4] If Orlando was the new middle-class mecca of Johannesburg, Alex was its poorer sibling. Yet it was still favored by many Black people as one of the few places in the city they could hold property rights. In contrast, Orlando housing was owned by the white-run municipality.[5]

Violaine Junod—with Hilda Kuper and Ellen Hellmann, who both advised the center—thought well of Regina's talents.[6] Upon Regina's graduation, the center's trustees appointed her to be its new assistant director. The organization was colloquially known by its staff and Alex residents as "Entokozweni," or Place of Happiness.[7] Regina's hours were from seven in the morning to five in the afternoon, and frequently evenings and weekends. She was to assist Junod oversee a small staff and supervise services offered for Alex's residents: a nursery, recreation for children, women's sewing and cooking clubs, pre- and postnatal classes, and an adult night school. Vusi—now a toddler—was enrolled in Entokozweni's nursery school, which must have neatly solved the problem of childcare for Regina as a working parent. Each day Junod—who lived nearby—would use her car to pick up and drop off Regina and Vusi from their Bantu Sports Club home.[8]

Regina's two years at Entokozweni were a bleak education in Black life in the city. The center was woefully overstretched—serving around seven hundred people—and unable to keep up with the intense demand on its services. Regina correctly identified nutrition as the key challenge for Alex residents. She introduced the same type of food clubs she'd pioneered in Orlando just a few years earlier, enabling straitened Alex residents to purchase fresh produce at less than what local shops charged exorbitantly.[9] Alex's deprivation was becoming the norm for all Africans in cities like Johannesburg. Around the time that Regina started her new job, the general election of May 1948 delivered a shock victory to the Afrikaner National Party. Its doctrine of apartheid proclaimed "separate development" for South Africa's races. In reality, apartheid meant far inferior "development" for all but the country's whites. Its promoters deployed slogans like "Swart Gevaar" ("Black Peril") to play to white South Africans' fears of extinction by a Black majority. Apartheid ideologues built on prior legislation by intensifying the message that Black people belonged in rural areas rather than cities. Proponents of the apartheid system presented Africans as the exotified other, mired in primitive ways since time immemorial. Fighting against the labor needs of urban industry and manufacturing, Afrikaner fanatics argued that cities, with their Western ways, were alien environments for "tribal" Africans.

From the 1950s onward, the government began to remove tens of thousands from urban "blackspots" and shunted the exiles to flatlands far from the cities. A flurry of legislation further undercut all but white South Africans' right to live in cities. Cosmopolitan neighborhoods like Johannesburg's Sophiatown disappeared over the next several years. The new government's introduction of a single, centralized identity document was especially hated. This was the Reference Book, a panopticon-like document sweeping away the older bureaucratic tangle of pass books, tax receipts, and permits, replacing it with the all-seeing *dompas* (or the "stupid book," as African holders called it). This little document listed the holder's race, their complete work and travel history, mug shot, and fingerprints. The stakes of the book could not have been higher: without it, any nonwhite would be ejected from the city.[10]

As a Black woman in Johannesburg, Regina experienced the indignities of apartheid in a multitude of personal ways. But one particular incident stands out. In 1949 Regina's boss, Violaine Junod, announced she was leaving the center for a PhD at the London School of Economics.[11] The search began for a new director. Regina had performed excellently and was popular with the staff. Junod encouraged her to apply. The center's board selected Regina as one of three finalists, although the race was really between her and one of the other two applicants, a white woman named Margaret Ryan who had also graduated from the social studies program at Wits. Regina's experience, her achievements, and the fact that she was liked by her colleagues and popular with Alex residents made her the natural choice. Indeed, Regina seemed the stronger candidate in all ways but one: her race.

But the center's all-white board—supported by Junod—decided that in the present political climate it would be too great a liability to have a Black woman as director. These were Junod's words: "The Centre's development would be affected. . . . The issue of efficient administration within the South African racial context was the very serious consideration that led the Board to appoint the white applicant." Junod personally delivered the bad news to Regina. In an account written some twenty years later, Junod remembered Regina was "very emotional and burst out saying [to Junod] 'you have stabbed me in the back' . . . accusing me of outright racism." Junod remembered she tried to "calm" Regina, explaining that while the board had wanted "to select on merit alone, they were forced to recognize the problems raised by the racial context." Regina would not accept this and resigned from her post.[12]

Violaine Junod's reflections display astonishing naïveté about African life under apartheid, especially considering she would shortly be a leading figure in the new Liberal Party with its antiapartheid platform.[13] Rather than focusing on Regina's disenfranchisement via apartheid's racist code—effectively making it impossible for Black professionals to hold senior positions—Junod instead focused on how this injustice created time-consuming responsibilities for whites. In her reading, the major tragedy of racial discrimination was that it increased her workload: "I could not delegate certain administrative tasks to staff like Mrs Twala as it would have made for inefficiency. . . . Africans like her would not have received the courteous and prompt service that I did." In Junod's analysis, Regina's passing over for promotion merely "illustrated the additional burdens that the white person had to carry."[14]

Regina's encounter with Junod illustrates how a self-professed progressive like Junod could both devote themselves to Black South Africa's "uplift" and be blind to the contradictions of Black life. Junod's conclusion was that she herself was the victim of an unfair charge of racism. She argued Black South Africans could be "racist" too, suggesting they did not appreciate the difference between "good" liberal whites who had the interests of Africans close to their hearts—in which camp she placed herself—and the run-of-the-mill National Party–voting Afrikaner. Did Regina not see Junod was not like other whites? The event only convinced Junod of "Mrs Twala's own racial prejudices . . . an inverted racial prejudice which no reason could dissuade."[15] Decades later, Dan Twala would tell Tim Couzens that "Regina was *hot* against whites. . . . She thought the moderate white was deceptive, worse than the Afrikaner."[16] Perhaps it was this botched job application at Entokozweni that Regina had in mind when she made such a comment. I date Regina's disgust with the white liberal cause that had nurtured her since childhood to this Entokozweni incident. Her disillusionment with progressive whites had been steadily growing—we can think of her time at the Hofmeyr School—but it is only after her break with Junod that Regina more openly voiced her criticism of white liberals.

Her Entokozweni chapter behind her, in 1951 Regina accepted a new post with the Council for Industrial and Scientific

Research. This was a government-funded body aiming to apply social-scientific research to urban problems, reflecting the big-state interventionist ethos undergirding apartheid ideology. It perhaps helped Regina that Hilda Kuper was also employed by the council in these years; Kuper may have put in a good word for her former student.[17] But the job meant leaving Johannesburg. The council deployed Regina to the coastal Cape Province city of Port Elizabeth—a two-day journey by train from Johannesburg—to conduct research into conditions of African housing in its large African township, New Brighton, a place as underprovisioned as Alex.[18] Regina's decision to take this far-off position was a sign she had few options; I cannot imagine she welcomed leaving the five-year-old Vusi in Johannesburg. Nevertheless, Dan and Vusi visited her at least once, making the long journey by rail to the city to spend Vusi's school vacation with her.[19]

Port Elizabeth was Regina's crucible moment, a time during which she shed her former affiliation with white liberalism and embraced the more radical tools of civil unrest. Indeed, after Regina's Entokozweni humiliation at the hands of Junod, she arrived in Port Elizabeth well primed for such political awakening.[20] She could hardly have selected a better city. By the early 1950s the city was one of South Africa's most radical environments. Its history of trade unionism, its liberal legacy of relatively relaxed segregation laws, and the dire living conditions in New Brighton all conspired to make it what the popular African magazine *Drum* called "a political time bomb."[21] Port Elizabeth was where the ANC was experiencing a major resurgence. After years of toothless gradualism and being dominated by older men who optimistically clung to ineffectual petitions and the chimera of reasoned debate with the government, the ANC had at last changed leadership. Young radicals like Nelson Mandela demanded change now, and they devised concrete strategies to make it happen.

By 1952 Port Elizabeth was one of the hubs of the ANC's Defiance Campaign, a nationwide mass protest that recruited volunteers to defy apartheid laws with an aim to clogging the judicial system by filling prisons. "No bail, no defence, no fine" was the campaign's slogan. Throughout 1952 officials arrested and imprisoned over eight thousand people for streaming into Europeans-only post offices and railways stations. The "Windy City," as the coastal Port Elizabeth was known, supplied more volunteers—tightly disciplined, carefully selected individuals—than anywhere else.[22] Women were especially active in the city's campaign, and Christianity infused the protests; volunteers would meet nightly for hours of fervent prayer to ready themselves for the next day's action.[23]

What did Regina make of this? Few letters exist between her and Dan from the 1950s (for reasons I shall explain below), and the surviving handful are all authored by Dan. But we can piece together her response to the political atmosphere from other sources. We know that during 1952 Regina started using her isiZulu name—Gelana—rather than Regina, something she maintained for the rest of her life. This shift is visible in the handful of articles she published in the newly founded *Drum* magazine in 1952, publicly signing off as "Mrs Gelana Twala."[24] This can, I think, be interpreted as her growing Africanist political orientation. (In respect of her choice, I use "Gelana" for the rest of her story.)[25] And although there is no record in newspapers like *Bantu World* of Gelana being imprisoned during a Port Elizabeth protest (newspapers supplied extensive lists of convictions), we also know that many volunteers in Port Elizabeth were arrested but never charged by the police.[26] The year, moreover, was when Gelana became actively involved in ANC women's activities. By 1953 she was sufficiently high up to be charged with forming a Women's League branch in the small but politically influential town of Queenstown, 250 miles from Port Elizabeth.[27]

Gelana was just as preoccupied with the injustices of gender as of race. She became particularly outspoken on the issue of women's representation within the ANC, denouncing it a patriarchal organization excluding women.[28] She is on record at the annual conference of the ANC in 1952 "strongly protesting" in a submission to the meeting that "women have been used as tools to raise money without representation in Congress" (probably referring here to the Shilling Campaign run by female ANC members).[29] Dan's memory is of a woman so critical of male comrades that those around were both attracted and repelled: "She was on fire, so that even the men were pulled around by her. Ah, she was very startling at that moment. She felt very strongly and she had an opinion that could not be defied. Even some men could not work with her because she was so straightforward."[30]

Gelana's baptism-by-fire came on December 8, 1952, four days before her forty-fourth birthday. Taking place in Germiston Location, an African area in eastern Johannesburg, this was one of the final acts of the Defiance Campaign. It was also one of the most high-profile. It was led by a group of about forty prominent Africans, Europeans, and Indians, symbolizing the ANC's shift to a multiracial alliance, repudiating its former Africanist "purity" for pragmatic collaboration with dissenters of all races. The leaders were Patrick Duncan—son of the former governor-general of South Africa—and Manilal Gandhi, son of the Mahatma (who had lived and worked in South Africa for over two decades). Gelana was one of fourteen Black volunteers who took part in the protest, many university students from Wits or Fort Hare.

Wearing the black, green, and gold ribbons of the ANC, the protesters entered Germiston Location through a back entrance. They were almost immediately met with the crowd's "cheers and great excitement," followed by a group of "about 1,000 singing Africans." More ominously, they were also trailed by uniformed policemen on foot and in police cars, as well as plainclothes Special Branch members who dealt with political dissidents.[31] This particular afternoon, the protesters aimed to defy two laws. The first was a law prohibiting political meetings with more than ten Black people. Their second goal, linked to the first, was to contravene a regulation against "[enticing] Africans to break laws." Hobbling on crutches after a recent car accident and addressing the crowd in English and seSotho, Patrick Duncan told those gathered, "We come with love for you and with peace."

It was then Gelana's turn to speak. She addressed them in frank personal terms. She spoke of her own years of training as a social worker—six in total—and she expressed her disillusionment with the futility of "uplifting" Black life when faced with the reality of apartheid South Africa: "Most of the theories for solving the problems I learned at the University only work according to skin colour." She continued: "Unless these obnoxious laws are exposed and their injustice opposed, there can be no hope for future of our South African nation." Speeches concluded, the protesters began to process out of Germiston. It looked as if no arrests would be made.

But as Gelana and her fellow protesters neared the exit, "squad cars raced up and encircled the crowd," screeching across the tarmac and blocking the road. The crowd started shouting "Afrika" and raising clenched fists—the symbol of antiapartheid resistance for the next forty years—as the protesters were bundled by policemen into cars and driven away for booking and processing. It was all over. Other than shouts and cheers, the protest had concluded peacefully, although the Afrikaner police commandant who oversaw the arrests would later make the dubious claim in the court hearing that women "were shouting war cries, which I recognized as a noise made by Natives before going into attack."[32]

Gelana would spend her birthday, Christmas, and New Year's Day 1953 in a Germiston prison. One of her companions during her two-month incarceration—the volunteers were imprisoned separately according to race—was the young daughter of Barney Ngakane, the headmaster of Orlando High School and himself a Hofmeyr School graduate.[33] This gives some sense of the middle-class respectability of the protesters. Many considered going to jail a mark of honor rather than a social stigma. Yet despite the prestige of this political arrest, upon her release Gelana found herself with a criminal record and without a job. She had been immediately fired by the Council for Industrial and Scientific Research, the standard fate for Defiance Campaign protesters, and for the next year struggled to find anyone who would employ her.[34]

We do not know what support Dan gave to Gelana while she was in prison—whether he visited her, sent her food and warm blankets, greeted her on the day the authorities released her, or drove her back to their sports club home. What we do know is Dan was resolutely apolitical, determined to steer clear of anything smacking of trouble. Yet he himself had already been adversely affected by apartheid. In 1949 the sports club's trustees sold their premises to the government, knowing the latter would soon close the club as part of the clamp-down on Africans in cities.[35] In the meantime, Dan's position at the club was progressively eroded. By 1952, the year of Gelana's arrest, the trustees booted Dan out of his office and told him to work from home. Meanwhile, his office was turned into a toolshed for the white groundsman. Club members "strongly resented" the insult to their popular "secretary" and sent deputations to the Native Affairs Department but to no avail.[36]

But Dan never pursued the path of public protest that Gelana chose. To her, this was inexcusable weakness. In later life, Dan recalled—perhaps sadly—that Gelana "used to say I was a coward."[37] The difference between the two was partly a question of personality. Easy-going Dan hated conflict. And once the trustees sold the club, he became a government employee, dependent upon Johannesburg Municipality for his livelihood. Entirely justified fear of losing his job—it had happened to Gelana—underlay Dan's reluctance to protest. And for his part, Dan neither sympathized with nor even accepted Gelana's politics. He felt the consequences would be disastrous for their domestic stability and professional and financial prospects. As he put it to Tim Couzens, he was "really disappointed when [Gelana] took up this Congress work," having thought that "she was going to go a long way" on account of her education, her talent, and her ambition.[38]

By the time of Gelana's arrest, further problems had arisen between the couple. At this point, the small family—Gelana, Dan, Vusi, and Mary—had left the loathed Orlando and were living a spacious house on the sports club's premises in downtown Johannesburg. But this was not a happy home. By 1953, the year after Gelana's arrest during the Defiance Campaign, Mary—now a teenager of thirteen—had become Dan's sidekick on what were frequent assignations with other women. In 2019 I spoke with Mary in her Orlando house, one year before her death. Mary—then seventy-nine—recounted to me how "I always used to go with Papa when he was going to visit the girlfriends. I knew all of Papa's girlfriends." On one ill-fated occasion, Dan had used Mary as a go-between, asking her to carry a love letter from himself to one Margaret Mmope, a domestic servant in a white household in Berea (a residential suburb north of the city). Margaret had started helping Dan with housework on account of Gelana being in Port Elizabeth, and an affair between the two had commenced. This is what Mary told me:

> Dan gave me a letter to go and give to Margaret. I had just come home from school. I took the letter. When I got to Berea I couldn't find Margaret. So I put the letter in my school blazer pocket. So, I got home and I hung my blazer behind the wardrobe. The letter was sticking out there. When Gelana came into the house, she saw this letter sticking out from my blazer! And that's how she found out about Margaret.

Family lore has it that after discovering the love letter, Gelana put a huge pot of water to boil on the stove, waited for Dan to come home from the sports club, and hurled her vat of boiling water into his face. Mary remembered, "Papa became PINK. It was terrible. His ears were glued to his head." Ever-practical, Gelana took Dan to their doctor in Johannesburg, a Dr. Hirschman, who did what he could for Dan's burns.[39] Evidently he succeeded, as later photographs of Dan show no scarring.

I have no other information about this event, as it is not referenced in Gelana and Dan's letters. But given its attestation to by several family members—some seventy years later—it seems likely that it contains at least a kernel of truth. Its shocking nature provokes many questions. Did Dan press charges against his wife, given her near murderous actions? What was the reaction of

Dr. Hirschman to the severely burned face of his patient? Did he alert the police? These are questions for which I have no answers. Yet whatever the facts, one can be sure that this violent episode would have created a lasting rift between the couple—an emotional scar long outlasting the physical wound.

When I asked Mary what the letter had contained to make Gelana so incandescently furious, she could not—or would not—tell me. Whatever its cause, Gelana's anger was far from quenched by that pot of hot water. Deciding the marriage was over, she engaged the services of a young African lawyer, one of two partners in the first Black-run law firm in South Africa. One partner was Oliver Tambo, soon to be an antiapartheid activist and president of the ANC during its years in exile. Personally representing Gelana was none other than the firm's second partner, Nelson Mandela, already one of the best-known Black politicians in the country and president of the Transvaal branch of the ANC. Regina knew Mandela well, both from her student days at Wits and as an Orlando neighbor. After discussions in the Mandela & Tambo offices in the art deco–inspired Chancellor House at 25 Fox Street, Gelana filed for divorce. The document, kept in Pretoria's National Archives, gives some clue as to what Dan may have written in the letter Gelana found stuffed into Mary's pocket. Dated October 23, 1953, Mandela's submission to the Native Divorce Court maintained that "on diverse occasions during 1951 and 1952, the Defendant [Dan] committed adultery with a woman known to the Plaintiff [Regina] as Miss Margaret Mmope, also known as Mrs Margaret Twala, in consequence whereof she became pregnant and was delivered of a child in March 1953 and of which child the Defendant is the father."[40]

Perhaps the letter in Mary's pocket mentioned Dan's newly born or soon-to-be-born child and this was the first time Gelana realized her husband had fathered a baby with another woman. Or perhaps Dan's letter referred to the fact he seems to have entered into some kind of marital relationship—legal or otherwise—with Margaret, judging from how Mandela's submission noted Dan's mistress was widely known as "Mrs Margaret Twala." Either way, Gelana's hurt would have been horrendous. This would have been made more so by the fact that Dan and Gelana had themselves been trying, unsuccessfully, to conceive a second child all throughout this time.[41]

But by 1953 Dan was also angry with Gelana. For all his promotion of her career in their early years, he now resented her for "failing" to meet his needs. Previously proud of his career wife (in 1939, Dan had defiantly proclaimed "I am not looking for a housemaid nor a domestic servant in my wife"[42]), a decade-older Dan now felt disenchanted that Gelana showed little interest in the traditional roles of a 1950s wife. He hated that she eschewed domesticity for a career—both in research and in politics—and that she had left Vusi when she moved to Port Elizabeth. As he put it, "Gelana cannot look after children. . . . [She has] failed lamentably as a mother."[43] Decades later, in his interview with Couzens, Dan's bitterness was still palpable: "Gelana wanted to do anything but be a housewife."[44] Dan repeatedly leveled accusations of bad mothering at Gelana over the following decade.[45] These accusations say more about the hypocritical sexism of the 1950s than about Gelana's mothering talents, as all evidence points to Gelana and Vusi having a close, loving relationship. Yet while a man could pursue a career while neglecting paternal duties, of course a woman of the 1950s had no such latitude. Public opinion cast her career as detrimental to housewifely responsibilities.

This was a complex topic for Gelana herself. It is true she had changed since she and Dan met in 1938. From an unconfident, abandoned wife, she had metamorphosed into an assertive career woman who did not hesitate to voice her opinions, including, and perhaps especially, to men. As Dan wrote sadly and self-pityingly in 1952, "The general opinion is that I am bossed by my wife."[46] But this transformation was not without tensions for Gelana herself, something we sense in articles she wrote for *Drum*. Founded in 1951, the magazine was a forum for Black writers, photographers, and readers. Most histories of *Drum* focus on the tight-knit set of male writers at the magazine's heart, a generation that would define South African literature. Historians characterize this literary set as a macho culture, marked by drinking and womanizing.[47] Silence reigns on women writers.[48] Yet the debut of "Mrs Gelana Twala" in 1952 indicates female writers were also part of this influential cohort. Gelana Twala wrote alongside celebrated male journalists like Bloke Modisane, Can Themba, and Lewis Nkosi (although relegated to the Women's Pages).[49] Throughout 1952, Gelana developed an agony column for female readers. This regular offering explored the expectations husbands and society laid upon urban Black working women. Gelana's verdict on the woes of professional mothers who relied on extended family to look after their children is harshly open-eyed, suggesting her own experience of being charged with "negligence" for pursuing work alongside mothering: "You must take care of your children, for you are responsible for bringing them into the world. If they are neglected the Child Welfare Society may find out and bring the matter to the Children's Court and you would be charged with negligence."[50] Dan was also angry that, as apartheid gripped tighter at the throats of Black people, his wife had woken to a new life of political militancy. The unconfident young teacher from eNdaleni had become a fearless activist. In Dan's view, all of this was a huge waste of Gelana's education and her talents. It was sure to end in disaster, probably for them both. It was no wonder, he most likely thought to himself, that he had sought refuge in the arms of another woman, Margaret Mmope.

Yet by January of 1954—three months after Mandela had submitted Gelana's divorce petition to the court—Gelana withdrew the suit. Equally suddenly, she moved to the country of Eswatini, a neighbor of South Africa that sat under the "protection" of Britain. Gelana had received momentous news: she'd been awarded a prestigious four-year research fellowship by the Nuffield Foundation in the United Kingdom. The award would enable her to conduct ethnographic research in an area of her choice. Although her fellowship would be hosted in Durban at the new Institute for Social Research (ISR) at the University of Natal (under the supervision of

Hilda Kuper), the fact that her research topic was cultural change and Swati women meant she could live in Eswatini.

Gelana effectively separated from Dan. In early 1954, at the invitation of the Swati monarch Sobhuza II, Gelana left Johannesburg and moved to Eswatini, a day's journey away. Dan was happy about an arrangement that ensured separation but legally preserved the marriage. Despite everything, he had never wanted to divorce his wife, and the two remained in regular—intermittently cordial—contact during Gelana's decades in Eswatini: "Luckily for me, she got that Nuffield Fellowship and went to live in Swaziland. . . . We never really split up, we just made the decision to let the other person do what they like."[51]

The move could not have come too soon. All signs were that Gelana was heading for trouble. Both Dan and Mary Twala believed that had Gelana not left the country in 1954, she would have been imprisoned in 1956 when Mandela and other ANC leaders were swooped up in an avalanche of arrests. Gelana did in fact show up during the Treason Trial of 1956.[52] For a reason we don't yet know, one of the accused—Duma Nokwe—had several letters from Gelana addressed to him, implying a close association or even friendship between them. But by the time these documents came under scrutiny by the government prosecutor, Gelana was safe in Eswatini, part of a growing wave of Black exiles who crossed the border into the British protectorate.[53]

Exile in Eswatini, and comfortable funding to conduct ethnographic research, presented Gelana with the opportunity to push her politics in new directions. On the surface, it's true that this research didn't much look like politics. Anthropology could be read—indeed, *was* read by some—as an apolitical distraction from revolution and the overthrow of the government. In Dan's words, "now that she was in Swaziland, Gelana became more attached to tradition . . . how people make medicine, spears etc."[54] Yet politics and anthropology were never that far apart—not for Gelana and certainly not for the Swati monarch, Sobhuza II, who paved her way to Eswatini.

# 12

## Eswatini

> Very little has been written on beads among the Bantu. The following information has been collected from the Swazi of the Swazi Protectorate and the Zulu of eMangwaneni, Bergville, Natal. All facts are from personal observation and conversation with the people of these tribes, in their own environment. [Presented] here are the various ways in which beads help to keep each person's behaviour within the prescribed sanctions of the group. Beads were sign posts which show a young individual exactly where danger lies, and by them he is constantly reminded of his duty to society.
>
> —R. G. Twala, "Beads as Regulating the Social Life of the Zulu and the Swazi," *African Studies* 10, no. 3 (1951), 113–23

Sobhuza II of Eswatini—Ingwenyama ("The Lion"), as his subjects called him, or the lesser paramount chief, as the British officials ruling Eswatini insisted he be called—was a well-known figure in Johannesburg. Befitting his status as Eswatini's monarch, Sobhuza owned two properties in Sophiatown, one of the oldest Black townships in Johannesburg. The larger was a five-bedroom house at 124 Bertha Street, which was purchased by his lawyer,

Pixley kaIsaka Seme, and which had previously belonged to the Zulu king, Solomon kaDinuzulu.[1] The house served as Sobhuza's base during his time in the city as well as headquarters for emaSwati in Johannesburg; it was also known as the Swazi National Royal Club, where large meetings for emaSwati were held.[2] But even the Swati monarch was not invulnerable to apartheid. By the 1950s both Sobhuza's Johannesburg houses were slated for demolition by the government. In 1950 the newly elected National Party passed its infamous Group Areas Act, designating specific areas for particular racial groups. Black residents of areas that the authorities deemed "white"—such as Sophiatown, right in the heart of Johannesburg—were expelled to areas allocated for Black occupation, always cynically located in places far from the city. In 1955 Sobhuza's houses were destroyed when two thousand policemen armed with guns and ridged truncheons called "knobkerries" descended upon Sophiatown residents to start the brutal process of "forceable removal" to the plains of Soweto.[3]

Although a younger Sobhuza could not have foreseen his properties' destruction, he did recognize as early as the 1930s the quickening march of racial segregation. For this reason, Sobhuza took keen interest in the newly emerging discipline of social anthropology, seeing it a potential ally in his struggle against white rule. Sobhuza was a frequent fixture at the city's intellectual offerings from the 1930s onward. He mingled with the cream of Black Johannesburg society at lectures hosted by the Bantu Sports Club and the Bantu Social Centre and attended joint council conferences where white and Black elites met to debate social problems. He was also frequently at Wits University anthropology seminars and subscribed to ethnographic journals like *Bantu Studies*. Sobhuza was close friends with the anthropologist Hilda Kuper, whom he'd first welcomed to his country in the 1930s when she did fieldwork in Eswatini. Additionally, Sobhuza frequently corresponded with Kuper's doctoral adviser in London, Bronisław Malinowski.[4]

Sobhuza's interest in anthropology was part of his lifelong quest for freedom for his subjects. By the mid-1950s, fertile and mineral-rich Eswatini faced forces threatening its survival. From without, the threat was the same as for the last half century: a land-greedy Union of South Africa wanted to amalgamate Eswatini—one hundred miles long, eighty miles wide—into its borders. The question of "incorporation of the protectorates" (not only Eswatini but also Basutoland [now Lesotho] and Bechuanaland [now Botswana]) had even been named as an impending reality by the architects of the 1910 constitution of the new Union of South Africa.[5] Since his inauguration as paramount chief in 1921 at the age of only twenty-two, Sobhuza had devoted himself to blocking South African ambitions to cannibalize his country. Much of this was persuasion. Sobhuza skillfully invoked a supposedly superior British sense of justice to protect Eswatini against its powerful South African neighbor. After the election of an avowedly racist government in South Africa in 1948, Sobhuza's chosen path was still diplomacy and deal brokering rather than outright opposition. It was for this reason that Sobhuza had commanded his subjects in South Africa not to take part in the Defiance Campaign of 1952. He correctly foresaw the campaign would not succeed and would result in further oppression and even loss of life. Why should his people languish in South African jails for nothing? he is said to have asked Hilda Kuper.[6]

Within Eswatini's border the threat came from the British administration. Since the early twentieth century, British officials had tried to limit the powers of the indigenous monarchy, forbidding Sobhuza's subjects to address their monarch as "King" and mandating the lesser nomenclature of "Paramount Chief." However, in recent years the administration's stance had changed. Post–World War II Britain displayed greater interest in allying with indigenous leaders in places like Eswatini, paired with a recognition that independence for African colonies was on the horizon. It was a question of when, not if. Responding to these political transformations, Sobhuza doubled down on a strategy he'd been pursuing since the 1930s. This was to play the game of ethnic nationalism: casting present-day Eswatini as a political entity laying claim to a glorious history and reviving cultural traditions as supposedly practiced by emaSwati since time immemorial. In this way, Sobhuza bolstered his argument for Eswatini's legitimacy as an independent nation-state of venerable standing—deserving of freedom from both British and South African interference—as well as pandered to British preference for dealing with "traditional" political authorities as part of their indirect-rule policy. Incidentally, after 1948 Sobhuza's project also resonated with Afrikaner officials' opinion that the state should govern Africans along "tribal" lines.[7]

Anthropologists were crucial allies. Malinowski at the London School of Economics became Sobhuza's adviser as the latter resuscitated the traditional age-grade system—in which "regiments" of young men were organized according to age, with each subgroup allocated certain duties linked to national welfare. Hilda Kuper also became a firm friend in this neotraditionalist endeavor, writing an article outlining the significance of the regimental system in 1937.[8] Also in the 1930s, in conversation with Kuper and Malinowski, Sobhuza was reviving the Incwala, a historic ceremony for soliciting rain that also served as a ritual of kingly power. Performed by thousands of young men at Sobhuza's Lobamba palace in the shadow of the Mdzimba Mountains, the ceremony underlay Sobhuza's effort to assert his status as the nation's rainmaker and hence his supreme political and spiritual authority. Kuper's publications on the Incwala—dating from the 1930s onward—were invaluable to Sobhuza, providing his innovations with the stamp of expert ethnographic approval.[9] Casting Eswatini as a bastion of traditional culture also meant repudiating Western ways. Sobhuza criticized missionary-run education, claiming it alienated emaSwati from their traditional ways. Instead, he instituted "national schools" in which teachers instructed children not to "despise their traditions."[10] By the 1950s Sobhuza's strategy was paying dividends. In 1950 the British administration passed several "native proclamations" that significantly enhanced Sobhuza's powers over his people under the guise of traditionalism.[11]

The Swati diaspora in South Africa was key to Sobhuza's nationalist project. By the middle of the twentieth century, more emaSwati lived outside of Eswatini than within (a situation that still prevails today). Partly this was due to Eswatini's disastrous loss of land to Afrikaner concessionaires in the nineteenth century.[12] But the diasporic community also increased because the British placed extraordinarily high taxation on emaSwati men and the largely rural economy still had scant employment opportunities. EmaSwati men—and increasing numbers of women—migrated to South Africa for work and especially to Johannesburg's gold mines. Sobhuza recognized the city was an important source of taxation revenue. After all, lining the coffers of the monarchy was a crucial part of ethnic patriotism. Sobhuza thus visited the city frequently, even appointing an influential chief, Michael kaDlamini, to oversee emaSwati affairs in Johannesburg during his absences.[13]

As prominent Johannesburg emaSwati, both Gelana and Dan knew Sobhuza. Dan, of course, was a liSwati, although born in South Africa in Barberton, a tiny village tucked in high mountains near the Swati border. His Methodist minister father, Reuben, had fluidly moved across the mountainous border as he tended to peoples' souls, suggesting the boundary's irrelevance for most people. Dan similarly exemplified a seamless loyalty to both Eswatini and South Africa: a lifelong resident of South Africa, he was nonetheless adviser to the Swazi National Royal Club and coordinated grand receptions for Sobhuza at the sports club.[14] He was also warmly welcomed by Sobhuza on his frequent trips to Eswatini. A 1950 visit with a Johannesburg soccer team for an away game resulted in an honorary "beast" (a cow), personally provided by Sobhuza, being ceremonially slaughtered for the visitors and devoured at a postmatch feast.[15]

Both as the wife of a prominent liSwati, and an exceptionally accomplished woman in her own right, Gelana became Sobhuza's close friend. As much as Sobhuza promoted the notion of Swati culture free from European influence, Western-style education was actually key to his project (evident also from the involvement of European-trained anthropologists like Kuper and Malinowski). Sobhuza's invented tradition was eclectic, and despite his professed repudiation of Western ways, he in fact sought to amalgamate the old and the new in a happy and intensely modern synthesis. For this reason, Sobhuza was interested in the small and growing group of Western-style educated emaSwati, individuals who had attended universities in South Africa and further afield and qualified as doctors, lawyers, and other professionals. Sobhuza recognized this class's significance in preparing the nation for independence from Britain (doubtless also discerning this was precisely the kind of person the British would do business with). A rare university-educated Black woman like Gelana—trained in anthropology, no less—was an enticing prospect for a Swati ruler determined to co-opt educated elites.

It was for this reason that Sobhuza had supplied an impressive delegation of emaSwati councillors and princes to Gelana's Wits graduation ceremony in 1948. While unable to attend, Sobhuza sent his sister, Princess Nkosi, to personally represent him at

FIGURE 12.1. Gelana Twala (*far left*) with Swati princesses at *Bantu World* offices, Johannesburg, 1945 (*Bantu World*, August 4, 1945, Historical Papers Research Archive, University of the Witwatersrand)

FIGURE 12.2. "The Swazi Royal Party at the 'Welcome Home' General Smuts Ceremony" with Gelana Twala (*seated on right*), Johannesburg, 1945 (Pinokie Twala)

Gelana's graduation ball at the Bantu Sports Club and hosted a reception for her in Eswatini to honor her achievement (claiming her as the first liSwati woman to gain a degree).[16] When Sobhuza's daughters visited Johannesburg in 1946, it was Gelana whom Sobhuza selected as the princesses' guide and chaperone on their tour of the city's highlights.[17] Gelana was also a member of the Swati royal party welcoming home Gen. Jan Smuts at the war's end. All these were unmistakable marks of royal favor. In 1950, when Sobhuza's Johannesburg representative, Chief Michael, died, and his new representative was installed in Johannesburg at a huge ceremony in Sophiatown, the only woman to stand and give a speech before the two thousand people was Gelana. Signaling her incorporation as an honorary liSwati, Gelana's promise made during the speech was that, as an educated pioneer, she would "pave the way by organizing Swazi women in the Transvaal."[18]

For Sobhuza, Gelana was much more than merely an inspiring example of what Black women could achieve against the odds. Even better, Gelana was developing with Sobhuza a shared interest in anthropology as the preeminent route to African emancipation.

This had already started percolating during Gelana's Wits days while taking anthropology classes with Hilda Kuper. While a university student (and also in the year or two after she graduated), Gelana did several bouts of fieldwork in Eswatini in connection with a research paper on the Incwala ceremony. While the paper is lost, we do have the letters she exchanged with Dan during these trips. Their correspondence shows the city-dwelling Gelana struggling with the conditions of the remote protectorate. She fretted about the rural setting (requesting that Dan post her a "lantern, torch, washing soap, bathing soap, ink, toothpaste, red and black boot polish"), Vusi's poor health—he was only a toddler at this point—in the hot weather ("Vusi sweats like a lizard. . . . I am so frightened he will take [the whooping cough]"), and her difficulties buying food ("things are very dear here").[19]

Yet throughout, the figure of Sobhuza shines through as a beacon of kindness, transforming inhospitable Eswatini into a welcoming refuge. Rueful references to the dire weather (December is the rainy season)—"it has been raining and thundering like Hell. I am frightened as usual"—sit alongside Gelana's warm mentions of the Ingwenyama: how "kind" he was, how he "called us to his office and explained everything about the Incwala to me from 4pm to 6pm, he was so well disposed and so kind."[20] Sobhuza attentively plied Gelana with gifts—a car and a driver, meat, potatoes and onions for her and Vusi's meals, one of his daughters to accompany her to ceremonies[21]—and instructed her in the mysteries of Swati culture and the little-known methods—the "secret science"—behind the Incwala ceremony: "He explained to me that to understand Incwala one must understand the secret science behind African Medicine."[22]

When in 1954 Gelana learned she'd landed four years of funding to continue her research in Eswatini, Sobhuza must have been thrilled. Gelana's project to undertake graduate-level research on Swati women was funded by the Nuffield Foundation to the extremely generous tune of £700 annually (about $16,000 in today's money).[23] She would be supervised by Hilda Kuper, who was attached to the Institute of Social Research at University of Natal as a consultant, this being a period during which Kuper was without a formal university post. Kuper brokered introductions between Gelana and British administrators. Gelana, of course, needed no introduction to Sobhuza.[24] By the mid-1950s, Gelana was living full time in Eswatini, only occasionally visiting Durban to see Kuper and institute colleagues.[25] Sobhuza warmly welcomed Gelana, giving her a plot of land on which to build a home in the new residential area of Kwaluseni and, according to Gelana's daughter-in-law, Anne, gifting materials to roof her new home.[26] Situated on the outskirts of the business hub of Bremersdorp (shortly to be renamed as Manzini), Kwaluseni was close to Sobhuza's palace, making it—as Sobhuza put it—"under the Royal one, part of the Royal Household."[27] Residents of the 1960s remember how Sobhuza was a regular presence in Bremersdorp, just down the road from Gelana's new home in Kwaluseni. His driver would ferry him from his nearby palace at Lozitha, park outside the Paramount Hotel—a popular watering hole—and

FIGURE 12.3. Gelana Twala's house, Kwaluseni, Eswatini, 2022 (Carla Cabrita)

Sobhuza would hold informal court from his car, "leaning out his window and calling people. . . . People would kneel on the pavement [i.e., sidewalk] and talk to him."[28]

Kwaluseni was where many members of the Black middle classes were making their home, but its appearance meant European observers snottily dismissed it a "slum."[29] These critics did not perceive that behind the lack of running water or electricity, its residents were BA degree holders like Gelana, whose neighbors were people like Ambrose Zwane—Eswatini's first Black doctor—and Douglas Lukhele, the first Swati lawyer and like Gelana a political exile from South Africa (having formerly worked in the Mandela & Tambo law firm).[30] Gelana set about making Kwaluseni her home, the first time she had lived separately from Dan in twenty years. With her, she had Vusi, Mary, and a six-month-old baby girl named Zanele.[31] The mother of both Zanele and Mary was Elizabeth, the wife of Dan's brother, Shadrack. After Shadrack's death, Dan had cared for Elizabeth and her children, including taking in Mary. Zanele, however, was subsequently fathered by Dan. When Gelana relocated to Eswatini, the decision was taken to send Baby Zanele to Eswatini with her stepmother, a move that suggests the expansive nature of family for Gelana, even when infidelity was involved. Zanele grew up thinking she was Gelana's biological daughter (only traumatically disabused of this the day of Gelana's funeral), and she has affectionate memories of a strict but loving mother.[32] While Zanele was too small to help, both Mary and Vusi helped Gelana build the house, mixing cement and setting bricks: "All the children helped build the Kwaluseni house," Mary Twala recounted to me.[33] A neat red-roofed structure rose up. Continuing the love of gardening she'd first showed in her Orlando yard, Gelana made the most of Kwaluseni's subtropical climate by planting fruit trees around her house—papayas, bananas, mangos, avocados—and cultivated maize to feed her family. Both Mary and Zanele remembered Gelana would be up at dawn, tending to her plants and hoeing her fields.[34]

Alongside homebuilding, Gelana's 1950s were largely devoted to research. Despite her Nuffield proposal's mention of "culture contact," in truth her research during these years presented Swati women as unchanged from time immemorial. Her research prospectus states she would investigate women's traditional food preparation ("wild food plants and fruits as well as garden vegetables" and "custom and taboo with preparing food") as well as traditional utensils women used in the kitchen ("grass containers, baked clay containers, gourds and calabashes"). An interest in women and cooking was not just theoretical for Gelana; her ideological commitment to African ingredients manifested in her own kitchen in Kwaluseni. When I interviewed Zanele in her Eswatini home in 2019, she fondly told me of childhood memories of cooking with her mother and especially cooking indigenous leafy greens—"which I hated, ugh!" Gelana even fashioned Zanele a small wooden stool so she could stretch up to the stove to help as Gelana cooked.[35] All in all, the traces of emaSwati undergoing the momentous cultural changes of the 1950s are slight. Gelana only briefly mentioned the "diet of urban Swazi women in Johannesburg" and "the impact of new institutions on Swazi society." Reflecting the nostalgic mood of the 1950s and Sobhuza's own preference for a romantic view of the past, most of Gelana's proposal dealt with "tradition" cast in a timeless mold.[36]

Research-wise, Gelana was especially interested in the craft of beadwork, which had a particularly robust existence in 1950s Eswatini. Gelana had been interested in beads since the early 1940s, bringing home to Johannesburg new purchases of beads each time she and Dan visited Eswatini.[37] Not content only to collect samples, Gelana also wanted to learn the craft (bringing to mind her fondness for dressmaking and other handwork that we first noted in the context of her Indaleni Mission days). In a letter written to Dan during a 1942 holiday in Eswatini, she confessed she wanted to use her time there "to learn beads, someone who has been in the kraals [traditional homesteads] will teach me."[38] But by 1948 Gelana still didn't possess this knowledge. When Violaine

Junod introduced beadwork as a women's activity at Entokozweni, she found none of her African staff, including Gelana, had any practical knowledge of this. So Junod learned beadwork herself and claimed that she then taught her Black employees (including Gelana), who then taught Alex's women.[39] Did Gelana learn this most "traditional" craft, a cornerstone of her belief in African emancipation via culture, from a white social worker of racist

FIGURE 12.4. Gelana Twala wearing a bead necklace she made, ca. 1940s (Pinokie Twala)

leanings? If so, this anecdote highlights the invented nature of the African traditions Gelana celebrated. Appeals to indigeneity often masked a messy hybrid of African and Western elements. We see something similar in Sobhuza's invocation of Swati tradition.

Whatever the source of her knowledge, beads now moved to the heart of Gelana's research. Beadwork exemplified for Gelana the beauty of African culture independent from European influence (despite the possible involvement of Junod as her instructor) and underscored Black women's dignity as economic and cultural producers. After her resignation from Entokozweni and during her years in Port Elizabeth, Gelana had begun to publish on beadwork—although where she found the time or the money prior to the Nuffield funding to finance trips to Eswatini is a mystery. The coexistence of Gelana's political activism and her anthropological research underscores that beadwork and defiance of the apartheid government were not on separate trajectories. Gelana both used the tools of political activism and made nostalgic reference to African tradition in service of a single goal of overturning a racist political system. Gelana's first article on beadwork—published by the renowned anthropological journal *African Studies*—appeared in 1951, the year before her arrest in the Defiance Campaign.[40]

In this and subsequent publications from the 1950s, beads were Gelana's way to argue for the resilience of traditional African society. While her arrest in 1952 spoke of her refusal to accept apartheid's dehumanizing terms, her beadwork publications emphasized the other side of the coin: her celebration of Black culture's dignity. Gelana examined different kinds of beads: those worn by women, by men, and by traditional healers and those used for decorative purposes and for utilitarian communication. (Young women would send male suitors intricately coded beaded messages.) All these showed her that "beads among the Bantu are used as a regulating agent . . . a method of controlling youth in society." Certain beads marked out certain stages of life. A young girl who had recently fallen in love gifted her beloved a bead necklace while herself wearing a single string of beads all in one color around her waist, wrist, and ankles. In this way she proclaimed her status as a girl transitioning to womanhood. And not only sex was regulated via beads. Commoners could not wear royal beads, for example, and thus Gelana argued beads maintained the aristocratic hierarchies of Swati society. While most bemoaned a Swati society that was dissolving due to "culture contact" with Europeans, Gelana showed how traditional "regulating agents"—beads, in this case—still powerfully gave societal coherence: "Beads help to keep each person's behavior within the prescribed sanctions of the group. . . . By beads, he is constantly reminded of his duty to society."[41] African society still worked, in other words. Gelana had swopped the politics of revolution for the politics of anthropology.

A fundamental paradox was that this was African politics that conservative white audiences could appreciate. Beadwork spoke to stereotypical white notions that Africans were intrinsically "other," tribal curiosities enmeshed in "queer customs" like beadwork. As well as publishing in academic journals, Gelana also wrote a popular series of articles in local newspapers aimed at white readers—who lauded her as "an expert on native lore."[42] Gelana's writings for the white press focused on the beaded "love letters," intricate multicolored creations that young women sent their male lovers. Through her textured descriptions of beads signaling the start of a romance or beads breaking off an engagement, Gelana made her case that beads preserved so-called traditional society, regulating romantic relations between women and men.[43] Gelana of course had her own long history as an ardent writer of love letters—to Dan Twala decades earlier. I like to imagine her attention to the nuances of passion-filled beadwork was informed by her intimate knowledge of the work such "letters" did in fanning longing for the other. Paradoxically (given Gelana's own mastery of the written letter), she also, surely incidentally, must have reinforced white prejudices of unschooled Africans, compelled to write in beads instead of with pen and paper.

White enthusiasts of African culture were not limited to professionally trained anthropologists like Hilda Kuper. A whole range of well-off white women of liberal leanings were establishing themselves as sympathetic promoters of "African art." A leading "expert" on beadwork was Killie Campbell, the daughter of a white Natal sugar baron and an eminent collector of so-called Africana, including Zulu and Swati beadwork.[44] Gelana was congratulated by Campbell on her "splendid articles."[45] Campbell's opinion of Gelana was she was "very worthwhile" and to this end supplied Gelana with reading lists on African beadwork. Of course, not a single African scholar was listed, a telling indictment of the all-white academic establishment Gelana was trying to break into. Campbell also brokered introductions for Gelana to other white enthusiasts. One of these was the artist Barbara Tyrrell, a painter from Richmond—located across the river from Gelana's hometown of eNdaleni—widely praised for her stylized drawings of African women and men in "traditional" dress, including beads.[46]

In positioning herself as an anthropologist of Swati culture and in gaining the novel and no doubt pleasant experience of acclaim from white readers, Gelana found herself in a curiously double position. She was both insider and outsider. On the one hand, as a Black African woman who spoke isiZulu (widely used in Eswatini of the 1950s) and as an honorary liSwati warmly welcomed by Sobhuza, Gelana enjoyed privileged access to the culture she was studying, far beyond what a white researcher would experience. Yet, as an ethnographer, Gelana was a scrutinizing outsider, armed with a university degree and a notebook, seeking an "objective" perspective on her research subjects. I find it significant that Gelana wrote her pieces on beadwork as "R. G. Twala," burying both "Gelana" and "Regina" in favor of gender-neutral and relatively anonymous initials. It was as if she were effacing Gelana by a new persona, that of the expert anthropologist. Gelana emphasized her ethnographic credentials—the learned R. G. Twala, BA, University of the Witwatersrand—to present herself to white South African readers as an authoritative explicator of African cultures.

Gelana's written work for white audiences leaned into this role of learned interpreter of Black culture. She occupied an ironic distance from the traditions she described, and as the expert ethnographer she claimed no part in them. Her ethnography published in *African Studies* recounted to readers the adventure of pretending "to be a Swati": how she "one day decided to dress myself up in tribal fashion. . . . I had on a lihhiya [traditional cloth worn by women] I had borrowed and I went into a fowl run and got some white feathers and arranged them in my hair as the Swazi do."[47] Although she might "pretend to dress [her]self in tribal fashion," if anything this only accentuated the divide between her and ema-Swati women. Gelana also parsed Swati custom in terms she imagined would be familiar to her white readers. In an article on the Umhlanga ceremony—an annual dance performed by unmarried girls—Gelana described how a girl whose hair was saturated in river mud as part of the preparations refused to appear in public. Gelana confidingly explained to her imagined reader why this reticence was entirely understandable: "In Western culture, you would not expect any sensible woman to go out amongst strangers with curlers in her hair."[48]

Despite her focus on the seemingly apolitical world of female dress, Gelana's interest in Swati tradition was not a retreat from politics. Nor should we take her shifting authorial voice and ethnographic distance from her research subjects as reflective of a lack of solidarity with Black Africans. Rather, in Gelana's reading, culture was political—even if it was culture imagined in an exoticized guise, ready-made for white consumption, and created to scrutinize Black life from a distance. For as Gelana worked on her study of ema-Swati women—their beadwork, dress, cooking, gardening, courtships, and childrearing—she was mobilizing this knowledge for political ends. From her Johannesburg training as a social worker, Gelana had held the view that Africans' progress depended upon the uplift of womenfolk. In her mind, traditional handicrafts, far from a nostalgic remnant of a fast-disappearing past, were also the way of the future. Women already knew how to make these items. If they could only be encouraged and helped to sell them by society at large, they would be set upon a path to economic independence.

Gelana hit upon the idea of launching a new organization to teach emaSwati women beadwork, one that would then help them sell their wares. Sobhuza was warmly supportive, deeming the project a perfect fusion of economic modernization with Swati tradition. Moreover, it would transform women into economically productive units without having them leave their homes, something in keeping with his patriarchal ethos. At a meeting launching the initiative in 1958, Sobhuza maintained "it has long been my question that girls leave school having learnt these crafts but could never use their knowledge profitably, they lacked a market for their crafts."[49] As a sign of his support, Sobhuza "gave" Gelana the woman widely rumored to be his favorite wife as the project's patron. This was La Masuku, of artistic bent and twenty years younger than Gelana. La Masuku was already interested in traditional crafts. Now Gelana began to teach La Masuku beadwork; from there, both fanned out throughout the country to train women to make these items in their own homes.[50] Sobhuza named their new organization Zakhe Ngwane—"Build Up Eswatini"—and gave the enterprising pair a site at the Bremersdorp Market, a few miles from Kwaluseni. Public opinion warmed to the project. When a nearby luxury hotel catering for wealthy South African tourists started selling beaded items, there was public outcry that this unfairly undercut Zakhe Ngwane.[51] Dan also helped the organization by accepting items to sell in Johannesburg, where they found an enthusiastic market.[52]

It was also around this time that Gelana initiated another project aimed at emaSwati women. This time, though, instead of emphasizing Swati culture, she appealed to the value of Western-style literacy. By the early 1960s there was not a single library for Black readers in the country (although whites in the protectorate could access books in a small private library in Mbabane).[53] Deeming this a great national failing, in 1960, Gelana founded a small one-room library for Black readers located in Kwaluseni opposite the Swazi National School, which had been founded decades earlier by Sobhuza as a corrective to Western missionary education. The postal services awarded Gelana a former post office building to house the library, and she procured books through a combination of fundraising (organizing rummage sales) and requesting donations of second-hand titles (although reminding the public that "care should be used that the standard is high").[54] Genius Aphane, the young son of her neighbor Janet Aphane, would help her out after his school day had ended (he was a boy who "liked to read"), and Gelana taught him how to "clean the library, clean the books, and put them back on the shelves."[55] Gelana named her new library the "Prince Mfanyana Memorial Library" (celebrating Abner Mfanyana Dlamini, a member of the Swati royal family and an educated liSwati teacher who had recently died), and she provided books clearly aimed at a female readership, on "embroidery, cooking, knitting, mothercraft." Her long-term and "most ambitious plan" was to use the structure for night classes for "those who were unable to finish their schooling." One imagines that, here again, women were her intended target. The public—both white settlers and emaSwati—applauded Gelana for her initiative. The *Times of Swaziland* praised her "valiant" work for the "advancement of her people," while the isiZulu-language *Izwi lama Swazi* [Voice of the Swati] lauded the "important" work that had caused Gelana to "become prominent, even overseas."[56]

Whether her projects were envisioned in a neotraditionalist or modernizing mode, key to both the Kwaluseni library and Zakhe Ngwane was Gelana's conviction that whites should not be involved. This was self-help by and for emaSwati women. A speech Gelana had given in Eswatini, some eight years earlier, was emphatic on this point: "To the Swazi people my message to you is that you must learn to do things for yourself. The Europeans among you should only guide you, but do not ask them to do things for you."[57] This was a growing feeling among emaSwati. A 1958 editorial in one of the country's two national newspapers maintained that insofar as women's activities such as Zakhe Ngwane went, "the wives of our European officials could do a lot to make such institutes a success but the main part of the work should be done by emaSwati themselves. . . . We know there are many Swati women who could do a great deal to help other women and girls."[58] Gelana's beadwork teacher may have been a white woman, but ten years later beadwork was her way to give this message to European women: stay out.

# 13

# God

I hope you will get something out of this. I have done my best.

—Gelana to Bengt Sundkler, July 26, 1958 (Bengt Sundkler Papers, box 110, Uppsala Archives)

God—as much as beadwork—was an ally for Black uplift. During the 1950s the newly radicalized Gelana underwent a religious conversion twinning her political awakening. In this latter-life conversion, Gelana rejected the Methodist Christianity of her early years. In its place, she embraced a more radical God, one who taught African believers to embrace their Black identity and reject Western Christianity's racism. While Gelana's spiritual revolution solidified during her early years in Eswatini, in fact this was a development that had begun earlier, during her time in Port Elizabeth. In addition to radical politics, Port Elizabeth was also where Gelana "got God"—as a useful Pentecostal phrase would have it.

This is not to say Gelana did not have a Christian faith before her time in the Windy City. As we have already seen, Gelana was raised as part of a long-standing Methodist family deeply rooted in the Indaleni Mission. She was no "Sunday Christian": Gelana played the organ for services at Indaleni, she led Bible studies and read Scriptures daily, and she prized her shared Methodist faith with Dan. Throughout the 1930s and 1940s, she punctuated her letters to Dan with mentions of her daily prayers and the Christian literature she pored over.[1] Her faith faltered during the hard years of her separation from Percy Kumalo, yet it ultimately endured stronger than ever, becoming a great solace during her efforts to conceive. Yet Gelana's faith of these decades was still a Christianity largely aligned with European missionary values. Old Indaleni missionaries like Reverend Cragg promulgated a harshly judgmental attitude toward African traditions, conflating Christianity with allegiance to conservative Edwardian norms.[2] Despite her own disillusionment with these norms (many of which she also bucked), I have no evidence that throughout the 1930s and 1940s Gelana ever contemplated leaving the Methodist church. She and Dan continued to attend services in Orlando, as well as ensured that their son, Vusi, was formally welcomed within the church soon after his birth.[3]

But by the early 1950s Gelana discovered a new God. This was a deity who symbolized Black pride, a god who denounced any correlation between Western-style Christianity and spiritual virtue. During her time in Port Elizabeth, Gelana started attending the services of Nicholas Bhengu, the popular founder and leader of a South African branch of the worldwide Pentecostal Assemblies of God church. By the 1950s Bhengu was widely known as the South African "Billy Graham." He had become famous throughout South Africa and internationally for his massive "Back to God" campaigns. Bhengu would pitch a tent in a town, hold a series of revival meetings over the course of several weeks, and invite largely working-class attendees to confess their sins and embrace Jesus Christ. In typical Pentecostal style, the services were renowned for criminals tearfully giving up their old lives and turning to God. Services ended with "piles of knives, blackjacks, brass knuckles, stolen goods"—all tokens of the old life of sin—heaped at the altar.[4]

We can partly understand Gelana's admiration for Bhengu in intimate terms. Her Pentecostal faith offered a language to criticize

Dan for his unfaithfulness. Bhengu was especially outspoken about the unraveling of traditional sexual mores and sympathetic to the predicament of women who found their husbands strayed amid the temptations of modern life in the city. Pentecostal-style Christianity, with its uncompromising stance on sexual virtue, became useful fodder for Gelana to attack Dan for his relationship with Margaret Mmope. Unfortunately, we have none of Gelana's letters to Dan on this topic (their correspondence significantly shrunk during their decades apart in the 1950s and 1960s), but we do have Dan's replies to her and their tone gives us some sense of the content of Gelana's missives. In April 1952 Dan instructed Gelana to "try more self-denying love, and you will not need your Bible, your prayers, your tears and your vindictiveness."[5] Several days later, Dan fumed that Gelana dared patronize him on matters of faith, despite his status as the son of Reuben Twala, one of the first Black Methodist ministers in Southern Africa. Dan condescendingly reminded Gelana of her place, elevating his membership in the Black religious aristocracy against her upstart Pentecostalism: "I am, for your information, a son of the [Methodist] Manse. I come from a family that boasts of having given to Christianity the best man power in Ministers, Prayer Women, Preachers and Devotees. You need not have any misgivings about that. In fact, you yourself owe what you are through my religious faith."[6]

Bhengu's church taught Gelana differently. Pentecostals like Bhengu spurned institutional Christianity like the supposedly respectable Methodist tradition Dan hailed from. What was important was purity of heart, dedicated commitment to Jesus, and a life of Christian virtue (all areas where the adulterous Dan fell short). Bhengu's church also became a means to further express Gelana's sense that Africans should be independent of white influence and free to develop more culturally authentic ways of being Christian. Bhengu was an ardent advocate of Black pride. Yet he was not explicitly political in orientation. He insisted Christians look to God rather than reform the secular political system.[7] During the 1952 Defiance Campaign, Bhengu was criticized by Manilal Gandhi (whom Gelana would march alongside in the Germiston protest) for being a sellout because he did not leverage his popularity for the cause.[8] But Bhengu *was* disturbed by the injustices of apartheid, something he vocally communicated to his huge following. Yet rather than political protest, Bhengu believed a crucial part of the struggle was strengthening Black self-confidence and dignity. For this reason, his sermons often stressed Christianity's African ancestry, telling listeners that Christianity had been in Africa long before Europe and that key biblical figures—Abraham, for example—had all sojourned in Africa.[9]

Gelana's connection with Bhengu continued after she moved to Eswatini. In 2018 I interviewed Elizabeth Shalala in Eswatini. By then a very elderly woman, Mrs. Shalala had been part of Bhengu's church in Port Elizabeth from its earliest days. Speaking to me from her Kwaluseni living room, she remembered how Gelana visited her Port Elizabeth church in 1956 (once Gelana was already living in Eswatini). Gelana stood up and shared her vision with the congregation. God had directly told her Bhengu should expand into Eswatini, leading her to plead with Bhengu and the church as a whole: "I am crying out for these revivals to come to Swaziland!"[10] Bhengu seems to have heeded the call from Gelana, God's messenger, as Gelana subsequently introduced Bhengu to Sobhuza II, who felt Bhengu's Black pride message chimed with his neotraditionalist agenda. She also helped Bhengu negotiate the expansion of his church into the country, leaning on her many connections to help him secure a plot for its first building.[11] It was no coincidence that Swati devotees built the first of Bhengu's Eswatini Assemblies of God churches in Kwaluseni around the corner from Gelana's home. Her daughter-in-law, Anne, told me that while the church was constructed, Gelana would host Sunday school in her front living room and play piano for the children's songs.[12] Throughout the 1950s and 1960s, Gelana attended Bhengu's large annual Christmas service in the town of East London, making the long pilgrimage from Eswatini to the Cape each December.[13]

Gelana's arrival in Eswatini also expanded her religious sensibilities in new directions. If Port Elizabeth had brought Gelana to Bhengu, it was Eswatini that now brought her to the Zionist churches. These were a loose federation of hundreds of evangelical churches, entirely African in leadership and membership, that had stemmed from a controversial faith-healing church in the American Midwest.[14] At the turn of the century, Illinois-based John Alexander Dowie—the self-proclaimed return of the prophet Elijah—had sent both testimonial literature and (white) missionaries to the Transvaal. The church quickly grew among both Blacks and whites of the whole Southern African region, many drawn by its promise of bodily health via prayer. By the 1950s the influence of the original midwestern church was slight. Its multiracial character had disappeared as white Zionists migrated to neighboring Pentecostal groups. Many now perceived Zionists as espousing a thoroughly Africanized Christianity, entirely forgetting their older links to white North American evangelicals. Zionists of this decade dubbed their leaders prophets—invoking their ability to diagnose the hidden spiritual cause of sickness—and combined indigenous medicine with Christian faith healing. European missionaries denounced these believers as backsliding sinners, syncretists who adopted African cosmologies.

Yet despite missionaries' censure (and the disapproval of Africans linked to more "respectable" churches), Zionists exponentially grew across Southern Africa. Navigating the restrictions placed upon them by colonial governments, churches rapidly mushroomed, meeting in cramped rooms in townships, praying on hillsides, and baptizing in rivers. Tired of lectures from missionaries for their supposed sin of syncretism, many African Christians welcomed Zionists' fusion of Christianity with indigenous religion. Not least due to the support of Sobhuza, as well as the heavy footfall of migrant laborers between South Africa and Eswatini, Zionists became especially formidable in Eswatini. By the 1940s Zionists accounted for half of all Swati Christians, and those numbers grew as the century progressed.[15]

By the 1950s an already close relationship between Zionist churches and Sobhuza had ripened. The Zionists were as close to a national church as it came. Zionist prophets argued that the Ingwenyama—Sobhuza—was divinely ordained, and they regularly lent their presence to key royal national rituals like Incwala. Each December, snowy-garbed Zionist prophets lined up shoulder to shoulder in support of Sobhuza, standing alongside emaSwati warriors wearing cloaks of cattle tails, heads studded with black and white feathers. Zionist leaders frequently used a biblical grammar of divinely ordained kingship to argue for Sobhuza's legitimacy. In 1956 a prominent Zionist published praises of Sobhuza in the national newspaper, *Izwi lama Swazi*: "Sobhuza is like Solomon of old in wisdom and his grandfather, Mbandzeni I, compares with Moses of old in Israel."[16] The queen mother—who coruled with Sobhuza and was enormously powerful—had herself converted to Zionism in the 1930s after being healed by a prominent Zionist healer in the country.[17] Zionists also gained standing in royal circles due to their ambivalent stance toward Western culture. While mission churches stressed book learning as part of the intertwined package of Christianity and civilization, Zionists insisted the only guidance for God's people was the Bible and the Holy Spirit.[18] Sobhuza welcomed Zionists' reluctance to partake in missionary education, seeing this a welcome sign of independence from Western influence. Zionists even sanctioned aspects of Swati culture that European missionaries denounced as satanic, including polygamy and venerating deceased ancestors. One prominent Zionist of the 1950s defended his church's adoption of indigenous practices on the grounds of patriotism: "One was worried whether the customs of the Swazi were found so wanting that it became necessary for customs of other nations to be superimposed on Swazis."[19]

Gelana took an intense interest in this. Even more than Bhengu's church perhaps, the Zionists seemed a compelling example of what a perfectly fused blend of African culture and Christianity might be.[20] They rejected European ways, paralleling Gelana's own fascination with Swati culture. And Zionists were also ardently Christian, preaching the necessity of salvation through Jesus Christ (much as Bhengu did). Moreover, living where she did in Kwaluseni, Gelana could hardly have ignored the Zionists. One of the oldest and largest Zionist denominations in the country, the Christian Catholic Apostolic Holy Spirit Church in Zion, had its headquarters in the small town of Ludzeludze, just over the rise and down a gentle valley from Kwaluseni, within earshot of her own house. (Zionists were a highly auditory church: weekends saw nightlong vigils punctuated with ecstatic prayers, speaking in tongues, and loud exorcisms.)[21] While she never became a Zionist herself, throughout all Gelana's years in Eswatini she allied with them on many occasions. In 1959, for example, she helped organize the Zionists' Easter service near Sobhuza's palace, persuading senior Zionists to invite her own religious mentor, Nicholas Bhengu, to address them.[22]

Gelana also aided Zionist leaders as they worked to fulfill a decades-long dream that their many denominations unite into a single national church. The Swati monarch had long identified a national church as crucial to his push for self-rule. Reconciling the squabbling denominations of Western missionaries, a single Swati church—named Isonto La Makrestu (Church of Christ)—would echo the unity of the emaSwati people and form a strong foundation for impending nationhood. Prince Madevu, the royal architect of the single-church idea, identified Gelana's unique talents as the most highly educated Black woman in the country as strategic for the movement. At Madevu's request, Gelana assisted in drawing up documents for the new national church, taking on "edit[ing] and put[ing] into good English the constitution of Isonto ke Makrestu [*sic*]."[23] In 1957 the League of Zionist Churches—the organization that worked for the creation of the single church—considered Gelana as a candidate for the influential position of secretary, but this never came to pass. Women—in the 1950s as today—did not hold formal leadership positions within this highly patriarchal structure.[24] Gelana was fast learning

Swati organizations had very little room for women in leadership roles, a bitter lesson she would continue to be exposed to throughout her political activity of the 1960s.

Gelana also began to undertake ethnographic research into the Zionist churches. Yet unlike her research into Swati beadwork, this was not her own project. She researched the Zionists as a paid assistant, the first time she had offered herself as a researcher-for-hire to another scholar. In 1958 Bengt Sundkler—the esteemed Swedish Lutheran church historian—affiliated with Gelana's own ISR in Durban.[25] Some ten years earlier, Sundkler had written the definitive ethnographic monograph on Zionist churches in South Africa, *Bantu Prophets in South Africa* (1948).[26] His interpretation of the Zionists was in keeping with the spirit of the time. As a

FIGURE 13.1. Bengt Sundkler, Uppsala University, 1957 (Upplandmuseet, Uppsala)

European missionary, he could only bemoan their syncretistic practices as "the bridge over which Africans are brought back to heathenism."[27] Yet by the late 1950s, with decolonization on the horizon for the African continent, many missionaries revised their hostile stance. Where previous missionaries had viewed Zionists as syncretistic, now they saw laudable indigenization, an Africanization of Christianity complementing an era of political independence. Echoing this newly celebratory spirit, Sundkler decided to update his book on Zionists by revising his older critical statements about syncretism. He also wanted to incorporate a chapter on Zionists in Eswatini in the second edition, recognizing their powerful role in the protectorate. But Sundkler was only in Southern Africa for six months in 1958, after which he had to return to his teaching duties at Uppsala University. As for his first book, Sundkler hired several African researchers to do much of the research, which largely involved conducting interviews with church leaders and supplying accounts of religious services they had attended.[28]

Already affiliated with the ISR and living in Eswatini, Gelana would have seemed a natural choice for a research assistant. Furthermore, by 1958 Gelana was in financial trouble; her Nuffield funding was fast running out.[29] Dan was struggling to support so many children (yet more had arrived with Margaret), and he could not offer much financial help to Gelana during these years.[30] But although there was a financial motivation for accepting the commission, there was also Gelana's genuine commitment to African religion free from European influence. She considered the Zionists a parallel to what she had celebrated in Swati beadwork—albeit in the realm of religion rather than the arts. So, throughout the late 1950s, Gelana attended numerous Zionist services and conducted interviews with prominent prophets, all at the behest of Sundkler. There was even an ultimately abortive plan for Gelana to assist Sundkler in making an ethnographic film on Swati Zionists; Gelana would have traveled with the film to Sweden and supplied "running commentary" on it during screenings.[31]

Bengt Sundkler's archives are in the Carolina Library at Uppsala University. His papers are copious and jumbled, still awaiting full cataloging. Gelana's research reports for Sundkler are hard to find but unmistakable when finally unearthed. Signed off by "R. D. Twala," there are twenty-five pages of carefully typed-out reports on Zionist life in Eswatini in 1958 and 1959. The writing is authoritative and the depth of knowledge unmistakable. In these pages, Gelana argues the Zionists were a thoroughly Africanized Christianity. She made her case meticulously. This was a body of work Gelana proudly confessed to Sundkler she had "done her best" with. As she explained to him, she had conscientiously "tried to give a tidious [*sic*] account of all that happened because I feel that what I may leave out as unimportant may perhaps give you a useful clue."[32] Her careful footnotes cited recent local newspaper reports, added elaborations on fine points of language and local botany, and comprehensively cited the work of other scholars of Eswatini, most of all Hilda Kuper. Due to Gelana's high personal standing with the Zionists, she could also supply Sundkler with official minutes of executive meetings, a precious resource I myself have used in my own writings on Zionist history.[33] Sundkler must have been thrilled with this rich cache from this exceptionally accomplished "assistant." Indeed, were it a different era, and were it not for the binds of race and gender, it is not inconceivable that Gelana herself would have occupied the role of the professional academic, commissioning her juniors to undertake paid research on her behalf.

Salaried scholar or not, Gelana used Sundkler's project to further develop her theories on African tradition. Her reports for him became a platform to argue for Swati Zionism as a form of Christianity in keeping with African values, much along the lines of what she had so valued in Nicholas Bhengu's Assemblies of God church. In late 1959, for example, Gelana attended services run by a Zionist prophet in her hometown of Kwaluseni. She transcribed, typed out, and translated the Christian hymns she had heard at these services, proclaiming one in particular "very popular with the Zionists." Through highlighting this composition, Gelana was partly underscoring for Sundkler the limitations of white missionary Christianity. The song criticized European missionary Christianity for its divisive factionalism as well as made a plea for unity among African churches, based on the unity they observed between the persons of the Trinity: "Jesus, united with Father and Spirit! They are united and love one another; They do not part. Well, whom do we copy?"

Gelana's exegesis of the hymn also conveyed her view that Zionists represented a truer African Christianity than mission religion. Gelana instructed Sundkler to "take note of the wording [of the song] which brings out the clearly African concept." She argued the specifically musical elements of the song—its rhythm and its pace—communicated a proudly African Christianity independent of European influence. As Gelana told Sundkler, "Zionists say European composed songs are too dull and out of context with the feelings of the people of Africa." Along these lines, Gelana added a small note to her research notes (handwritten in the margins, almost as an afterthought, scribbled by her as she read over by paraffin lamp what she had written late at night, before sending it off in the morning at the Kwaluseni post office), informing Sundkler to "note in tribal life the songs are always accompanied by dancing or some other bodily movement or the swaying of the body, the characteristic which the Negroes of America took over with them, rhythm is in their veins. Western classics are not appreciated by our people."[34]

Yet even in the midst of Gelana's effusive appreciation for "tribal life," she still wrote about the emaSwati as an outsider. Gelana *was* an outsider. Despite her marriage to a prominent liSwati and her personal ties to Sobhuza, Gelana found the emaSwati unwilling to accept her, a Zulu woman, as one of their own. Gelana was one of hundreds of thousands of South Africans who had left their country due to the worsening political situation in the 1950s and 1960s; a good number of those fled to neighboring British protectorates like Eswatini. Many never truly acclimatized to their new countries, reporting feeling shunned even after many years.

We see a similar sentiment in Gelana's letters, despite her growing commitment to the country and her conviction that bolstering up Swati tradition was vital to autonomy from Britain. Gelana, for example, ruefully confessed to Sundkler that emaSwatis' still intact institution of kingship made them feel decidedly superior to more "lowly" Zulus such as herself: "There is no getting away that they really feel aristocratic, far more than the Zulu."[35] As she also told Sundkler in a tone of semihumorous frustration, "Swazis never hurry an affair. They leave for a period of time until you think you are out of trouble. Then one day they remember you and call you up to come and explain your behaviour."[36]

Yet at other moments, Gelana writes as one who identifies closely with her research subjects, even with the landscape within which they move. This is her account to Sundkler of a Zionist church calling its faithful to worship: "When Prophet Sibiya rings the bell for services the sound is carried as far as my house because of the echo of the hills."[37] Her own home was one of many Kwaluseni residences drawn into the auditory world of the Zionists. Gelana's more intimate tone in her Eswatini research contrasts with the self-consciously detached feel of her prior publications on beadwork. In this later work, she seems more willing to insert herself as an involved participant in rituals. Gelana's accounts for Sundkler have her kneeling, praying, and sitting alongside Zionist believers as one of them. To my mind, this suggests Gelana's growing affinity with emaSwati, despite the challenges she encountered as a Zulu woman. But this newly engaged tone also speaks of Gelana's new ethnographic style, a commitment to ethnography as an act of solidarity with those whom she studied (contrasting with more traditional conceptions of the ethnographer as a neutral and objective scholar). We will later see how this new ethnographic voice came to full maturity in her journalistic writings of the 1960s, under the pseudonym Intombazana. Solidarity yielded certain advantages. As an insider (at least in some senses), Gelana could access areas undoubtedly blocked to Sundkler or indeed to any white researcher. As she kneels and prays with Zionists and members of the royal family, her voice is a notable "we," rather than the more common ethnographic "they": "The Indlovukazi (Queen Mother) and two of her attendants rose and left, as did the ministers. . . . I followed them. We found the Indlovukazi on her verandah of her house and said 'Nkosi!' (Hail!). Then we knelt and prayed in concerted action."[38]

Gelana's work for Sundkler was also characterized by new intellectual confidence. Leaning on her privileged access to her research subjects, combined with her university education, she presented herself in her dealings with Sundkler as an accomplished expert. Despite her status as "assistant," there is no submissiveness in her letters: she addresses Sundkler as her intellectual equal rather than her employer. They are both ethnographers, after all, and Gelana is entirely confident in her scholarly authority. Gone is the deference she showed to Hilda Kuper in decades past. Gelana freely gives Sundkler advice on the future direction of his research ("I feel some of the film I took for the University of Natal should really belong to your research") as well as corrects his misperception of events.[39] Her tone is authoritative. She includes her own

FIGURE 13.2. Zionists, Eswatini, 1970s (Ludo Kuipers)

scholarly work in the roster of scholarship on Eswatini cited in her footnotes. On more than one occasion, Gelana directs Sundkler to her own research on Swati women, carried out under the auspices of the Nuffield grant. She is also obliged to note that it is as yet unpublished—something she passionately hoped to rectify in coming years. In the meantime, though, Gelana would continue to insert herself into the scholarly historiography, published or not. This is Gelana's handwritten footnote, supplied in support of her discussion of the role of the queen mother in the Zionist churches: "Noone [*sic*] should lay hands on the head of the Indlovukazi because it wears ematinta—sacred symbols of the Swazi Nation. Water cannot be poured on her head as a sign of baptism for the same reason [Handwritten note: See R. D. Twala THE SWAZI WOMAN—chapter on Indlovukazi. Unpublished yet.]"[40]

While Gelana lamented the unpublished status of her own work, her employer, Bengt Sundkler, had no such struggles. Oxford University Press published his book on Zionism in Eswatini and South Africa more than fifteen years later as *Zulu Zion and Some Swazi Zionists* (1976). Reviewers immediately hailed the chapter on Zionism as one of the most innovative and groundbreaking sections of the book.[41] In this chapter, and throughout the book, Sundkler revised his earlier condemnation of Zionist churches. Now he argued "the strait-jacket of White worship did not suit [Africans]. . . . There was a search for a place where the individual could feel 'at home' and where African rhythm and conviction could be expressed freely, convincingly, and worthily."[42] The chapter on Eswatini showed how Zionism—with its sanction of Sobhuza as divinely ordained—was a major force in soliciting loyalty of emaSwati to their king, thereby maintaining the so-called traditional order.[43] Gelana's material—services, songs, and sermons—allowed Sundkler to make this argument. As Sundkler noted in his preface to the book, "participating observation has been my ambition . . . in the circumstances, much less of it was possible than I would personally have wished."[44] Yet far from supplying merely raw data to Sundkler from which he drew his own learned conclusions, Gelana presented Sundkler with ready-made arguments. The portrayal of Zionists as a "tribalistic" force in the country was first her own, as was the richly textured detail of synergy between royal family and church.

But Sundkler's book barely mentions Gelana. His preface to *Zulu Zion* briefly references "the late Mrs. Regina D. Twala [who] established many contacts which I could not have made on my own."[45] But that is all. Sundkler reduces Gelana to a "fixer" who procured contacts for him rather than a coresearcher in her own right. Neglecting to properly acknowledge his research assistants was something Sundkler had a habit of doing, including with his previous book, *Bantu Prophets in South Africa*.[46] Doubtless this was common academic practice of the 1950s. Still, at least one contemporary South African scholar of the period criticized Sundkler for failing to acknowledge the work done for him by Black researchers.[47] Appropriation of others' work was thus a point Sundkler would surely have been sensitive about. Indeed, he even writes of his own "anticipation of the study to be made one day by an African scholar living much closer to the anguish and jubilation of the movement than [he] ever could be."[48] Seemingly, it did not cross his mind that one African scholar had already conducted a study, right under his very nose—and that was Gelana Twala. For Sundkler, scholars were only legible if white and of equal social footing.

A line-by-line reading of Sundkler's forty-page chapter on Swati Zionism reveals a shocking and entirely unattributed reliance upon Gelana's material. Sundkler constructed his historical narrative of the growth of Zionism in Eswatini relying on factual data Gelana supplied to him, entirely without acknowledgment. His presentation of rich primary material—songs, sermons, and interviews—implies these were the fruit of his own personal efforts. He presents her rich ethnographic observations from his perspective, audaciously drawing upon the first person as if he had attended these services rather than Gelana.[49] Most of all, though, Sundkler repeatedly appropriated Gelana's reports nearly word by word, passing her prose off as his own. Compare Gelana's research report for Sundkler written in 1958 with the published text of *Zulu Zion,* which appeared in 1976:

> *Gelana, sent to Sundkler in 1958:* A bell was rung, and that was a signal for all to find their staves and set out for Lobamba [Sobhuza's palace], then when the women began singing the congregation began marching in circles. The women with flags, emagosa, always led the way. This parade before the Church House is called kuhlehla, same term as used for warriors or age-groups when they dance or give a display before royalty.
>
> *Sundkler, published in 1976:* A bell was rung, the signal for all to find their "holy sticks" and to set out for Lobamba. The lady wardens (emagosa) bore flags and led the way. The women with sticks, while marching, would walk in circles, kuhlehla. This was the term used for warriors or age-groups when giving a dancing display before royalty.[50]

Gelana would die in 1968, nearly ten years before Sundkler published his book. I have found no correspondence giving any indication of her feelings on Sundkler's plagiarism of her work or any mention of it elsewhere. It seems painfully ironic that anthropology—Gelana's chosen medium for articulating African autonomy—became another venue where unequal power structures continued to silence her. And another irony: while Gelana struggled—and ultimately failed—to publish her own ethnographic book on Swati women, her research for Sundkler did appear in published form. But her published work was not attributed to Gelana Twala, its rightful author. Instead, it was subsumed into a book that established Bengt Sundkler—rather than Gelana—as a widely acclaimed expert on religion in Africa, unabashedly passed off by him as his own research. Gelana's experiences seem sadly in keeping with a lifelong pattern of her exploitation at the hands of white academics. The epithet I cited at the chapter's outset—Gelana's comment to Sundkler that "I hope you will get something out of this. I have tried my best"—seems nothing short of tragic.

But this is not solely a story of defeat. Gelana also put the research she completed for Sundkler to work in other channels. She kept copies of everything she posted to him in Uppsala. This material she recycled into fodder for her weekly column in the country's national newspaper, the *Times of Swaziland*, a forum for ideas about Swati identity, race, and religion. Although her voice was nearly extinguished through the published work of white anthropologists, throughout the decade of the 1960s Gelana still found other ways to make herself heard.

# 14

# Politics and Patriarchy

> Let us mention a few ways for a young husband to copy to feel secure in his "divine right" of being the head of the female species. It is strange that a man so robustly built and with so terrorising a voice reinforced by a big beard and whiskers should fear so feeble and delicate a creature with so squeaky a voice as a woman. Yet it is so. A man is forever on guard not to lose his dignity and rights in the face of a woman.
>
> —Intombazana, "For Men Only," *Times of Swaziland*, December 28, 1962

Friday was newspaper day. Manzini—which in 1960 discarded its colonial name of Bremersdorp in favor of a siSwati name—was suffused with a party atmosphere as white settlers poured into the agricultural hub from surrounding farms, eager to catch up with friends and get the latest news from the country's weekly English newspaper, the *Times of Swaziland*. Copies were bought from Bennett's, the white art deco store fringed with palm trees, and then consumed over drinks at the Paramount Hotel in the company of other well-lubricated white farmers and businessmen. (The

South African proprietor maintained separate bars for whites and Blacks—a "very hard somebody," in the words of Abel Mngomezulu, a former employee at the Paramount.)[1]

The *Times of Swaziland* was Eswatini's oldest newspaper. It had been established in 1897 by Allister Miller, a pernicious exploiter of Swati territory. (The protectorate's whites held a different view, revering him as a pioneer settler-explorer.)[2] The newspaper targeted the protectorate's white population, being funded by the colonial administration as a vehicle to deliver local and British Empire news to Eswatini's several-thousand-strong white community.[3] Some viewed the paper as little more than an organ of white government, similar to countless others funded by British officials across colonial Africa.[4] But this misses an important fact. Beyond white officials, farmers, and businesspeople, the *Times* enjoyed a very different readership. Since the 1930s a small group of middle-class emaSwati—teachers, clerks, nurses, doctors, lawyers—had read its pages and contributed letters to the editor, news items, and opinion pieces. Many defended Black aspirations against the racist views of many settlers (despite the fact that Eswatini's whites frequently boasted of their more enlightened attitudes compared to their South African neighbors), mounting impassioned arguments against the unequal treatment emaSwati still received.

Throughout 1961 to 1965 one of the most prolific of these Black writers was Gelana Twala, who wrote nearly seventy columns under the pen name of Intombazana ("Young Lady" in isiZulu). Surely a deliberate invocation of her old pseudonym of Mademoiselle, Gelana's choice of Intombazana encapsulated her shift from venerating European culture to celebrating the vernacular. No longer the cosmopolitan Parisian Mademoiselle, Gelana now created a public identity that emphasized her Zulu heritage (parallel to her earlier shift from using "Regina" to "Gelana"). And in an era where formal publication of books eluded many Black authors—let alone Black women—Gelana turned to newspapers' weekly cycle to get her views in print. Over five years, she published nearly fifty-five thousand words as Intombazana, the length of a short monograph. Much as *Bantu World* and *Umteteli wa Bantu* had provided her means for publication in the 1930s, thirty years later the *Times* became Gelana's route to disseminate her writing to the nation. (For the British, allowing "native" contributors—drawn from the better-educated class, of course—meant they could present themselves as reasonably enlightened.)

Gelana's early Intombazana articles offered to enlighten white readers on Swati tradition. In her column's debut, the *Times*'s editor, Will Talbott, presented her as an authority on Swati custom, reprising the same role of informant for the curious Westerner that she had played for Sundkler. Talbott promised his mainly white readers an insider's view into the mysterious workings of an unknown culture. Intombazana's column would be "of interest for European readers who want to know more about the ordinary life of Swazis among whom we live."[5] Indeed, Gelana's identification with emaSwati—already discernible in her work for Bengt Sundkler—was here even more apparent. Her 1962 *Times* column on the Incwala inserted herself, South African Gelana Twala, into the ranks of the "Swazi," juxtaposing a communal Swati "we" against the ignorant Westerner who mistook sacred ritual for a mere "concert": "One asked: 'Don't they get tired of singing one thing over and over again?' as if it is singing in a concert. . . . We the Swazi do not sing for entertainment but we identify ourselves with the occasion, we are part of it and by repetition we get the rhythm right into our bone and marrow."[6]

There was little of anything groundbreaking about Gelana's early clutch of columns from 1961 and 1962, little that would have unsettled white settlers' complacent assumptions about seemingly exotic African tradition. For these early articles, Gelana's topics read like an old-style functionalist anthropology syllabus. She wrote on traditional marriage, Swati etiquette customs, the relationship between the king and the state, choosing an heir, and the Incwala.[7] She communicated an impression of timeless

Swati rituals, practices meaning the same in 1961 as in 1861. Intombazana's comment on the Swati state—"the concept of a State among the Swazi has a different background from that of Western culture"—presented this political entity as static and fixed (it was a distinct capital *S* "concept"), intrinsically different since time immemorial from the state "of Western culture."[8]

But Gelana's romanticized portrayals of Swati custom should not be read as statements of fact. Rather, they were desperate efforts to shore up a society changing quicker than Gelana could type her articles. Eswatini of the early 1960s was experiencing a painful transition period. Old uncertainties were uprooted, and new orthodoxies were yet to emerge. As elsewhere across the continent, whispers of African independence from European colonial powers were growing into a roar. Ghana's independence from Britain in 1957 and British prime minister Harold Macmillan's "Winds of Change" speech of 1960, in which he predicted the end of empire was nigh, gave momentum to increasing calls by Sobhuza II for independence from Britain.[9]

But emaSwati were not united about the nature of an independent Eswatini. On one hand, Sobhuza thought independence should consolidate his powers as absolute monarch. On the other, educated emaSwati and non-Swati Africans (many refugees from South Africa), called for a constitutional monarchy and a reduction of the king's powers. Preeminent among this latter group of voices was John Nquku's. A Zulu from Pietermaritzburg, Nquku had come to Eswatini in 1930, appointed by the colonial administration to the prestigious position of the first African inspector of schools. From Nquku's base in Msunduza—a township nested in the green hills overlooking the capital city, Mbabane—he carved out a massive presence in the country, sitting on the Swazi National Council advising Sobhuza and spearheading the project to create a national church. Since 1945 Nquku presided over the first cultural organization for educated emaSwati, the Swaziland Progressive Association. This gave a mouthpiece for Africans' bitter complaints about racism and unequal wages.[10] By 1960, despite his earlier links with Sobhuza, Nquku transformed his Swaziland Progressive Association into the country's first political party, the Swaziland Progressive Party (SPP).[11] To the horror of both Sobhuza and Eswatini's conservative white population, the SPP advocated a common voters' roll; one man, one vote; and eradicating the powers of chiefs (although Nquku shied short of criticizing the popular Sobhuza).[12]

Sobhuza was wary of parties like Nquku's SPP and cast them in carefully timed public speeches as "unSwazi," characterizing them as "carbon copying of cultures of other people, like dung beetles who feed on excreta."[13] Sobhuza argued Western-style parties were not applicable to the Eswatini context and would breed division in the nation. Of course, Sobhuza also stood to lose many of his hereditary privileges if independent Eswatini transitioned to parliamentary democracy. Addressing SPP members at his Masundvwini residence in 1960, Sobhuza counseled, "The policy of one man, one vote, can only lead us into hardship," calling for parties' "immediate abolition."[14] Sobhuza's suspicion of democratic politics found widespread support among traditionalists, many in rural areas. There was, for example, an "open letter to all the political leaders" written by A. Z. Khumalo and published in the *Times:* "What race are the political parties going to make us? Black Europeans, devoid of their nationhood, their laws and customs, mere mimics of the Western way of life?"[15] Ever strategic, Sobhuza worked to combat the perceived threat of impending democracy. For one, he forged an alliance with the minority group of white settlers who also stood to lose by parliamentary democracy and a transition to majority rule.[16]

Gelana now became embroiled in Sobhuza's efforts to rout democratic reform. In either 1960 or 1961, Sobhuza planted Gelana as a spy within the SPP. Confident she was a loyal promoter of Swati tradition and the monarchy, he requested she "join" the party and report back to him on their doings.[17] Beyond a brief mention of this fact by Dan in an interview conducted with him by Tim Couzens in the 1970s, I have frustratingly little information on this startling turn of events.[18] Gelana was surely not the only spy employed by Sobhuza throughout this period (even in contemporary Eswatini, rumors abound of spies strategically placed to report back to the monarchy on dissenting citizens). As Couzens did not ask Dan to further elaborate upon this fact, it is entirely speculative as to what Gelana made of her appointment as a double agent. Yet there is something fitting in Gelana's new role as a spy. Reinvention and fluidity of identity are themes that mark much of her life; playing the role of pro-democratic political activist does not seem a great stretch for her.

Sobhuza's scheme rapidly paid dividends. A woman of Gelana's caliber rose up the ranks: by 1962, she became secretary of the SPP's Women's League.[19] This was clever planning on Sobhuza's part, not least because as an educated non-Swati formerly politically active in South Africa, Gelana had exactly the profile of many SPP members. Gelana also lived in Kwaluseni, the second hub of urban opposition politics, along with Nquku's base in Msunduza. Nquku's number-two in the SPP was Eswatini's first Black doctor, Ambrose Zwane, Gelana's Kwaluseni neighbor, whom she used to visit for discussions about Swati politics and history.[20] A 1962 photograph confirms Gelana's standing within the SPP: she is pictured (in a demure white-collared dress) alongside the party's leader, a standing John Nquku (the seated man is Ethan Mayisela, future governor of the Bank of Swaziland after independence; the woman is possibly his wife, Constance).[21]

But Sobhuza's strategy had a crucial flaw. He did not account for a change of heart in his old ally. Who could have guessed Gelana would lose faith in the sanctity of an African monarchy? Yet omens of her skepticism were there from the start. Traditionalist politics were both "traditional"—which Gelana loved—and patriarchal—which she hated. Women had no political representation in the traditional order as practiced during colonial times. With the exception of the queen mother, there were no female chiefs who reported to Sobhuza, no female members of the Swazi National Council advising Sobhuza, or any women on

FIGURE 14.1. Gelana Twala (*right*) with the SPP's John Nquku (*standing*) and Ethan Mayisela (*seated*), 1962 (Pinokie Twala)

the traditional advisory body to the king—the Liqoqo—rumored to exercise the real power in the protectorate.[22] Outside politics, women's rights were curtailed. Women could not own property, meaning a widow would lose everything if her husband died.[23]

As early as 1961, there were signs of Gelana's changing attitude toward traditional politics. Already an SPP member, in August she staged a lone protest outside the heart of royal power—the Lobamba Royal Kraal, where the highest echelons met to address state matters. Inside, Sobhuza, his advisers, and representatives of the political parties were holding a meeting suffused with gravitas, discussing the country's future direction. But tradition forbade women to enter this sacred space. So, Gelana folded her legs sideways, in the traditional manner, and sat patiently outside "to listen to discussions inside" and pose for the photographer from *Izwi lama Swazi*—Eswatini's isiZulu-language newspaper—as she made her silent challenge to patriarchy.[24]

N ECURDAY AUGUST 19, 1961 PAGE 7

hi the news

# TURES

## eaders who 't arrive

This, it was apparently felt, might be a suitable opportunity for the Progressive Party to air what views might occur to them and explain their differences with the Swazi National Council.

They didn't like the Constitution, the Progressives explained—it gives rights to the Europeans—and they wanted their freedom. Apparently only the Progressives, an alleged 2,000 of them, were aware of the Swazi chains.

But they stuck to their guns and the Party conference, a little off schedule, got off to its opening the following day—Nyerere or no Nyerere.

In the end, it was Mr. T. Musi, former Treason Trialist from South Africa and now leader of the Bechuanaland People's Party, who was good enough to stand in for Mr. Nyerere.

But in spite of the dancing and singing, only about 500 entered the hall, some from an adjoining football field.

In an opening address, Mr. Musi attacked the Swaziland Central Government, Sir John Maud, Seretse Khama, Chief Bathoen, other chiefs and the constitution.

Lending an admiring ear was President Nquku, this time dressed in robes given to him by President Nkrumah of Ghana.

When his own turn came, Mr. Nquku demanded a constitution acceptable to the Progressive Party and the Swazi Nation—an incompatibility not overlooked by some members of the audience.

The party's invitation to foreign guests was also not overlooked by some critics. If guests arrived in Swaziland without the authority of the Paramount Chief, they should be dealt with, it was sugested.

But, in spite of the embarrassing disappointment, it was the Progressive's "glorious hour."

There was dead silence when Mr. Nquku, shown standing in the centre of the gathering at Lobamba, stood up to speak but towards the end there was a murmur of disapproval of his speech. The complaint in most cases was that he should not have acted against the majority vote of the Constitutional Committee and later resigned without consultation with the Paramount Chief. The feeling was that he should have fought within the Committee to avoid causing confusion and division in the nation.

Mrs. D. R. Twala was photographed at Lobamba Royal Kraal listening to discussions inside. She sat lonely at the entrance because Swazi Tradition does not allow women to enter the Royal Kraal where national gatherings are held. Mrs. Twala, who holds a B.A. degree in Social Science (Wits) takes keen interest in constitutional developments in Swaziland. She is building a library. She told a reporter of The World that she was struggling, her appeal for funds and books seemed to have fallen on deaf ears.

Listening attentively is Mr. Polycarp Ka-Dlamini, national secretary. Beside him is Mr. J. S. M. Mathebula, laison officer between the Swazi National Administration and the Central Government of Swaziland. Mr. Dlamini opened the gathering at Lobamba and explained the controversy before Chief Sozisa Dlamini addressed the gathering. Mr. Mathebula was taking the minutes.



FIGURE 14.2. Gelana Twala outside the Lobamba Royal Kraal (*Izwi lama Swazi*, August 19, 1961)

We also know from her Intombazana articles that Gelana was increasingly outspoken about race relations. Sobhuza's coziness with the white settler community sat ill with her. Her earliest articles sought to "inform" white audiences; soon, she used the persona of Intombazana to denounce them. A caustic article recalled her conversation with a "Swazilander"—a white settler—who "said to me, 'I like to work with the Swazi, but I do not wish to mix with them socially.'"[25] In the same column she opined that E. M. Forster's *Passage to India,* a critique of Britons in India, should be read by all "Swazilanders." She took swipes at whites' assumed superiority, calling them out for attending sacred ceremonies such as Incwala dressed as oafish tourists: "the slovenly, careless, holiday attire of the Europeans."[26] She criticized white Christians for not worshipping with Swati believers, observing, "We are divided not only according to denomination but also colour."[27]

Accra, Ghana, changed Gelana. Ten years ago, she had spent a transformative year in Port Elizabeth. Now it was the West African metropolis that infused fresh vision into her politics. In 1962 party officials selected Gelana, as the Women's League's secretary, to be part of a SPP delegation to Ghana for Kwame Nkrumah's Conference for African Freedom Fighters. Since Ghana's independence in 1957, Nkrumah had positioned the country as a beacon for other African countries striving for independence. The government initiated an African Affairs Bureau, which provided support for independence movements throughout the continent. Prominent nationalists—Patrice Lumumba from the Belgian Congo, Tom Mboya from Kenya, ANC activists in exile—were all hosted by the bureau.[28]

In 1962 Gelana entered their ranks.[29] She stayed in the African Affairs Center, housed in modest bungalows near the airport, while attending training sessions. She and the other emaSwati delegates were impressed. Joshua Mzizi visited in 1964 through a scholarship program for young SPP members. He remembered an exciting pan-Africanist buzz: "That country was alive. . . . It did not belong to Ghanaians but to all Africa."[30] We have a single

FIGURE 14.3. Gelana Twala, Ghana, 1962, alongside a man in traditional clothes of the Dagaaba of northwestern Ghana. (RTP; thanks to Charles Prempeh for identifying the clothing)

photograph of Gelana in the delegates' hall, seated next to Ambrose Zwane, listening intently as Nkrumah spoke, cautioning delegates, "The forces arrayed against us are formidable. . . . They operate using agents who are often unpatriotic sons of Africa, buying personal satisfaction with the betrayal of their countries."[31] Was this the first time the thought occurred to Gelana that Sobhuza's promotion of indigenous monarchy and his "unholy alliance" with white settlers was "unpatriotic"?

Gelana's time in Accra also showed her that women could be major players in national affairs. After her return, Intombazana glowingly wrote of Ghanaian women: "The women of Ghana are the lifeblood of the social structure of their country. . . . They play a very important role in socio-economic problems." She admiringly mentioned the National Council of Ghana Women's active role in politics and the many female Ghanaian parliamentarians and successful businesswomen: "A married woman runs her own business, banks her own money and runs all her own affairs without having to go begging to her husband for aid." She held up women like Margaret Martei, president of the National Council of Women, and Mary Laryea, a prominent entrepreneur, as models for emaSwati women.[32] Intombazana's description of Laryea is a paean to independent women: "An example of an independent prosperous woman is Mary Laryea of Accra. She owns property and is a trader, being chairman of the Market Women. She has two shops and a stone crushing machine with her own lorries for carting the gravel. She has her own driver, her own car and lives in her own family unit with children and mother. The husband, a well to do man, lives elsewhere with another wife who is also independent."[33]

Gelana came back to Eswatini charged with a new vision for women's role in the nation. From 1962 we can track changes in Intombazana's estimation of "tradition," revising her earlier veneration of the indigenous. Instead, she developed a more nuanced view of Swati identity as ever-changing and contested, newly charting the impact of modernity upon Swati people and especially its women. An excellent example of her changing tone is the quartet of articles Gelana published on Swati marriage throughout 1963. The first of the four is old-style Intombazana. Titled "Swazi Traditional Wedding," it presents Swati weddings as carried out since time immemorial.[34] So far, so familiar.

The rest of the quartet was an exciting divergence. Intombazana's second article was an account of the wedding of Sobhuza's daughter, Gcinaphi, a qualified nurse, to a liSwati businessman. Intensely covered in the press, the event attracted attention for its blend of "tradition" and "modernity," what Intombazana dubbed a "successful salad of Swazi and Western culture." A traditional ceremony in Lobamba's cattle kraal was followed by dancing the twist and drinking champagne in a school hall.[35] Intombazana's third article described a wedding in Johannesburg, a "cosmopolitan city that is a cauldron of various tribal customs so pure traditional practices are hard to find." In true Mademoiselle style, Intombazana lovingly detailed the bride's Afro-modern clothing: "the expensive Paris creation, the leopard skin pattern, top long coat in gold."[36] Her final article, "Arranged Marriages," destabilized any notion of "traditional" marriage by discussing new forms of pragmatic marriage in South African townships, largely ways of accessing housing from a city municipality that only allocated married couples' accommodations.[37] Gelana's portrayals of these marriages show her frustration with the static categories beloved by many anthropologists and her advocacy for greater sensitivity to social change: "Anthropologists will say the cause of these marriages is what they term 'detribalization,' but I say, tribe or no tribe, what can you do if you wish to work in a town for your starving children in the 'native area' and are told that the hostels are all full up?"[38]

Alongside marriage, fashion was a favorite topic of Intombazana's, helping her describe the convergence of the old and the new she now saw as the hallmark of contemporary Swati life. In early 1963 Intombazana wrote on "Fashions at the Incwala." She celebrated the eclectic outfits leading Swati women selected for the ritual, a mixture of traditional, black, heavy skin skirts, and haute couture hats:

> There was the Princess Royal, looking elegant in a gossamer-like hat with a light dress to match and of course a perfect fit. Over there was Mrs Nkambule in her snow-white curved-brim hat and full of smiles. A pleasant surprise was the wife of the National Secretary who had discarded her nurses' uniform for a full matronly Swazi attire: isicholo hair-bun, isidziya skin apron and isidwaba skin-skirt. Didn't she look pretty! You could have seen her with Mrs Zondi, who came all the way from Durban. She too had decided to appear in proper national attire for this greatest of all gatherings.[39]

Intombazana also commented that married women shied away from wearing "the weight of the skin-skirt. . . . They tell us that it is so heavy and that it gives on excruciating pain around the waist." Her sage solution was perfectly in keeping with her new interest in hybrids of old and new, advising manufacturers to create synthetic fabrics for modern women: "I am sure a firm making artificial furs will soon try its luck by devising a skin-skirt and apron of nylon fur. I am sure it would sell like hot cakes."[40]

Intombazana also became increasingly critical of Sobhuza—a controversial thing, given his undoubted popularity among many emaSwati. Dan Twala testified to Gelana's change of heart, remembering that "she was giving Sobhuza a dirty time because he was becoming a capitalist more than a Saint of the Africans" (here Dan alluded to Sobhuza's monetary interests in maintaining the royalist status quo).[41] There are few letters between Gelana and Dan during the 1960s, testimony to their marriage's fraught state. (Dan to Gelana in 1963: "I am convinced you have nothing to do in Swaziland but to torment me and make my remaining days miserable and a torture.")[42] The existing letters speak to Gelana's tense relationship with Sobhuza and Dan's worries about his own compromised reception in Eswatini due to the perception of Black South Africans as political troublemakers: "Do you think Sobhuza will be in a good frame of mind to receive any Republic [of South Africa] Swazi with magnanimity when he is living on pins and needles?"[43] Rumors circulated that the apartheid president Hendrik Verwoerd was buying Sobhuza off in return for the latter quashing antiwhite political parties.[44]

Gelana was careful not to confront Sobhuza outright. But she made her suspicions known, nonetheless. Again, Intombazana gave voice to this criticism. An article titled "Valediction to Manzana" eulogized the pristine hot springs in the Ezulwini Valley that Sobhuza had sold to a South African company for development into an exclusive tourists' spa. The Manzana springs were a popular destination for emaSwati wanting to soak in their rejuvenating waters. (Gelana had visited them in the 1940s during her fieldwork in Eswatini.)[45] Now they would be fenced off, available only to paying guests. Intombazana wrote sadly about her final visit to the springs, enjoying one last swim before they were closed to line Sobhuza's pockets: "This was our last dip in the Zulwini Springs and we cry all of us who have known these Springs. This was our Manzana, made by God, shooting from the bowels of the earth . . . but now we are to have an off-sale of the Casino de Luxe and Spa."[46]

In the fraught 1960s Gelana's Intombazana articles marked her out as an opponent of the status quo. Many educated young women became keen followers of her column. The young Stella Lukhele, teacher and future MP for Kwaluseni, read Intombazana's column and was so inspired she started contributing articles to the *Times* herself, under the pseudonym "Khulelaphi" (Where Are You Raised?). As Lukhele explained to me, it was too dangerous to write under her own name, given "she was being critical and might offend some people." (Interestingly, the opposite was true for Gelana. It seems that—as with Mademoiselle in years old—Intombazana was a nom de plume rather than a truly anonymous pseudonym; readers knew Intombazana was Gelana Twala of Kwaluseni. Thirty years older than Lukhele and more professionally established, Gelana seems to have felt sufficiently confident to reveal her true identity to the country.) Lukhele would send Gelana her articles for comment, and the older woman became a mentor to this radical young politician.[47] Intombazana's articles started to gain notice more widely, with the *Times* noting "requests for copies of [Twala's] articles were received from many parts of the world."[48] That Gelana started inserting a short note—"All Rights to the Reproduction of this Article Reserved"—at the end of her columns is surely a sign of their popularity.[49]

As Gelana's fame grew, her political career became more radical. In 1963 she announced her departure from the SPP. Gelana's reason was "I want to continue with work concerning women." She found "we can do it without having to be part of groupings where there are men."[50] Gelana did not consider the SPP sufficiently supportive of women's issues. Inequity was reflected in the leadership: Gelana was the lone woman in any authority. The SPP's president, John Nquku, made vitriolic women-shaming comments in *Izwi*—flagellating women for wearing makeup and laying the cause of failed marriages on their overburdened shoulders. Nquku wrote as "Kadebona" (the Farsighted One), a moniker reflective of his outsized ego and that contrasts with the humility of Gelana's identity as Intombazana (the Young Girl). While Kadebona savaged women for "modern" clothing, Intombazana toasted novel fashion choices.[51]

Gelana found a new home in the Ngwane National Liberatory Congress (NNLC), formed in early 1963 and composed of a group of disgruntled SPP members, including Ambrose Zwane and Dumisa Dlamini, Sobhuza's nephew. By late 1963 Gelana joined her old friend Zwane in the NNLC, again appointed as Women's League secretary.[52] The NNLC sat considerably to the left of the SPP, distinguishing itself as the country's most radical party.[53] It stood for universal suffrage (most other parties only pushed for suffrage for men), was explicitly socialist, and had close links to Nkrumah's Ghana. It was also outspoken in denouncing Sobhuza's alleged links to apartheid South Africa, maintaining, "Verwoerd's purpose is to back up the traditionalist and reactionary elements in our nation to destroy us as a nation."[54]

Just how radical the NNLC was soon became evident for a horrified Sobhuza. March to June 1963 saw waves of NNLC-led strikes ripple through Mbabane, Manzini, and industrial centers like the Havelock asbestos mine. Workers demanded increased pay and protested the unpopular British-imposed constitution (a road map for independence that had Britain retain considerable power). In June 1963 a huge NNLC-coordinated strike had the whole country at a standstill. Temperatures rose. British police used tear gas to dispel protesters; Dumisa Dlamini led a crowd of furious women—perhaps including Gelana—to march on the British residency in Mbabane, shouting "Afrika—one man, one vote!" Prisoners in the Mbabane jail broke out and looted shops.[55] Usually peaceful Eswatini had never seen anything like it.

Sobhuza tried to calm things, broadcasting that strikes were "un-Swazi," a "foreign infectious germ." But no one listened.[56] It was only after a panicked Brian Marwick, British resident commissioner, appealed for British troops from Kenya that the situation calmed down. EmaSwati were deeply shocked at the airborne arrival of hundreds of Gordon Highlanders, adding to anti-British sentiment and giving many the impression their country was under military occupation by a foreign power for the first time. Intombazana was right there, covering people's responses to the crisis, including quoting one old man who exclaimed in horror: "Oh Mbandzeni [an ancient liSwati king], we are locked in indeed! Flying machines buzzing over us!"[57]

In the strike's aftermath, the British arrested much of the NNLC leadership, including Ambrose Zwane and Dumisa Dlamini. We know Gelana was not in their number, although she had taken part in the protests. But NNLC lawyers used Gelana for their defense; she took the stand to testify that strike leaders had not, in fact, threatened violence. In an ironic role reversal, Gelana invoked her status as ethnographic "expert" to defend her NNLC comrades who sought to undo the traditional Swati order. She told the court Dlamini and other leaders carried sticks while they marched but not because they were about to attack the British police. Rather, stick-carrying was part of Swati "tradition": "I could not imagine people in a crowd singing without sticks. . . . If Swazis

FIGURE 14.4. Gelana Twala (*front, third from right*) during Eswatini's 1963 general strike (RTP)

wanted to threaten they would be giving war cries and they would not be singing." In her own defense, Gelana reminded the court, "I have published various papers on this topic" (although noting her book was still forthcoming), and she also took a swipe at the professional anthropological establishment, noting, "I regard the work of Hilda Kuper and Brian Marwick dated."[58] She was, of course, right. Kuper had not done fieldwork in Eswatini since the 1930s, although many still regarded her works as authoritative. Likewise, Resident Commissioner Marwick's monograph on the emaSwati dated to the 1930s.[59]

Gelana became even bolder. In January 1964 Sobhuza and his advisers organized a referendum to gauge opinion on the unpopular British constitution. Sobhuza knew he had little chance of reversing Britain's imposition of the constitution, but he hoped the referendum would convince the British of the support of emaSwati for the traditional regime. The political parties were scathing of the exercise, denouncing it a royalist bid for power and instructing members not to take part. Sobhuza arranged matters so the outcome was not in doubt. Voters had to choose on the ballot between two pictures. One was a lion, Sobhuza's traditional symbol, indicating opposition to the constitution. The other was a reindeer, an animal totally unknown in Eswatini. This indicated assent to the constitution. Not surprisingly, the referendum was a massive popular vote for Sobhuza: 122,000 voted for the lion, 154 for the reindeer.[60]

Traditionalists hailed the outcome a "complete expression of loyalty of the Swazi people to the Ngwenyama."[61] But Gelana was skeptical. Her Intombazana column in the referendum's aftermath narrated events from the perspective of rural women commanded by their chief to cast their ballot for Sobhuza. As with her previous writing, Intombazana experimented with a range of vantage points, merging her identity as prominent Gelana Twala with an unschooled rural woman. Titled "Swazi Women's World: The Day of the Plebiscite," Intombazana's account, ostensibly in the voice of a rural woman, describes a population taught since birth their king was "umlomo ongaqambi manga"—"the mouth that never tells lies." Although they could ill afford to take a day off from the fields, "we go because we are called, we dare not stay away, we have no beasts to pay a fine." Intombazana described a corrupt process whereby she was presented with the ballot by a "man in authority who knows me well" and asked whether she supported the king. When she asked questions, the official gave her an answer she did not understand: "I grinned and nodded and said I understood so as to hide my ignorance."[62] Royalists responded sharply to the column, none fooled this was an uneducated rural woman. A. K. Hlophe, powerful in the Swazi National Council, wrote to the *Times* refuting Gelana's account: "It is difficult to believe all the details of the story as she has given it." Implying Gelana's political affiliations biased her, Hlophe wrote that she "has tried to discount the Plebiscite for reasons she does not state." He patronizingly concluded: "Intombazana may be one of the very very very few Swazi who prefer to think that the Ngwenyama does not represent the great mass of the people."[63]

Gelana knew the cost of crossing the monarchy. Around this time, her niece, Mary Twala, was expelled from school for the crime of insulting one of Sobhuza's daughters in schoolyard banter. Perhaps the fact that her aunt was a known critic of Sobhuza's worked against Mary. Mary remembers Gelana was "furious" at the school.[64] There were also many emaSwati men who thought women should not be in politics and attacked Gelana for her outspokenness. Once again, newspapers were the forum for these debates. In 1963 Gelana outlined for *Izwi lama Swazi* a meeting between emaSwati women (including herself) and a high-ranking colonial official, M. J. Fairlie. The women asked Fairlie why the constitution cut women out of any representative role, arguing that "the constitution will be incomplete if women are not included; we want women to be able to vote, even in their tinkundla [rural councils]."[65] Outraged male readers immediately responded. One suggested, "Women cannot restrain themselves, especially when talking, and thus ruin everything. . . . It is foolish to talk about women and the law!"[66] Then came Gelana's icy response that "this person who says women do not know the law is worthy of dislike," citing the venerable old queen mother, La Botsibeni, "who ruled well in Swaziland, even though males were in conflict with her."[67]

Those who had known Gelana recounted just how unpopular she was with men. Her Kwaluseni neighbor, Janet Aphane, remembered that "Gelana used to argue with men, they would say she was enlightening the women too much," while her stepdaughter Zanele recollected that "men didn't like her, they said she was teaching women to disrespect men." Zanele recalled how, during meetings, Gelana would insist chairs be brought for women rather than have them sit at their menfolk's feet in the "traditional" style.[68] Zanele also said that Gelana drilled into her the importance of autonomy, insisting Zanele focus on her studies to "get out of this subservient mentality. . . . She just couldn't understand why women were not making decisions of their own. It used to irritate the hell out of her!"[69] There were also, of course, the provocative Intombazana articles Gelana published on this topic. Intombazana's grimly humorous "For Men Only" provided a sarcastic manual for the ways men could abuse their wives: a spate of psychological terrorizing (throwing his things on the floor and demanding his wife pick them up; pitting wife against mother-in-law) as well as financial tyranny (squeezing income from a working wife so she was a "dispossessed individual").[70]

Despite the public outcry she caused, Gelana resolved to run in the 1964 elections, the first ever where the whole country would vote.[71] Women may have voted, but Gelana was the sole female candidate out of nearly sixty contenders.[72] Ironically, her symbol (voters selected candidates via their emblems) was a pair of trousers.[73] The stakes were high: the results of this election would determine the legislative council seeing Eswatini to independence and beyond. Sobhuza, recognizing he could not change the constitution, which allowed for political parties, had decided to join them. Sobhuza and the traditionalists had formed a new party, which, given their former denigration of parties as un-Swati, they dubbed a "movement." The Imbokodvo National Movement ran on Eswatini's independence and Sobhuza's retention of absolute power. Imbokodvo threw the full weight of the monarchy and the funds of the Swazi National Treasury behind its campaign. In contrast, many NNLC leaders were still in jail, the organization was burdened with legal fees, and it had failed to make inroads in hard-to-reach rural constituencies.[74]

The outcome was a clean sweep for Imbokodvo and defeat for all the parties, although the NNLC put up the most respectable showing. Gelana ran as the NNLC candidate for Manzini. Yet even in Manzini, a hotbed of political activism, the Imbokodvo's A. K. Hlophe and Amos Kumalo each defeated Gelana by a margin of eleven to one. Nonetheless, Gelana gained 908 votes, more than any other candidate except Ambrose Zwane. By way of comparison, the father of Swati politics, John Nquku, gained only 56 votes.[75] Imbokodvo hailed the outcome a great victory for Sobhuza and Swati traditionalism and a refutation of Gelana and her colleagues, of "unscrupulous parties [who] fought us with vicious false propaganda."[76]

Some sounded notes of caution. Rumors circulated that chiefs had threatened their subjects with dispossession of their lands if they voted against Imbokodvo.[77] After the election, Gelana wrote a single, bitter Intombazana column, describing an imagined conversation between two baffled voters who grasped the unfairness of the elections but dared not say anything. One asked his friend, "Tell me this, in whose land will this work, because Swaziland is a feudal land, the tikhulu [chiefs] exercise their powers in his name, who-that-never-tells-a-lie, umlomo ongaqambi manga?" His friend replied, "My friend, I feel scared. I have no land of my own, let us part. I have no voice of my own, yet the truth is there."[78]

Gelana was weary. Throughout the next year, prominent NNLC leaders defected to Imbokodvo, seeing the writing on the wall and the impossibility of maintaining resistance to Sobhuza. He now possessed nearly hegemonic control over the political process.[79] Gelana would not betray her principles in this way. But she felt she could not continue along the same path either. In 1965 Gelana announced her resignation from politics, using the *Times* to inform the country that "she had decided to spend her full time doing social welfare work, which had always been her calling."[80]

# 15

## Social Worker

> The question is how can one revive the esprit de corps of the Swazi womanhood. The new group affiliations should be purified and worked to fit in with the present daily life of the emerging educated and Christian Swazi woman.
>
> —"Choosing a Partner by Intombazana," *Times of Swaziland*, October 15, 1965

Dan Twala was fed up. In his eyes, Gelana's departure from politics was just the latest evidence of her lack of direction. As he scathingly wrote to her in 1964, shortly after her failed election, "the pity of your life is that you have not yet started knowing what your profession in life is. Not housewife—not a literary sage—not a farmer—not a priest—not an MP—just ageing Regina Twala."[1] Dan's frustration was in large part financial. Despite her manifold professional commitments—ethnography, politics, journalism—Gelana was still not earning sufficiently to support herself and the children, Vusi, Mary, and Zanele. Dan was feeling the strain of sending money to Eswatini as well as of supporting his new family in Johannesburg.[2] Time and time again, he lamented his loss of the respectable teacher and social worker of early decades. *That* Regina could have brought a steady income to their family budget. But instead he had Gelana—a flighty God-loving writer—as his wife: "I had hoped that when I sent you to University that by now I would be reaping the results of this investment but you have chosen to worship other Gods before Me."[3]

But where Dan saw a dilettante or a "beggar and parasite" (in the words of one cruel letter), the truth was that for Gelana all these roles—her journalism, her ethnography, her Christian faith, and her political ambitions—were a seamless whole.[4] That her professional identity defies categorization was partly because her work was an extension of her very self: her interest in women's welfare amid a patriarchal society, her concern for ordinary people repressed by elites (of whom, paradoxically, as an educated, relatively well-off woman she was nonetheless a part), her faith in God, and her commitment to African values and to defying white supremacy. It is this, I believe, that partly explains Gelana's many professional reinventions over the years: from teacher, to writer, to social worker, to ethnographer, to politician and columnist, and now, finally, back to social worker. All were different routes to the same ends. The other part of the puzzle is that Gelana was *obliged* to reinvent herself. Her career path was impeded by multiple prejudices. Professional dexterity was a survival technique. And in these final years of Gelana's life, all her interests merged in a complex crescendo. Disillusioned with the corruption of Eswatini's political process, Gelana felt it was through hands-on social work she could best serve the country's ordinary women.

After years of unpaid politicking, this was a position that came with an actual salary. In 1966, at the age of fifty-eight, Gelana became a member of the executive committee of the new Swaziland Council of Social Service. In the following year, she was appointed as the salaried secretary of the council. Gelana was replacing a British woman in this role, and her appointment reflected the new Africanization of the civil service as Eswatini neared the date of independence from Britain (scheduled for September 1968).[5] Installed in an office of her own in Mbabane, with a dedicated phone line, Gelana would have been delighted at this coup, although we have no record of any correspondence between her and Dan or anyone else on this achievement. The appointment suggested that Gelana was poised to play a leading role in soon-to-be-independent Eswatini, even—according to her daughter-in-law, Anne (who would marry Gelana's son, Vusi, in 1968)—rumored to be possibly the first female senator in the new Parliament. Certainly, her unique achievements would have marked her out as a natural choice, were it not for the fact that her politics were too far left for Sobhuza's taste.[6]

Indeed, evidence of Gelana's fall from grace in royal circles can be found in the decline of her Kwaluseni library. By 1966, it had fallen into such severe disrepair that one letter to the editor in the *Times* disdainfully called it a "slum." Gelana quickly replied in defense of herself and of her project. The reason for the library's sad state lay not with her, but with the monarchy, which had withdrawn its previous financial support. Sobhuza now claimed there was "no money" to support the library any further. Gelana professed matters out of her hands: "As one who initiated the idea of a national library, I have done my best: the rest I leave to the

FIGURE 15.1. Gelana Twala (far left) with prominent white philanthropists and social workers in Eswatini, ca. 1964 (RTP)

powers that be."[7] Given that "the powers that be" no longer favored her, it must have been a great relief to find a secure salaried position in the transitionary government (appointed by the British, rather than by Sobhuza).

Alongside Gelana's formal work from her Johnstone Street office in Mbabane, she also used Eswatini's weekly newspaper to work in the service of the country's female population. Around the time of her resignation from politics and in the following years, Gelana's Intombazana articles turned away from any mention of politics.[8] Instead, she now addressed women's matters, highlighting marginalized women who lacked support in 1960s Eswatini, with its still embryonic social services. As Intombazana announced in 1964, "A country is as advanced as its social services. Where there are no social services, there is unheeded suffering among the poorest of the population."[9] Her articles of these years were inventories of female misfortune and pleas to those in power for change: stories of poverty-level elderly women bereft of a social support structure, descriptions of broken homes and laments for the children left to fall through the cracks in the absence of legislation protecting mothers who left husbands, jeremiads against the state for the shortage of school places for children, and heart-rending accounts of rural women unable to afford life's basics.[10]

In the absence of a robust state institution, newspapers became social welfare. Gelana mobilized the *Times* as a platform to bring visibility to specific cases as well as channel monetary donations. In 1964 Intombazana wrote an article titled "The Poor among Us," in which she profiled an elderly woman called Alvina Nxumalo, who "softly knocked" at the door of her Kwaluseni house, disturbing Gelana from a nap on her couch.[11] Alvina was a grass widow, as so many emaSwati women were. Her children had died in their youth, and she was now caring for her surviving grandchild, a young boy called Sipho. A childhood illness had left Sipho paralyzed on one side. Alvina was herself in poor health and spent her nights worrying, "If I die now, what will become of Sipho?" But, as she explained to Gelana, "all of a sudden the idea clearly came to my mind. . . . Yes, there is that Intombazana, and she writes in the famous paper that is read all over the world, it could be that the hand of God may touch one of them to wish to take my Sipho [when I die]." Deeply moved by Alvina's predicament, Intombazana lamented the absence of a "Child Welfare Society" in Eswatini and announced her determination to mobilize the press in lieu of this: "I am appealing to the public to help us in this matter and give Alvina the peace of mind and an assured future for Sipho."[12]

The Swati public warmly responded to these pleas. For example, Intombazana's article on the plight of female prison inmates ended with a plea to women readers to donate materials for warm winter clothes: "If you happen to be female, answer the following question practically not theoretically: How many women prisoners have we got? How many pounds of wool and pairs of needles to go round? How many odd ounces will you donate?"[13] A few weeks later, her next Intombazana piece appeared with a note stating, "As a result of the article by Intombazana, she has received a donation of wool and R1," and instructing future donations to be sent to her Kwaluseni post office box.[14] The isiZulu-language newspaper *Izwi lama Swazi* also served as Gelana's platform to send out social welfare SOS alerts, calling those "who are touched by this message to send their names so they can be shown where help is needed."[15]

As well as drawing attention to—and mending—female hardship, Intombazana also used her copy to celebrate female accomplishment. Intombazana regularly profiled prominent Black women in Eswatini who were engaged in social work of one kind or another. One article celebrated the rural nurse Mary Abner—"a member of the Coloured community"—"who knows exactly what Florence Nightingale stood for."[16] The death in August 1964 of the prominent social worker Mildred Malie was a chance for Intombazana to eulogize someone who had been "a live wire in bettering the habits of women in their homes all over the territory. . . . Mrs Malie did not merely exist: she lived a packed hurried life of service that reformed the whole of Swazi womanhood."[17] Intombazana's paeans were not insular. Mother's Day 1964 celebrated international social workers, showing "the women of Swaziland are proud that their social and spiritual problems can be solved with women in other lands."[18] Intombazana praised women in Ghana and farther afield; one piece exulted female accomplishment around the world and specifically in Russia, South Africa, and Sri Lanka: "Yes, women! Women! Brave beautiful women! Valentine [*sic*] the Sputnik Woman did it. Mrs Helen Suzman is doing it just beyond our borders. The Ceylon Prime Minister is doing it."[19]

Yet it is inaccurate to portray Gelana as a thoroughgoing progressive on issues of gender—at least by the standards of contemporary Western feminism. As much as she fought for the equality of the sexes, Gelana-as-Intombazana held very particular views regarding what a "good woman" looked like. In the context of the Swinging Sixties, politics was not the only area in ferment; gender and sexual norms were being upended as emaSwati negotiated what femininity meant in postcolonial Africa. We already know that women's involvement in politics caused consternation. Both men and women now also debated the new sexual freedoms that some women laid claim to, brought into being by the demise of "traditional" marriage and the increasing migration of women to towns. As the economy opened up, the influx into Eswatini of white workers and businessmen also caused a panic about the sexual ruination of Swati women, thought to gravitate to these well-paid foreigners.[20]

Gelana wholeheartedly concurred with these worries. In this sense, she was still the same Miss Mazibuko of Indaleni who escorted a shamed young schoolgirl to Durban. Now in her fifties, and as much as she raged against the patriarchal structures that dictated a woman should sit at a man's feet, Gelana still participated in much of its logic, especially the belief that young women's sexuality required policing. Gelana's Intombazana articles on this topic used the device of conversations "overheard" between ordinary emaSwati women as they went about their business, gossiping and bemoaning the sexual laxity of their juniors. Gelana's long-standing interest in playing with perspective and voice, blending ethnography and fiction, here came to full fruition. These articles entirely efface the author, Gelana—indeed, they even render her pseudonym-self, Intombazana, invisible—and instead present themselves as authentic transcripts of actual dialogues between Swati women.

The device added a textured realism to Intombazana's writings. It also gave the erroneous impression that these criticisms of supposedly dissolute young women were not issuing from her but rather from ordinary women. As Gelana had done in the 1950s with her ethnographic appropriation of a Swati identity in her research for Bengt Sundkler, she now experimented with inhabiting the voice of a "common woman." Of course, the reality was full of tensions. As one of the most educated women in the country and the possessor of an emancipated lifestyle—living solo in a house to all intents and purposes her own—Gelana's privileged life couldn't have been further from the reality of the rural women she purported to speak for. Yet laying claim to a quotidian identity gave her powerful moral leverage to criticize young women. In this respect, then, Gelana's earlier radicalism was morphing into a harshly judgmental conservatism.

Toward the end of 1964, Intombazana wrote a column lamenting, "What can be done about our girls?" The format was a conversation "overheard" by Intombazana between two rural women chatting as they got water from a nearby spring: "Since there are no cocktail parties, the only meeting places for gossip are when we go to fetch water from the spring or wood from the forest." While getting water, the women discuss "what is happening to our girls, with these white men around. . . . Girls move loosely up and down the country not knowing what they are doing. They want pretty clothes and cosmetics. When our own sons try to make love to them, they say, 'You have no money. Sorry.'"[21] Presenting these statements as neutral ethnographic reportage, Gelana was in fact skewering the liberated women of the 1960s. She was also reprising her lifelong interest in clothing. Foremost among the pretty clothes young girls desired were the much-hated miniskirts, which had arrived in Eswatini around this time. In the following article, written in the late 1960s, Gelana took aim at them. In this case, the setting was a long bus journey, whereby one woman was "heard" by Gelana—riding the same fictitious bus—to say to another: "If you look around you feel nauseated by what they call isimanjemanje—modernism—you find married women doing emanyala—disgusting things—wearing such short dresses called mini-skirts showing to the public their mansweba, back upper-leg muscles, with all the marks and strains of child birth. We Swazi say they are badunusile, they are badly exposed."[22]

Yet her criticism of modern women and their fashionable miniskirts ("shamefully" exposing the scars of childbirth) did not mean Gelana was recommending a return to traditional Swati norms. Far from it. As the 1960s progressed and keeping pace with her disillusionment with the politics of her adopted country, Gelana increasingly felt the salvation of Eswatini, and especially the salvation of Swati women, lay in God alone. Her involvement with Nicholas Bhengu's church had continued unabated since her conversion in the 1950s, with Gelana regularly making the long journey to the Assemblies of God annual Christmas service in South Africa.[23] She continued to work tirelessly to facilitate his expansion in Eswatini, helping organize large revival services and continuing to broker Bhengu's introductions to royalty, although as we have seen, Gelana's standing with Sobhuza declined after 1964.[24]

Gelana's Christian faith continued to poison the waters between her and Dan.[25] Around 1962 she had instigated a new push for a divorce, which he adamantly resisted. (She would die married to him.) Dan angrily wrote, "I am not prepared to give you DIVORCE because you are too old to benefit from it. So you can close that." His suspicion was this was a ploy to gain the deed to the Kwaluseni property—still held by Dan—so that Gelana's church could inherit the property upon her death: "I know you want to give it to your Church of the Assemblies so that they can make you their saint. I am not falling for that joke."[26]

In these her "postpolitical" years, Gelana felt the traditional rituals of Swati womanhood, which she had written about at such length since the 1950s, could only be retained if thoroughly Christianized. Gelana's diagnosis of the problem of "too many illegitimate children born to young girls" was this: "The reason is that because Swazis have left their own custom and have taken nothing in its place." Yet her answer was not what she would have advocated a decade earlier—namely, a nostalgic return to womanhood ceremonies of the past. In an article titled "Choosing a Partner," Intombazana presented the church—in particular, Bhengu's Assemblies of God—as the new forum within which wholesome relations between men and women could be restyled. She described how young couples' courtship would be mediated, overseen, and approved by the church, arguing that "group affiliations [traditional age-based groups that oversaw courtship, akin to female versions of the age-grade regiments discussed in chapter 12] should be purified and worked to fit in with the present daily life of the emerging educated and Christian Swazi woman. To meet this half way, I feel that such customs as Umhlanga ceremony [a annual ritual for girls], if they have to survive, must have as their foundation basic Christian principles."[27] Traditionalists would have read with horror this suggestion that indigenous ceremonies be Christianized.

But just as Gelana was successfully positioning herself as the outspoken czar of social services in an Eswatini on the brink of independence, everything came crashing down. In either 1966 or 1967, she was diagnosed with cancer of the stomach and intestines. Gelana desperately hoped this was just a momentary obstacle in her newly defined career path. She traveled regularly to Johannesburg to receive chemotherapy, and Dan would also frequently visit Eswatini during this difficult period, their animosities of previous years seemingly set aside. Gelana's stepdaughter, Zanele, remembers these years as ones when Dan regularly visited Kwaluseni, staying for a week or so at a time. While Gelana lived in the shadow of death, newly peaceful harmony prevailed between her and Dan: "[they] would play piano duets in the living room." They returned to their easy playfulness of years past, punning affectionately on each other's initials, with Gelana calling Dan "RD" and him calling her "DR." Zanele, then just a girl of eight or so, had no inkling her mother was deathly ill; she was told by everyone, including Gelana, that her mother was suffering from the flu, although Vusi—now a teenager just out of high school—would have known the truth.[28] By the end of 1967, doctors declared Gelana beyond help. Mary Twala remembers how Gelana was discharged from Baragwanath Hospital in Johannesburg and sent by ambulance for the long journey back to Eswatini. First, the ambulance dropped by the Orlando house where Mary lived for Gelana to say goodbye to her and other family members. Mary had bought her a "beautiful night dress," which she gave to her. She remembered Gelana was terribly thin but very brave and "still talking."[29]

Gelana spent the last months of her life resting quietly in her Kwaluseni house. She was cared for by her Vusi and his new bride, Anne. Her old friend Janet Aphane visited her daily, bringing food, and toward the end she would sleep in the house overnight to help Gelana.[30] While Gelana's body slowly shut down and her world narrowed for the first time since infancy to the confines of four walls, life continued apace in the outside world. Kwaluseni and Eswatini crackled with excitement. Independence was scheduled for September 6, 1968, and the whole country was alive with joy. Poignantly, Anne remembers Gelana, who probably was following events via radio and newspaper, still hoped to survive for the much-anticipated day and even selected her outfit, instructing her to lay out her carefully chosen hat, dress, and shoes.[31] Deathly ill (Genius Aphane remembers she was in a "very, very bad way" by that time), Gelana still took interest in fashionable outfits.[32]

As Gelana lay in bed, she also found the strength to write a little. Once again, she reached for her favorite device of "listening" to ordinary women. In this case, it was again women traveling on a bus, now chatting about the coming independence of Eswatini. This is one of the last things Gelana would write, and it is achingly reminiscent of her first writing as Mademoiselle, thirty years earlier. Clothing was once again her focus, as it had been for both Mademoiselle and Intombazana on so many occasions. Gelana recounted how the women on the bus excitedly planned what they would wear for the big day. Yet it was neither Western fashion nor traditional Swati dress that Intombazana overheard the women talking about, but a creative hybrid of both: "The women at the palace were taking orders from those who wanted new costumes. . . . They decided on inventing a new skirt made of towelling dyed black and to sew an apron with a gold design; the colours of Indlovukazi [Queen Mother]. Some orders were from white Swazis; those European women who had taken up partaking in National dances."[33] Reinvention, role-playing, feminine costumes, and the malleability of tradition—these were all themes that had been in Gelana's life from the start, and they would stay with her to the very end.

In her last month of her life, Gelana was admitted to Raleigh Fitkin Memorial, Manzini's sole hospital, run by the Nazarene missionaries responsible for introducing top-notch medical care to Eswatini. She was cared for by their lead physician, the Scottish Dr. David Hynd, who would also tend to Sobhuza II in the last years of his illness. Dr. Hynd would be one of the pallbearers at Gelana's funeral.[34] Some years earlier, Gelana had written about the gardens surrounding the hospital for an Intombazana article. She described the avenue leading up to the hospital as made up of "majestic trees . . . just in the right place as a wind breaker and sound absorber, with pines that grow up spire-like pointing the way to heaven and to salvation, so trim and beautiful."[35]

Perhaps Gelana could have seen the pines from her hospital room window. Even if she could not, she would have been reminded of heaven and of salvation by her Assemblies of God friends who visited her daily, for prayers and for ministrations, and who were with her at the moment of death on the chilly winter night of August 15, 1968. (Vusi did not make it in time and was anguished to receive a phone call from the hospital during the early hours informing him that his mother had just died.)[36] Gelana died during a season when Eswatini's sun-dried grass contrasts with a rainless sky. Gelana may have heard the harsh cry of the hadada ibis from her window, and she may have caught a glimpse of the petals of the coral-red flame trees that still grow in the Raleigh Fitkin Memorial gardens. She breathed slower; she slipped to peace and to rest.

# 16

# The Gatekeepers

> From my deathbed I am appealing to you to do all within your power to get the book on the Swazi as I have compiled printed to be sold on Independence Day. . . . It is my last legacy to Swazi progress and the Nation. I am so ill that I doubt if I will reach the day of Independence. But how I wish I could leave this one present to the nation that I have and still love so well, the SWAZI.
>
> —Gelana to J. S. M. Matsebula, July 1, 1968 (box 24, Hilda Kuper Papers, UCLA)

I like to think that Gelana's death was peaceful. But the truth is harder to accept. In her last weeks, she was agitated and anxious; in her own words, she was "in great distress." As life seeped out of her, Gelana agonized about the fate of her book manuscript, a selection of her favorite Intombazana articles. Six weeks before her death, Gelana wrote to J. S. M. Matsebula, Sobhuza's private secretary, an author in his own right, and a longtime acquaintance: "From my deathbed I am appealing to you to do all within your power to get the book on the Swazi that I have compiled printed to be sold on Independence Day."[1]

This was Gelana's frantic eleventh-hour push to release her work to the world. She knew September 1968—the month of independence—would see a renewed interest in Swati tradition and history, and she hoped to harness the patriotic fervor around the event to generate interest in her book: "The point is that if [the book] misses the Independence no one will be interested in it afterwards." She appealed to Matsebula as a fellow writer, hinting at her bitterness about her failure thus far in publishing: "Like uzame [keep trying] Matsebula—you are a writer yourself and you know just how people never understand. . . . Otherwise, I die with all this information of the nation." Gelana's desire was that now, at the end of her life, her book would be her final love letter—although this time addressed to her adopted country rather than to Dan Twala: "How I wish I could leave this one present to the nation that I have and still will love so well the SWAZI."[2]

While her impending death gave her fresh urgency, Gelana's efforts to publish her Intombazana book were not new. She had been trying to find a publisher for the past five years, since she first started penning the column for the *Times*. In 1963 she wrote to the Africa Service Institute in New York to inquire about North American publishers of books about Africa. (She was advised to try Praeger; nothing seems to have come of this.)[3] The following year, she corresponded with one G. B. Smith, an Australian writer who had lived in Eswatini and knew her Intombazana articles. Gelana sought her advice about book publishing. Smith confidently informed Gelana that "New York or London are the only true markets for books, I believe," a comment that, if nothing else, indicates contemporary prejudices around publishing venues. The politics of publishing were heavily skewed toward northern metropolises. While she thought Gelana's articles were "beautifully written," she feared they wouldn't sell as a book "unless written from a more personal angle." But, she went on, this personal angle "should not be from the angle of an educated woman such as yourself but through the eyes of a girl like my dear Housegirl [from Swaziland] with whom I am in regular touch."[4]

Was this part of the reason Gelana turned in 1964 to adopting the voice of a "common woman" in her Intombazana columns, hoping this would aid her publication chances? If so, her decision to write in this style then not only reflected her ethnographic training but also the sentiment of a European readership that educated, elite African women were somehow less authentic literary voices than the working classes. It is an exchange that exemplified, once again, the many prejudices that Gelana faced. Embarking upon a publishing career in mid-twentieth-century Southern Africa meant negotiating contradictions and obstacles at every turn: too female, too Black, too radical, and now, seemingly, too educated.

Matsebula was Gelana's final hope. Whether Matsebula tried and failed or never tried at all, we will never know. What we do know is that Gelana's manuscript was entirely forgotten in the flurry of preparations for independence. If Sobhuza did see it, we can only assume he passed over his erstwhile friend's deathbed wish, doubtless not wishing a staunch antiroyalist to occupy limelight at independence celebrations. Despite her optimistic prediction to Matsebula that "it would sell like hot buns at R1.20 a copy" (around $5 in today's money), the book never appeared. Overshadowed by national political events, Gelana's funeral in Manzini passed without fanfare. It was a quiet affair attended by Dan (arriving with Margaret in train), a distraught Vusi, and Gelana's other children. Vusi, described by his wife, Anne, as deeply attached to his mother, was angry that Margaret attended the funeral. Less than a decade later, Vusi himself would die in a car crash in Eswatini. His mother's funeral was also attended by church members and the leaders of the political parties, including Ambrose Zwane. Underscoring the distance Gelana had traveled since her earlier warmer relationship with Sobhuza, members of the royal family were pointedly absent.[5] Gelana was buried on a shady slope of Manzini's cemetery, with a headstone erected by Vusi—and on which Dan as husband was not mentioned—"in loving memory of my beloved mother Gelane R. D. Twala. . . . Lala Ngoxolo [Rest in Peace]."

FIGURE 16.1. Gelana Twala's grave, Manzini, Eswatini (Ibrahim Ameen Al-Hashimi)

This was not the first of Gelana's many burials. She, and her work, had already been buried many times over: when the Zulu Society sank her novella, when she was passed over for promotion by Junod, when Sundkler plagiarized her work, when she resigned from politics. As we shall shortly see, Gelana would be buried yet again, even after this bodily interment.

Eswatini was too busy preparing for its historic moment to take much notice of Gelana's death. The only public announcement was a brief paragraph appearing in the *Times* two weeks afterward. (By 1968 *Izwi lama Swazi* had folded; otherwise, it would surely have announced something too.) The paper informed readers of "The Death of a Former Times Contributor" who had "contributed articles for many years published under the pen name of 'Ntombazana [*sic*].'" This briefly factual paragraph is nonetheless colored by a poignant note. The author, probably the editor, Bill Talbott, noted that although "Mrs Twala's writing reflected a keen sense of humour," at the same time "she tended to be almost bitter in contrasting the lives of the 'haves' and the 'have nots.'" Given the "haves" in 1960s Eswatini—as is still the case fifty years later—tended to be connected with the royal family or members of the white settler community, this was a tactful reference to the criticisms Gelana had made of the monarchy and of the British in her last decade of life. The notice also referenced her efforts to publish her book, noting that "shortly before her death Mrs Twala selected a number of her articles and was anxious to have them published in book form before she died."[6]

A week after the *Times* published this announcement, Eswatini officially became independent from Britain. For Dan, one of the saddest moments of Gelana's illness and death was that she had not survived to enjoy this, the event toward which she had committed so much of her life: "I am so sorry she died before she saw the independence of Swaziland. She had based all her life that there would be a state where we Africans would run the country ourselves."[7] The queen's commissioner, Sir Francis Loyd, oversaw the celebrations from the British side. Colonial officials in Eswatini typically wore whites, so immaculate that Gelana had commented in one Intombazana article of 1963 that they "reminded one of being on board a ship."[8] But today Loyd was in full empire regalia: black military dress, epaulets, medals, sword, with a nodding pink plume of feathers atop his cocked hat. And in pointed contrast to the three-piece suit he had donned on prior state occasions, for this historic moment Sobhuza made the unmistakable statement of donning traditional Incwala dress, what Hilda Kuper—who with her family attended the independence celebrations as guests of honor—gushingly called in a letter to Sobhuza "a magnificent symbolic expression of your awareness there was no need to accept Western culture uncritically."[9]

I wonder what Gelana would have made of the event had she lived to see it. The celebrations were watched by tens of thousands in the new Somhlolo Stadium, freshly built in the Ezulwini Valley (site of the Manzana hot spring she had previously eulogized as Intombazana). To the east lay the rolling Mdzimba Mountain Range, where royal kings past lay. This whole area—known as Lobamba—was the historical seat of power of the Dlamini dynasty represented by the present-day royal family. Sobhuza's choice of this site for Independence Day celebrations (and that his new parliament building was built across the road, a stone's throw from the stadium) was his signal to the nation—and to the departing British—that independence marked a restoration of precolonial authority.[10] The moment was a triumph for Sobhuza and for his decades-long quest to promote Swati tradition as the status quo. The British were out, the opposition was nearly silenced, and key NNLC figures such as the once outspoken Dumisa Dlamini had been successfully absorbed into the new regime, a pattern that would continue over the next decade.[11]

Instead of Gelana's Intombazana book, a publication on Eswatini that did come out around the time of independence was that of the white artist and ethnographer Barbara Tyrrell, containing her watercolor paintings of "tribal people" of Southern Africa, including of the emaSwati. This was a glossy-paged coffee-table book that certainly did not sell for "R 1.20."[12] It is hard not to see the two women as a fateful pair. Born within a few years of each other, both hailed from the same region of isiZulu-speaking Natal, yet from different sides of the Mjintini River—Gelana from eNdaleni, Tyrrell from Richmond—a bifurcation that symbolized the divergent paths that race and class carved out for these two female intellectuals of twentieth-century Southern Africa.

Both Gelana and Tyrrell were promoted by Killie Campbell, yet it was Tyrrell who would have an international career as a renowned expert of "tribal people."[13] And Tyrrell's stylized drawings of emaSwati in traditional dress exemplified precisely the anthropological tradition that Gelana had separated herself from in the final years of her life. While Tyrrell's images froze her emaSwati subjects in a mythologized past, Gelana's nuanced portraits of emaSwati women of the 1960s told a different story about tradition, casting it as innovative and ever-changing. There is no evidence that Sobhuza patronized Tyrrell's book, but Tyrrell's was certainly the timeless image of Eswatini he wanted to promote. While Gelana's manuscript languished on Matsebula's desk, Tyrrell's book was applauded by the *Times* as a triumph; readers celebrating independence were advised that "it had a place in every self-respecting library."[14] Tyrrell had achieved the acclaim from the Swati nation had Gelana had so long and unsuccessfully sought.

I end Gelana's story by twinning her with another white female ethnographer: Hilda Kuper. The diligent Matsebula had not forgotten the deathbed charge laid upon him by Gelana's letter. Once the independence hullabaloo had died down, Matsebula posted Gelana's manuscript to Kuper, now professor of anthropology at UCLA, after explaining in a letter that "Mrs Regina Twala, who was well known to you," had "left in my custody for the King a manuscript she had written, anthropological material." Matsebula went on thus: "This being your line, may I please send it to you and you try to edit it for publication."[15] Matsebula's decision to approach Kuper suggests a lack of local support for Gelana's manuscript; Sobhuza could easily have smoothed the way for its publication with a number of Mbabane publishers. (The small private printing houses Websters and Apollo were both publishing local books.) Kuper, as the most renowned living scholar of Eswatini, was a likely next choice. Her links to UCLA and the University of California Press, as well as the fact that Gelana was her former student, all presented her to Matsebula as a more hopeful prospect for publication.

The snag was this: as noted, relations between the two women had not been warm. Gelana was irked by Kuper's status as the authoritative "expert" of Eswatini, an identity that Kuper occupied, by all accounts, with some relish.[16] When Kuper visited Eswatini in 1966, two years before independence, and the first time she had returned to the country in many decades, she was feted by the public as an intellectual celebrity, warmly welcomed by Sobhuza (he hosted her in the home of his daughter, Princess Gcinaphi), and hailed by the *Times* as "the well-known authoress of books on Swaziland" and an "anthropologist of renown." Kuper was invited to give public talks, including the Speech Day address at Salesian High School, which Gelana's own Vusi had attended. Kuper's ethnographic play *Inhliziyo Ngumthakathi* (*A Witch in my Heart*) had already been for some years on the syllabus for Eswatini's junior certificate pupils.[17]

Kuper, in other words, was exactly what Gelana had wished throughout her life to be: a well-regarded intellectual, an acclaimed expert on African custom, and a celebrated author of books. It rankled Gelana that this was not to be for her. It specifically rankled her that Kuper had occupied—as many white scholars had done then and continue to do—positions as authoritative experts of African culture. We remember Gelana had already dismissed Kuper's scholarship as "out-dated" in the NNLC trial of 1963. This is Dan's memory of his conversations with Gelana about her former teacher, reflecting her resentment that white academics studying Africa were self-appointed gatekeepers for Black lives and that they were considered the true "scientists," delivering supposedly authoritative knowledge on societies of which they were not members: "She was unhappy with Dr Hilda Kuper. She thought they allowed their [white] communities to see what they said as sufficient [as best] because they were regarded as the 'scientists.'"[18]

The ill-feeling was mutual. Kuper didn't like Gelana. During her visit to Eswatini, there is no evidence the two made plans to see each other, something that would be usual given their old student-teacher relationship and the fact they hadn't seen each other in twenty years. We only know that when Kuper was seated next to Gelana at a formal lunch in 1966, she lamented her bad luck in being "caught between the American Consul (not an engaging personality) and Mrs Regina Twala who has grown more stupid and opinionated with the years."[19] And when sent Gelana's work by Matsebula, with a plea to aid publication, Kuper made her feelings known. She wrote back to Matsebula that "unfortunately the articles are not of sufficient general interest to be published by the University." She then really twisted the knife in: "I am disappointed that they have so little that is rich in depth and new material. I was under the impression Mrs Twala had collected far more data. There is almost nothing new and nothing substantial enough for any academic journal to accept."[20] In fact, Kuper's astonishment at the contents of Gelana's manuscript is itself surprising. Her archived papers at UCLA show she had read several of Gelana's Intombazana articles, as some had been carefully clipped out and pasted into one of her scrapbooks.[21]

How should we interpret Kuper's lack of support for the posthumous publication of her former student's work? Kuper could indeed be supportive of younger academics (which Gelana, being three years older than Kuper, was not) as well as of junior scholars, including Matsebula, whose own forthcoming history of Eswatini she warmly inquired about, being "sure it will be very useful for students."[22] Then there was also Thoko Ginindza, a liSwati woman who earned a master's degree in African studies at UCLA and for whom Kuper helped procure a scholarship.[23] Jenny Kuper, Hilda's daughter, remembers her mother as a generous academic mentor who invited students to meals at her house and "made them a part of their family."[24] Furthermore, the literary method Gelana was experimenting with—semifictional ethnography—was one Kuper herself was deeply interested in.[25]

But there were also grounds for profound disagreement between the two women. For one, these were conflicts over the very nature of anthropology as a scholarly discipline. As we have seen, Gelana had increasingly pivoted toward a realization that Swati tradition was no single thing: it was as messy and contradictory as any other identity of the contemporary world. As Intombazana, Gelana told the stories of emaSwati of the 1960s, painting them as modern people seeking new ways of living in a fast-changing world. Tradition was flexible, adaptive, endlessly innovative. On this count, Gelana's views starkly contrasted with Kuper's own view of Swati tradition. Kuper drew a clear line between what was "Swati" and what was "Western," believing the rituals and customs of the emaSwati—as they had supposedly been practiced since time immemorial—created a functional and cohesive society, delicately balanced in all respects.

The two women's divergent takes on anthropology had real-life consequences. Gelana's anthropological change of heart occurred in tandem with her political awakening, her conviction that tradition could also be a pretext for repressive patriarchal rule. By contrast, in Kuper's opinion, it was absolute monarchy along "traditional" lines that was the answer to the problems colonialism had created for Swati society. In Kuper's view, the leaders of the political parties—especially the NNLC—were dangerous extremists who unjustly sought to cast Sobhuza and the Imbokodvo—the natural customary rulers of the people—as repressive and anti-democratic.[26] Accusations of politicians like Gelana and Ambrose Zwane that the royalists were "ultra-conservative" was mere "propaganda."[27] Kuper's negative feelings toward the political parties are revealed in a violent dream she said she had on the eve of independence. She dreamed of "extremists" who used the pretext of an independence fireworks display to torch and destroy the royal kraal. She was so shaken she immediately wrote to Sobhuza to warn him: "There are, as you know, people in the country who are hostile and who could easily do great damage by lighting fires in wrong places. As a friend deeply committed to your welfare, and progress and peace in Swaziland, I urge you to reconsider this [fireworks] display."[28]

Kuper's conservative political stance and her unease with "extremist" politicians were crystallized in her official biography of Sobhuza, embarked upon in the early 1970s. The book was adulatory in tone, casting Sobhuza as "a good king, a wise statesman, a gracious man. Bayethe [Hail]."[29] Kuper compared the Swati monarch to "an elegant Gandhi," bravely fusing traditional and modern in his challenge of colonial rule.[30] Given Sobhuza's highly repressive domestic policies (and things were about to get worse), some scholars have excused this on the grounds the biography was official and Kuper was thus constrained in what she could write.[31] This was doubtless true (something Kuper's daughter, Jenny, remembers irked her mother on occasion). Kuper's correspondence with the commissioning committee in Eswatini shows every word she wrote was vetted by these proroyalist figures.[32] But these *were* Kuper's own views. She was personally friendly with Sobhuza and all the key royalist personalities in the 1960s and 1970s. Why else would the politically sensitive task of a royal biography have been entrusted to her? The comment about Sobhuza being "the Gandhi of Africa" was first made by her in conversation with Sobhuza. This was no public statement for the benefit of the committee.[33]

FIGURE 16.2. Hilda Kuper and Sobhuza II, Eswatini, 1981 (Hilda Kuper Papers, UCLA Archives)

Kuper's commitment to Swati tradition even allowed her to give a positive spin to Sobhuza's autocratic suspension of the constitution in 1973. Since the exit of the British, Sobhuza had continued to be plagued by political opposition. Startled and worried by the NNLC's success in the 1972 elections, the king abolished the constraining inconvenience of parliamentary procedure by declaring a state of emergency in early 1973.[34] He named himself the holder of "supreme power" and outlawed all political parties on the grounds they were "highly undesirable political practices alien to and incompatible with the way of life in our society . . . designed to disrupt and destroy our own peaceful, constructive and essentially democratic methods of political activity."[35]

Kuper admitted to "the restrictions on individual freedom" this entailed: all political meetings were banned by the government, and detention without trial was now legal. Yet in her eyes this was the ultimate victory for an undiluted version of Swati tradition, a full reversal of colonial-era Westernization: "This was not a military coup but an effort to turn nominal political independence into full sovereignty under a leader who had proved his wisdom and moral courage over the years."[36] Kuper declared herself opposed to a "self-satisfied belief in the West that the traditional African king is a tyrant."[37] Sobhuza's assumption of absolute rule showed his unwavering commitment to "traditional" politics against Westminster-style constitutions: he has the "courage to express unpopular opinions for unselfish reasons."[38]

The emaSwati scholars whom Kuper supported throughout the 1960s and beyond espoused a similar proroyalist stance. Behind her lifelong warm relationship with Matsebula was the fact he was the king's personal secretary. Matsebula's history of Eswatini, published in 1976, followed the official line. His depiction of Sobhuza verged on the sycophantic, and he dismissed all political opposition as espousing "foreign ideas and institutions which were quite irrelevant to Swazi life."[39] Kuper's former MA student at UCLA, Thoko Ginindza, was likewise also enmeshed in royalist networks. Ginindza sat on the commissioning committee for Sobhuza's biography and upon her return to Eswatini from the United States was appointed government ethnographer and curator at the new national museum, a position surely reserved for regime supporters.[40] These were the scholars of Swati life and history to whom Kuper lent her patronage.

Finally, there was the issue of personality. Gelana was forceful and not afraid of conflict. She was not going to take direction from Kuper as she had done decades earlier. She was also, by temperament, incapable of playing the game of deference and clientelism. Her critical views of white liberal academics rendered her unwilling to do so.[41] On the other hand, a figure like Ginindza was dependent upon Kuper—first as sponsor of her UCLA scholarship while in the United States and second as a paid employee of Kuper's, undertaking research for her in the 1970s. Historian Abby Gondek has shown how Kuper reworked Ginindza's UCLA master's thesis to cast it as more proroyalist and celebratory of Swati tradition than Ginindza had initially suggested. There is no evidence Ginindza resisted this—how could she have done so as a client of her powerful employer?[42] Kuper also used Gindinza's notes and fieldwork reports with little acknowledgment, a dynamic all too familiar to Gelana from her interactions with Bengt Sundkler.[43] Gelana of the 1960s would not allow herself to be dictated to as in earlier decades. All this, I speculate, turned Kuper against her former student, leading her to make the intriguing accusation that Regina was both "stupid" and "opinionated." Was she "stupid" because she spoke against the monarchy and tradition, and was she "opinionated" because she did not accept Kuper's place as ethnographer queen of the emaSwati?

Kuper had been Gelana's last hope. Gelana's star had briefly flamed in the 1950s and 1960s. By the 1970s it had been quenched by forces arrayed against her. Patriarchal royalist Eswatini had no room for memorializing antimonarchy "foreign" women—this despite Gelana's deathbed declaration of love for her adopted nation, "the SWAZI." Virtually the only mention I've managed to find of Gelana in the decades since was in an article published in the 1980s by Mbuso Mathenjwa, a writer for the monthly magazine for Swati television—itself owned by the monarchy. Mathenjwa warmly commemorated Gelana's handicraft work and her interest in women's welfare. But on Gelana's politics, her NNLC membership, and her criticism of the monarchy, he was silent. If anything, Eswatini in the 1980s was even more repressive than during the 1970s; Sobhuza had died in 1982, and a tussle between his successors plunged the country into crisis.[44] Political dissent was whispered about behind closed doors, not published in widely read publications. But Mathenjwa could not entirely suppress the subversive truth of Gelana Twala. He noted, almost in passing, almost casually, that she was remembered by mourners at her funeral "as a strong woman who used to be volatile at meetings of the Swazi National Council."[45] Gelana is similarly absent in other accounts of the period. Not a single history of Eswatini or South Africa mentions her, and although one of the very first Black alumna of the University of the Witwatersrand, she is absent from the authoritative two-volume history of the university.[46] A Google search yields as many references to Regina Twala, a contemporary street vendor of "cooked treats and dishes," as to Regina Gelana Twala, writer, politician, and social worker.[47] Gelana's derelict Kwaluseni library seems to encapsulate the erasure of her legacy: situated on a busy road, it is ignored by those who pass it daily.

Hilda Kuper died in 1992. As she was a decades-long employee of UCLA and a prominent anthropologist of Southern Africa, Kuper's papers were archived in the university's special collections. Gelana's unpublished Intombazana manuscript was silently enfolded within Kuper's papers, a documentary microcosm of Gelana's struggles to assert her own scholarly voice against the more dominant voices of others. Reaching Gelana is only possible via Kuper's archived papers; Kuper is quite literally gatekeeping access to the defining work of this important figure of Swati history. And in this case, archiving at ULCA—just as in the private home of Tim Couzens—was a double-edged sword. On the one hand, it preserved Gelana's manuscript for posterity, making it possible for future generations to recover her lost legacy. On the other hand, archiving seemed the worst kind of slight to Gelana. After all, it was not even her own papers that were archived—Gelana's manuscript was only preserved as an unintended consequence of Kuper's more illustrious reputation. Archiving also seemed to say something about the significance of Gelana's writing. It suggested that although she may be of interest to the scholars one day poring through the boxes of the Kuper collection, her writings were not "current," nor would they appeal to contemporary audiences. Publishing was a very different statement to archiving, one that argued for the relevance and the potential popularity of Gelana's writings.

I am certain that Gelana—an author hungry throughout her life for recognition and readers—would have preferred the visibility of publication to the invisibility of being archived. Here, then, is the equivocal meaning of Gelana Twala's identity as a Black Southern African writer and intellectual: an author forever destined to have her story told by everyone except herself, to be remembered through her proximity to those whom the world privileged more than her, and to be written about in the books of white intellectuals rather than in her own.

What you have just read is my account of Gelana's life—ironically, a further example of access to her life being mediated through a white academic. I have shone a biographer's light on aspects of a life that has ended up in dusty boxes and distant memories. However, the lived experience is Gelana's alone. Her full story—an autobiography of sorts—exists in her letters, her hundreds of articles, and her one surviving book manuscript. For Gelana wrote of her experiences nearly every day since childhood. And from this perspective, she was indeed the author of her own life. We are just awaiting this story's publication.

# Postscript

I had not planned to write Gelana Twala's biography. When I first read her Intombazana manuscript in the UCLA archives during the summer of 2017, my initial thought was to secure a publisher for this unique book, to help find a platform for a work that I believed merited a far wider audience than what it could find as part of a manuscript collection in a scholarly library. After making some inquiries about possible viable partners for this project—publishers who might be interested in a forgotten writer-scholar of the 1950s and 1960s—I contacted Gill Berchowitz, then editor in chief at Ohio University Press. The press has a strong African studies catalog, and I knew Gill was committed to supporting and promoting the stories of African women. Plus, Ohio University Press frequently enters into copublishing agreements with presses in southern Africa, meaning there would be the possibility of a more affordable edition in that region. Gill heard me out sympathetically. But to her mind, the major problem was the obvious one. Gelana was entirely unknown. How to make a case for publishing the corpus of a writer whose significance and reputation were so uncertain?

Gill suggested an alternative. Since 2012 the press had been pioneering a new book series called Ohio Short Histories of Africa. The goal was—in the words of the press's website—to present a "series of informative and concise guides, lively biographies and succinct introductions to important topics in African history."[1]

But the series was lacking in female subjects. When I first emailed Gill about Gelana's manuscript in 2018, the Short Histories series only had three titles focusing on women out of a total of eighteen.[2] Gill's suggestion was that I prepare a proposal for Gelana's inclusion in the series, not least because she wanted to feature more biographies of African women.

For my part, I felt once a biography had been written of Gelana, it might then be easier to make a case for having her manuscript released to the world. Yet once I started working on Gelana's biography for the Short Histories series, I realized how—thanks to Gelana's own prolific writing career—a biography of her would have much more material than would typically be the case for titles in this series, which ranged from thirty thousand to forty thousand words. Gill was open to publishing the biography as a stand-alone book of longer word length, rather than being constrained by the rubric of the series. (This book is over twice as long.)

Yet although my biography of Gelana is now complete, I have not forgotten my original aim of publishing Gelana's own work. And the more of her work I have found in the course of writing the present book—including her early newspaper columns from the 1930s as well as the many Intombazana articles that she had not included in her final manuscript sent to Matsebula—the more convinced I felt that her work should be published. The first step, however, was to work out who owned Gelana's estate. For someone like myself unversed in copyright law, this involved a frequently overwhelming morass of complex legal issues. Gelana died without leaving a will, so the question of who held her intellectual property was unclear to me as well as to her family. Not least, the issue was complicated by the transnational nature of her situation—a writer who lived and died in Eswatini but who was South African and whose papers are located in both those countries as well as the United States and Sweden. Which country's copyright laws apply here? I finally ended up consulting a lawyer in Eswatini who determined that according to both Roman-Dutch law and Swati customary law, "the rightful beneficiary of the estate of the late Mrs. Regina Twala is her granddaughter Pinokie Twala, with whom all copyright, royalties, and other benefits derived from the use of her grandmother's intellectual property should be discussed and negotiated."[3]

Gelana's letters presented me with a different set of questions. While Pinokie Twala agreed that they should be deposited at the archives of Wits University—her grandmother's alma mater—this involved negotiating access to the letters with Diana Wall (Tim Couzens's widow), who has had the letters at her Johannesburg home since Couzens' death. Because I know both "sides" (as it were), and also due to my own interest in having the letters professionally archived, I have adopted the role of mediator between Diana Wall and Pinokie Twala, their rightful proprietor. In September 2021, a legal agreement between Pinokie Twala and Wits University was finally signed, and the letters have recently been deposited by Wall into the safekeeping of the Wits Historical Papers collection.

Questions of access, ownership, and archiving aside, what should be the platform of releasing these materials to the world? Since first coming across Twala's letters in Johannesburg, I had moved from my post at the University of Cambridge in the United Kingdom to Stanford University in California. Perhaps by virtue of its location in Silicon Valley, digital humanities are especially strong at Stanford, a new experience for me. I soon contacted Stanford's Center for Spatial and Textual Analysis, the digital humanities hub for the university. My exposure to the relatively new field of digital humanities gave me the idea of digitizing Gelana's output and publishing it virtually via a dedicated website. With the consent of Pinokie Twala, I planned to draw upon digital humanities techniques to make sure this was not just a data-heavy text dump. Rather, I hoped that new technology could assist in designing thought-provoking ways for readers to engage with Gelana's writings. If traditional publishers would not take on the risky enterprise on publishing her book in hard copy, then why should I not explore digital platforms, especially given my current geographical location? I gained a Stanford University grant to support the work of digitizing and curating Gelana's work as a virtual archive and commenced work on the project in the summer of 2020.

Almost immediately several paradoxes presented themselves. On one hand, a digital archive seemed the antithesis of the hierarchies of the traditional publishing world. This could be a populist way of bringing neglected texts to the attention of potentially worldwide audiences—and at a significantly lower cost than traditional hard-copy publishing. On the other, the digital world clearly had its own inequities. Not least there was the fact that digital access was by no means equal across the world, especially in sub-Saharan Africa, where I hoped Gelana's writings would find their most significant audience. We are a long way away from the tech-utopianism of the early twenty-first century when many naively believed in the leveling powers of digital innovation.

Yet a further contradiction is linked to the issue of revenue. Digital access is typically free of charge, something usually held up as evidence of the egalitarian nature of online texts. Might this be the solution that topples the exclusionary publishing edifice that Gelana struggled with her whole life? But the claim to free internet of course doesn't account for the significant cost of accessing the internet, depending on where you live in the world. And in addition to not truly being free, open-access publishing also erases profits from those who may seek them. Gelana's family, especially Pinokie, felt strongly that Gelana would have wished that some kind of financial benefit accrue to her family via her writings. An open-access digital archive and publishing platform would clearly not achieve that. What would Gelana have thought, in any case—a woman who died decades before the birth of the internet—of a publishing platform that she would have been scarcely able to imagine during her lifetime?

Some of these challenges have been successfully navigated, while others are still pending. Yet whether resolved or not, the complexities to both publishing Gelana's work and ensuring its long-term safety and accessibility to the public in the Wits Historical Papers seem to me a painful affirmation of the racial hierarchies of the academic knowledge industry as well as an echo of the intellectual gatekeeping that constrained Gelana during her lifetime. Gelana's failure in publishing while alive is now echoed in my difficulties encountered in releasing her work to the world. From beyond the grave, Gelana Twala is still striving to write herself into history, and she is still restlessly seeking an audience for her many thousands of words.

# Notes

The following is a list of common abbreviations used throughout the notes section.

| | |
|---|---|
| BSP | Bengt Sundkler Papers, University of Uppsala |
| CL | Methodist Collection, Cory Library, Rhodes University |
| HKP | Hilda Kuper Papers |
| ISR | Institute for Social Research, University of Natal |
| KCL | Killie Campbell Library |
| KZN | University of KwaZulu-Natal Archives |
| LSE | London School of Economics and Political Science Archives |
| RTP | Regina Twala Papers, Historical Papers Research Archive, University of the Witwatersrand |
| UCLA | University of California, Los Angeles Archives |
| SAIRR | South African Institute of Race Relations Archives |
| SOAS | School of Oriental and African Studies Archives |

## Introduction

1. Swaziland was renamed Eswatini (the siSwati-language rendering of Swaziland) in 2018. Throughout the book I use Eswatini, save when quoting historical sources that use the older name of Swaziland.
2. In keeping with the fact that this is a biography, the rest of the book refers to Regina Twala by her first name (Regina, and later in life, as Gelana, which can also be spelled "Gelane"). I also refer to all other members of the Twala family (Dan, Vusi, Anne, Mary, Zanele, and Pinokie) by their first names.
3. "liSwati" (singular) and "emaSwati" (plural) refer to people of the country of Eswatini (formerly known as Swaziland). During the period when the country was known as Swaziland, its peoples were known as Swazi (singular) or Swazis (plural). I use "liSwati/emaSwati" throughout for the people of Eswatini, as well as the adjectival form of "Swati." All the historical sources refer to "Swazi/Swazis."

4. Tim Couzens, *The New African: A Study of the Life and Works of H. I. E. Dhlomo* (Johannesburg: Ravan, 1985). Couzens's pioneering research on early twentieth-century Black literature would remain firmly androcentric—a chronicle of notable literary men—despite the contrary evidence posed by a female figure like Regina Twala.
5. Belinda Bozzoli and Mmantho Nkotsoe, *Women of Phokeng: Consciousness, Life Strategy, and Migrancy in South Africa, 1900–1983* (Portsmouth, NH: Heinemann, 1991).
6. Pumla Dineo Gqola, ed., *Miriam Tlali, Writing Freedom* (Cape Town: HSRC Press, 2021), 4.
7. Hilda Kuper, *Sobhuza II, Ngwenyama and King of Swaziland: The Story of an Hereditary Ruler and His Country* (London: Duckworth, 1978).
8. Nancy J. Jacobs and Andrew Bank, "Biography in Post-Apartheid South Africa: A Call for Awkwardness," *African Studies* 78, no. 2 (2019): 168. These are Rebecca Reyher, *Zulu Woman: The Life Story of Christian Sibiya* (New York: Feminist Press at CUNY, 1999); Clifton Crais and Pamela Scully, *Sara Baartman and the Hottentot Venus: A Ghost Story and a Biography* (Princeton, NJ: Princeton University Press, 2009); Bob Edgar, *Josie Mpama/Palmer: Get Up, Get Moving* (Athens: Ohio University Press, 2020); Zubeida Jaffer, *Beauty of the Heart: The Life and Times of Charlotte Mannya Maxeke* (Bloemfontein: SUN Media, 2016); Shireen Hassim, *Voices of Liberation: Fatima Meer* (Pretoria: HSRC Press, 2019); Margaret McCord, *The Calling of Katie Makhanya: A Memoir of South Africa* (Cape Town: David Philip, 1999); Sisonke Msimang, *The Resurrection of Winnie Mandela* (Johannesburg: Jonathan Ball, 2018); Anné Mariè du Preez Bezdrob, *Winnie Mandela: A Life* (Cape Town: Zebra, 2003); and Louise Viljoen, *Ingrid Jonker: Poet under Apartheid* (Athens: Ohio University Press, 2013). There are also a few "collective biographies" of women—e.g., M. M. Nthunya, K. L. Kendall, E. Kuzwayo, *Singing Away the Hunger: Stories of a Life of Lesotho* (Bloomington: Indiana University Press, 1997) and Shula Marks, *Not Either an Experimental Doll: The Separate Worlds of Three South African Women* (Bloomington: Indiana University Press, 1988).
9. Jaffer, *Beauty of the Heart.*
10. Heather Hughes, "Lives and Wives: Understanding African Nationalism in South Africa through a Biographical Approach," *History Compass* 10, no. 8 (2012): 562–73.
11. Msimang, *Winnie Mandela;* du Preez Bezdrob, *Winnie Mandela;* Nancy Harrison, *Winnie Mandela* (London: Gollancz, 1985).
12. Crais and Scully, *Sara Baartman.*
13. Athambile Masola, "A Footnote and a Pioneer: Noni Jabavu's Legacy," in *Foundational African Writers: Peter Abrahams, Noni Jabavu, Sibusiso Nyembezi, and Es'kia Mphahlele,* ed. Bhekizizwe Peterson, Khwezi-Mkhize, and Makhosazana Xaba (Johannesburg: Wits University Press, 2022).

14. Michel-Rolph Trouillot, *Silencing the Past: Power and the Production of History* (Boston: Beacon, 1995), 48.
15. Jean Allman, "The Disappearing of Hannah Kudjoe: Nationalism, Feminism, and the Tyrannies of History," *Journal of Women's History*, 21, no. 3 (2009): 13–35.
16. Moya Bailey, "They Aren't Talking about Me . . . ," *Crunk Feminist Collective* (blog), March 14, 2010, https://www.crunkfeministcollective.com/2010/03/14/they-arent-talking-about-me/.
17. Frances M. Beal, "Double Jeopardy: To Be Black and Female," *Meridians: Feminism, Race, Transnationalism* 8, no. 2 (2008): 166–76.
18. Barbara Boswell, *And Wrote My Story Anyway: Black South African Women's Novels as Feminism* (Johannesburg: Wits University Press, 2020), 37; Barbara Boswell, *Lauretta Ngcobo: Writing as the Practice of Freedom* (Cape Town: HSRC Press, 2022). Boswell's research on South African writers like Miriam Tlali and Lauretta Ngcobo details these female authors' conflicts with husbands, fathers, editors, and publishers. See also Gqola, *Miriam Tlali*; and Caroline Davis, "A Question of Power: Bessie Head and Her Publishers," *Journal of Southern African Studies* 44, no. 3 (2018): 491–506.
19. Gqola, *Miriam Tlali*, 18.
20. Goretti Kyohumendo, interview by author, September 18, 2021, via Zoom between San Francisco and Kampala.
21. Shireen Hassim, *The ANC Women's League: Sex, Gender and Politics* (Auckland Park, South Africa: Jacana, 2014).
22. "Gelana" can also be spelled "Gelane" (Pinokie Twala, for example, prefers "Gelane").
23. Rebecca Skloot, *The Immortal Life of Henrietta Lacks* (New York: Broadway Paperbacks, 2011).
24. Lynn Thomas, "Historicizing Agency," *Gender and History* 28, no. 2 (2016): 324–39.
25. Naminate Diabate, *Naked Agency: Genital Cursing and Biopolitics in Africa* (Durham, NC: Duke University Press, 2020), 19.

## Chapter 1: eNdaleni

1. In isiZulu, the spelling is "eNdaleni"; the Anglicized rendering of the word is "Indaleni." I use eNdaleni unless I am referring to the mission station or school.
2. Norman Etherington, "Mission Station Melting Pots as a Factor in the Rise of South African Black Nationalism," *International Journal of African Historical Studies* 9, no. 4 (1976): 600–601.
3. Dan Magaziner, *The Art of Life in South Africa* (Athens: Ohio University Press, 2016), 315n1.

4. Norman Etherington, *Peasants, Peasants and Politics in Southeast Africa, 1835–1880: African Christian Communities in Natal, Pondoland and Zululand* (London: Royal Historical Society, 1978), 122.
5. E. M. Preston-Whyte, "Land and Development at Indaleni: A Historical Perspective," *Development Southern Africa* 4, no. 3 (1987): 408.
6. Etherington, *Preachers, Peasants, and Politics*, 95–99.
7. Richard Elphick, *The Equality of Believers: Protestant Missionaries and the Racial Politics of South Africa* (Charlottesville: University of Virginia Press, 2012).
8. Etherington, "Mission Station Melting Pots," 603–4.
9. Jeff Guy, *The Maphumulo Uprising: War, Law and Ritual in the Zulu Rebellion* (Pietermaritzburg: University of KwaZulu-Natal Press, 2005), 48.
10. Sol Plaatje, *Native Life in South Africa* (Athens: Ohio University Press, 1991), chap. 4, chap. 5.
11. Dan Twala, interview by Tim Couzens, July 26, 1979, Dube, Soweto, RTP.
12. *Umteteli wa Bantu*, December 9, 1922.
13. Regina to Dan, July 2, 1938, RTP. I am grateful to Dan Magaziner for sharing his memories of present-day Ndaleni with me.
14. *Times of Swaziland*, April 17, 1964.
15. *Natal Mercury* (Pietermaritzburg), June 1, 1926.
16. A. W. Cragg, *The Story of Indaleni* (N.p.: Natal District Missionary Committee of the Wesleyan Methodist Church, South Africa, 1924), photograph between p. 5 and p. 6.
17. Studies of Missionaries and Missionary Institutions, series II, no author, n.d., p. 90, CL.
18. Diary of A. W Cragg, May 12–13, 1927, CL.
19. Cragg, *Story of Indaleni*, photograph between p. 3 and p. 4.
20. Regina to Dan, July 2, 1939, RTP.
21. Diary of A. W. Cragg, April 18, 1929, CL.
22. Cragg, *Story of Indaleni*, 16–17.
23. D. Mck. Malcolm, "Zulu Literature," *Africa: Journal of the International African Institute* 19, no. 1 (1949): 39.
24. *Times of Swaziland*, April 17, 1964.
25. Dan Twala, interview, RTP.
26. Les Switzer, "*Bantu World* and the Origins of a Captive Commercial Press in South Africa," *Journal of Southern African Studies* 14, no. 3 (1988): 351.
27. Prospectus of the Indaleni Wesleyan Training and Industrial School for Girls (1907), n.p., Methodist pamphlet box 10, CL.
28. Megan Healy-Clancy, *A World of Their Own: A History of South African Women's Education* (Charlottesville: University of Virginia Press, 2013), 89.
29. Cragg, *Story of Indaleni*, 10.

30. *Times of Swaziland*, April 17, 1964.
31. *Ilanga lase Natal*, October 2, 1931.
32. Corinne Sandwith, "'The Appearance of the Book: Towards a History of the Reading Lives and Worlds of Black South African Readers," *English in Africa* 45, no. 1 (2018): 25.
33. "Never Read a Bad Book," *Bantu World*, January 6, 1940.
34. Regina to Dan, June 7, 1938, RTP.
35. Alan M. Kent, *Pulp Methodism: The Lives and Literature of Silas, Joseph and Salome Hocking, Three Cornish Novelists* (Cornwall, UK: Cornish Hillside Publications, 2002), 119.
36. Regina to Dan, June 28, 1938, RTP. Dan Twala's favorite Hocking novel was the decidedly more gender-normative *Nancy Molesworth*, which showed him "how noble a woman can be. . . . What a life of bliss a man can have should he only get a proper loving dear woman." Dan to Regina, June 23, 1938, RTP.
37. Shula Marks, *Divided Sisterhood: Race, Class, and Gender in the South African Nursing Profession* (New York: St. Martin's, 1994), 100.
38. Healy-Clancy, *World of Their Own*, 88–89.
39. *Times of Swaziland*, April 17, 1964.
40. Susan Michelle Du Rand, "From Mission School to Bantu Education: A History of Adams College" (MA thesis, University of Natal, 1990), 62–63.
41. Tim Couzens, *The New African: A Study of the Life and Work of H. I. E. Dhlomo* (Johannesburg: Ravan, 1985), 51.
42. Couzens, 52.
43. Ellen Kuzwayo, *Call Me Woman* (London: Women's Press, 1985), 85–89.
44. Du Rand, "From Mission School," 97; Shula Marks, *Not Either an Experimental Doll: The Separate Worlds of Three South African Women* (Bloomington: Indiana University Press, 1988), 25.
45. *Iso loMuzi* (Adams College, Amanzimtoti) 3, no. 2 (May 1934); *Umteteli waBantu*, February 10, 1934.
46. *Iso loMuzi* 3, no. 2 (May 1934).
47. "Our Native Work in Natal," *Wesleyan Methodist Church News*, April 1930, 31.
48. Dan Twala, interview, RTP.
49. Diary of A. W. Cragg, May 10, 1931, CL; Dan Twala, interview, RTP.
50. "Sporting and Social News from Indaleni," March 24, 1934; "Thrilling Tennis Played in Natal," *Bantu World*, May 12, 1934.
51. Dan Twala, interview, RTP.
52. Farieda Khan, "Anyone for Tennis? Conversions with Black Women Involved in Tennis during the Apartheid Era," *Agenda* 24, no. 85 (2010): 77–78.
53. Nicholas Cope, *To Bind the Nation: Solomon kaDinuzulu and Zulu Nationalism, 1913–1933* (Pietermaritzburg: University of Natal Press, 1993), 213.

54. *Ilanga lase Natal,* November 1, 1929.
55. Diary of A. W. Cragg, September 8, 1930, CL.
56. Healy-Clancy, *World of Their Own,* 107.
57. Tammy M. Proctor, "A Separate Path: Scouting and Guiding in Interwar South Africa," *Comparative Studies in Society and History* 42, no. 3 (2000): 620; Deborah Gaitskell, "From Domestic Servants to Girl Wayfarers at St Agnes', Rosettenville: Phases in the Life of a South African Mission School, 1909–1935," *Southern African Review of Education* 19, no. 2 (2013): 105.
58. Healy-Clancy, *World of Their Own,* 93; Paul la Hausse de Lalouviere, *Restless Identities: Signatures of Nationalism, Zulu Ethnicity and History in the Lives of Petros Lamula (c. 1881–1948) and Lymon Maling (1889–c. 1936)* (Pietermaritzburg: University of Natal Press, 2000), 143.
59. Marks, *Experimental Doll,* 31; Healy-Clancy, *World of Their Own,* 107.
60. Nicholas Cope, "The Zulu Petit Bourgeoisie and Zulu Nationalism in the 1920s: Origins of Inkatha," *Journal of Southern African Studies* 16, no. 3 (1990): 439.
61. *Ilanga lase Natal,* July 24, 1931.
62. Diary of A. W. Cragg, March 30, 1928, CL.
63. Anne Twala, interview, July 29, 2019, Kwaluseni, Eswatini.
64. *Bantu World,* May 18, 1935.
65. Diary of A. W. Cragg, July 22, 1933, CL.
66. *Umteteli wa Bantu,* July 8, 1932; February 1, 1936.
67. *Times of Swaziland,* April 17, 1964.

## Chapter 2: Mademoiselle

1. *Bantu World,* February 2, 1935.
2. Les Switzer, "*Bantu World* and the Origins of a Captive African Commercial Press in South Africa," *Journal of Southern African Studies* 14, no. 3 (1988): 356.
3. Ray Phillips, *Bantu in the City: A Study of Cultural Adjustment on the Witwatersrand* (Alice: Lovedale, 1938), esp. 91–99.
4. Switzer, "*Bantu World,*" 358.
5. Marijke du Toit and Palesa Nzuzu, "Isifazane Sakiti Emadolebheni: The Politics of Gender in *Ilanga lase Natal,* 1933–1938," *Journal of Natal and Zululand History* 33, no. 2 (2019): 64.
6. Regina to Dan, April 28, 1938, RTP.
7. Regina to Dan, August 5, 1938, RTP.
8. Philip Bonner, "Desirable or Undesirable Sotho Women? Liquor, Prostitution, and the Migration of Sotho Women to the Rand" (African studies seminar paper, University of Witwatersrand, May 1988), https://core.ac.uk/download/pdf/39667365.pdf.

9. *Bantu World,* May 12, 1935.
10. *Bantu World,* September 5, 1936; Modern Girl around the World Research Group, *The Modern Girl around the World: Consumption, Modernity and Globalization* (Durham, NC: Duke University Press, 2008), esp. 96–119.
11. *Bantu World,* February 5, 1938.
12. *Bantu World,* May 20, 1933.
13. *Bantu World,* May 8, 1937.
14. *Bantu World,* May 14, 1932. For Cecilia Tshabalala, see Megan Healy-Clancy, "Women and the Problem of Family in Early African Nationalist History and Historiography," *South African Historical Journal* 64, no. 3 (2012): 450–71.
15. *Bantu World,* March 11, 1933.
16. Anne Twala, interview by author, July 29, 2019, Kwaluseni.
17. Dan Twala, interview by Tim Couzens, July 26, 1979, Dube, Soweto, RTP.
18. Regina to Dan, August 1938, RTP.
19. Miss R. D. Mazibuko, "Teachers Do Know How to Cook," *Umteteli wa Bantu,* May 18, 1935.
20. Sister Kollie, "African Women and Character," *Umteteli wa Bantu,* June 15, 1935.
21. Regina to Dan, April 28, 1938, RTP.
22. Dan to Regina, April 1938, RTP.
23. *Ilanga lase Natal,* May 1, 15, 1937.
24. Jeff Peires, "The Lovedale Press: Literature for the Bantu Revisited," *History in Africa* 6 (1979): 158–59.
25. N. W. Visser, "HIE Dhlomo: The Re-emergence of an African Writer," *English in Africa* 1, no. 2 (1974): 1.
26. *Bantu World,* November 23, 1935.
27. *Umteteli wa Bantu,* June 8, 1935.
28. Jeff Opland, trans. and ed., *The Nation's Bounty: The Xhosa Poetry of Nontsizi Mgqwetho* (Johannesburg: Wits University Press, 2007), xiv.
29. *Umteteli wa Bantu,* December 23, 1933.
30. *Ilanga lase Natal,* November 13, 1931.
31. Sister Kollie, "African Women and Character," *Umteteli wa Bantu,* June 15, 1935.
32. *Bantu World,* January 20, 1934.
33. *Bantu World,* December 23, 1936.
34. *Bantu World,* March 18, 1939.
35. Christopher Ballantine, "Concert and Dance: The Foundations of Black Jazz in South Africa between the Twenties and the Early Forties," *Popular Music* 10, no. 2 (1991): 141.
36. *Bantu World,* December 29, 1934. For "Lady Porcupine," see Tsitsi Ella Jaji, *Africa in Stereo: Modernism, Music and Pan African Solidarity* (New York: Oxford University Press, 2014), 125.

37. *Bantu World,* May 18, 1935.
38. Low teachers' salaries were frequently bemoaned in the African press. "Unapologetic Native Teacher," *Ilanga lase Natal,* October 16, 1931.
39. *Bantu World,* December 21, 1935.
40. Stephanie Newell, "Literary Activism in Colonial Ghana: A Newspaper-Novel by 'A. Native,'" *Current Writing: Text and Representation in Southern Africa* 31, no. 2 (2001): 25.
41. *Bantu World,* July 21, 1934.
42. *Bantu World,* August 25, 1934.
43. *Bantu World,* May 12, 1934.
44. *Bantu World,* May 5, 1934.
45. *Bantu World,* April 14, 1934.
46. *Bantu World,* December 1, 1934.
47. *Bantu World,* December 1, 1934.
48. *Bantu World,* January 19, 1935.
49. *Bantu World,* January 19, 1935.
50. *Bantu World,* August 25, 1934.
51. *Bantu World,* February 2, 1935.
52. *Bantu World,* November 24, 1934.
53. *Bantu World,* December 21, 1935.
54. *Umteteli wa Bantu,* September 2, 1939.
55. *Umteteli wa Bantu,* March 30, 1935.
56. *Umteteli wa Bantu,* April 13, 1935.
57. *Umteteli wa Bantu,* April 6, 1935.
58. *Umteteli wa Bantu,* March 23, 1935.
59. *Umteteli wa Bantu,* April 13, 1935.
60. Regina to Dan, July 2, 1938, RTP.
61. *Umteteli wa Bantu,* March 24, 1934; *Umteteli wa Bantu,* July 20, 1935.
62. *Bantu World,* March 23, 1935.
63. *Bantu World,* December 21 and 28, 1935; "Isambulelo," 2 pages, n.d., RTP.
64. Regina to Dan, May 15, 1938, RTP.
65. Email correspondence with Liz Thornberry, July 20, 2021.

## Chapter 3: Johannesburg

1. Clive M. Chipkin, *Johannesburg Style: Architecture and Society, 1880s to 1960s* (Cape Town: David Philip, 1993), 80–81.
2. Chipkin, *Johannesburg Style,* 82.
3. Dan to Regina, May 15, 1938, RTP.
4. *Bantu World,* May 31, 1941.
5. Chipkin, *Johannesburg Style,* 146 ff.
6. Dan Twala, interview by Tim Couzens, July 26, 1979, Dube, Soweto, RTP.

7. *Bantu World*, March 10, 1934; *Bantu World*, February 9, 1935.
8. R. T. Mazibuko, interview by Tim Couzens, September 15, 1992, Edendale, RTP.
9. *Bantu World*, March 24, 1934.
10. Dan to Regina, September 1, 1938, RTP.
11. *Bantu World*, June 27, 1935.
12. Natasha Erlank, "The White Wedding: Affect and Economy in South Africa in the Early Twentieth Century," *African Studies Review* 57, no. 3 (2014): 29–50.
13. Marriage certificate of Percy Cameron Kumalo and Regina Doris Mazibuko, Indaleni, Richmond, July 1, 1936, RTP. The American Board was the American Board of Commissioners for Foreign Missions, an early Christian mission organization active in South Africa.
14. Ellen Hellmann, "Urban Areas," in *Handbook on Race Relations in South Africa*, ed. Ellen Hellmann (Oxford: Oxford University Press, 1949), 233–34; *Report of the Native Affairs Commission, 1921* (Cape Town: Native Affairs Commission, 1922), 25.
15. Tim Couzens, *The New African: A Study of the Life and Work of H. I. E. Dhlomo* (Johannesburg: Ravan, 1985), 134.
16. *Bantu World*, March 6, 1937.
17. Ray Phillips, *Bantu in the City: A Study of Cultural Adjustment on the Witwatersrand* (Alice: Lovedale, 1938), 5.
18. Deidre Pretorius, "AmaPasi Asiwafuni: Class, Race, and Gender Identities in the Anti-Pass Laws Cartoons Published in Umsebenzi / South African Worker, 1933–1936," *Image and Text: A Journal for Design* 13 (2007): 5.
19. *Bantu World*, April 21, 1934.
20. Regina to Dan, May 16, 1938, RTP.
21. Deborah Gaitskell et al., "Class, Race, and Gender: Domestic Workers in South Africa," *Review of African Political Economy* 10, nos. 27–28 (1983): 96.
22. The average monthly wage for an African family man was £4, 2s, 6d, and a minimum monthly family budget £7, 10s. Ray Phillips, *The Bantu Are Coming: Phases of South Africa's Race Problem* (London: Student Christian Movement Press, 1930), 62; Phillip Bonner, "The Transvaal Native Congress, 1917–1920: The Radicalization of the Black Petit Bourgeoisie on the Rand," in *Industrialization and Social Change in South Africa*, ed. Shula Marks and Richard Rathbone (London: Longman, 1982), 275.
23. Bonner, "Transvaal Native Congress," 272, 276.
24. Dan to Regina, September 1938, RTP. Throughout this work, I have chosen not to print out racial slurs in full. Where the original sources gave the words in full, I have replaced some letters with asterisks. The K-word is a highly offensive racial slur in South Africa. Since 2000, its use has been

actionable under the Promotion of Equality and Prevention of Unfair Discrimination Act.

25. Bonner, "Transvaal Native Congress," 272.
26. Marks and Rathbone, "Introduction," *Industrialization and Social Change,* 167.
27. Iris Berger, "From Ethnography to Social Welfare: Ray Phillips and Representations of Urban Women in South Africa," *Social Sciences and Missions,* no. 19 (2006): 97–98.
28. Phillips, *Bantu Are Coming,* 127.
29. Richard John Haines, "The Politics of Philanthropy and Race Relations: The Joint Councils of South Africa, 1920–1955" (PhD diss., University of London, 1991), 1.
30. Couzens, *New African,* 88.
31. Phillips, *Bantu Are Coming,* 7 (foreword by Charles Loram).
32. Phillips, 93.
33. Phillips, 109.
34. Berger, "From Ethnography," 98–99.
35. *Umteteli Wa Bantu,* February 22, 1930.
36. Bantu Men's Social Center Records, 1923–1975, A1058, Annual Report 1936, 11–12, Wits Historical Papers.
37. Berger, "From Ethnography," 92.
38. *Bantu World,* February 1, 1941.
39. Phillips, *Bantu Are Coming,* 149.
40. Regina to Dan, October 1938, RTP.
41. *Ilanga lase Natal,* August 5, 1927.
42. *Bantu World,* April 9, 1932.
43. David Coplan, *In Township Tonight: South African Black City Music and Theatre* (Chicago: University of Chicago Press, 1985), 146.
44. Christopher Ballantine, "Concert and Dance: The Foundations of Black Jazz in South Africa between the Twenties and the Early Forties," *Popular Music* 10, no. 2 (1991): 122; Es'kia Mphahele, *Down Second Avenue* (London: Faber & Faber, 1959), 99.
45. *Umteteli wa Bantu,* December 28, 1940.
46. Regina to Dan, May 22, 1938, RTP.
47. R. T. Mazibuko, interview, RTP.
48. Regina to Dan, February 1938, RTP.
49. Regina to Dan, May 20, 1938, RTP.
50. *Bantu World,* February 16, 1935.
51. *Bantu World,* February 5, 1938.
52. *Bantu World,* September 25, 1937.
53. *Umteteli wa Bantu,* November 9, 1935.
54. Regina to Dan, February 1938, RTP.

55. Regina to Dan, June 7, 1938, RTP.
56. Regina to Dan, May 15, 1938, RTP.
57. Miriam Basner, *Am I an African? The Political Memoirs of H. M. Basner* (Johannesburg: Wits University Press, 1993); Nomfundo Manyathi-Jele, "Farewell to One of the Greatest Moral Compasses," *De Rebus*, no. 538 (2014): 6.
58. *Bantu World*, August 21, 1937.
59. Sasha Claude Rai, "Laws of Love: The Transvaal Native Divorce Court and the Urban African" (MA thesis, University of the Witwatersrand, 2018), 41–42.
60. Rai, "Laws of Love," 41.
61. Couzens, *New African*, 13, 15.
62. Regina to Dan, September 18, 1938, RTP.
63. Noor Nieftagodien, *Orlando West, Soweto: An Illustrated History* (Johannesburg: Wits University Press, 2012), chap. 2, "A Right to Live in the City."
64. Regina to Dan, November 24, 1938, RTP.
65. E. J. Verwey, *New Dictionary of South African Biography* (Pretoria: HSRC Publishers, 1995), 187–88.
66. Dan Twala, interview, RTP.
67. Regina to Dan, August 16, 1938, RTP.
68. Regina to Dan, May 24, 1938, RTP.
69. Regina to Dan, August 1938, RTP.
70. Chipkin, *Johannesburg Style*, 165.
71. Regina to Dan, April 1938, RTP.
72. Regina to Dan, 1938, RTP.
73. *Bantu World*, August 5, 1933; Megan Healy-Clancy, "Politics of Marriage in New Segregationist South Africa," *African Studies Review* 57, no. 2 (2014): 15.
74. Alan Gregor Cobley, *Rules of the Game: Struggles in Black Recreation and Social Welfare Policy in South Africa* (Westport, CT: Greenwood, 1997), 88.
75. Regina to Dan, May 1938, RTP.
76. Regina to Dan, August 28, 1938, RTP.
77. Regina to Dan, October 10, 1938, RTP.

## Chapter 4: Dan

1. Dan Twala, interview by Tim Couzens, July 26, 1979, Dube, Soweto, RTP; *Bantu World*, February 23, 1935.
2. *Bantu World*, February 27, 1937.
3. *Bantu World*, February 27, 1937.
4. Dan Twala, interview, RTP.

5. C. M. Badenhorst and C. M. Rogerson, "Teach the Native to Play: Social Control and Organized Black Sport on the Witwatersrand, 1920–1939," *GeoJournal* 12, no. 2 (1986): 201.
6. Dan Twala, interview, RTP; Deborah Gaitskell et al., "Class, Race, and Gender: Domestic Workers in South Africa," *Review of African Political Economy* 10, nos. 27–28 (1983): 96; Clive Glaser, "Managing the Sexuality of Urban Youth: Johannesburg, 1920s–1930s," *International Journal of African Historical Studies* 38, no. 2 (2005): 308.
7. Dan to Regina, September 1, 1938, RTP.
8. Dan Twala, interview, RTP.
9. Dan Twala, interview, RTP.
10. Badenhorst and Rogerson, "Teach the Native to Play," 200.
11. Dan Twala, interview, RTP; Peter Alegi, "Playing to the Gallery: Sport, Cultural Performance, and Social Identity in South Africa, 1920s–1945," *International Journal of African Historical Studies* 35, no. 1 (2002): 24.
12. Alegi, "Playing to the Gallery," 24–25.
13. My female interviewees were unanimous in their high estimation of Dan's physical charms. Stella Lukhele, Kwaluseni, July 31, 2019; Mary Twala, Johannesburg, August 20, 2019.
14. *Bantu World*, December 3, 1932.
15. Vukile Khumalo, "Ekukhanyeni Letter Writers: A Historical Enquiry into Epistolary Networks and Political Imagination in KwaZulu-Natal South Africa," in *Africa's Hidden Histories: Everyday Literacy and Making the Self*, ed. Karin Barber (Bloomington: Indiana University Press, 2006), 122, 140n22.
16. *The Foreign Field: 1919* (London: Wesleyan Methodist Mission House, 1919), 95; Dan Twala, interview, RTP.
17. *Bantu World*, February 3, 1940.
18. Dan to Regina, April 1938, RTP.
19. *Bantu World*, March 7, 1936; Dan to Regina, April 1938, RTP.
20. Dan to Regina, 1943, RTP; Dan O'Meara, "The 1946 African Mine Workers' Strike and the Political Economy of South Africa," *Journal of Commonwealth and Comparative Politics* 13, no. 2 (1975): 146–73.
21. Dan to Carroll, September 23, 1941, RTP.
22. Phillips cited in Iris Berger, "From Ethnography to Social Welfare: Ray Phillips and Representations of Urban Women in South Africa," *Social Sciences and Missions*, no. 19 (2006): 99.
23. Dan to Regina, April 30, 1938, RTP; "Domestic Servants, 1939–1945," J4.8, Wits Historical Papers, South African Institute of Race Relations.
24. "The African Domestic Servants' League, J. G. Coka, November 1939," AD 843/RJ/J4.8, South African Institute of Race Relations.
25. Baruch Hirson, *Yours for the Union: Class and Community Struggles in South Africa, 1930–1947* (Johannesburg: Wits University Press, 1989), 52.

26. Dan to Regina, April 1938, RTP.
27. Dan to Regina, May 26, 1938, RTP.
28. Dan to Regina, March 28, 1938, RTP.
29. Dan to Regina, February 25, 1938, RTP.
30. Dan to Regina, February 25, 1938, RTP.
31. Dan to Regina, April 1938, RTP.
32. Tim Couzens, *The New African: A Study of the Life and Works of H. I. E. Dhlomo* (Johannesburg: Ravan, 1985), 68.
33. Regina to Dan, 1938, RTP.
34. Dan to Regina, April 1938, RTP.
35. Dan's first child was Alice Simangele Twala, born to Chloe, in Ermelo, Eastern Transvaal. Zanele Twala, interview by the author, July 5, 2018, Mbabane, Eswatini.
36. Dan to Regina, 1941, RTP.
37. T. Dunbar Moodie, Vivienne Ndatshe, and British Sibuyi, "Migrancy and Male Sexuality on the South African Gold Mines," *Journal of Southern African Studies* 14, no. 2 (1988): 228–56.
38. Dan to Regina, September 1, 1938, RTP.
39. Carroll to Dan, 1938, RTP.
40. Dan to Regina, June 17, 1938, RTP.
41. Dan to Regina, August 1938 and April 24, 1938, RTP.
42. Carroll to Dan, July 18, 1941.
43. Regina to Dan, May 1938, RTP.
44. Regina to Dan, October 1938, RTP.
45. Dan to Regina, September 1938, RTP.
46. Dan to Regina, September 1, 1938, RTP.
47. Regina to Dan, September 1938, RTP.
48. Dan to Regina, April 24, 1938, RTP.
49. Dan to Regina, February 25, 1938, RTP.
50. Dan to Regina, April 24, 1938, RTP.
51. Dan to Regina April 1938, RTP.
52. Dan to Regina, February 1938, RTP.
53. Regina to Dan, February 17, 1938, RTP.
54. Dan to Regina, February 1938, RTP.
55. Regina to Dan, February 17, 1938, RTP.
56. Dan Twala, interview, RTP.
57. Regina to Dan, August 21, 1938, RTP.
58. Regina to Dan, April 26, 1938, RTP.
59. Regina to Dan, August 21, 1938, RTP.
60. Regina to Dan, 1938, RTP.
61. Dan to Regina, February 18, 1938, RTP.
62. Regina to Dan, February 21, 1938, RTP.

63. Dan to Regina, 1940, RTP.
64. Dan to Regina, 1940, RTP.
65. Regina to Dan, December 1939, RTP.
66. *Bantu World*, September 8, 1934.
67. Dan to Regina, April 30, 1938, RTP.
68. Dan to Regina, July 25, 1938, RTP.
69. Couzens, *New African*, 16.
70. Eric Naki, "The Humble House Where Winnie Found a Second Home," *The Citizen*, April 13, 2018, https://citizen.co.za/news/south-africa/1892403/the-house-where-winnie-found-a-second-home/.
71. Dan to Regina, April 1938, RTP.
72. Dan to Regina, April 1938, RTP.
73. Regina to Dan, April 28, 1938, RTP.
74. Regina to Dan, April 4, 1938, RTP.
75. Regina to Dan, May 26, 1938, RTP.
76. Regina to Dan, August 28, 1938, RTP.
77. Regina to Dan, August 3, 1938, RTP.
78. *Bantu World*, September 4, 1937.
79. Dan to Regina, April 1938, RTP.
80. Regina to Dan, February 23, 1938, RTP.
81. Regina to Dan, March 1938, RTP.
82. Dan to Regina, April 1938, RTP.
83. Dan to Regina, April 1938, RTP.
84. Regina to Dan, April 28, 1938, RTP.
85. Regina to Dan, June 7, 1938, RTP.
86. Regina to Dan, August 2, 1938, RTP.
87. Regina to Dan, August 2, 1938, RTP.
88. Regina to Dan, September 13, 1938, RTP.

## Chapter 5: Letters

1. Isaac Schapera, *Married Life in an African Tribe* (New York: Sheridan House, 1941), 9.
2. Keith Breckenridge, "Love Letters and Amanuenses: Beginning the Cultural History of the Working Class Private Sphere in Southern Africa, 1900–1933," *Journal of Southern African Studies* 26, no. 2 (2000): 345.
3. Regina to Dan, August 21, 1938, RTP.
4. Regina to Dan, June 27, 1938, RTP.
5. Dan to Regina, September 1938, RTP.
6. Regina to Dan, September 13, 1938, RTP.
7. Regina to Dan, August 16, 1938, RTP.
8. Regina to Dan, February 1938, RTP.

9. Regina to Dan, August 21, 1938, RTP.
10. Regina to Dan, October 1938, RTP.
11. Regina to Dan, August 21, 1938, RTP.
12. Regina to Dan, August 21, 1938, RTP.
13. Regina to Dan, August 1938, RTP.
14. Keith Breckenridge, "Reasons for Writing: African Working-Class Letter Writing in Early Twentieth-Century South Africa," in *Africa's Hidden Histories: Everyday Literacy and Making the Self*, ed. Karin Barber (Bloomington: Indiana University Press, 2006), 148–49; Rebecca Earle, ed., *Epistolary Selves: Letters and Letter-Writers, 1600–1945* (Aldershot, UK: Ashgate, 1999), 6.
15. Regina to Dan, September 1938, RTP.
16. Regina to Dan, October 29, 1938, RTP; Regina to Dan, November 1938, RTP.
17. Regina to Dan, April 1938, RTP.
18. Dan Twala, interview by Tim Couzens, July 26, 1979, Dube, Soweto, RTP.
19. Dan to Regina, October 28, 1938, RTP.
20. Regina to Dan, October 1938, RTP.
21. Regina to Dan, July 1938, RTP.
22. Dan to Regina, July 1938, RTP.
23. Regina to Dan, June 23, 1939, RTP.
24. Dan to Regina, July 25, 1938, RTP.
25. Dan to Regina, June 1939, RTP.
26. Regina to Dan, July 6, 1939, RTP.
27. Dan to Regina, September 18 and 19, 1939, RTP; Regina to Dan, December 25, 1940, RTP.
28. Dan to Regina, December 30, 1940, RTP.
29. Dan to Regina, October 21, 1938, RTP.
30. Regina to Dan, April 26, 1938, RTP.
31. Dan to Regina, October 1938, RTP.
32. Gary Schneider, *The Culture of Epistolarity: Vernacular Letters and Letter Writing in Early Modern England, 1500–1700* (Newark: University of Delaware Press, 2005), 133.
33. Breckenridge, "Love Letters and Amanuenses," 337–48.
34. *Bantu World*, May 6, 1933; *Bantu World*, May 23, 1936; *Bantu World*, April 22, 1939.
35. Dan to Regina, November 19, 1940, RTP; *Bantu World*, February 17, 1940.
36. Regina to Dan, April 1938, RTP.
37. Dan to Regina April 1938, RTP.
38. Dan to Regina, May 25, 1938, RTP.
39. Dan to Regina, July 1939, RTP.
40. Regina to Dan, November 13, 1939, RTP.

41. Dan to Regina, May 2, 1938, RTP.
42. Ray Allen and George P. Cunningham, "Cultural Uplift and Double-Consciousness: African American Responses to the 1935 Opera Porgy and Bess," *Musical Quarterly* 88, no. 3 (2005): 342–69.
43. Dan to Regina, April 1938.
44. Dan to Regina, April 1938.
45. Katherine Ann Jensen, *Writing Love: Letters, Women and the Novel in France, 1605–1776* (Carbondale: Southern Illinois University Press, 1995), 3.
46. Dan to Regina, June 17, 1938, RTP; Regina to Dan, October 1938, RTP; Dan to Regina December 1939, RTP; Regina to Dan, June 12, 1941, RTP.
47. Dan to Regina, June 17, 1935, RTP.
48. Regina to Dan, December 25, 1942, RTP.
49. Vukile Khumalo, "Ekukhanyeni Letter Writers: A Historical Enquiry into Epistolary Networks and Political Imagination in KwaZulu-Natal South Africa," in *Africa's Hidden Histories: Everyday Literacy and Making the Self*, ed. Karin Barber (Bloomington: Indiana University Press, 2006), 122.
50. Dan Twala, interview, RTP.
51. Dan Twala, interview, RTP.
52. Regina to Dan, October 1938, RTP.
53. Regina to Dan, October 1938, RTP.
54. Dan to Regina, July 5, 1939, RTP.

## Chapter 6: Kufa

1. Regina to Dan, June 7, 1938, RTP.
2. Regina to Dan, June 7, 1938, RTP.
3. Regina to Dan, August 1938, RTP.
4. Regina to Dan, August 2, 1938, RTP.
5. Regina to Dan, August 1938, RTP.
6. Regina to Dan, June 12, 1938, RTP.
7. Regina to Dan, October 23, 1938, RTP.
8. Regina to Dan, August 1938, RTP; Dan to Regina, August 18, 1938, RTP.
9. Regina to Dan, September 25, 1938, RTP.
10. Regina to Dan, September 25, 1938, RTP.
11. Regina to Dan, May 26, 1938, RTP.
12. Isabella Venter, "The Modern Girl and the Lady: Negotiating Modern Womanhood in a South African Magazine, 1910–1920," *South African Historical Journal* 71, no. 2 (2019): 173.
13. Jeff Opland, "The First Novel in Xhosa," *Research in African Literatures* 38, no. 4 (2007): 108; Regina to Dan, May 9, 1938, RTP. The three women were Letitia Kakaza, Victoria Swartbooi, and Violet Dube.

14. Brian Willan, *Sol Plaatje: A Life of Solomon Tshekisho Plaatje* (Auckland Park, South Africa: Jacana, 2018), 522.
15. Jeff Peires, "The Lovedale Press: Literature for the Bantu Revisited," *History in Africa* 6 (1979): 156.
16. Peter McDonald, "The Book in South Africa," in *The Cambridge History of South African Literature*, ed. David Attwell and Derek Attridge (Cambridge: Cambridge University Press, 2012), 804.
17. *Bantu World*, November 25, 1933.
18. David Attwell, "Modernizing Tradition / Traditionalizing Modernity: Reflections on the Dhlomo-Vilakazi Debate," *Research in African Literatures* 33, no. 1 (2002): 94.
19. Norman Etherington, "Mission Station Melting Pots as a Factor in the Rise of South African Black Nationalism," *International Journal of African Historical Studies* 9, no. 4 (1976): 592–605.
20. Regina to Dan, September 10, 1938, RTP.
21. Regina to Dan, November 1938, RTP.
22. Regina to Dan, November 1938, RTP.
23. Regina to Dan, September 10, 1938, RTP.
24. Regina to Dan, September 10, 1938, RTP.
25. Elizabeth le Roux, "Black Writers, White Publishers: A Case Study of the Bantu Treasury Series in South Africa," *Revue électronique d'études sur le monde anglophone* 11, no. 1 (2013): 26.
26. Regina to Dan, August 1938, RTP.
27. Regina to Dan, October 19, 1938, RTP.
28. Regina to Dan, May 24, 1938, RTP.
29. Regina to Dan, October 1938, RTP.
30. Attwell, "Modernizing Tradition / Traditionalizing Modernity," 100.
31. *uDingane kaSenzangakhona* (Pietermaritzburg: Shuter & Shooter, 1936); *uShaka* (Pietermaritzburg: Shuter & Shooter, 1937); *uMpande kaSenzangakhona* (Pietermaritzburg: Shuter & Shooter, 1938); *uCetshwayo* (Pietermaritzburg: Shuter & Shooter, 1952); *uDinuzulu kaCetshwayo* (Pietermaritzburg: Shuter & Shooter, 1968).
32. R. R. R. Dhlomo, *An African Tragedy* (Alice: Lovedale, 1928).
33. Regina to Dan, 1938, RTP.
34. Regina to Dan, September 10, 1938, RTP; Regina to Dan, October 1938, RTP.
35. Regina to Dan, October 1938, RTP.
36. Regina to Dan, October 29, 1938, RTP.
37. Regina to Dan, October 9, 1938, RTP.
38. Dan to Regina, April 1938, RTP.
39. Dan to Regina, November 19, 1938, RTP.
40. Dan to Regina, May 13, 1938, RTP.

41. Dan to Regina, December 1938, RTP; Andrew Bank, *Pioneers of the Field: South Africa's Women Anthropologists* (Cambridge: Cambridge University Press, 2016), 189–238.
42. Regina to Dan, May 9, 1938, RTP.
43. Dan to Regina, May 13, 1938, RTP; David Attwell, *Rewriting Modernity: Studies in Black South African Literary History* (Athens: Ohio University Press, 2006), 77ff.
44. Regina to Dan, May 1938, RTP.
45. Regina to Dan, May 1938, RTP.
46. Dan to Regina, May 3, 1939, RTP.
47. Regina to Dan, May 2, 1938, RTP.
48. Dan to Regina, September 1938, RTP.
49. Dan to Regina, April 1938, RTP.
50. Regina to Dan, December 30, 1938, RTP.
51. Dan to Regina, April 1938, RTP.
52. Regina to Dan, September 9, 1938, RTP.
53. Dan to Regina, July 31, 1938, RTP.
54. Regina to Dan, May 9, 1938, RTP.
55. Regina to Dan, October 1938, RTP.
56. Dan to Regina, September 9, 1938, RTP.
57. Dan to Regina, April 28, 1939, RTP.
58. Dan to Regina, June 3, 1938, RTP.
59. Dan to Regina, April 1938, RTP.
60. Dan to Regina, October 28, 1938, RTP.
61. Dan to Regina, March 20, 1939, RTP.
62. Regina to Dan, October 23, 1938, RTP.
63. Regina to Dan, June 23, 1939, RTP.
64. Regina to Dan, April 28, 1938, RTP.
65. Regina to Dan, September 27, 1940, RTP.
66. Regina to Date, April 1939, RTP.
67. Regina to Dan, October 23, 1938, RTP.
68. Regina to Dan, August 1938, RTP.

## Chapter 7: Failed

1. Regina to Dan, 1938, RTP.
2. *Umteteli wa Bantu*, April 30, 1940.
3. D. Mck. Malcolm, "Zulu Literature," *Africa: Journal of the International African Institute* 19, no. 1 (1949): 39.
4. Regina to Dan, August 1938, RTP.
5. Shula Marks, "Patriotism, Patriarchy and Purity: Natal and the Politics of Zulu Ethnic Consciousness," in *The Creation of Tribalism in Southern*

*Africa*, ed. Leroy Vail (Berkeley: University of California Press, 1989), 217–18.

6. Regina to Dan, August 1938, RTP. See also Regina to Dan, August 16, 1938, RTP.
7. R. T. Mazibuko, interview by Tim Couzens, September 15, 1992, Edendale.
8. Regina to Dan, September 1938, RTP.
9. Dan to Regina, September 9, 1938, RTP.
10. Regina to Dan, September 1938, RTP. Debates around the standardization of African languages' orthography raged during the 1930s. Jeff Peires, "The Lovedale Press: Literature for the Bantu Revisited," *History in Africa* 6 (1979): 155–75.
11. Regina to Dan, September 9, 1938, RTP.
12. Regina to Dan, August 16, 1938, RTP.
13. Regina to Dan, October 1938, RTP.
14. Regina to Dan, May 9, 1938, RTP.
15. Regina to Dan, February 17, 1938, RTP.
16. Regina to Dan, April 1938, RTP.
17. Regina to Dan, November 6, 1938, RTP.
18. Dan to Regina, September 9, 1938, RTP.
19. Bhekizizwe Peterson, "HIE Dhlomo," in *Encyclopedia of African Literature*, ed. Simon Gikandi (London: Routledge, 2003), 193.
20. Regina to Dan, October 29, 1938, RTP.
21. *Umteteli wa Bantu*, April 13, 1940.
22. *Bantu World*, February 25, 1939. For other complaints about the censorship experienced by African authors, see *Umteteli wa Bantu*, June 10, 1939, January 27, 1940, and April 13, 1940. For poor treatment of African writers by commercial publishers of the day, see *Umteteli wa Bantu*, April 30, 1940.
23. Regina to Dan, October 29, 1938, RTP.
24. Regina to Dan, November 6, 1938, RTP.
25. Regina to Dan, October 29, 1938, RTP.
26. Regina to Dan, October 1938, RTP.
27. Regina to Dan, December 30, 1940, RTP.
28. Regina to Dan, November 11, 1938, RTP.
29. *Bantu World*, May 2, 1936.
30. Regina to Dan, April 28, 1939, RTP.
31. Dan to Regina, April 29, 1939, RTP.
32. Regina to Dan, January 31, 1939, RTP; Clive Glaser, "Managing the Sexuality of Urban Youth: Johannesburg, 1920s–1960s," *International Journal of African Historical Studies* 38, no. 2 (2005): 305.
33. Dan to Regina, July 31, 1938, RTP.

34. Saul Dubow and Alan Jeeves, eds., *South Africa's 1940s: Worlds of Possibilities* (Cape Town: Double Storey, 2005), 7.
35. Dan to Regina, September 1, 1938, RTP.
36. Hilda Kuper, *An African Aristocracy: Rank among the Swazi* (Oxford: Oxford University Press, 1947).
37. Dan to Regina, April 19, 1939, RTP.
38. Dan to Regina, April 26, 1939, RTP.
39. Regina to Dan, May 18, 1939, RTP.
40. Dan to Regina, probably February 1939, RTP.
41. Brian Willan, *Sol Plaatje: A Life of Solomon Tshekisho Plaatje, 1876–1932* (Auckland Park: Jacana, 2018), 540.
42. Dan to Regina, February 22, 1939, RTP.
43. Dan to Regina, April 23, 1939, RTP.
44. Dan to Regina, March 23, 1939, RTP.
45. Dan to Regina, March 29, 1939, RTP.
46. Dan to Regina, March 29, 1939, RTP.
47. *Bantu World*, October 18, 1941.
48. *Um-Afrika*, November 5, 1949, cited in Lindiwe Dovey and Angela Impey, "*African Jim*: Sound, Politics and Pleasure in Early 'Black' South African Cinema," *Journal of African Cultural Studies* 22, no. 1 (2010), fn 10. See also *Bantu World*, October 29, 1949, for a review.
49. *Rand Daily Mail*, November 2, 1949.
50. This paragraph relies upon Tim Couzens's account in Couzens, "The Courtship of Regina and Dan Twala" (unpublished paper, n.d.), p. 20, RTP.

## Chapter 8: Orlando

1. *Umteteli wa Bantu*, November 2, 1940.
2. *Umteteli wa Bantu*, August 2 and October 18, 1941.
3. Ray Phillips, *Bantu in the City: A Study of Cultural Adjustment on the Witwatersrand* (Alice, South Africa: Lovedale, 1938), 112.
4. *Umteteli wa Bantu*, October 4, 1941.
5. *Umteteli wa Bantu*, October 4 and 18, 1941.
6. Gerhard Van der Waal, *From Mining Camp to Metropolis: The Buildings of Johannesburg, 1886–1940* (Johannesburg: Chris Van Rensburg, 1987), 171.
7. Keith Beavon, *Johannesburg: The Making and Shaping of the City* (Pretoria: University of South Africa Press, 2004), 78, 82, 103.
8. Noor Nieftagodien, *Orlando West, Soweto: An Illustrated History* (Johannesburg: Wits University Press, 2012), 6.
9. *Bantu World*, September 16, 1933.

10. Alan Paton, *Cry, the Beloved Country* (New York: C. Scribner's Sons, 1948), 56.
11. Nieftagodien, *Orlando West, Soweto*, 9.
12. Es'kia Mphahlele, *Down Second Avenue* (London: Faber & Faber, 1959), 203.
13. T. Dunbar Moodie, "The Moral Economy of the Black Miners' Strike of 1946," *Journal of Southern African Studies* 13, no. 1 (1986): 1–35.
14. Jordan K. Ngubane, *Should the Native Representative Council Be Abolished?* (Cape Town: African Bookman, 1946), 13.
15. Beavon, *Johannesburg*, 125–27.
16. Mphahlele, *Down Second Avenue*, 201; Trevor Huddleston, *Naught for Your Comfort* (London: Collins, 1956), 54.
17. Deborah Posel, "The Case for a Welfare State: Poverty and the Politics of the Urban African Family in the 1930s and 1940s," in *South Africa's 1940s: World of Possibilities*, ed. Saul Dubow and Alan Jeeves (Cape Town: Double Storey, 2005), 64–66.
18. Regina to Dan, June 16, 1939, RTP.
19. *Bantu World*, September 13, 1941; *Bantu World*, April 7, 1944.
20. *Umteteli wa Bantu*, February 7, 1942.
21. Regina to Dan, July 1942, RTP.
22. Regina to Dan, December 30, 1940, RTP.
23. Regina to Dan, August 21, 1942, RTP.
24. Regina to Dan, August 21, 1942, RTP; *Bantu World*, January 10, 1948.
25. Dan to Regina, 1942, RTP.
26. Regina to Dan, July 14, 1941, RTP.
27. Regina to Dan, March 11, 1940, RTP.
28. Regina to Dan, February 24, 1940.
29. Andrew Bank, *Pioneers of the Field: South Africa's Women Anthropologists* (Cambridge: Cambridge University Press, 2016), 224–25.
30. Regina to Dan, July 12, 1942, RTP.
31. Mary Twala, interview by author, August 20, 2019, Orlando East.
32. Dan to Regina, December 8, 1939, RTP.
33. Non-European Hospital, Hospital Street, Johannesburg, May 10, 1940, RTP.
34. Regina to Dan, March 24, 1940, RTP.
35. Dan to Regina, 1941, RTP.
36. Dan to Regina, November 18, 1940, RTP.
37. Regina to Dan, August 16, 1940, RTP.
38. Dan to Regina, 1940, RTP.
39. Dan to Regina, 1940, RTP.
40. Dan to Regina, 1940, RTP.
41. Dan to Regina, 1940, RTP.

42. Dan to Regina, 1940, RTP.
43. Phillips, *Bantu in the City*, 309.
44. Regina to Dan, February 11, 1943, RTP.
45. Regina to Dan, December 1940, RTP.
46. *Bantu World*, May 3, 1941; *Umteteli wa Bantu*, November 23, 1940.
47. *Umteteli wa Bantu*, October 4, 1941. For the Blue Lagoon restaurant, see Philip Bonner and Noor Nieftagodien, *Alexandra: A History* (Johannesburg: Wits University Press, 2016), 118.
48. Dan to Regina, 1941, RTP.

## Chapter 9: Jan Hofmeyr School

1. Dan to Regina, January 3, 1941, RTP; Bruce Murray, *Wits, the "Open" Years: A History of the University of the Witwatersrand, Johannesburg, 1939–1959* (Johannesburg: Wits University Press, 1997), 16.
2. *Umteteli wa Bantu*, January 18, 1941.
3. Dan to Regina, January 3, 1941, RTP.
4. Regina to Dan, February 2, 1941, RTP.
5. "Matric" refers to "matriculation," the final result obtained on graduating from South African high schools.
6. Regina to Dan, September 25, 1938, RTP.
7. Dan to Regina, September 28, 1938, RTP.
8. Alan Gregor Cobley, *The Rules of the Game: Struggles in Black Recreation and Social Welfare Policy in South Africa* (Westport, CT: Greenwood, 1997), 125–33.
9. Iris Berger, "An African American Mother of the Nation: Madie Hall Xuma in South Africa, 1940–1963," *Journal of Southern African Studies* 27, no. 3 (2001): 547–66; Shula Marks, ed., *Not Either an Experimental Doll: The Separate Worlds of Three South African Women* (Bloomington: Indiana University Press, 1988).
10. Andrew Bank, *Pioneers of the Field: South Africa's Women Anthropologists* (Cambridge: Cambridge University Press, 2016), 116ff. Over a decade later, Hellmann would publish this research as *Rooiyard: A Sociological Survey of an Urban Native Slum Yard* (Cape Town: Oxford University Press, 1948).
11. Bank, 104.
12. Dan to Regina, October 29, 1940, RTP.
13. Cobley, *Rules of the Game*, 135.
14. *Bantu World*, October 19, 1940.
15. *Bantu World*, August 17, 1940.
16. Cobley, *Rules of the Game*, 76.
17. Cobley, 146.
18. *Bantu World*, February 1, 1941.

19. Hofmeyr School, Revenue and Expenditure Account July 1–December 31, 1941, AD 1715, Wits Historical Papers, SAIRR.
20. Cobley, *Rules of the Game*, 147.
21. *Bantu World*, February 1, 1941.
22. Cobley, *Rules of the Game*, 148.
23. *Umteteli wa Bantu*, February 8, 1941.
24. See chapter 3, note 61.
25. "Jan H. Hofmeyr School of Social Work," 1941, no author (probably a promotional pamphlet for the school), 4, A1444 file no. 2, Phillips Papers, 1940–48, Wits Historical Papers.
26. Ray Phillips, "Phillips News," April 1, 1948, A1444 file no. 2, Phillips Papers, 1940–48, Wits Historical Papers.
27. Hofmeyr School, Courses of Study, 1941 and 1942, SAIRR.
28. Ray Phillips, "Philips News," June 30, 1945, A1444 file no. 2, Phillips Papers, 1940–48, Wits Historical Papers.
29. Bank, *Pioneers of the Field*, 127.
30. "Jan H. Hofmeyr School of Social Work," 4.
31. That is, receive a better grade than her classmates.
32. Cobley, *Rules of the Game*, 144.
33. Hofmeyr School, Courses of Study, 1941 and 1942, SAIRR. Also see Iris Berger, "From Ethnography to Social Welfare: Ray Phillips and Representations of Urban Women in South Africa," *Social Sciences and Missions* 19 (2004): 106ff.
34. Berger, "Ethnography to Social Welfare," 107.
35. Berger, 107.
36. Hofmeyr School, Courses of Study, 1941 and 1942, SAIRR.
37. *Bantu World*, November 2, 1946.
38. Regina to Dan, February 2, 1941, RTP.
39. Regina to Dan, August 13, 1941, RTP.
40. Regina to Dan, December 25, 1942, RTP.
41. Ray Phillips, "Phillips News," 1943, Phillips Papers, 1940–1948, A1444 file 2, Wits Historical Papers.
42. Regina to Dan, December 21, 1942, RTP.
43. Murray, *Wits, the Open Years*, 3–4.

## Chapter 10: Wits

1. Mervyn Shear, *Wits: A University in the Apartheid Era* (Johannesburg: Wits University Press, 1996), 9.
2. Bruce Murray, *Wits, the "Open" Years: A History of the University of the Witwatersrand, Johannesburg 1939–1959* (Johannesburg: Wits University Press, 1997), 35, 47; Shear, *Wits*, 9.

3. Murray, *Wits*, 27.
4. Murray, 14, 28.
5. A law degree was £48 per annum. Bruce Murray, "Nelson Mandela and Wits University," *Journal of African History* 57, no. 2 (2016): 274.
6. Dan to Trustees of Bantu Sports Club, 1941, RTP; Dan to Regina, January 2, 1940, RTP; Dan to Regina, 1941, RTP.
7. Dan to Regina, 1941, RTP.
8. *Bantu World*, October 10, 1942, RTP.
9. Regina to Dan, December 21, 1942, RTP.
10. Regina Gelana Doris Twala, Wits Student Record, 1947, list of bursaries received, RTP.
11. Regina to Dan, March 8, 1943, RTP.
12. Murray, "Nelson Mandela," 276.
13. Regina to Dan, January 9, 1945, RTP.
14. Murray, *Wits*, 5.
15. Murray, 56–57.
16. Regina to Dan, January 17, 1943, RTP.
17. *Umteteli wa Bantu*, July 8, 1939.
18. Regina to Dan, February 11, 1943, RTP.
19. Hilda Kuper, "Function, History, Biography: Reflections on Fifty Years in the British Anthropological Tradition," in *Functionalism Historicized*, ed. George Stocking (Madison: University of Wisconsin Press, 1988), 206ff.
20. Andrew Bank, *Pioneers of the Field: South Africa's Women Anthropologists* (Cambridge: Cambridge University Press, 2016), 214ff.
21. Murray, *Wits*, 255.
22. By 1945 women were one quarter of a student body of three thousand. Murray, 14, 28.
23. Richards to Mother, April 17, 1939, Family Correspondence 18.2, file 2, Audrey Richard Papers, University of Cambridge. My thanks to Andrew Bank for sharing this reference.
24. Dan Twala, interview by Tim Couzens, July 26, 1979, Dube, Soweto, RTP.
25. Murray, *Wits*, 234.
26. Andrew Bank, "Audrey Richards: Life and Letters" (MS in progress), citing letter from Richards to Godfrey Wilson, March 1 and March 9, 1938.
27. Murray, *Wits*, 53.
28. Regina to Dan, February 11, 1943, RTP.
29. Regina to Dan, February 11, 1943, RTP.
30. Luli Callinicos, *Who Built Jozi? Discovering Memory at Wits Junction* (Johannesburg: Wits University Press, 2012), 139, 145.
31. Dan Twala, interview, RTP.
32. Regina to Dan, February 11, 1943, RTP; Regina to Dan, July 1943, RTP.

33. This assessment method was based on the British "class" system, whereby a first-class grade was awarded for 70 percent or higher, a second-class for 50–69 percent, and a third-class for 40–49 percent. Anything below that was a fail.
34. Wits Student Record, Regina Twala, 1947, RTP.
35. *Bantu World*, January 12, 1952.
36. University of the Witwatersrand Examination Results, Summer Examinations, 1943, Faculty of Arts, First Year Examination for the Degree of Bachelor of Arts in Social Studies, RTP.
37. *Bantu World*, January 12, 1952.
38. Santu Mofokeng, *Stories No. 1: Train Church* (Göttingen, Germany: Steidl, 2015).
39. Murray, "Mandela and Wits," 276.
40. Theo Twala to Dan, July 9, 1942, RTP; Regina to Dan, February 17, 1943, RTP; Steven Gish, *Desmond Tutu: A Biography* (Westport, CT: Greenwood, 2004), 9.
41. Regina to Dan, July 18, 1943, RTP.
42. Regina to Dan, February 11, 1943, RTP.
43. Theo Twala to Dan, March 25, 1943, RTP; Regina to Dan, July 1943, RTP; Regina to Dan, July 1943, RTP.
44. Regina to Dan, July 21, 1943, RTP.
45. Report on the case, first interview, September 9, 1946, Transvaal House, Alberton, Johannesburg, RTP.
46. Intombazana, "A Place Where You Get Things Cheap," *Times of Swaziland*, September 4, 1964.
47. Intombazana.
48. *Bantu World*, February 9 and March 9, 1946.
49. Dan also mentioned this to Tim Couzens. Dan Twala, interview, RTP.
50. Dan Twala, interview, RTP.
51. *Bantu World*, September 28, 1946. Notice of christening (with accompanying photograph), September 22, 1946, Methodist Church Pimville, property of Shado Twala. My thanks to Pinokie Twala for sharing these documents with me.
52. *Bantu World*, March 23, 1946.
53. *Bantu World*, January 17, 1948.
54. *Bantu World*, March 27, 1948.
55. *Umteteli wa Bantu*, February 1948.

## Chapter 11: Regina to Gelana

1. Bruce Murray, "Wits at War" (unpublished African studies seminar paper, University of the Witwatersrand, 1990), 28, http://wiredspace

.wits.ac.za/bitstream/handle/10539/9374/ISS-312.pdf?sequence=1&isAllowed=y.

2. Philip Bonner and Noor Nieftagodien, *Alexandra: A History* (Johannesburg: Wits University Press, 2008).
3. Violaine Junod, "Entokozweni: Managing a Community Service in an Urban African Area," *Human Organization* 23, no. 1 (1964): 31.
4. "Report of a Budget Study of Four African Families in Alexandra Township, May–June 1952, Entokozweni, Alexandra Township," Federation of African Women, 1954–63, AD 1137, Wits Historical Papers; *Bantu World*, June 7, 1952.
5. Bonner and Nieftagodien, *Alexandra*, 17–18.
6. Andrew Bank, *Pioneers of the Field: South Africa's Women Anthropologists* (Cambridge: Cambridge University Press, 2016), 141.
7. Dan Twala, interview by Tim Couzens, July 26, 1979, Dube, Soweto, RTP.
8. Junod, "Entokozweni," 29.
9. Junod, 31.
10. Keith Breckenridge, "Verwoerd's Bureau of Proof: Total Information in the Making of Apartheid," *History Workshop Journal*, no. 59 (2005): 83.
11. *Bantu World*, July 2, 1949.
12. "Report of a Budget Study."
13. Violaine Junod, "Last Chance for Whites," *Africa Today* 4, no. 6 (1957): 36–40.
14. Junod, "Entokozweni," 32.
15. Junod, 34.
16. Dan Twala, interview, RTP.
17. Records of the Institute of Social Research, Hilda Kuper, BIOS 836/1/1, University of KwaZulu-Natal Archives, Pietermaritzburg.
18. Tom Lodge, *Black Politics in South Africa since 1945* (New York: Longman, 1983), 50.
19. Dan to Regina, May 25, 1952, RTP.
20. Dan Twala, interview, RTP.
21. "The Eastern Province Is a Political Time Bomb," *Drum*, October 1956.
22. Lodge, *Black Politics*, 42.
23. Gary Fred Baines, "New Brighton, Port Elizabeth, c. 1903–1953: A History of an Urban African Community" (PhD diss., University of Cape Town, 1994), 214.
24. *Drum*, December 1951, 1, 9.
25. For consistency's sake, the notes will continue to refer to her letters with "Regina."
26. Baines, "New Brighton, Port Elizabeth," 215.
27. Yengwa Manuscript, 77 Luthuli Museum, Groutville, KwaZulu-Natal. I am grateful to Jill Kelly for generously providing me with this reference. Queenstown was also the site of the 1921 Bulhoek Massacre.

28. Shireen Hassim, *The ANC Women's League: Sex, Gender and Politics* (Auckland Park, South Africa: Jacana, 2014).
29. *Drum*, February 1954, 10.
30. Dan Twala, interview, RTP.
31. *Bantu World*, December 13, 1952; *Advance*, December 11, 1952, collection CULL001, Wits University Research Archives.
32. *Bantu World*, January 31, 1953.
33. *Advance*, December 11, 1952.
34. Director of the South African Council for Industrial and Science Research, to Mrs R. Twala, February 25, 1953, RTP.
35. *Bantu World*, June 18, 1949.
36. *Bantu World*, February 21, 1952; "Talk of the Rand," *Drum*, April 1953, 8.
37. Dan Twala, interview, RTP.
38. Dan Twala, interview, RTP.
39. Mary Twala, interview, August 20, 2019, Orlando East.
40. Case no. 593, 1953, Regina Twala (born Kumalo) versus Dan Twala, Native Divorce Court, Pretoria National Archives.
41. Regina to Dan, January 9, 1950, RTP.
42. Dan to Regina, July 5, 1939, RTP.
43. Dan to Regina, January 24, 1961, RTP.
44. Interview with Dan Twala, RTP.
45. Dan to Regina, December 10, 1962, RTP.
46. Dan to Regina, April 20, 1952, RTP.
47. Benjamin Lawrance and Vusumuzi R. Kumalo, "A Genius without Direction: The Abortive Exile of Dugmore Boetie and the Fate of Southern African Refugees in a Decolonizing Africa," *American Historical Review* 126, no. 2 (2021): 600.
48. Lindsay Clowes, "Are You Going to Be MISS (or MR) Africa? Contesting Masculinity in *Drum* Magazine, 1951–1953," *Gender and History* 13, no. 1 (2001): 6, 9.
49. Lawrance and Kumalo, "Genius without Direction," 600.
50. *Drum*, January 1952, 2, 1.
51. Dan Twala, interview, RTP.
52. The Treason Trial (1956–61) accused 156 South Africans, including Nelson Mandela, of treason against the South African apartheid state. All were ultimately found not guilty.
53. "Duma Nokwe Interrogation," 1956 Treason Trial Papers, AD 1812, 2821, Wits Historical Papers. For South African exiles in Eswatini during this period, see Thula Simpson, "The Bay and the Ocean: A History of the ANC in Swaziland, 1960–1979," *African Historical Review* 41, no. 1 (2009): 90.
54. Dan Twala, interview, RTP.

## Chapter 12: Eswatini

1. Shireen Ally, "If You Are Hungry and a Man Promises You Mealies, Will You Not Follow Him? South African Swazi Ethnic Nationalism, 1931–1986," *South African Historical Journal* 63, no. 3 (2011): 416.
2. Ally.
3. Ivan Evans, *Bureaucracy and Race Administration in South Africa* (Berkeley: University of California Press, 1997), 145–55.
4. "Hilda Beemer/Matthews, African Fellows II," Malinowski 7/39, LSE; Miss H. Beemer to the International Institute of African Languages and Cultures, January 30, 1935, Malinowski 7/39, LSE; "First Report on Field Work," Malinowski 7/39, LSE; Paul Cocks, "The King and I: Bronislaw Malinowski, King Sobhuza II of Swaziland, and the Vision of Culture Change in Africa," *History of the Human Sciences* 13, no. 4 (2000): 25–47.
5. Alan Booth, "Lord Selbourne and the British Protectorates, 1908–1910," *Journal of African History* 10, no. 1 (1969): 137.
6. Hilda Kuper, *Sobhuza II, Ngwenyama and King of Swaziland: The Story of an Hereditary Ruler and His Country* (London: Duckworth, 1978), 191.
7. Hugh Macmillan, "Swaziland, Decolonization and the Triumph of Tradition," *Journal of Modern African Studies* 23, no. 4 (1985): 643–66. See also Hugh Macmillan, "A Nation Divided: The Swazi in Swaziland and the Transvaal, 1865–1986," in *The Creation of Tribalism in Southern Africa*, ed. Leroy Vail (Berkeley: University of California Press, 1989), 289–323.
8. "Hilda Beemer/Matthews, African Fellows II"; Marwick to Malinowski, October 29, 1934, Malinowski 7/39, LSE; Hilda Kuper, "The Development of the Military Organization in Swaziland," *Africa: Journal of the International African Institute* 10, no. 1 (1937): 55–74.
9. Hilda Kuper, "Ritual of Kingship among the Swazi," *Africa: Journal of the International African Institute* 14, no. 5 (1944): 230–57.
10. Macmillan, "Triumph of Tradition," 650–51.
11. J. S. M. Matsebula, *A History of Swaziland*, 3rd ed. (Cape Town: Longman, 1973), 221
12. Philip Bonner, *Kings, Commoners and Concessionaires: The Evolution and Dissolution of the Nineteenth-Century Swazi State* (Cambridge: Cambridge University Press, 1983).
13. *Bantu World*, May 29, 1948.
14. Letterhead for the Swazi National Royal Club lists D. R. Twala as "Consultant," n.d., RTP.
15. R. G. Twala, "Umhlanga (REED) Ceremony of the Swazi Maidens," *African Studies* 11, no. 3 (1952): 97n1.
16. *Bantu World*, March 27, 1948.
17. *Bantu World*, July 28, 1945.

18. *Bantu World,* May 27, 1950.
19. Regina to Dan, December 25, 1949, RTP; Regina to Dan, January 9, 1950, RTP.
20. Regina to Dan, December 31, 1944, RTP.
21. Regina to Dan, January 7, 1945, RTP.
22. Regina to Dan, December 31, 1944, RTP.
23. ISR, University of Natal, Durban, to Dr. Stanley Jackson, Nuffield Foundation, South Africa Liaison Committee, University of the Witwatersrand, December 13, 1954, RTP. See also the report in the *Times of Swaziland,* December 31, 1955.
24. "The Swazi Women: A Study in Culture Contact (Visit by Mrs R. D. Twala)," file 3355, Lobamba Archives, Eswatini; Hilda Kuper, ISR, University of Natal, King George V Avenue, Durban to Dan Fitzpatrick, District Commissioner, Mbabane, April 4, 1955, file 3355, Lobamba Archives, Eswatini.
25. *Ilanga lase Natal,* August 24, 1957.
26. Anne Twala, interview with author, July 29, 2019, Kwaluseni.
27. *Izwi lama Swazi,* June 28, 1958.
28. James Hall, *Speak Manzini: An Autobiography of an African City* (Manzini, Eswatini: Landmark, 2000), 86.
29. *Times of Swaziland,* January 30, 1960; *Izwi lama Swazi,* May 18, 1963; *Izwi lama Swazi,* October 5, 1963.
30. Anne Twala, interview, July 29, 2019. Anne would marry Vusi in the late 1960s.
31. Zanele Twala, interview by author, August 8, 2019, Siphocosini, Eswatini.
32. Zanele Twala, interview by author, April 13, 2019, Mbabane.
33. Mary Twala, interview by author, August 20, 2019, Orlando East.
34. Mary Twala, interview, August 20, 2019; Zanele Twala, interview by author, August 8, 2019, Siphocosini.
35. Zanele Twala, interview, August 8, 2019.
36. Memorandum of Proposed Research on the Swazi Women, by Mrs. R. D. Twala, May 24, 1957, RTP.
37. Dan to Regina, January 17, 1951, RTP.
38. Regina to Dan, 1942, RTP.
39. Violaine Junod, "Entokozweni: Managing a Community Service in an Urban African Area," *Human Organization* 23, no. 1 (1964): 33.
40. R. G. Twala, "R. G. Twala, 'Beads as Regulating the Social Life of the Zulu and Swazi,'" *African Studies* 10, no. 3 (1951): 113–23.
41. Twala, 12.
42. "Expert on Native Lore," *Natal Mercury* (Pietermaritzburg), no. 10 (1955).
43. "Fascinating Secrets of Zulu Letters," *Sunday Times* (Johannesburg), February 7, 1954, 22; "I Come to You with a Clean Heart," *Sunday Times* (Johannesburg), February 14, 1954; R. G. Twala, "Coloured Beads Tell Their

Tale of Love," *Sunday Tribune* (Durban), March 13, 1955; R. G. Twala, "Expert on Native Lore," *Natal Mercury* (Pietermaritzburg), no. 10 (1955).

44. *Times of Swaziland*, February 27, 1954; *Times of Swaziland*, July 8, 1960.
45. Campbell, 220 Marriott Road, Durban, May 20, 1954, to Twala, PO Box 6975, Johannesburg, KCM 5969, KCL.
46. Campbell to Mr. Tings Robson, Municipal Department of Native Affairs, Box 154, Durban, May 20, 1954, KCM 5969, KCL; Campbell, 220 Marriott Rd., Durban to Twala, c/o Swazi National School, Matapa, Swaziland, May 3, 1955, KCM 5969, KCL; Barbara Tyrrell, *Tribal Peoples of Southern Africa* (Cape Town: Books of Africa, 1968).
47. Twala, "Beads as Regulating Social Life," 121.
48. Twala, "Umhlanga," 98.
49. *Izwi lama Swazi*, May 1958.
50. On La Masuku, see Kuper, *Sobhuza II*, 177–79, and *Izwi lama Swazi*, May 1958. Regina's instruction of La Masuku in beadwork was confirmed by Anne, Zanele, and Mary Twala.
51. *Times of Swaziland*, September 28, 1957.
52. Dan to Regina, July 15, 1959.
53. Mvubo Kingsley, interview by author, August 10, 2019, Mbabane.
54. *Times of Swaziland*, June 17, 1960.
55. Genius Aphane, interview by author, August 12, 2018, Kwaluseni.
56. *Times of Swaziland*, June 17, 1960, and February 10, 1961; *Izwi lama Swazi*, July 9, 1960.
57. *Izwi lama Swazi*, October 1950.
58. *Izwi lama Swazi*, May 3, 1958.

## Chapter 13: God

1. Regina to Dan, August 21, 1938, RTP; Regina to Dan, August 28, 1938, RTP; Regina to Dan, September 18, 1938, RTP.
2. Cragg's diary—maintained from 1928 to 1940—gives a full picture of his theological and political commitments. Diary of Rev. A. W. Cragg, CL.
3. Mary Twala, interview by author, August 20, 2019, Orlando East, Johannesburg.
4. Anthony Balcomb, "From Apartheid to the New Dispensation: Evangelicals and the Democratization of South Africa," *Journal of Religion in Africa* 34, no. 1 (2004): 24; "No Room for Half a Million Christians," *Drum*, February 1956.
5. Dan to Regina, April 17, 1952, RTP.
6. Dan to Regina, April 20, 1952, RTP.
7. Bhengu's *Back to God* magazine, 1958, cited in Balcomb, "From Apartheid to the New Dispensation," 24.

8. Balcomb, 25.
9. Balcomb, 23.
10. Elizabeth Shalala, interview by author, August 12, 2018, Kwaluseni.
11. Mrs. Ndwandwe, interview by author, June 18, 2018, Kwaluseni.
12. Nicholas Bhengu to Regina, April 28, 1960, RTP; Mrs. Ndwandwe, interview by author, July 10, 2018, Kwaluseni.
13. Dan to Regina, September 10, 1962, RTP.
14. For an account of the Zionists' relationship with the church in the United States, see Joel Cabrita, *The People's Zion: Southern Africa, the USA and a Transatlantic Faith-Healing Movement* (Cambridge, MA: Harvard University Press, 2018).
15. Hilda Kuper, *The Uniform of Color: A Study of White-Black Relationships in Swaziland* (Johannesburg: Wits University Press, 1947), 122.
16. *Izwi lama Swazi,* December 8, 1956, cited in Bengt Sundkler, *Zulu Zion and Some Swazi Zionists* (Oxford: Oxford University Press, 1976), 233.
17. Sundkler, *Zulu Zion,* 210.
18. Simon/Dabete Mavimbela, interview with author, July 11, 2016, Mbabane.
19. "The Swazi National Council Challenges Statutory Marriage," June 18, 1959, box 92, BSP.
20. Dan Twala, interview by Tim Couzens, July 26, 1979, Dube, Soweto, RTP.
21. This was the Ekuphileni Church in Zion, founded by Stephen Mavimbela. Herbert Mavimbela, interview with author, June 23, 2016, Ludzeludze, Eswatini.
22. R. D. Twala, typewritten report, ca. 1959, box 110, BSP.
23. Twala.
24. Fiona Armitage, "The Zionist Movement in Swaziland: Origins and Bid for League Recognition, 1936–1958" (unpublished paper, Botswana History Workshop, August 1973).
25. "Brief History of the Institute for Social Research, 1956–1965," Records of the ISR, KZN.
26. Bengt Sundkler, *Bantu Prophets in South Africa* (London: Lutterworth, 1948).
27. Sundkler, 297.
28. Joel Cabrita, "Writing Apartheid: Ethnographic Collaborators and the Politics of Knowledge Production in Twentieth-Century South Africa," *American Historical Review* 125, no. 5 (2020): 1668–97.
29. "Statement of Expenditure from 1st January 1958 to 30th June 1958: Nuffield Grant—Mrs Twala," Records of the ISR, KZN.
30. Dan to Regina, July 22, 1959, RTP
31. Regina to Sundkler, July or August 1958, box 110, BSP.
32. R. D. Twala, "Saturday 26 July 1958, Lobamba Royal Kraal, Ibandla le League of African Churches," 6, box 110, BSP.

33. R. D. Twala, "The New Baprofitha at Kwaluseni, Bremersdorp, Swaziland, October 1959," 6, box 110, BSP.
34. Twala, 9–10.
35. Twala, 15.
36. Twala, 2.
37. Twala, 3.
38. Twala, "Saturday 26 July 1958," 4.
39. E.g., Regina to Sundkler, August 11, 1958, box 110, BSP.
40. Twala, "Saturday 26 July 1958," 5.
41. E.g., David Rycroft, "Zulu Zion and Some Swazi Zionists by Bengt Sundkler," *Bulletin of the School of Oriental and African Studies* 41, no. 1 (1978): 205–6; George Shepperson, "Review: Ethiopianism and Zionism in Southern Africa," *Journal of African History* 20, no. 1 (1979): 142–45.
42. Sundkler, *Zulu Zion,* 7.
43. Sundkler, 206–43.
44. Sundkler, 6.
45. Sundkler, 8.
46. Cabrita, "Writing Apartheid," 1681–82.
47. Sundkler to G. C. Oosthuizen, February 10, 1952, box 97, BSP.
48. Sundkler, *Zulu Zion,* 7.
49. Sundkler, 230.
50. Twala, "Saturday 26 July 1958," 1; Sundkler, *Zulu Zion,* 230.

## Chapter 14: Politics and Patriarchy

1. James Hall, *Speak Manzini: An Autobiography of an African City* (Manzini: Landmark, 2000), 71–72, 88.
2. Philip Bonner, *Kings, Concessionaries and Commoners: The Evolution and Dissolution of the Nineteenth-Century Swazi State* (Cambridge: Cambridge University Press, 1983), 185; J. R. Masson, "The First Map of Swaziland," *Geographical Journal* 155, no. 3 (1989): 335–41.
3. Sandile Simelane, "Politics and the Press: A Case Study of the Times of Swaziland and the Swazi Observer" (master's thesis, University of KwaZulu-Natal, 1995), 28.
4. Simelane, chap. 3.
5. "Marriage Contract as Swazis See It by Intombazana," *Times of Swaziland,* November 3, 1961.
6. "Incwala by Intombazana," *Times of Swaziland,* January 2, 1962.
7. "Marriage Contract as Swazis See It by Intombazana"; "Choosing an Heir by Intombazana," *Times of Swaziland,* November 10, 1961; "The State by Intombazana," *Times of Swaziland,* November 17, 1961; "Etiquette by

Intombazana," *Times of Swaziland*, December 1, 1961; "Incwala by Intombazana," *Times of Swaziland*, January 2, 1962.

8. "State by Intombazana."
9. Christian P. Potholm, *Swaziland: The Dynamics of Political Modernization* (Berkeley: University of California Press, 1972), 47–50.
10. Potholm, 51.
11. Brian Marwick to Sobhuza II, July 28, 1958, Lobamba Archives, Lobamba.
12. "Editorial: The Political Scene in Swaziland," *Times of Swaziland*, February 24, 1961.
13. J. S. M. Matsebula, *A Tribute to the Late His Majesty King Sobhuza II* (Mbabane: Webster, 1983), 28.
14. "Ingwenyama Warns Swazi Nation," *Times of Swaziland*, October 14, 1960.
15. "Open Letter to All the Political Leaders by Mr A. Z. Khumalo," *Times of Swaziland*, January 4, 1963,
16. Potholm, *Swaziland*, 104–5.
17. Dan Twala, interview by Tim Couzens, July 26, 1979, Dube, Soweto, RTP.
18. Dan Twala.
19. *Times of Swaziland*, August 31, 1962.
20. Dudley Barker, *Swaziland* (London: H. M. Stationery Office, 1965), 131. Anne Twala, interview by author, July 29, 2019, Kwaluseni.
21. My thanks to Phumzile van Damme for identifying her grandfather, Mr. Mayisela.
22. Potholm, *Swaziland*, 22–23.
23. Thoko Ginindza, *Swazi Women: Sociocultural and Economic Considerations; Final Report March–May 1989* (Washington, DC: US Agency for International Development, 1989).
24. *Izwi lama Swazi*, August 19, 1961.
25. "Parallelism by Intombazana," *Times of Swaziland*, December 22, 1961.
26. "Fashions at the Incwala by Intombazana," *Times of Swaziland*, February 1, 1963.
27. "Prayer, Churches and Unity by Intombazana," *Times of Swaziland*, February 8, 1963. See also "Old African Way of Worship by Intombazana," June 21, 1963, *Times of Swaziland*, for similar criticism.
28. Matteo Grilli, "Nkrumah, Nationalism and Pan-Africanism: The Bureau of African Affairs Collection," *History in Africa* 44 (2017): 301–2.
29. *Times of Swaziland*, June 1, 1962.
30. Joshua Mzizi, *Man of Conscience: The Life History of Albert Shabangu and Selected Speeches* (Mbabane: Websters, 1990), 30.
31. "Now Is the Time to Win!," *New Age*, June 14, 1962, AG 2877, Wits Historical Papers.
32. "The Women of Ghana by Intombazana," *Times of Swaziland*, August 3, 1962.

33. "Women of Ghana."
34. "Swazi Traditional Wedding by Intombazana," *Times of Swaziland*, July 19, 1963.
35. "Turning Point in the Swazi Way of Life by Intombazana," *Times of Swaziland*, August 2, 1963.
36. "An Urban Wedding by Intombazana," *Times of Swaziland*, August 16, 1963.
37. Deborah Posel, "Marriage at the Drop of a Hat: Housing and Partnership in South Africa's Urban African Townships, 1920s to 1960s," *History Workshop Journal* 61, no. 1 (2006): 57–76.
38. "Arranged Marriages by Intombazana," *Times of Swaziland*, August 30, 1962. For new forms of pragmatic urban marriage, see also Hilda Kuper and Selma Kaplan, "Voluntary Associations in an Urban Township," *African Studies* 3, no. 4 (1944): 178–86.
39. "Fashions at the Incwala by Intombazana," *Times of Swaziland*, February 1, 1963
40. "Fashions at the Incwala."
41. Dan Twala, interview, RTP.
42. Dan to Gelana, November 7, 1963, RTP.
43. Dan to Gelana, November 7, 1963, RTP.
44. *Izwi lama Swazi*, November 30, 1963; Potholm, *Swaziland*, 98.
45. Regina to Dan, January 3, 1945, RTP.
46. "Valediction to Manzana by Intombazana," *Times of Swaziland*, March 26, 1965,
47. Stella Lukhele, interview by author, Kwaluseni, July 31, 2019.
48. "Death of Former Times Contributor," *Times of Swaziland*, August 30, 1968.
49. E.g., *Times of Swaziland*, August 2 and August 16, 1963 (her wedding series).
50. "I Have Left the Progressive Party by R. D. Twala," *Izwi lama Swazi*, April 13, 1963.
51. "Ukuzendisa namalobolo ngu Kadebona," *Izwi lama Swazi*, January 19, 1963; "Izintombi ezineterylene ebusweni ngu Kadebona," November 9, 1963.
52. Dumisa Dlamini to Regina, July 10, 1960, RTP.
53. Barker, *Swaziland*, 131.
54. *Times of Swaziland*, December 13, 1963.
55. Potholm, *Swaziland*, 91–93.
56. *Times of Swaziland*, March 29, 1963.
57. "This Passport Business by Intombazana," *Times of Swaziland*, July 12, 1963.
58. "Zwane Gives Evidence," *Times of Swaziland*, December 13, 1963.

59. B. A. Marwick, *The Swazi: An Ethnographic Account of the Natives of the Swaziland Protectorate* (Cambridge: Cambridge University Press, 1940).
60. Hilda Kuper, *Sobhuza II, Ngwenyama and King of Swaziland: The Story of an Hereditary Ruler and His Country* (London: Duckworth, 1978), 248.
61. *Times of Swaziland*, January 24, 1964.
62. "Swazi Women's World: The Day of the Plebiscite by Intombazana," *Times of Swaziland*, January 24, 1964.
63. "SNC Replies to Intombazana," *Times of Swaziland*, February 7, 1964.
64. Mary Twala, interview by author, August 20, 2019, Orlando East, Johannesburg.
65. "Zenzele Women at Matsapha by R. D. Twala," *Izwi lama Swazi*, April 20, 1963.
66. Letter to the editor (unsigned), *Izwi lama Swazi*, May 4, 1963.
67. "In What Way Do Women Not Understand the Law? By R. D. Twala," *Izwi lama Swazi*, May 18, 1963.
68. Janet Aphane, interview by author, August 12, 2018, Kwaluseni; Zanele Twala, interview by author, August 8, 2019, Siphocosini.
69. Twala, interview, August 8, 2019.
70. "For Men Only by Intombazana." *Times of Swaziland*, November 30, 1962.
71. "Ngwenyama Urges All to Register," *Times of Swaziland*, February 14, 1963.
72. "58 Candidates for Swaziland's First Legco," *Times of Swaziland*, May 22, 1964.
73. "58 Candidates."
74. "Swaziland Fighting News: Issued by NNLC, 21 September 1964," PP.SQ Ngwane National Liberatory Congress, SOAS.
75. Potholm, *Swaziland*, 112; "Clean Sweep for Sobhuza," *Times of Swaziland*, July 4, 1964; Christian Potholm, "Changing Political Configurations in Swaziland," *Journal of Modern African Studies* 4, no. 3 (1966): 316.
76. "Victory Message from Imbhokodvo," *Times of Swaziland*, July 3, 1964.
77. Richard Levin, *When the Sleeping Grass Awakens: Land and Power in Swaziland* (Johannesburg: Wits University Press, 1997), 77.
78. "Our Elections by Intombazana," *Times of Swaziland*, July 10, 1964.
79. Potholm, *Swaziland*, 115.
80. "Mrs Twala Resigns," *Times of Swaziland*, May 14, 1965.

## Chapter 15: Social Worker

1. Dan to Regina, July 22, 1964, RTP.
2. November 8, 1960, RTP; Dan to Regina, December 10, 1962, RTP.
3. Dan to Regina, December 10, 1962, RTP.
4. Dan to Regina, 1962, RTP.

5. "Swaziland Council of Social Service," July 29, 1966; "Mrs Twala New Social Service Secretary," *Times of Swaziland,* May 12, 1967.
6. Anne Twala, interview by author, July 29, 2019, Kwaluseni.
7. *Times of Swaziland,* November 26 and December 10, 1966.
8. An exception is Gelana's 1966 eulogy for deceased SPP member Sifunti Matsebula, "Illiterate but Enlightened by Intombazana," *Times of Swaziland,* February 4, 1966.
9. "The Poor among Us by Intombazana," *Times of Swaziland,* April 24, 1964.
10. "Poor among Us by Intombazana"; "System of Checks and Balances against Broken Homes by Intombazana," *Times of Swaziland,* July 16, 1965; "Mothers, Children, Education by Intombazana," *Times of Swaziland,* March 13, 1966; "A Place Where You Can Get Things Cheap by Intombazana," *Times of Swaziland,* September 4, 1964.
11. According to Zanele, Alvina was one of many women who would call upon the Kwaluseni house with pleas for help from her mother. Zanele Twala, interview by author, August 8, 2019, Mbabane,
12. "Poor among Us."
13. "Zenzele YWCA Helps Women in Jail by Intombazana," *Times of Swaziland,* June 28, 1963.
14. "Zenzele YWCA Helps Women in Jail by Intombazana," *Times of Swaziland,* July 12, 1963.
15. "Mothers of the Nation," *Izwi lama Swazi,* July 20, 1963.
16. "May Her Tribe Increase by Intombazana," *Times of Swaziland,* May 10, 1963.
17. "A Nation Bereaved by Intombazana," August 14, 1963. See the follow-up column on the first anniversary of Malie's death: "Give Honour Where It Is Due by Intombazana," *Times of Swaziland,* September 24, 1965.
18. "Zenzele Women and Mother's Day by Intombazana," *Times of Swaziland,* May 22, 1964.
19. "The Women of Ghana by Intombazana," *Times of Swaziland* August 3, 1962; "Zenzele YWCA Helps Women by Intombazana," *Times of Swaziland,* June 28, 1963.
20. "Ingosi Yabesifazane," *Izwi lama Swazi,* July 6, 1963; "By Kadebona," *Izwi lama Swazi,* January 26, 1963; "There Are Many Women Moving Around," *Izwi lama Swazi,* April 6, 1963.
21. "What Can Be Done about Our Girls? By Intombazana," *Times of Swaziland,* November 27, 1965. For a similar article, see "Intombazana Takes Stock," *Times of Swaziland,* January 1, 1965.
22. R. D. Twala, "Independence," unpublished book manuscript, n.p., HKP, UCLA.
23. Dan to Regina, December 20, 1962, RTP; *Times of Swaziland,* July 30, 1965.

24. Nicholas Bhengu to Regina, April 28, 1960, RTP; Stella Lukhele, interview by author, July 31, 2019, Kwaluseni. See correspondence between Myra Lindiwe Nkosi and Gelana Twala regarding her dilapidated Kwaluseni library, *Times of Swaziland,* November 26 and December 10, 1965.
25. Dan to Regina, 1962, RTP.
26. Dan to Regina, December 10, 1962, RTP.
27. "Choosing a Partner by Intombazana," *Times of Swaziland,* October 15, 1965.
28. Zanele Twala, interview by author, August 8, 2019, Mbabane.
29. Mary Twala, interview by author, August 21, 2019, Orlando East.
30. Janet Aphane, interview by author, August 12, 2018, Kwaluseni.
31. Anne Twala, interview by author, July 29, 2019, Kwaluseni.
32. Genius Aphane, interview by author, August 12, 2018, Kwaluseni.
33. Twala, "Independence," n.p.
34. "Death of Former Times Contributor," *Times of Swaziland,* August 30, 1968.
35. "Making Our Towns and Villages Beautiful by Intombazana," *Times of Swaziland,* July 23, 1965.
36. Anne Twala, interview by author, July 29, 2019, Kwaluseni.

## Chapter 16: The Gatekeepers

1. "A Report on the Swazi Nation's Library Work at Kwaluseni by R. D. Twala," *Izwi lama Swazi,* July 2, 1960. Matsebula's poems had been published in 1957 as *Iqoqo lezinkondlo ziqoqwe zahlelwa* (Pietermaritzburg: Shuter & Shooter, 1957), which Regina quoted in the *Izwi* article.
2. Gelana to Matsebula, July 1, 1968, HKP, UCLA; Dan Twala, interview by Tim Couzens, July 26, 1979, Dube, Soweto.
3. Regina to Africa Service Institute, New York, November 1, 1963, RTP.
4. Mrs. G. B. Smith, 41 Cremorne Road, New South Wales, Australia, to Regina, August 21, 1964, RTP.
5. Anne Twala, interview with author, July 29, 2019, Kwaluseni.
6. "Death of Former Times Contributor," *Times of Swaziland,* August 30, 1968.
7. Dan Twala, interview by Tim Couzens, July 26, 1979, Dube, Soweto, RTP.
8. "Fashions at the Incwala by Intombazana," *Times of Swaziland,* February 1, 1963.
9. Kuper to Sobhuza II, September 30, 1968, HKP.
10. R. D. Twala, unpublished book manuscript, chap. on Swaziland independence, n.p., HKP, UCLA.
11. Hilda Kuper, *Sobhuza II, Ngwenyama and King of Swaziland: The Story of an Hereditary Ruler and His Country* (London: Duckworth, 1978), 276.

12. Barbara Tyrrell, *The Tribal People of Southern Africa* (Cape Town: Books of Africa, 1968).
13. Elwyn Jenkins, "Barbara Tyrrell, 1912–2015," *Natalia*, no. 45 (2015): 117–19.
14. "Triumph for Author and Publisher," *Times of Swaziland*, April 19, 1968.
15. Matsebula to Kuper, February 11, 1969, HKP, UCLA.
16. See Kuper's early conflict with Pieter Johannes Schoeman, who published on the Incwala in 1935, in Andrew Bank, *Pioneers of the Field: South Africa's Women Anthropologists* (Cambridge: Cambridge University Press, 2016), 202–4.
17. "Hilda Kuper on Visit to Swaziland," *Times of Swaziland*, October 7, 1966; "Hilda Kuper's Fine Novel about Swazis, Bite of Hunger," *Times of Swaziland*, December 30, 1966.
18. Dan Twala, interview, RTP. This sentiment was confirmed by Gelana's daughter, Zanele.
19. Kuper to Leo and Girls, October 28, 1966, box 35, HKP, UCLA.
20. Kuper to Matsebula, June 2, 1969, box 24, HKP, UCLA.
21. E.g., "The Incwala by Intombazana," *Times of Swaziland*, January 5, 1962, box 50, newspaper clippings, HKP, UCLA. Kuper's PhD student Sondra Hale helped clip and sort newspaper articles. Sondra Hale, Dawn Chatty, and Beth Rosen-Prinz, Zoom interview by author, December 11, 2020.
22. Kuper to Matsebula, March 3, 1969, box 24, HKP, UCLA.
23. Thoko Ginindza application material, UCLA 1970, box 24, HKP, UCLA.
24. Jenny Kuper, telephone interview by author, November 21, 2020.
25. Bank, *Pioneers of the Field*, 189–238.
26. Kuper to Mr. Chris Pappas, American consul, June 28, 1967, box 24, HKP, UCLA.
27. Kuper to William Talbott, August 9, 1967, box 25, HKP, UCLA.
28. Kuper to Sobhuza, April 1, 1968, box 24, HKP, UCLA.
29. Kuper, *Sobhuza II*, 347.
30. Kuper, 284.
31. See Bank, *Pioneers of the Field*, 232.
32. Kuper to Polycarp Dlamini, V. S. Hiller, J. S. M. Matsebula, and Msindazwe Sukati, September 24, 1976, box 24, HKP, UCLA.
33. Hilda Kuper interview with Sobhuza II, with J. S. M. Matsebula present, August 9, 1970, Etsheni, HKP, UCLA; Hale, Chatty, and Rosen-Prinz, Zoom interview, December 11, 2020.
34. Richard Levin, *When the Sleeping Grass Awakens: Land and Power in Swaziland* (Johannesburg: Wits University Press, 1997), 95–103.
35. Kuper, *Sobhuza II*, 336.
36. Kuper, 337.
37. Kuper, 347.
38. Kuper, 347.

39. J. S. M. Matsebula, *A History of Swaziland* (Cape Town: Longman, 1972), 236.
40. Kuper, *Sobhuza II*, 14.
41. Bank, *Pioneers of the Field*, 233.
42. Abby Gondek, "The Swazi Clothing and Adornment Collection at the UCLA Fowler Museum: A Transnational Collaboration between Hilda Kuper and Thoko Ginindza" (paper presented at the American Anthropological Association meeting, Vancouver, BC, November 22, 2019), https://abbysgondek.com/portfolio/the-swazi-clothing-and-adornment-collection-at-the-ucla-fowler-museum-a-transnational-collaboration-between-hilda-kuper-and-thoko-ginindza/. There are also reports of similar dynamics between Kuper and Fatima Meer, who worked as Kuper's research assistant in Durban in the 1950s. Personal Zoom communication with Shireen Hassim, November 7, 2020.
43. Abby Gondek, "Jewish Women's Transracial Epistemological Networks: Representations of Black Women in the African Diaspora" (PhD diss., Florida International University, 2018), 124.
44. Levin, *When the Sleeping Grass Awakens*, 144–66.
45. *Swazi TV Times*, n.d., Zanele Twala papers, property of Zanele Twala.
46. Bruce Murray, *Wits: The Early Years* (Johannesburg: Wits University Press, 1982); Bruce Murray, *Wits, the "Open" Years: A History of the University of the Witwatersrand, Johannesburg, 1939–1959* (Johannesburg: Wits University Press, 1997).
47. I am grateful to an anonymous reviewer for my manuscript making this point.

## Postscript

1. Ohio Short Histories of Africa, accessed July 22, 2022, https://www.ohioswallow.com/series/Ohio+Short+Histories+of+Africa.
2. Louise Viljoen, *Ingrid Jonker: Poet under Apartheid* (Athens: Ohio University Press, 2013); Pamela Scully, *Ellen Johnson Sirleaf* (Athens: Ohio University Press, 2016); Shireen Hassim, *ANC Women's League: Sex, Gender and Politics* (Auckland Park, South Africa: Jacana, 2014).
3. S. C. Zondi Attorneys, "Legal Opinion: Regina Gelane Twala," May 2021.

# Bibliography

## Primary Sources

### *Archives*

Killie Campbell Library, University of KwaZulu-Natal, Durban
Campbell, Correspondence KCM 5969
Lobamba National Archives, Eswatini
File No. 3355
London School of Economics Archives
Malinowski Collection 7/39
Luthuli Museum, Groutville, South Africa
Yengwa Collection
National Archives of South Africa, Pretoria
Records of the Native Divorce Court
Rhodes University, Cory Library Archives
Methodist Collection
School of Oriental and African Studies, University of London
Methodist Collection
Ngwane National Liberatory Congress Collection
University of California at Los Angeles Archives
Hilda Kuper Papers
University of KwaZulu-Natal Archives, Pietermaritzburg
Records of the Institute of Social Research
University of Uppsala Archives
Bengt Sundkler Papers
University of the Witwatersrand, Wits Historical Papers
Advance Newspaper, CULL001
Bantu Men's Social Center Records, 1923–75, A1058
End Conscription Campaign Collection, AG 1977
Federation of African Women, 1954–63, AD 1137
Regina Twala Papers
South African Institute of Race Relations, AD 1715
Treason Trial Papers, AD 1812

Zanele Twala Papers, Siphocosini, Eswatini
Photographs and newspaper/magazine articles

*Newspapers*

*Bantu World*
*The Citizen* (online)
*Drum*
*Ilanga lase Natal*
*Iso lo Muzi* (Adams College)
*Izwi lama Swazi*
*Natal Mercury* (Pietermaritzburg)
*Rand Daily Mail*
*Sunday Times* (Johannesburg)
*Sunday Tribune* (Durban)
*Swati Newsweek* (online)
*Times of Swaziland*
*Umteteli wa Bantu*

## Published Secondary Sources


Alegi, Peter. "Playing to the Gallery: Sport, Cultural Performance, and Social Identity in South Africa, 1920s–1945." *International Journal of African Historical Studies* 35, no. 1 (2002): 17–38.

Allen, Ray, and George P. Cunningham. "Cultural Uplift and Double-Consciousness: African American Responses to the 1935 Opera Porgy and Bess." *Musical Quarterly* 88, no. 3 (2005): 342–69.

Allman, Jean. "The Disappearing of Hannah Kudjoe: Nationalism, Feminism, and the Tyrannies of History." *Journal of Women's History* 21, no. 3 (2009): 13–35.

Ally, Shireen. "If You Are Hungry and a Man Promises You Mealies, Will You Not Follow Him? South African Swazi Ethnic Nationalism, 1931–1986." *South African Historical Journal* 63, no. 3 (2011): 414–30.

Asad, Talal. *Genealogies of Religion: Discipline and Reasons of Power in Christianity and Islam.* Baltimore: Johns Hopkins University Press, 1993.

Attwell, David. "Modernizing Tradition / Traditionalizing Modernity: Reflections on the Dhlomo-Vilakazi Debate." *Research in African Literatures* 33, no. 1 (2002): 94–119.

———. *Rewriting Modernity: Studies in Black South African Literary History.* Athens: Ohio University Press, 2006.

Badenhorst, C. M., and C. M. Rogerson. "Teach the Native to Play: Social Control and Organized Black Sport on the Witwatersrand, 1920–1939." *GeoJournal* 12, no. 2 (1986): 197–202.

Balcomb, Anthony. "From Apartheid to the New Dispensation: Evangelicals and the Democratization of South Africa." *Journal of Religion in Africa* 34, no. 1 (2004): 5–38.

Ballantine, Christopher. "Concert and Dance: The Foundations of Black Jazz in South Africa between the Twenties and the Early Forties." *Popular Music* 10, no. 2 (1991): 121–45.

Bank, Andrew. *Pioneers of the Field: South Africa's Women Anthropologists.* Cambridge: Cambridge University Press, 2016.

Barker, Dudley. *Swaziland.* London: H.M. Stationery Office, 1965.

Barnes, Julian. *Flaubert's Parrot.* London: Jonathan Cape, 1984.

Basner, Miriam. *Am I an African? The Political Memoirs of H. M. Basner.* Johannesburg: Wits University Press, 1993.

Beal, Frances M. "Double Jeopardy: To Be Black and Female." *Meridians: Feminism, Race, Transnationalism* 8, no. 2 (2008): 166–76.

Beavon, Keith. *Johannesburg: The Making and Shaping of the City.* Pretoria: University of South Africa Press, 2004.

Berger, Iris. "An African American Mother of the Nation: Madie Hall Xuma in South Africa, 1940–1963." *Journal of Southern African Studies* 27, no. 3 (2001): 547–66.

———. "From Ethnography to Social Welfare: Ray Phillips and Representations of Urban Women in South Africa." *Social Sciences and Missions,* no. 19 (2006): 91–116.

Bischoff, Paul-Henri. "Why Swaziland Is Different: An Explanation of the Kingdom's Political Position in Southern Africa." *Journal of Modern African Studies* 26, no. 3 (1988): 457–71.

Bonner, Philip. "Desirable or Undesirable Sotho Women? Liquor, Prostitution, and the Migration of Sotho Women to the Rand." African studies seminar paper, University of Witwatersrand, May 1988. https://core.ac.uk/download/pdf/39667365.pdf.

———. *Kings, Commoners and Concessionaires: The Evolution and Dissolution of the Nineteenth-Century Swazi State.* Cambridge: Cambridge University Press, 1983.

———. "The Transvaal Native Congress, 1917–1920: The Radicalization of the Black Petit Bourgeoisie on the Rand." In *Industrialization and Social Change in South Africa,* edited by Shula Marks and Richard Rathbone, 270–313. London: Longman, 1982.

Bonner, Philip, and Noor Nieftagodien. *Alexandra: A History.* Johannesburg: Wits University Press, 2008.

Booth, Alan. "Lord Selborne and the British Protectorates, 1908–1910." *Journal of African History* 10, no. 1 (1969): 133–48.

Boswell, Barbara. *And Wrote My Story Anyway: Black South African Women's Novels as Feminism.* Johannesburg: Wits University Press, 2020.

———. *Lauretta Ngcobo: Writing as the Practice of Freedom.* Cape Town: HSRC Press, 2022.

Bozzoli, Belinda, and Mmantho Nkotsoe. *Women of Phokeng: Consciousness, Life Strategy, and Migration in South Africa, 1900–1983.* Portsmouth, NH: Heinemann, 1991.

Breckenridge, Keith. "Love Letters and Amanuenses: Beginning the Cultural History of the Working-Class Private Sphere in Southern Africa, 1900–1933." *Journal of Southern African Studies* 26, no. 2 (2000): 337–48.

———. "Reasons for Writing: African Working-Class Letter Writing in Early Twentieth-Century South Africa." In *Africa's Hidden Histories: Everyday Literacy and Making the Self,* edited by Karin Barber, 143–54. Bloomington: Indiana University Press, 2006.

———. "Verwoerd's Bureau of Proof: Total Information in the Making of Apartheid." *History Workshop Journal,* no. 59 (2005): 83–108.

Cabrita, Joel. *The People's Zion: Southern Africa, the USA and a Transatlantic Faith-Healing Movement.* Cambridge, MA: Harvard University Press, 2018.

———. "Writing Apartheid: Ethnographic Collaborators and the Politics of Knowledge Production in Twentieth-Century South Africa." *American Historical Review* 125, no. 5 (2020): 1668–97.

Callinicos, Luli. *Who Built Jozi? Discovering Memory at Wits Junction.* Johannesburg: Wits University Press, 2012.

Chipkin, Clive M. *Johannesburg Style: Architecture and Society, 1880s to 1960s.* Cape Town: David Philip, 1993.

Ciuraru, Carmela. *Nom de Plume: A (Secret) History of Pseudonyms.* New York: Harper, 2011.

Cobley, Alan. *Rules of the Game: Struggles in Black Recreation and Social Welfare Policy in South Africa.* Westport, CT: Greenwood, 1997.

Cocks, Paul. "The King and I: Bronislaw Malinowski, King Sobhuza II of Swaziland, and the Vision of Culture Change in Africa." *History of the Human Sciences* 13, no. 4 (2000): 25–47.

Cooper, Helene. *Madame President: The Extraordinary Journey of Ellen Sirleaf Johnson.* New York: Simon & Schuster, 2017.

Cope, Nicholas. *To Bind the Nation: Solomon kaDinuzulu and Zulu Nationalism, 1913–1933.* Pietermaritzburg: University of Natal Press, 1993.

———. "The Zulu Petit Bourgeoisie and Zulu Nationalism in the 1920s: Origins of Inkatha." *Journal of Southern African Studies* 16, no. 3 (1990): 431–51.

Coplan, David. *In Township Tonight: South African Black City Music and Theatre.* Chicago: University of Chicago Press, 1985.

Couzens, Tim. *The New African: A Study of the Life and Work of H. I. E. Dhlomo.* Johannesburg: Ravan, 1985.

———. "Pseudonyms in Black South African Writing, 1920–1950." *Research in African Literatures* 6, no. 2 (1975): 226–31.

———. *Tramp Royal: The True Story of Trader Horn*. Johannesburg: Ravan Press, 1993.

Cragg, A. W. *The Story of Indaleni*. N.p.: Natal District Missionary Committee of the Wesleyan Methodist Church, South Africa, 1924.

Crais, Clifton, and Pamela Scully. *Sara Baartman and the Hottentot Venus: A Ghost Story and a Biography*. Princeton, NJ: Princeton University Press, 2009.

Davis, Caroline. "A Question of Power: Bessie Head and Her Publishers." *Journal of Southern African Studies* 44, no. 3 (2018): 491–506.

Daybell, James. "Letters." In *The Cambridge Companion to Early Modern Women's Writing*, edited by Laura Knoppers, 181–93. Cambridge: Cambridge University Press, 2010.

Diabate, Naminate. *Naked Agency: Genital Cursing and Biopolitics in Africa*. Durham, NC: Duke University Press, 2020.

Dhlomo, R. R. R. *An African Tragedy*. Lovedale: Lovedale Institution Press, 1928.

Dineo Gqola, Pumla, ed. *Miriam Tlali, Writing Freedom*. Cape Town: HSRC Press, 2021.

Dovey, Lindiwe, and Angela Impey. "*African Jim*: Sound, Politics and Pleasure in Early 'Black' South African Cinema." *Journal of African Cultural Studies* 22, no. 1 (2010): 57–73.

Dubow, Saul, and Alan Jeeves, eds. *South Africa's 1940s: Worlds of Possibilities*. Cape Town: Double Storey, 2005.

du Preez Bezdrob, Anné Mariè. *Winnie Mandela: A Life*. Cape Town: Zebra, 2003.

du Toit, Marijke, and Palesa Nzuzu. "Isifazane Sakiti Emadolebheni: The Politics of Gender in *Ilanga lase Natal*, 1933–1938." *Journal of Natal and Zululand History* 33, no. 2 (2019): 62–86.

Earle, Rebecca, ed. *Epistolary Selves: Letters and Letter-Writers, 1600–1945*. Aldershot, UK: Ashgate, 1999.

Edgar, Bob. *Josie Mpama/Palmer: Get Up, Get Moving*. Athens: Ohio University Press, 2020.

Elphick, Richard. *The Equality of Believers: Protestant Missionaries and the Racial Politics of South Africa*. Charlottesville: University of Virginia Press, 2012.

Erlank, Natasha. "*Umteteli wa Bantu* and the Constitution of Social Publics in the 1920s and 1930s." *Social Dynamics* 45, no. 1 (2019): 75–102.

———. "The White Wedding: Affect and Economy in South Africa in the Early Twentieth Century." *African Studies Review* 57, no. 3 (2014): 29–50.

Etherington, Norman. "Mission Station Melting Pots as a Factor in the Rise of South African Black Nationalism." *International Journal of African Historical Studies* 9, no. 4 (1976): 592–605.

———. *Peasants, Peasants and Politics in Southeast Africa, 1835–1880: African Christian Communities in Natal, Pondoland and Zululand*. London: Royal Historical Society, 1978.

Evans, Ivan. *Bureaucracy and Race Administration in South Africa.* Berkeley: University of California Press, 1997.

First, Ruth, and Ann Scott. *Olive Schreiner: A Biography.* London: A. Deutsch, 1980.

Gaitskell, Deborah. "From Domestic Servants to Girl Wayfarers at St Agnes', Rosettenville: Phases in the Life of a South African Mission School, 1909–1935." *Southern African Review of Education* 19, no. 2 (2013): 92–110.

Gaitskell, Deborah, Judy Kimble, Moira Maconachie, and Elaine Unterhalter. "Class, Race, and Gender: Domestic Workers in South Africa." *Review of African Political Economy* 10, nos. 27–28 (1983): 86–108.

Gengenbach, Heidi. "Truth-Telling and the Politics of Women's Life History Research in Africa: A Reply to Kirk Hoppe." *International Journal of African Historical Studies* 27, no. 3 (1994): 619–27.

Gish, Steven. *Desmond Tutu: A Biography.* Westport, CT: Greenwood, 2004.

Glaser, Clive. "Managing the Sexuality of Urban Youth: Johannesburg, 1920s–1960s." *International Journal of African Historical Studies* 38, no. 2 (2005): 301–27.

Griffin, Robert J. "Anonymity and Authorship." *New Literary History* 30, no. 4 (1999): 877–95.

Grilli, Mateo. "Nkrumah, Nationalism and Pan-Africanism: The Bureau of African Affairs Collection." *History in Africa* 44 (2017): 295–307.

Guy, Jeff. *The Maphumulo Uprising: War, Law and Ritual in the Zulu Rebellion.* Pietermaritzburg: University of KwaZulu-Natal Press, 2005.

Hall, James. *Speak Manzini: An Autobiography of an African City.* Manzini, Eswatini: Landmark, 2000.

Harrison, Nancy. *Winnie Mandela.* London: Gollancz, 1985.

Hassim, Shireen. *The ANC Women's League: Sex, Gender and Politics.* Auckland Park, South Africa: Jacana, 2014.

———. *Voices of Liberation: Fatima Meer.* Pretoria: HSRC Press, 2019.

Healy-Clancy, Megan. "Politics of Marriage in New Segregationist South Africa." *African Studies Review* 57, no. 2 (2014): 7–28.

———. "Women and the Problem of Family in Early African Nationalist History and Historiography." *South African Historical Journal* 64, no. 3 (2012): 450–71.

———. *A World of Their Own: A History of South African Women's Education.* Charlottesville: University of Virginia Press, 2013.

Hellmann, Ellen. "Urban Areas." In *Handbook on Race Relations in South Africa,* edited by Ellen Hellmann, 233–34. Oxford: Oxford University Press, 1949.

Hirson, Baruch. *Yours for the Union: Class and Community Struggles in South Africa, 1930–1947.* Johannesburg: Wits University Press, 1989.

Hoppe, Kirk. "Whose Life Is It Anyway? Issues of Representation in Life Narrative Texts of African Women." *International Journal of African Historical Studies* 26, no. 3 (1993): 623–36.

Huddleston, Trevor. *Naught for Your Comfort*. London: Collins, 1956.

Hughes, Heather. "Lives and Wives: Understanding African Nationalism in South Africa through a Biographical Approach." *History Compass* 10, no. 8 (2012): 562–73.

Jacobs, Nancy J., and Andrew Bank. "Biography in Post-Apartheid South Africa: A Call for Awkwardness." *African Studies* 78, no. 2 (2019): 165–82.

Jaffer, Zubeida. *Beauty of the Heart: The Life and Times of Charlotte Mannya Maxeke*. Bloemfontein: SUN Media, 2016.

Jaji, Tsitsi Ella. *Africa in Stereo: Modernism, Music and Pan African Solidarity*. Oxford: Oxford University Press, 2014.

Jenkins, Elwyn. "Barbara Tyrrell, 1912–2015." *Natalia*, no. 45 (2015): 117–19.

Jensen, Katherine Ann. *Writing Love: Letters, Women and the Novel in France, 1605–1776*. Carbondale: Southern Illinois University Press, 1995.

Junod, Violaine. "Entokozweni: Managing a Community Service in an Urban African Area." *Human Organization* 23, no. 1 (1964): 28–35.

———. "Last Chance for Whites." *Africa Today* 4, no. 6 (1957): 36–40.

Kanongo, Tabitha. *Wangari Maathai*. Athens: Ohio University Press, 2020.

Kent, Alan M. *Pulp Methodism: The Lives and Literature of Silas, Joseph and Salome Hocking, Three Cornish Novelists*. Cornwall: Cornish Hillside Publications, 2002.

Khan, Farieda. "Anyone for Tennis? Conversions with Black Women Involved in Tennis during the Apartheid Era." *Agenda* 24, no. 85 (2010): 77–78.

Khumalo, Vukile. "Ekukhanyeni Letter Writers: A Historical Enquiry into Epistolary Networks and Political Imagination in KwaZulu-Natal South Africa." In *Africa's Hidden Histories: Everyday Literacy and Making the Self*, edited by Karin Barber, 113–42. Bloomington: Indiana University Press, 2006.

Kuper, Hilda. *An African Aristocracy: Rank among the Swazi*. Oxford: Oxford University Press, 1947.

———. "Function, History, Biography: Reflections on Fifty Years in the British Anthropological Tradition." In *Functionalism Historicized*, edited by George Stocking, 192–213. Madison: University of Wisconsin Press, 1988.

———. "Ritual of Kingship among the Swazi." *Africa: Journal of the International African Institute* 14, no. 5 (1944): 230–57.

———. *Sobhuza II, Ngwenyama and King of Swaziland: The Story of an Hereditary Ruler and His Country*. London: Duckworth, 1978.

———. *The Uniform of Color: A Study of White-Black Relationships in Swaziland*. Johannesburg: Wits University Press, 1947.

Kuper, Hilda, and Selma Kaplan. "Voluntary Associations in an Urban Township." *African Studies* 3, no. 4 (1944): 178–86.

Kuzwayo, Ellen. *Call Me Woman*. London: Women's Press, 1985.

la Hausse de Lalouviere, Paul. *Restless Identities: Signatures of Nationalism, Zulu Ethnicity and History in the Lives of Petros Lamula (c. 1881–1948) and Lymon Maling (1889–c. 1936)*. Pietermaritzburg: University of Natal Press, 2000.

Lawrance, Benjamin, and Vusumuzi R. Kumalo. "A Genius without Direction: The Abortive Exile of Dugmore Boetie and the Fate of Southern African Refugees in a Decolonizing Africa." *American Historical Review* 126, no. 2 (2021): 585–622.

le Roux, Elizabeth. "Black Writers, White Publishers: A Case Study of the Bantu Treasury Series in South Africa." *Revue électronique d'études sur le monde anglophone* 11, no. 1 (2013).

———. "Miriam Tlali and Ravan Press: Politics and Power in Literary Publishing during the Apartheid Era," *Journal of Southern African Studies* 44, no. 3 (2018): 431–46.

Levin, Richard. *When the Sleeping Grass Awakens: Land and Power in Swaziland*. Johannesburg: Wits University Press, 1997.

Lodge, Tom. *Black Politics in South Africa since 1945*. New York: Longman, 1983.

Macmillan, Hugh. "A Nation Divided: The Swazi in Swaziland and the Transvaal, 1865–1986." In *The Creation of Tribalism in Southern Africa*, edited by Leroy Vail, 289–323. Berkeley: University of California Press, 1983.

———. "Swaziland, Decolonization and the Triumph of Tradition." *Journal of Modern African Studies* 23, no. 4 (1985): 643–66.

Magaziner, Dan. *The Art of Life in South Africa*. Athens: Ohio University Press, 2016.

Malcolm, D. Mck. "Zulu Literature." *Africa: Journal of the International African Institute* 19, no. 1 (1949): 33–39.

Manyathi-Jele, Nomfundo. "Farewell to One of the Greatest Moral Compasses." *De Rebus*, no. 538 (2014): 6.

Marks, Shula. *Divided Sisterhood: Race, Class, and Gender in the South African Nursing Profession*. New York: St. Martin's, 1994.

———. *Not Either an Experimental Doll: The Separate Worlds of Three South African Women*. Bloomington: Indiana University Press, 1988.

———. "Patriotism, Patriarchy and Purity: Natal and the Politics of Zulu Ethnic Consciousness." In *The Creation of Tribalism in Southern Africa*, edited by Leroy Vail, 215–40. Berkeley: University of California Press, 1989.

Marwick, B. A. *The Swazi: An Ethnographic Account of the Natives of the Swaziland Protectorate*. Cambridge: Cambridge University Press, 1940.

Masola, Athambile. "A Footnote and a Pioneer: Noni Jabavu's Legacy." In *Foundational African Writers: Peter Abrahams, Noni Jabavu, Sibusiso Nyembezi, and Es'kia Mphahlele*, edited by Bhekizizwe Peterson, Khwezi-Mkhize, and Makhosazana Xaba, 95–116. Johannesburg: Wits University Press, 2022.

Masson, J. R. "The First Map of Swaziland." *Geographical Journal* 155, no. 3 (1989): 335–41.

Matsebula, J. S. M. *A History of Swaziland*. 3rd ed. Cape Town: Longman, 1972.

———. *Iqoqo lezinkondlo ziqoqwe zahlelwa*. Pietermaritzburg: Shuter & Shooter, 1957.

———. *A Tribute to the Late His Majesty King Sobhuza II*. Mbabane: Websters, 1983.

McCord, Margaret. *The Calling of Katie Makhanya: A Memoir of South Africa*. Cape Town: David Philip, 1999.

McDonald, Peter. "The Book in South Africa." In *The Cambridge History of South African Literature*, edited by David Attwell and Derek Attridge, 800–817. Cambridge: Cambridge University Press, 2012.

Mirza, Sarah, and Margaret Strobel. *Three Swahili Women: Life Histories from Mombasa, Kenya*. Bloomington: Indiana University Press, 1989.

Modern Girl around the World Research Group. *The Modern Girl around the World: Consumption, Modernity and Globalization*. Durham, NC: Duke University Press, 2008.

Mofokeng, Santu. *Stories No. 1: Train Church*. Göttingen, Germany: Steidl, 2015.

Moodie, T. Dunbar. "The Moral Economy of the Black Miners' Strike of 1946." *Journal of Southern African Studies* 13, no. 1 (1986): 1–35.

Moodie, T. Dunbar, Vivienne Ndatshe, and British Sibuyi. "Migrancy and Male Sexuality on the South African Gold Mines." *Journal of Southern African Studies* 14, no. 2 (1988): 228–56.

Mphahele, Es'kia. *Down Second Avenue*. London: Faber & Faber, 1959.

Msimang, Sisonke. *The Resurrection of Winnie Mandela*. Johannesburg: Jonathan Ball, 2018.

Mthembu, Maxwell Vusumuzi. "The Political and Economic History of Swaziland's First Indigenous-Language Newspaper, Izwi lama Swazi." *African Journalism Studies* 41, no. 1 (2020): 17–34.

Murray, Bruce. "Nelson Mandela and Wits University." *Journal of African History* 57, no. 2 (2016): 271–92.

———. *Wits: The Early Years*. Johannesburg: Wits University Press, 1982.

———. *Wits, the "Open" Years: A History of the University of the Witwatersrand, Johannesburg, 1939–1959*. Johannesburg: Wits University Press, 1997.

Mzizi, Joshua. *Man of Conscience: The Life History of Albert Shabangu and Selected Speeches*. Mbabane: Websters, 1990.

Newell, Stephanie. "Literary Activism in Colonial Ghana: A Newspaper-Novel by 'A. Native.'" *Current Writing: Text and Representation in Southern Africa* 31, no. 2 (2001): 20–30.

———. *The Power to Name: A History of Anonymity in Colonial West Africa*. Athens: Ohio University Press, 2013.

Ngubane, Jordan K. *Should the Native Representative Council Be Abolished?* Cape Town: African Bookman, 1946.

Nieftagodien, Noor. *Orlando West, Soweto: An Illustrated History*. Johannesburg: Wits University Press, 2012.

Nthunya, M. M., K. L. Kendall, and E. Kuzwayo. *Singing Away the Hunger: Stories of a Life of Lesotho.* Bloomington: Indiana University Press, 1997.

O'Meara, Dan. "The 1946 African Mine Workers' Strike and the Political Economy of South Africa." *Journal of Commonwealth and Comparative Politics* 13, no. 2 (1975): 146–73.

Opland, Jeff. "The First Novel in Xhosa." *Research in African Literatures* 38, no. 4 (2007): 87–110.

———, trans. and ed. *The Nation's Bounty: The Xhosa Poetry of Nontsizi Mgqwetho.* Johannesburg: Wits University Press, 2007.

Paton, Alan. *Cry, the Beloved Country.* New York: C. Scribner's Sons, 1948.

Peires, Jeff. "The Lovedale Press: Literature for the Bantu Revisited." *History in Africa* 6 (1979): 155–75.

Personal Narratives Group, ed. *Interpreting Women's Lives: Feminist Theory and Personal Narratives.* Bloomington: Indiana University Press, 1989.

Peterson, Bhekizizwe. "HIE Dhlomo." In *Encyclopedia of African Literature,* edited by Simon Gikandi, 193–94. London: Routledge, 2003.

Phillips, Ray. *The Bantu Are Coming: Phases of South Africa's Race Problem.* London: Student Christian Movement Press, 1930.

———. *Bantu in the City: A Study of Cultural Adjustment on the Witwatersrand.* Alice, South Africa: Lovedale, 1938.

Plaatje, Sol. *Native Life in South Africa.* Athens: Ohio University Press, 1991.

Posel, Deborah. "The Case for a Welfare State: Poverty and the Politics of the Urban African Family in the 1930s and 1940s." In *South Africa's 1940s: World of Possibilities,* edited by Saul Dubow and Alan Jeeves, 64–86. Cape Town: Double Storey, 2005.

———. "Marriage at the Drop of a Hat: Housing and Partnership in South Africa's Urban African Townships, 1920s to 1960s." *History Workshop Journal* 61, no. 1 (2006): 57–76.

Potholm, Christian. "Changing Political Configurations in Swaziland." *Journal of Modern African Studies* 4, no. 3 (1966): 313–22.

———. *Swaziland: The Dynamics of Political Modernization.* Berkeley: University of California Press, 1972.

Preston-Whyte, E. M. "Land and Development at Indaleni: A Historical Perspective." *Development Southern Africa* 4, no. 3 (1987): 401–27.

Pretorius, Deidre. "AmaPasi Asiwafuni: Class, Race, and Gender Identities in the Anti-Pass Laws Cartoons Published in *Umsebenzi / South African Worker,* 1933–1936." *Image and Text: A Journal for Design* 13 (2007): 4–19.

Proctor, Tammy M. "A Separate Path: Scouting and Guiding in Interwar South Africa." *Comparative Studies in Society and History* 42, no. 3 (2000): 605–31.

Reyher, Rebecca. *Zulu Woman: The Life Story of Christian Sibiya.* New York: Feminist Press at CUNY, 1999.

Rycroft, David. "Zulu Zion and Some Swazi Zionists by Bengt Sundkler." *Bulletin of the School of Oriental and African Studies* 41, no. 1 (1978): 205–6.

Sandwith, Corinne. "The Appearance of the Book: Towards a History of the Reading Lives and Worlds of Black South African Readers." *English in Africa* 45, no. 1 (2018): 11–38.

———. "Progressing with a Vengeance: The Woman Reader/Writer in the African Press." In *Comparative Print Culture: A Study of Alternative Literary Modernities*, edited by R. Aliakbari, 143–63. London: Palgrave Macmillan, 2020.

———. "Well-Seasoned Talks: The Newspaper Column and the Satirical Mode in South African Letters." *Social Dynamics: A Journal of African Studies* 45, no. 1 (2019): 103–20.

Sapire, Hilary, and Robert Edgar. *African Apocalypse: The Story of Nontheta Nkwenkwe, a Twentieth-Century South African Prophet*. Athens: Ohio University Press, 2000.

Schapera, Isaac. *Married Life in an African Tribe*. Evanston, IL: Northwestern University Press, 1940.

Schneider, Gary. *The Culture of Epistolarity: Vernacular Letters and Letter Writing in Early Modern England, 1500–1700*. Newark: University of Delaware Press, 2005.

Scully, Pamela. *Ellen Johnson Sirleaf*. Athens: Ohio University Press, 2016.

Shear, Mervyn. *Wits: A University in the Apartheid Era*. Johannesburg: Wits University Press, 1996.

Shepperson, George. "Review: Ethiopianism and Zionism in Southern Africa." *Journal of African History* 20, no. 1 (1979): 142–45.

Shepperson, George, and Tom Price. *Independent African: John Chilembwe and the Origins, Setting and Significance of the Nyasaland Native Rising of 1915*. Edinburgh: Edinburgh University Press, 1958.

Simpson, Thula. "The Bay and the Ocean: A History of the ANC in Swaziland, 1960–1979." *African Historical Review* 41, no. 1 (2009): 90–117.

Skloot, Rebecca. *The Immortal Life of Henrietta Lacks*. New York: Broadway Paperbacks, 2011.

Stead Eilersen, Gillian. *Bessie Head: Thunder behind Her Ears—Her Life and Writing*. Johannesburg: Wits University Press, 2007.

Sundkler, Bengt. *Bantu Prophets in South Africa*. London: Lutterworth, 1948.

———. *Zulu Zion and Some Swazi Zionists*. Oxford: Oxford University Press, 1976.

Suresh Roberts, Ronald. *No Cold Kitchen: A Biography of Nadine Gordimer*. Johannesburg: STE Publishers, 2005.

Switzer, Les. "*Bantu World* and the Origins of a Captive Commercial Press in South Africa." *Journal of Southern African Studies* 14, no. 3 (1988): 351–70.

Thomas, Lynn. "Historicizing Agency." *Gender and History* 28, no. 2 (2016): 324–39.

Thompson, Leonard. *Survival in Two Worlds: Moshoeshoe of Lesotho 1786–1870*. Oxford: Oxford University Press, 1975.

Trouillot, Michel-Rolph. *Silencing the Past: Power and the Production of History*. Boston: Beacon, 1995.

Tyrrell, Barbara. *Tribal Peoples of Southern Africa*. Cape Town: Books of Africa, 1968.

Twala, R. G. "Beads as Regulating the Social Life of the Zulu and Swazi." *African Studies* 10, no. 3 (1951): 113–23.

———. "Umhlanga (REED) Ceremony of the Swazi Maidens." *African Studies* 11, no. 3 (1952): 93–104.

Van Baalan, Sebastian, and Kristine Hoglund. "So the Killing Continued: Wartime Mobilization and Post-War Violence in KwaZulu-Natal, South Africa." *Terrorism and Political Violence* 31, no. 6 (2019): 1168–86.

Van der Waal, Gerhard. *From Mining Camp to Metropolis: The Buildings of Johannesburg, 1886–1940*. Johannesburg: Chris Van Rensburg, 1987.

Venter, Isabella. "The Modern Girl and the Lady: Negotiating Modern Womanhood in a South African Magazine, 1910–1920." *South African Historical Journal* 71, no. 2 (2019): 170–96.

Verwey, E. J. *New Dictionary of South African Biography*. Pretoria: HSRC Publishers, 1995.

Viljoen, Louise. *Ingrid Jonker: Poet under Apartheid*. Athens: Ohio University Press, 2013.

Visser, N. W. "HIE Dhlomo: The Re-emergence of an African Writer." *English in Africa* 1, no. 2 (1974): 1–10.

White, Tim. "The Lovedale Press under the Directorship of R. H. W. Shepherd, 1930–1955." *English in Africa* 19, no. 2 (1992): 69–84.

Willan, Brian. *Sol Plaatje: A Life of Solomon Tshekisho Plaatje*. Auckland Park, South Africa: Jacana, 2018.

Wright, Marcia. *Strategies of Slaves and Women: Life Stories from Central/East Africa*. London: James Currey, 1993.

Wylie, Diane. *Art + Revolution: The Life and Death of Thami Mnyele, South African Artist*. Charlottesville: University of Virginia Press, 2008.

## Unpublished Secondary Sources, Conference Papers, Reports, and Dissertations

Armitage, Fiona. "The Zionist Movement in Swaziland: Origins and Bid for League Recognition, 1936–1958." Unpublished conference paper, Botswana History Workshop, August 1973.

Baines, Gary Fred. "New Brighton, Port Elizabeth, c. 1903–1953: A History of an Urban African Community." PhD diss., University of Cape Town, 1994.

Couzens, Tim. "The Courtship of Regina and Dan Twala." Unpublished conference paper, University of the Witwatersrand, 1992.

Du Rand, Susan Michelle. "From Mission School to Bantu Education: A History of Adams College." MA thesis, University of Natal, 1990.

Ginindza, Thoko. *Swazi Women: Sociocultural and Economic Considerations; Final Report March–May 1989*. Washington, DC: US Agency for International Development, 1989.

Gondek, Abby. "Jewish Women's Transracial Epistemological Networks: Representations of Black Women in the African Diaspora." PhD diss., Florida International University, 2018.

———. "The Swazi Clothing and Adornment Collection at the UCLA Fowler Museum: A Transnational Collaboration between Hilda Kuper and Thoko Ginindza." Paper presented at the American Anthropological Association Meeting, Vancouver, BC, November 22, 2019.

Haines, Richard John. "The Politics of Philanthropy and Race Relations: The Joint Councils of South Africa, 1920–1955." PhD diss., University of London, 1991.

Murray, Bruce. "Wits at War." Unpublished African studies seminar paper, University of the Witwatersrand, 1990, http://wiredspace.wits.ac.za/bitstream/handle/10539/9374/ISS-312.pdf?sequence=1&isAllowed=y.

Rai, Sasha Claude. "Laws of Love: The Transvaal Native Divorce Court and the Urban African." MA thesis, University of the Witwatersrand, 2018.

Simelane, Sandile. "Politics and the Press: A Case Study of the Times of Swaziland and the Swazi Observer." Master's thesis, University of KwaZulu-Natal, 1995.

# Index

Numbers in *italics* indicate pages with illustrations.